KT-294-507

B.S.U.C. - LIBRARY

00304204

Prostitution and Irish Society, 1800–1940

This is the first book to tackle the controversial history of prostitution in Ireland in the nineteenth and early twentieth centuries. Maria Luddy uncovers the extent of prostitution in the country and examines how Irish women came to work as prostitutes, their living conditions and their treatment by society. She provides new insights into the contentious history of Magdalen asylums in Ireland and reveals the inability of both the churches and the government to eliminate prostitution from the streets of Irish towns and cities right through until the mid 1920s. She shows that, while prostitution and venereal disease were viewed as social and moral problems, these issues were politicised by nationalists who linked them to the presence of the British garrison in Ireland and used them to argue for the withdrawal of the British. Once independence was achieved these problems were expected to disappear. However, the apparent increase in illegitimacy and VD rates suggested that something was amiss in the new State.

Revealing complex social and religious attitudes towards prostitution, prostitutes and the expression of sexuality in Irish society, this important study provides new perspectives on Irish social, cultural and political history.

MARIA LUDDY is Professor of Modern Irish History in the Department of History, University of Warwick. Her previous publications include *Women and Philanthropy in Nineteenth-Century Ireland* (1995) and, as editor, *The Crimean Journals of the Sisters of Mercy, 1854–56* (2004).

Prostitution and Irish Society, 1800–1940

Maria Luddy
University of Warwick

CAMBRIDGE
UNIVERSITY PRESS

CAMBRIDGE UNIVERSITY PRESS
Cambridge, New York, Melbourne, Madrid, Cape Town, Singapore, São Paulo,
Delhi

Cambridge University Press
The Edinburgh Building, Cambridge CB2 8RU, UK

Published in the United States of America by Cambridge University Press,
New York

www.cambridge.org
Information on this title: www.cambridge.org/9780521709057

© Maria Luddy 2007

This publication is in copyright. Subject to statutory exception
and to the provisions of relevant collective licensing agreements,
no reproduction of any part may take place without
the written permission of Cambridge University Press.

First published 2007

Printed in the United Kingdom at the University Press, Cambridge

A catalogue record for this publication is available from the British Library

ISBN 978-0-521-88241-5 hardback
ISBN 978-0-521-70905-7 paperback

Cambridge University Press has no responsibility for the persistence or
accuracy of URLs for external or third-party internet websites referred to
in this book, and does not guarantee that any content on such
websites is, or will remain, accurate or appropriate.

BATH SPA UNIVERSITY
NEWTON PARK LIBRARY
Class No.
3 01.4154 LUD
3/11/10

Contents

Figures

Maps

Tables

Abbreviations

CDAs	Contagious Diseases Acts
CSORP	Chief Secretary's Office Registered Papers
DDA	Dublin Diocesan Archives
DMP	Dublin Metropolitan Police
DORA	Defence of the Realm Act
GSC	Good Shepherd convent
LGB	Local Government Board
NAI	National Archives of Ireland, Dublin
NAL	National Archives, London
NLI	National Library of Ireland, Dublin
NUWW	National Union of Women Workers of Great Britain and Ireland
NVA	National Vigilance Association
OPW	Office of Public Works
PHS	Presbyterian Historical Society, Belfast
PRONI	Public Record Office of Northern Ireland, Belfast
RCB	Representative Church Body Library, Dublin
RCPI	Royal College of Physicians of Ireland
RCVD	Royal Commission on Venereal Disease
RIC	Royal Irish Constabulary
WL	Women's Library, London

Acknowledgements

Many individuals, organisations and institutions have assisted me with research for this book over the years. I am particularly grateful to the various religious congregations, the Good Shepherd Sisters, the Sisters of Mercy, the Sisters of Charity and the Order of Our Lady of Charity of Refuge who allowed me to work in their archives and gave me access to the important material they hold on Magdalen asylums in Ireland. Mr Robert Mills, archivist of the Royal College of Physicians of Ireland, facilitated my research in the college's magnificent library room. The staffs of the Bodleian Library, and particularly the Radcliffe Science Library, in Oxford were very helpful in informing me of obscure articles and journals. Similarly, the staffs of the National Library of Ireland, the National Archives in Dublin, the Public Records Office of Northern Ireland, the Presbyterian Historical Society, the Theological Union College in Belfast, the Cork Archives Institute, and other various libraries in Ireland, including those of Tralee and Kildare, offered congenial surroundings in which to conduct research. My thanks to the many archivists and librarians who took a real interest in what I was researching, among them Tom Quinlan, who brought my attention to the newly available material generated by the Carrigan Committee held in the National Archives in Dublin, and Rena Lohan who suggested I look at material from the Office of Public Works where copious correspondence exists on the 'wrens of the Curragh'. I am especially grateful to David Sheehy, formerly of the Dublin Diocesan Archives, for locating relevant material for me and engaging in much stimulating, and entertaining, discussion whenever I visited the archive. Seattle's gain is Dublin's loss. I would also like to thank Professors Mark Finnane and Elizabeth Malcolm for their assistance in locating source material. Many friends and acquaintances have over the years kept an eye out for material they thought might be of use to me. Larry Walsh, of the Limerick Museum sent me material on Limerick's lock hospital and Sr Cabrini Delahunty, of the Cloyne Diocesan Archive, provided me with copies of relevant material from that archive. Others, Mary Burke, Catherine Cox, Rosemary Cullen Owens, Lindsey Earner-Byrne, Kevin

James, Kevin O'Neill, Margaret Ó hÓgartaigh, Rosemary Raughter, Anne Wickham and Joanna Wydenbach, led me to fictional and archival sources. I am very grateful for the advice offered by Cliona Rattigan on the issue of infanticide and her comments on chapter 3 eased my anxieties on this subject. Jim Smith and I discussed Magdalen asylums, and much else about Irish society, over the months I was based in Boston College. I am grateful to the Arts and Humanities Research Board for providing me with a study leave award which gave me time to work on the book, as did a visiting professorship at the Burns Library, Boston College.

For assistance with illustrations I want to thank Patrick Gallagher of the Valuations Office, the staff at the Irish Architectural Archive, Sandra McDermott of the National Library of Ireland, and the staff of the Gilbert Library in Dublin. Fintan Cullen suggested Harry Clarke's depiction of Liam O'Flaherty's *Mr Gilhooley* as a suitable image for the cover and Nicola Gordon Bowe helped me track it down. My thanks to them both. Lisa Lavender was 'ace' with scanning and editing images.

My thanks to Leeann Lane for reading and commenting on the manuscript while in the process of finishing her own book on Rosamond Jacob. The anonymous readers of Cambridge University Press gave me pause for thought and I have tried to incorporate some of their suggestions into the text.

Des Marnane, Marianne Cosgrave and Gobnait Ní Chrulaioch always asked how it was going. Geraldine and Vic will be as glad, and maybe as relieved as I am, that the book is finally finished. Virginia Crossman read the whole thing through, again and again, and made all kinds of suggestions for improvements. Both she and Rosemary Clarke, in different ways, helped me to finish this project. Their wisdom, love and support allows me to keep some perspective on those things that really matter.

Introduction

In the late 1980s, having completed some preliminary work on the history of Magdalen asylums in Ireland, I gave two talks, one at Limerick and the other in Galway, on the general theme of prostitution in Ireland. In Galway I was told that a number of shops refused to put up the poster advertising the talk because the words 'prostitution' and 'Ireland' appeared together in the same space. In Limerick two members of the audience approached me after my talk and asked, in quite an aggressive manner, how I could possibly talk about such a subject, and thanked God the British had gone, as there had been no prostitution in Ireland since. The idea of Irish purity, particularly sexual purity, has long had a strong hold on the population. Various published accounts by travellers to the country in the nineteenth and twentieth centuries stressed the morality of Irish women. The bishop of Galway, Dr McHale, in his testimony to the Poor Law Inquiry Commission of the 1830s noted that 'there are instances of parishes in this province [Connaught], in which there are more than a thousand families in which there has not been one illegitimate child for ten years'.[1] Other witnesses observed that any 'failure in chastity' on the part of a woman meant that she 'forfeited for life her character and caste'.[2] In 1835 Monsignor Kinseley, of Kilkenny, in a conversation with Alexis de Tocqueville observed in relation to morality that 'twenty years in the confessional have made me aware that the misconduct of girls is very rare, and that of married women almost unknown'.[3] With regard to vice in London one commentator remarked in 1872 that 'Irish virtue is the only prophylactic which resists it'.[4] Writing in 1914, when prostitution was strongly evident on the streets of Dublin, Harold Begbie observed the city to be

almost entirely free of the common vice which disfigures cities. There is nothing in the whole town that suggests for a moment anything approaching to the central and unblushing shame of London. Indeed, a man might live all his life in Dublin and never see a single tragedy of this kind. Girls fall, perhaps willingly take to that way of getting money, but they do not remain in Dublin. Dublin does not pay.[5]

While some travellers did acknowledge that vice, and especially prostitution, existed in Ireland, few commented on it much.[7] Within Irish
nationalism there was a degree of puritanism and moral righteousness.
C. S. Andrews, recalling his associates in the nationalist movement of the
early twentieth century, wrote that

> we held strongly to the social ethos of republicanism in that . . . we were puritani-
> cal in outlook and behaviour. We didn't drink. We respected women and . . . knew
> nothing about them. We disapproved of the wearing of formal clothes . . . of
> anyone who took an interest in food . . . of women 'making up' or wearing
> jewellery.[8]

The Irish Christian Brothers proclaimed in 1924 that 'purity is the
national virtue of Ireland'.[6] At a court case held in Newbridge in 1928 a
judge, sentencing a soldier from the Curragh camp to prison for assault
on a young girl, stated that he was 'glad to say that cases of indecent
assault were uncommon in this country, and that was attributable to the
manhood of the country. It had rightly been said that Irishmen had
greater respect for women than the men of any other country in Europe.'[9]
The moral superiority of the Irish people was emphasised in the *Irish Press*
in 1931 when, explicitly linking Catholicism and morality, it declared that
'not only do our sons rule over scores of millions of Catholics throughout
the world, but they play a part in the formation of the character of many
nations that may yet save civilisation from the moral suicide it has planned
for itself'.[10]

This self-belief in Irish purity and moral superiority has rarely been
challenged. The perpetuation of the image of Ireland as a sexually pure
nation, and one in which an unrelentingly puritanical attitude existed to
sexual expression, has in fact been bolstered by the work of a number of
historians. Hasia Diner, for instance, observes in her study of female emigration that 'Irish women rarely crossed the line when it came to sexual
deviance . . . In Ireland, illegitimacy was virtually unknown, and prostitution extremely rare.'[11] K. H. Connell's work on illegitimacy in pre-famine
Ireland states unequivocally that the incidence of illegitimacy was abnor-
mally low. He observes that the harsh treatment meted out to unmarried
mothers made premarital sexual activity unwelcome and this, united
with parental and Church condemnation, constrained such activity.
Repression and purity went hand in hand, a view that has been accepted
almost uncritically.[12] An investigation into the history of prostitution
in Ireland problematises this image and suggests that resistance to the
Catholic Church's teaching on celibacy and sexual continence, as reflected in the levels and extent of prostitution in the nineteenth and twentieth
centuries, was far more common than generally believed.

For many influential commentators prostitution was a problem that could never be eliminated. Dr William Acton's influential study, *Prostitution Considered in its Moral, Social, and Sanitary Aspects in London and other Large Cities*, first published in 1857, argued that prostitution would exist as long as there was a 'demand for the article supplied by its agency'.[13] One of the witnesses to an 1854 committee of inquiry on Dublin hospitals believed that 'prostitution is absolutely necessary; if it is discouraged amongst the soldiers, you would reduce the moral character of the men. It is much better that soldiers have free access to women, or they will have worse.'[14] Frank Duff, the founder of the Legion of Mary, believed that a prostitute class was necessary to protect 'respectable' women. In a government inquiry into the extent of venereal disease he observed that 'it is probable that solicitation on the streets will never be completely prevented . . . there will always be some [prostitutes] left who will meet the needs of the man with utterly depraved appetites'.[15]

There was a considerable debate in England as to why women became prostitutes, a debate more muted in Ireland. Within England the effects of industrialisation were for many a major cause of prostitution, as were poverty and unemployment. Ireland, of course, was never industrialised to any great extent, although poverty was rife and understood, when allied to unmarried motherhood, to be a major cause of prostitution. The evidence given to the poor law inquiry sustains this link. As one witness claimed, 'most of the females who infest the streets of cities are such persons';[16] reinforcing that view another stated that 'almost all prostitution may be traced to that cause'.[17] In all countries prostitution offered women a means of making a living where they could not find alternative employment, or where that employment did not offer them a subsistence wage. The structure of the Irish economy offered few opportunities to women. The expansion of the domestic linen industry in the eighteenth and early nineteenth centuries increased the earning power of young men and women, although it did not give women increased status in the community. In many cases a woman's earnings were absorbed into the household income. In the nineteenth century the spread of the factory system undermined domestic industry, especially in textiles. The 1841 census recorded over 600,000 textile and clothing workers, over 500,000 of whom were women. By 1881 textiles employed fewer than 90,000 women. Post-famine Ireland experienced considerable industrial decline with linen mills and textile factories, mostly based in Ulster, providing one of the few forms of employment for married women outside the home. The brunt of the fall in industrial employment bore on women and they had few alternative sources of employment.

The major forms of employment for women in the post-famine period were domestic service and agriculture. But the number of women recorded in employment fell steadily from 29 per cent in 1861 to 19.5 per cent by 1911. The 1911 census reveals that of the 157,146 women who made up the female population of Dublin, 116,307 were enumerated as having no specified occupation. Of this number 33,623 were aged between twenty-five and forty-five.[18] The majority of domestic servants in Ireland in the pre- and post-famine period were young, single women. While domestic service was considered a respectable form of employment it appears to have been a major route into prostitution for many women.[19] This was the only area of female employment that expanded in the post-famine years. By 1911 one working woman in three was a servant, although the number of female servants began to decline from the 1890s. Other opportunities were emerging for women of the middle classes by this time and they were finding openings as schoolteachers, clerks, shop assistants and hospital matrons. Women were also involved in other forms of paid work. For instance, many women ran huxter shops or engaged in street selling, while others helped to run pubs, grocery shops and other retail businesses. Many worked as laundresses or took in lodgers. In Goldsmith's Street in Dublin in 1911 the census records twenty-eight of the fifty-four houses containing boarders.[20] The fact of single women keeping rooms was to become a source of anxiety for the moralists who saw single, independent women as a threat to morality.[21] Such women were believed to use their rooms for immoral purposes, and thus all single women living alone were suspect.

Women were more vulnerable to economic hardship than men. Poor pay, lack of skills, children and lack of suitable employment all had an impact on how well women could survive economically. For poorer women it was more difficult to remain economically independent and they were more likely than men to use welfare institutions to support them. From the beginnings of the poor law system in Ireland women were to be found in workhouses in greater numbers than men. According to the 1881 census there were 148 hospitals, asylums and almshouses which provided a permanent residence for the ill and distressed. The total number of places available in these institutions was 5,575 and women took up 72 per cent of them. In 1870 there were 6,338 able-bodied females in Irish workhouses as compared with 2,666 men. By 1900 the numbers were 3,338 able-bodied women and 2,386 men.[22] Women entered workhouses for a number of reasons: some were ill, others incapacitated by pregnancy or injury. Some were destitute and used the workhouse as a means of shelter and sustenance. The connection between poverty and prostitution has often been made. That prostitution was a less than lucrative business is evident from the hundreds of Irish prostitutes who were homeless, and whose poverty is witnessed in their entrance to workhouses and Magdalen asylums. In the period after the famine there were a growing number of single women in Irish society. In 1871, 43 per cent of all women aged between fifteen and forty-five were married; by 1911 that had dropped to 36 per cent.[23] By 1926, 24 per cent of women aged between forty-five and fifty-four were single.[24] Poor employment prospects and poor marriage prospects were factors that help to account for the high levels of emigration among Irish women in the nineteenth and twentieth centuries. Between 1790 and 1914 the gender balance between male and female emigrants from Ireland was fairly even. However, the number of women believed to have emigrated from Ireland in the nineteenth century is thought to be over 3 million. This exceeded the number of women actually living in Ireland as recorded in the 1901 census. By the 1870s, as Mary Daly has shown, women accounted for half of all emigrants, and women were to remain the majority of emigrants, with the exception of the years 1911–26, until the Second World War.[25]

The period covered by this study, the nineteenth to mid-twentieth centuries, saw the rise of prostitution as a social issue of concern to moralists, public health advocates and the police. From the early nineteenth century, as Jill Harsin has noted, the policing of prostitution underwent significant changes.[26] In many European countries and US cities regulatory systems were introduced which attempted to control the levels of prostitution and the spread of venereal diseases, systems overseen by the police and the medical profession. In France such regulation originated in Paris in 1802 as a means of examining public prostitutes for venereal disease and it quickly developed into a mandatory system of surveillance.[27] This kind of regulation became common in other places: the Italian, German and Scandinavian states, Belgium, the Netherlands and Poland, among other countries, introduced regulatory systems which followed the French model.[28] In contrast to the rest of Europe a regulatory system was not put in place in Britain until the 1860s, under the Contagious Diseases Acts (CDAs), and Ireland was part of that system, in this instance being treated as an integral part of the United Kingdom rather than as a colony.[29] Regulation was not without its critics and in the United Kingdom a concerted attempt by feminists, liberal and political activists, with active support from Ireland, eventually led to the suspension of the CDAs in 1883 and their repeal in 1886.

Ireland was a predominantly Catholic country in this period. Catholics made up about 80.9 per cent of the population in 1834, 74.2 per cent by 1901 and 92.6 per cent by 1926. The modern Irish Catholic Church was built in the nineteenth century. Under the leadership of Cardinal Paul Cullen the morale and professional competence of Irish priests was raised, the hierarchical leadership was centralised and as the century proceeded the Church took control of education and a myriad of welfare institutions which bound the people to it. The result was a politically conservative, religiously aggressive and highly centralised and bureaucratised Church. Nuns were to play a formative role in Catholic expansion and reorganisation.[30] Tom Inglis has argued that the priest, 'by his mere physical presence as a civilised, disciplined and well-mannered Catholic man' controlled all aspects of Irish social life.[31] He argues that the Catholic Church's control of sexuality 'became centred on gaining control of women's sex'.[32] Through confession, sermons and the institution of societies and confraternities the Church, it has been argued, gained control over the expression of sexuality in Ireland. Inglis, however, fails to acknowledge the resistance that existed to this formulation. Prostitution, for instance, survived with little interference from the Church. Levels of unmarried motherhood, where women choose to leave Ireland and have their babies in England, remained a concern and a problem for Church and state until, arguably, the 1960s.[33] Priests were challenged in their attempts to control the activities of the Catholic population.[34] Even when legislation, for example to control dancehalls, was put in place many judges refused to accede to a local priest's objections.[35] This is not to say that the Catholic Church did not have a profound impact on how individuals understood their own sexuality and how they expressed that sexuality. But we still know too little about the expression of sexuality in nineteenth- and twentieth-century Ireland to judge the nature of its repression.

'Before 1980, the prostitute was "pornographic"', states Timothy Gilfoyle in his review essay on the historiography of prostitution.[36] Few historians were willing to engage with the subject and until the 1990s it was a topic untouched by Irish historians.[37] Since the 1980s there have been numerous studies of prostitution reflecting the changing landscape of social and cultural history, and the development of women's history and gender history. In her now classic study, *Prostitution and Victorian Society: Women, Class and the State*, Judith Walkowitz[38] explores in detail the impact of the CDAs in shaping class relations in England. She argues that prostitution offered many women better economic opportunities than they could find within industrial employment. These women were not, she contends, necessarily forced into prostitution; many of them were active agents in their own lives and controlled their labour through their sexuality.[39] While few Irish prostitutes appear to have become financially independent through their work, there is evidence to show that for some at least prostitution was a chosen occupation and often a seasonal one. It was also an occupation very much dictated by poverty and lack of employment opportunities. Walkowitz shows how prostitutes often exploited their customers within the subculture they occupied. Clients, for instance, were robbed or assaulted when they went to the lodging-houses or brothels where prostitutes worked. This is also evident in the case of Irish prostitution. For many, in England, prostitution appears to have been a temporary occupation and working-class communities seem to have accepted former prostitutes into their midst without moralising. The same appears to be true for Ireland, particularly in the working-class districts of Dublin. Walkowitz reveals that while social reformers demanded more extensive anti-prostitution legislation, a strong feminist lobby successfully agitated for the repeal of the CDAs. The campaign for both the extension and repeal of the CDAs in Ireland was very much influenced by their British counterparts. Though neither movement was strong in Ireland, the campaigns offered Irish women an opportunity to argue for their political rights, as the best way in which vice could be eliminated from society.

Walkowitz's study is among a number of important works that have influenced this current book. Explorations of prostitution in the United States, for example, reveal the complex intertwining of urban life, social growth and class and gender identity. Ruth Rosen in *The Lost Sisterhood* investigates prostitution in the USA from 1900 to 1918.[40] She argues that the narratives on prostitution cannot be taken at face value and that for the period she is discussing prostitution was the 'symbol of an age' and that the narratives around it were a means for people to express their anxieties about the changing nature of US society. Prostitution was constructed to represent everything from the breakdown of traditional values to the growth of a youth culture centred around new forms of leisure.[41] To some extent similar trends can be seen in Ireland, particularly in the years after independence, when there was considerable anxiety about social change in the country. Rosen argues that the construction of the prostitute as a 'lost soul' was a creation of the progressive reform-driven society that attempted to rescue these women. In Ireland the prostitute was constructed as a 'seduced and abandoned' woman, who was in need of, and deserved, rescue. She was also, and at the same time, an infectious creature, a carrier of disease and immorality which was transferable to the respectable men and women of society. By the early twentieth century the prostitute in Ireland was, for some at least, an innocent corrupted by the presence of the British garrison, in need of saving from the British soldier. In time she became associated with unmarried motherhood, 'separation' women and the expression of sexuality by young Irish women. These constructions of the prostitute served the interests of rescue workers, advanced nationalists, suffragists and welfare workers. The real individual behind these constructions was often lost. There is nothing exceptional in the ways in which prostitution in Ireland was understood or dealt with. Its meanings, whether in political or moral terms, are echoed in many other countries which were dealing with the problem of prostitution in this period. Rosen argues that for many women prostitution 'was simply a form of work; an obvious means of economic survival which occasionally offered some small degree of upward mobility'.[42] Prostitutes did not see themselves as outcasts. Rosen reveals the prostitute as a social actor, and through interviews conducted by progressive reformers marks prostitution as an occupation of choice for many women who later left it and went on to make other lives for themselves.

In her introduction to *The Comforts of Home* Luise White made a significant point by noting the ways in which historians dealt with the agency of individual prostitutes. White argued that many academic studies and descriptions of prostitution had adopted the language and attitudes of nineteenth-century reformers. The 'biological and cultural absolutes' expressed towards prostitutes 'in the clichés of nineteenth century outrage and control', have found a place in twentieth-century accounts of prostitution, where pollution and passivity seem to articulate the essence of a prostitute.[43] By adopting these terms, White argued, historians had missed more complex issues that demonstrated agency or economic influence in the towns and cities where prostitutes worked. The best histories, like White's own work, gives us some indication of who the women really were, what their day-to-day lives were like or how they saw themselves within their social and political frameworks. White argues that the economic power that women working as prostitutes wielded was a very significant feature of their impact on their communities and a vital part of the women's work. However, the quality of interpretation also depends on the availability of source material – a point Walkowitz drew attention to in 1980. The prostitute revealed by most of the documentary records is a woman created by those who watched and discussed her. In the case of Ireland these included the police, court reporters, workhouse officials, military authorities, priests and nuns and at times the general public. The resultant images are sometimes varied and contradictory and say as much about middle-class society and its fears and anxieties about health, discipline and order as they do about the women themselves. Our views on the nineteenth- and twentieth-century prostitute come from those who feared, despised, pitied or tolerated her.

Gail Hershatter's *Dangerous Pleasures: Prostitution and Modernity in Twentieth-Century Shanghai* identifies the major trends in the study of prostitution. Some studies evaluate the use of prostitution as a symbol of fear and change; other scholars of prostitution look for subjects with agency not just the victims of circumstances. However, whatever the approach it is the lack of sources that hampers most studies of prostitution. As Hershatter explains, prostitutes found a place in the historical record because of the reformers who wished to change, save, hide, relocate or cure them.[44] She argues that 'prostitution is always about the sale of sexual services, but much more can be learned from that transaction: about sexual meaning, about other social relations, about sex as a medium through which people talked about political power and cultural transformations, about nationhood and cultural identity'.[45] These are aspects that I attempt to cover in this book. A study of prostitution in Ireland adds to our understanding of Irish society more generally in this period; it also problematises the idea of Ireland as a nation of pure women and gallant men. It offers a history of a group of women who were often rejected by 'respectable' Irish society and a way of understanding how many Irish women survived in a hostile economic environment. It questions the control the Catholic Church had on the moral life of the very poor and destitute in nineteenth-century Ireland in particular. It is telling that it was a lay Catholic organisation, in association with a small number of clerics, rather than the civil authorities, who managed to close down the brothel system in Dublin in the 1920s. Prostitution was a subject that the Catholic Church appeared to have difficulty in controlling. Reform efforts, mainly concerned with 'saving' the prostitute from her life of sin, are most evident in the myriad of Magdalen asylums and rescue homes that were established in Ireland from the mid-eighteenth century. These institutions did not offer a solution to prostitution or its causes, merely the possibility of reform to the women who decided to enter these establishments. The civil authorities did little to end prostitution and rarely intervened in this business unless public opinion forced them to act.

For Ireland we have no interviews or personal reminiscences of women who worked as prostitutes in the period of this study, 1800–1940. All that we know about prostitution in this period is mediated through police and criminal statistics, newspaper accounts of court scenes in which prostitutes appear and the opinions of medical men on women who worked as prostitutes. Indeed, much of the discussion that takes place around prostitution and sexual immorality in Ireland in this period is about issues other than prostitution. How prostitutes are represented in these sources is often shaped by the opinions and needs of those either writing letters to the press or by reporters often keen to amuse the readers of the paper with lively court cases. Concerns about disease, the encroachment of prostitutes into respectable geographical spaces, such as the main streets of Dublin, and the prominence of British soldiers on the streets are allied to the apparent corruption of young Irish women by the soldiers and the fight for suffrage among Irish women. In Ireland from the nineteenth century and into the twentieth century attitudes to prostitution were shaped by an amalgam of public health, moral, religious and legal concerns. At times some of these elements predominated, that predomination often being influenced by the context of political events. Hence, in the period after the foundation of the state religious and moral concerns came to the fore within the framework of political and social upheaval.

Reconstructing the story of prostitution in Ireland has involved exploring sources not often exploited by Irish historians. Among the most useful and valuable sources for this study have been the registers of Magdalen asylums that operated in Ireland from the eighteenth to the twentieth centuries. The public's interest in Magdalen asylums surfaced in the 1990s and particularly in 1998 with the broadcast of a Channel Four documentary entitled *Sex in a Cold Climate* which relied on the evidence of a number of women who had been incarcerated in the Magdalen asylums in Ireland in the 1940s and 1950s.[46] It was a powerful programme which provoked considerable controversy. It was this documentary which aroused Peter Mullan's interest in the Magdalen asylums and his film, *The Magdalene Sisters*, released in Ireland in October 2002, is based very closely on the stories told by the women in the documentary.[47] Mullan's film was well received by the critics, winning a major prize at the Venice film festival in 2002. The film took in over £250,000 in its first two weeks in Irish cinemas, and had earned over 2 million euros by the end of November 2002, an enormous sum in Irish film terms. It played in Ireland until January 2003.[48]

It is a passionate piece of film making. The story is set in Ireland in the mid-1960s and focuses on the plight of three young women, a rape victim, an unmarried mother and a young woman in an orphanage who is clearly an 'enticement' to young men. The young women are brutalised within the asylum. The nuns who run the asylum, particularly the nun in charge, are presented as greedy for money and we see the mother superior counting the laundry takings in a number of scenes. The nuns keep order through sarcasm and a belt, and the women are physically and spiritually abused, with one woman being sexually abused by a priest. They are not paid for their labour, are dressed in drab brown uniforms, sleep in a locked dormitory and are poorly fed while the nuns, witnessed behind a screen, eat well. Mullan uses some of the dialogue from the *Sex in a Cold Climate* documentary and transposes the stories of the women in the documentary from the 1930s, 1940s and 1950s to the 1960s.

The film was released in Ireland at a time when the country was coming to terms with a decade of revelations of clerical sexual abuse and the physical and sexual abuse of children in Church-run industrial and reformatory schools. There is no doubt that the state, through its reliance on Catholic religious orders and congregations to run industrial and reformatory schools, and indeed Magdalen asylums, abrogated its duty to care for the weakest individuals in society. From the beginning of the nineteenth century all Catholic welfare enterprises refused to allow any public accountability for their work, and this did not change in the twentieth, even when these institutions, it has been claimed, were asked to account for the use of public funds by the state.[49] Though the state did not fund or support Magdalen asylums, it did, as we will see, acquiesce in suggestions as to the value of the use of their facilities to control the sexuality of young women.

The film had a considerable impact in Ireland. It has again raised interest in Ireland's 'hidden' history and made the public more aware of Magdalen asylums than any of the media attention devoted to this subject since 1993. Since 1991 Magdalen asylums have been written about in newspapers and women's magazines; plays have been produced, and two novels and a work of history have been published on these institutions.[50] But the most lasting and powerful impact has been made by a work of film fiction. There is no doubt that the context in which the film was released in Ireland in 2002 assisted its promotion. This was an Ireland racked by stories of clerical abuse, the mistreatment of children in orphanages, industrial schools and reformatories throughout the country. There was an audience ready and willing to hear more. The story is an emotional one and it is on that level that it has made its greatest impact on Irish audiences. Mullan is quite clear in stating that his interest in the issue of the Magdalen laundries was aroused by the documentary *Sex in a Cold Climate*. It is also evident from various interviews that he has given that he was unaware of the history of these institutions and was apparently 'surprised' at the numbers of people who wrote to tell him about their experiences in them.[51] The popularity of the film raises a number of interesting questions for the historian, not least how to provide a balanced history of a very difficult subject. We know very little about Magdalen asylums in twentieth-century Ireland. Mullan's film, based as it is on a documentary, relies for its evidence on interviews with four women who were held within these institutions. There is no doubt that Magdalen asylums were harsh institutions, that women were made to work in laundries without pay and apparently kept against their will. They were, at least in a number of instances, abused.

At the end of Mullan's film we are told that over 30,000 women were kept in these asylums. It is not clear whether this figure refers to the last half of the twentieth century, or the entire twentieth century (as noted in the documentary *Sex in a Cold Climate*). If so it seems an extraordinarily high figure. We are given no idea how such a figure was reached, but it has become the standard used when referring to the numbers of women held in Magdalen asylums.[52] One of the interesting aspects of the Mullan film is that some of the women escape and make new lives for themselves. In the documentary one of the women escaped, another was taken home by a relative and another stayed in the refuge for a year. The stories we have are of women who have left, yet the common understanding and much publicised 'fact' about these asylums is that women never left. In this study I explore the history of Magdalen asylums in Ireland, from their origin in 1765 up to the 1940s. These institutions need to be placed within the context of the period in which they operated. It is important for us to know how they were organised and managed and what they offered to the women who used them. What is clear is that Magdalen asylums were not institutions of incarceration in the nineteenth and early twentieth centuries. There is some evidence to suggest that they may have changed their function in the twentieth century to become institutions of confinement. However, at this time welfare and rescue workers were becoming more concerned with preventative work, and the 'unmarried mother' became a major focus of concern. By the 1920s this concern had evolved into a serious consideration of the need to confine women who had more than one illegitimate child, for their 'protection' and for the protection of society. The Magdalen asylum appeared to offer the ideal institutional form for such incarceration.

In her study of Magdalen asylums in Ireland, Frances Finnegan offers an interpretation of these institutions in the nineteenth century.[53] This study has received a generally uncritical reception, even from historians.[54] However, Finnegan's work is limited and flawed. It examines the history of four Good Shepherd asylums that operated in the country in the nineteenth and twentieth centuries. She makes comparisons between Irish and English asylums but ignores the social, political and cultural contexts in which Irish institutions operated during this period. Finnegan claims that the arrival of the Good Shepherd order in Ireland had 'repercussions for Irish society [which] were far reaching, as the French order was to be the driving force in the country's Magdalen movement for almost a century and a half'.[55] This, however, is an exaggeration. The Good Shepherd nuns had no impact on the ways in which other Magdalen asylums evolved in Ireland and they operated only five out of the forty-two asylums that existed in the country between 1765 and 1960. They were as representative of the ways in which Magdalen asylums functioned in this period as any other religious-run asylum was. Finnegan implies that the women who used these institutions in the nineteenth century were somehow forced into them and detained against their will. While many of the convent asylums wished their inmates to remain for life, Finnegan's own figures, and those provided in this current study, reveal these institutions to have been flexible, in the nineteenth century at least.

Women entered and left them on a regular basis and the institutions offered respite when few other welfare organisations would care for prostitutes. Finnegan views these women as victims of the nuns, women without any agency or control over their own lives, where her statistics actually prove the opposite. She also makes assertions about these asylums in the twentieth century using nineteenth-century data. The ways in which Magdalen asylums are now understood in Irish society have been shaped primarily by a film, and to date historians have made little attempt to question that understanding.[56]

One purpose of the present study is to examine the extent of prostitution in Ireland in the years between 1800 and 1940. Police and criminal statistics provide us with some indication of the places where police were active in combating prostitution. It is clear that the police were often inactive in this area and that prostitution thrived, particularly in Dublin, until the mid-1920s when a lay Catholic organisation, with assistance from Catholic clerics, managed to close down the majority of brothels in the notorious red-light district of the city. Prostitutes were to be found in almost every town in Ireland, particularly in garrison towns. Containment and visibility were the factors that influenced both public and police reaction to prostitution. Prostitution was most often tolerated when it was not evident on the public streets. One of the solutions most regularly proposed for the problem of prostitution was the institution of rescue homes and Magdalen asylums. These, of course, were dealing with the symptoms of prostitution rather than its causes. There were no major investigations into vice in Ireland and as long as prostitutes remained out of public sight the majority of the population showed little interest in ending their trade. It is evident also that Catholic clerics became more vocal and active in ridding the streets of prostitution after 1850, though they were not always successful in this endeavour and clerical action depended very much on the disposition of the individual priest. Many did not to wish to get involved with prostitutes or prostitution in case they would somehow be tainted by the experience. One refuge which was readily available to prostitutes was the workhouse and many women found their way to this institution. Again, issues of contamination and infection decided how they were treated in workhouses, where they were generally separated from the 'respectable' poor. From the 1870s and into the 1880s there was a growing movement against prostitution evident in the organisation of vigilance and purity groups. Many of these took an active interest in closing down brothels, but seem to have had little to give to the women who worked as prostitutes either in terms of shelter or a way out of prostitution.

Who were the women who made up the prostitute population in Ireland? Much of what we know of prostitutes comes to us through court reports and the examples provided in this study give us some indication of the women who worked as prostitutes and the ways in which the authorities dealt with them. One of the dominant voices in the construction of the prostitute was that of the rescue worker or reformer, who characterised prostitutes as 'seduced' women, vulnerable and naive country girls who needed protection. However, women came to prostitution from a variety of life experiences. Individual women who worked as prostitutes had often been working as such for decades; many were addicted to alcohol and of those who walked the streets many were homeless and destitute. One group of women who worked as prostitutes for whom we have a substantial amount of information are the 'wrens of the Curragh'. These women lived in ditches and bushes around the Curragh army camp and a journalist, James Greenwood, who visited the area in the 1860s has left us his account of their lives. This information allows us to see these women shaping their own community. It also allows us to view how the military authorities dealt with the problem of prostitution; while they publicly condemned the vice they rarely did anything practical to stem its presence at the Curragh and other military garrisons.

Venereal diseases were an occupational hazard for women who worked as prostitutes. As for many other aspects of medical history we have no sustained secondary studies of venereal disease in nineteenth- and early twentieth-century Ireland. This work begins the exploration of that history by examining the various advertisements that appeared in the national press regarding cures for venereal diseases. Prostitutes were considered the main sites of venereal infection and the establishment of the Westmoreland lock hospital in 1755, and its existence as a hospital dealing only with women from 1820, make the link between female sexuality and disease very clear. The treatment provided in the hospital, together with an exploration of the hospital's regime, provides us with information on attitudes towards prostitution and disease in this period. Issues of containment and confinement loom large in this discussion and the perceived proliferation of venereal disease saw the implementation of the CDAs, which leads into an exploration of the political aspects of those Acts in Ireland. The campaign to repeal these Acts allowed Irish women a way of entering the public domain of politics to argue for the rights of women and for political citizenship.

This argument for political rights extends into the twentieth century when suffragists also use prostitution as a means of advancing the political cause of women. While the level of prostitution evident on the streets of Dublin becomes a rallying point for moralists and nationalists, the issues were again ones of visibility and contamination. But a new element enters the picture: the corrupting morality of the British soldier. For advanced nationalists the presence of the British garrison in Ireland becomes the major source of immorality and disease. Irish women are seen as pure, corrupted only by the soldier. Suffragists used the panic over 'white slavery' as a way to argue for their political rights. It is also from this period that the feminist voice, either male or female, argued that criminalising prostitutes and prostitution was useless as long as women could not support themselves through legitimate employment. Limited work opportunities, poor wages and exploitation were what many believed drove women into prostitution; as long as those conditions prevailed then prostitution would continue to exist. 'Separation women' and the 'amateur', especially women who engaged in sexual activity without monetary recompense, joined the prostitute as symbols of decay.

As Lucy Bland has noted, the moral panic that emerged around venereal disease during the First World War was in essence about promiscuity.[57] The threat to the health of soldiers from the 'amateur prostitute' saw that figure become a scapegoat and cause of the spread of venereal disease in Britain in this period. As Bland observes, sexual regulation 'exposes an ambivalence towards the display of female sexual initiative and the double-sided nature of the desire to protect – its underside being the supervision of women's sexual behaviour'.[58] This reflects similar attitudes towards sexual display by women in Ireland. The First World War brought middle-class women a new kind of surveillance in the form of women's patrols. This, together with the surveillance that took place in court proceedings, focused its attention on the sexuality of young women. The rise of vigilance societies in this period marks a new direction in attitudes to immorality. At this stage vigilance societies focused their attention on supposedly immoral newspapers and books. Their campaign was not very successful but was to reap real benefits with the establishment of the Irish Free State in 1922. Venereal disease also became a serious issue, particularly with the ending of the war in 1918. The Royal Commission on Venereal Disease suggested that this disease was a serious public health problem and allowed for the institution of treatment schemes throughout the United Kingdom. There was considerable delay in establishing such treatment centres in Ireland.

The final focus of this study is the history of prostitution and venereal disease within the context of the establishment of the Irish Free State. There was considerable concern about what appeared to be rising levels of immorality in the country, seen in high rates of illegitimacy and venereal disease. There was extensive discussion about the ways in which unmarried mothers might be dealt with and the sexuality of young women, particularly those who were unmarried mothers, became equated with that of prostitutes. This was a period when the Catholic

Church had considerable influence on social and moral legislation. There was a campaign to protect Irish morality which, it was believed, had been endangered by years of political and social upheaval. The campaigns and discussions that took place around censorship, around the supposedly immoral press, the cinema, the evils of dancehalls, contraception, unmarried motherhood and about prostitution were also discussions about how to deal with the very real social and political changes that were occurring in a newly independent Ireland and how to return to 'normality', a time when women knew their place in society, before the disruption of the war of independence and civil war. Anxiety about change, particularly concern about women in public life, focused on the expression of sexuality by young women. Unmarried mothers, the 'amateur' and the prostitute became the focus of intense scrutiny, with particular emphasis on how these women could be made to conform to a stricter sexual code. It is also during the early to mid-1920s that the brothel system in Dublin comes under final attack. The lay religious organisation, the Legion of Mary, focused its attention on the red-light district of the city and in the space of a few years managed to end the open brothel system. In spite of all the inquiries, the prostitute was not criminalised to any greater extent by the legislation introduced during the period, notably the Criminal Law Amendment Act of 1935. Penalties were increased for soliciting and brothel-keeping but the status of the prostitute as an individual had not changed.

This book opens up another frontier in Irish history. The Irish have for too long ignored the destitute, marginalised and outcast of Irish society. As yet, for example, there is no history of poverty and its impact on Irish men, women and children in either the nineteenth or twentieth century. We know little about how the destitute and poor actually lived their lives on a day-by-day basis. Prostitution was an occupation engaged in by women because of their poverty. This book explores their lives, examines how sexuality was viewed in this period, and the ways in which control was exerted, especially on young women, in the expression of their sexuality. Issues of class form an important element in how women were judged in Ireland, and may have been the deciding factor in normalising institutionalisation as a way of dealing with 'wayward' girls. A study of prostitution is also an investigation of power and authority in Ireland. The forces of law and order did not always win out against prostitution; women who worked as prostitutes were not always hapless victims but were quite capable of resisting, often in subtle ways, attempts to control them.

1 'Frowsy, shameless women': an overview of prostitution in Ireland in the nineteenth and twentieth centuries

Prostitutes in the nineteenth and twentieth centuries were referred to in many ways by commentators and rescue workers. Among the descriptive names used were 'women of bad character', 'prostitutes', 'women of abandoned character', 'unfortunate women', 'dirty persons', 'destitute women', 'night walkers', 'nymphs of the pave', 'cyprians', 'Hecates' and 'paphian nymphs'.[1] Linking the religious with the profane you could also be a 'mother abbess' if you ran a brothel and, of course, prostitutes were also called the 'fallen'. Within the rescue homes they were termed penitents, Magdalens and children. The range of names applied to women who worked as prostitutes reflects the ambiguity, ambivalence, hypocrisy and disgust the public often felt towards them. Ideally, the public preferred not to refer to them at all. Common to studies of prostitution in other countries, two themes emerge clearly when exploring the history of prostitution in Ireland.[2] Issues of visibility and contamination were the central features shaping reaction to prostitution in Ireland. It was most often the visibility of prostitutes which caused anxiety, an anxiety not only about the use of public space but the contamination of that space. The discussions which developed around prostitution focused on the idea of contagion, either in the spread of disease and/or immorality; prostitution was itself believed to be contagious. But how extensive was prostitution in Ireland and what efforts were made to reduce the problem? Where were prostitutes to be found? How did the authorities define prostitution and how did the public recognise women to be prostitutes? How did the authorities deal with these women? It is very difficult to know what women who worked as prostitutes thought of their lives. They did not leave records of their own and their actions and words come to us mediated through police and court records, newspaper accounts, and asylum, prison, hospital and workhouse records. Nevertheless, it is through a critical examination of these sources that we can begin to answer some of these questions.

Criminal statistics

There are few, if any, reliable statistics regarding the extent of prostitution in the nineteenth or twentieth century. The two best sources in this context are the police statistics that exist for the Dublin Metropolitan District[3] from 1838 to 1919, and the criminal and judicial statistics that exist from 1863, the latter covering the entire country. But while apparently objective and full, these records are not as reliable as they would at first appear. Often the DMP figures do not correlate with the figures provided within the criminal and judicial statistics for the area. The figures themselves are also sometimes incorrectly computed with totals that do not match the individual figures given in the statistics. Official criminal and judicial statistics were not kept with any consistency between one place and another, and between one time period and another. Category titles of certain offences also change in this period. For instance in 1882 changes were made to the ways in which the general criminal and judicial figures were presented.[4] By 1900 prostitution, which had most often appeared under vagrancy charges, was now entered as a separate offence. The figures available account for arrests and convictions of women accused of soliciting; they do not record the number of re-arrests made. Considering that many women were arrested dozens of times within any one year, the figures supplied by the police inflate the numbers of women operating as prostitutes because they do not account for repeat arrests. The figures can also fluctuate widely, giving the impression that prostitution diminishes or increases; yet other evidence fails to confirm such fluctuations. On the other hand it is unlikely that the police arrested every woman who worked as a prostitute within the country. For our purposes the available figures can give us a general idea of where and when the police were most vigilant in arresting prostitutes, but they rarely give us an exact figure for the numbers of women who were actually working as prostitutes at any one time.

The earliest figures, for Dublin, come from the DMP statistics and cover the years 1838–1919. The statistics begin with a figure of 2,849 arrests in 1838 (see appendices 1–2) increasing yearly to a maximum of 4,784 in 1856 and decreasing to 1,672 in 1877, fluctuating around the 1,000 from then to the 1890s and reaching a low of 494 in 1899. In the twentieth century the highest number of arrests, no doubt a result of the publicity afforded by the Criminal Law Amendment Bill,[5] is evident in 1912, with 1,067 detentions; the arrest figures then gradually decrease to a low of 198 by 1919. Not all of the women arrested were actually convicted of soliciting and generally in the earlier period an average of 18 per cent were released without being charged. From the 1870s only about 1 per cent were discharged. If we look at the figures for the entire country we find that in 1863 (and these figures would include Dublin) there were 3,318 arrests for prostitution. Of this number 3,115 women were convicted, and of the total number brought before the courts, 2,791 were within the DMP district. Leinster consistently had the highest number of arrests for prostitution, and Connaught always had the lowest number. Galway City rarely features in the returns, but prostitution certainly existed there. For instance, the 1851 census listed twenty-seven prostitutes and brothel-keepers in County Galway, with four in the city; these go unrecorded in the crime statistics.[6] In 1881, when no arrests for prostitution were returned for Galway City, a police officer stationed there described a brothel in Middle Street as 'the worst house in Ireland'.[7] In the same year the *Galway Express* reported a number of arrests of women who were clearly prostitutes, but who did not find their way into the official statistics.[8] Women were often arrested on a number of occasions. Sarah Wilson, for example, had been imprisoned forty times on various dates between 2 September 1875 and 2 August 1877. Committed by magistrates at Newbridge, the Curragh and Naas, her offences included trespass, being drunk and disorderly, escaping from the lock hospital,[9] insubordination in the lock hospital and obstructing the footpath. Her sentences ranged from three days to three months.[10] Similarly, a prostitute who had tried to hang herself in Limerick jail in 1876 had spent all but four and a half months of the previous four years in jail for a variety of petty offences.[11] Such cases highlight the inadequacies of the official statistics as reliable indicators of active levels of prostitution in Ireland in the period.

The statistics do allow us to see in which towns the police were most active in pursuing prostitutes. In 1863 Drogheda had the most arrests (see appendix 2) after Dublin, but from 1867 it is evident that outside Dublin prostitution was most vigorously pursued in Belfast. It is not until the twentieth century that the arrest statistics for Cork City consistently climb beyond 200 annual arrests. The difficulty with the figures can be highlighted by looking a little more closely at these arrest figures. Dr James Curtis, who gave evidence before the Select Committee on the CDAs, informed the committee that in 1869, when the Acts came into force, 'there were 500 or 600 registered prostitutes' and forty-eight brothels in the city.[12] According to the criminal and judicial statistics the police arrested eight prostitutes there in 1869. Indeed, there is a curious absence in the official figures of arrests for prostitution in Cork City between 1898 and 1900. Does this suggest that prostitution had ceased to exist in Cork in those years, or that the police had not bothered to arrest any women, or that they simply made no returns? Had they given up pursuing prostitutes? An examination of the Good Shepherd Magdalen asylum entrants for 1898 and 1899 reveals that a total of 107 women made their way into the asylum, a number quite in excess of the usual entry figures for the 1890s.[13] This may be an example of the police encouraging young women on the streets to enter an asylum – a collusion between religious and secular authorities which was to become such a feature of Irish life from the 1920s.

Nationally, arrests for prostitution had gone from a high of 4,427 in 1865 to a low of 582 by 1919. In 1899 there were, for the entire country, 626 persons arrested. Of that number 494 were from the Dublin Metropolitan District. There were 132 arrests for the rest of the country. By the end of the nineteenth century there is quite a decrease in overall arrest figures, but these figures go up again in the twentieth century, particularly during the period prior to and during the First World War. Given the political climate in Ireland at the end of the nineteenth century and the fact that the attention of the police was focused on agrarian and political crime, arresting prostitutes would certainly not have been a priority. Issues of morality, and particularly the spread of venereal diseases, made the police more vigilant in making arrests during the period of the First World War. By 1918 the number of arrests for prostitution in Belfast made up 55 per cent of all arrests, a sign that even in the political upheaval of that time the Belfast police were carefully guarding the morals of the city. Likewise, the state of the country from 1919 meant that again police attention was focused elsewhere and no statistics are available between 1920 and 1926.

Not all women who worked as prostitutes would have been arrested, but women who were thought to be prostitutes were also to be found among other women arrested. For example in 1871 the police instigated proceedings against 17,153 women (many of these were re-arrests) whom they deemed 'bad characters'. These included vagrants, drunkards and thieves, but 10,456 or 61 per cent were known prostitutes. If these figures are accurate this would form about 0.57 per cent of the total adult female population over the age of fifteen in 1871. The number of women arrested for offences other than soliciting in 1900 included 2,970 believed to be prostitutes. However, some indication of the numbers of individual women (see appendix 3) engaged in prostitution in Dublin can be gauged from the figures provided by the DMP on the statistics for women either residing in brothels or in other residences but working as prostitutes between 1838 and 1894.[14] The greatest number of prostitutes is evident for the first year that figures are available, 1838, when 1,630 were so identified.[15] That the numbers of women claimed to be working as prostitutes remained above the thousand mark during the period of the famine, 1845–50, is hardly surprising. The figures begin to decline from 1855, but rise above the thousand mark again between 1862 and 1867. After that there is a general decline, with some peaks, until 436 women are deemed to work as prostitutes in the DMP district by 1890. These figures, provided by the DMP, of individual women who worked as prostitutes in Dublin, excluded those known to be in prison, for which no figures were supplied.[16] Again these figures suggest that in the region of 0.5 per cent of the adult female population over the age of twenty living in Dublin engaged in prostitution. Using contemporary police arrest figures John V. O'Brien asserts that up to 2 per cent of the adult female population in Dublin worked as prostitutes and that it is not unreasonable to conclude, if one includes women in Magdalen asylums and the lock hospital, that as many as 3,000 to 4,000 women (3 to 4 per cent of the adult female population) over the age of twenty operated as prostitutes in the city in the early years of the twentieth century.[17] However, this seems to me to be an exaggeration. It is likely, as previously noted, that the numbers of individual women working as prostitutes never matched the numbers of those arrested. Although it is impossible to provide an exact figure for the number of women actively engaged in prostitution, accepting the police figures as a guide and including the women who were maintained in Magdalen asylums and the lock hospital, the number of possible prostitutes may well have reached between 1,000 and 1,500, though the women in these institutions would be temporarily, and sometimes permanently, removed from their occupation.

In gauging the extent of prostitution and its effect upon the local population it is important to look at the number of brothels that existed. Generally, it appears that women ran more brothels than did men. In Limerick in July of 1836 nine women were found guilty of keeping brothels in the city.[18] According to the 1861 census 131 of the 134 brothel-keepers listed were women.[19] The infamous Mrs Mack, who appears in the 'Nighttown' episode of *Ulysses*, kept a brothel at 85 Tyrone Street in the heart of the red-light (Monto) district of Dublin. She was so well known that the area was often referred to as 'Macktown'.[20] Brothels, recorded in the police statistics as of either a 'superior' or 'inferior' variety, were most common in Dublin but they also existed in other towns and cities in Ireland. In 1838 there were 402 brothels, or houses frequented by prostitutes, in Dublin; the highest number recorded was for 1845 when there were 419 such establishments. During the famine years the number of brothels, houses occupied or frequented by prostitutes, hovered between 330 and 419 (and the number of women deemed to live in them was in excess of 1,300) (see appendix 3). For the rest of the century the numbers fluctuated between 124 and 311.

We also have some information on the suppression of brothels by the police, although it is clear that they were not always vigilant or active in closing them down. For instance, a complaint made by a resident about the 'numerous brothels' in Digges Lane and Goat Alley in Dublin in 1835 initiated an inquiry. The ensuing report noted the existence of 'twenty-one houses in that lane; sixteen of which, as they have been informed by their officers, are brothels', and it was observed that the magistrates found it impossible to 'abate the nuisance complained of, because as soon as the keeper of one brothel is committed, another comes in his or her place'. The original complainant, John Bramble, had lived in Digges Lane for about fourteen years and observed that brothels had existed in the area prior to and throughout his residence. In his original memorial he declared the area a 'second Gomorrah'. The Catholic curate agreed with his assessment and noted an 'annual increase of those miserable outcasts and their companions, robbers and resurrection men'.[21] While the police did nothing in that instance sporadic efforts were made to close brothels. The greatest number suppressed in one year, 1855, was 77, when 196 brothels operated in the city. The criminal and judicial statistics tell us that on only seventeen occasions between 1838 and 1900 did the police suppress any brothels. Of the 506 operating in 1873 they managed to close 4. In 1879, the DMP closed 17 brothels in Bull Lane but observed that the effect of this suppression 'was their establishment in other parts of the city where their presence had been hitherto unknown'. This was considered a 'practice the wisdom of which may be open to question'.[22] From 1907 the police appear to have been more vigilant in arresting brothel-keepers, and between that year and 1912 over fifty arrests were made annually for this offence. In 1912, fifty-nine brothels were reported to exist in the DMP district, with Belfast having seven such establishments and Fermanagh two. By 1916 the DMP district reported the existence of fourteen brothels; Cork City had two, Armagh one, Belfast nineteen and Derry four. In the same year twenty-nine individuals were convicted of keeping brothels.[23] For 1918 the numbers of brothels reported in the DMP district was eight, while ten establishments were reported for Belfast and none was reported to exist in any other part of the country.[24] It is difficult to gauge exactly how many women worked from brothels. Figures for the Dublin Metropolitan District show that, for instance, an average of 5 prostitutes resided in 157 brothels in 1838. In the same year it was reported that 758 prostitutes resided in houses not considered to be brothels (see appendix 3). In 1863 the average number of women residing in 121 brothels was 8, with 141 women working outside the brothel system. By 1894, the last year when figures are available, an average of 3 women worked from 74 brothels, while 118 prostitutes operated as 'privateers'. It is also very clear that brothels, particularly in the nineteenth century, existed without too much interference from the authorities. It is evident that at times the police were vigilant in arresting prostitutes and closing brothels, at other times less so. Their vigilance was often a reaction to public pressure for them to act, but for much of the nineteenth, and into the early years of the twentieth, century prostitutes in Dublin at least went about their business with relatively little police interference.

Contemporary accounts of prostitution

Besides statistics there are also some contemporary accounts of prostitution in Ireland. William Logan, a Scottish mission worker who had experience of mission life and work in Leeds, Glasgow and elsewhere, visited Ireland in 1845 and reported on prostitution there.[25] It is notable that his book was not published until 1870, at the beginning of a decade that saw public interest and concern about prostitution and the CDAs become significant issues. He claimed that Cork contained eighty-five regular brothels and 356 public prostitutes. He observed that 'a large number of procuresses abound . . . individuals have been known to tender their daughters and other relatives to brothel keepers for money. A man in 1841 voluntarily offered his daughter for £3.' In addition to these women there were thought to be one hundred 'privateers' who operated from houses not designated as brothels. The nun in charge at the Sisters of Charity Magdalen asylum informed him that intemperance, dancing parties and a love of dress were the major causes of prostitution. Of brothels he noted that

prostitutes are not received into the superior brothels except upon a sort of recommendation from another of the same class. If it is known that any of them had been on the streets, they are never afterwards received in these houses. They pay their mistress about 8s a week for their board; their surplus earnings are appropriated to their own use.[26]

Logan was also told by the Rev. William Robertson, superintendent of the Dublin City Mission, that there were 1,700 prostitutes operating in Dublin at the same time. (The DMP noted 1,494 women working as prostitutes in 1845.) In Belfast he met Dr John Edgar who informed him that 236 prostitutes lived in brothels in that city.[27] Edgar himself became involved in rescue work and was to claim that he knew of a small 'village, where ten sisters in four families are prostitutes, I know four sisters who support their father, mother and younger brother, by the wages of iniquity.'[28]

Whether figures provided by rescue workers are to be relied on is open to question. It was clearly advantageous for them to overstate the numbers of women working in prostitution. Yet while their figures might not be entirely accurate there are enough incidental accounts to confirm the suggestion that large numbers of women engaged in prostitution.

Michael McCarthy recalled that when he was a boy in Cork in the 1870s, he saw women in North Street 'bare-headed and bare-breasted, in coloured dresses disporting themselves at the quay end of the street, within sight of Patrick's Bridge, the most central point of the town'.[29] A newspaper report of the notorious area around Barrack Street in Cork City remarked in 1878 that the area had 'been totally abandoned by the police'.[30] In the same year a traveller, staying in the Victoria Hotel in Cork, claimed he could not sleep because of the numbers of prostitutes outside on the street. He was kept awake by 'a series of noises consisting of cries, curses, howlings and screams the most appalling accompanied with language the most abominable that human lips can utter or human ears can listen to'.[31]

Large-scale public events such as fairs and race meetings attracted prostitutes. In 1868 the Naas poor law guardians wrote to the Poor Law Commissioners about the number of persons, including prostitutes, who obtained temporary relief in the workhouse on the nights of 24 and 25 April when the Punchestown races were held. Many of these individuals, the guardians complained, 'merely visit this locality for the purpose of attending the races'.[32] One witness to a committee of inquiry into the operation of the CDAs remembered 'a time when, if a ship or a regiment came into Queenstown, and a letter was thrown over the wall of that refuge [a Protestant refuge in Cork], they would all be out of it in 24 hours'.[33] Donnybrook Fair, an annual event since 1204, had become a source of annoyance to the Church and the authorities from the level of drunkenness, riot and immorality evident there. In 1834, in a submission to a parliamentary inquiry on intoxication, the police suggested that every year after the fair a number of young women, ruined by 'its intemperate orgies' ended up as unfortunates on the streets.[34] The professional classes and the local clergy began to place considerable pressure on the government to close the fair, observing that 'the scenes of immorality, prostitution, and the sickness which originate in it are too appalling and too forcible to believe that these proceedings which have led to the destruction of thousands, could ever be considered entertainment by the moral and discerning portion of the community'.[35] The reforming cleric Fr John Spratt observed the impact of the fair, noting that despite drunkenness 'many, many an unfortunate female [who] now rolls in the abyss of prostitution, would have been [an] honourable member of society but for that sink of pestilence and carnival of crime'.[36] The fair gradually declined and was gone by the 1860s.[37] Its suppression was due to an alliance between the Catholic Church, evangelical Protestants and the police who sought to control the behaviour of the lower classes, along with the spaces in which they sought entertainment. Fergus D'Arcy has noted that the decline of the fair 'was the cultural consequence of class formation in Dublin'.[38] The growth of the respectable classes and their increasing social and moral power saw members of this class assail what they understood as immorality, whether evident in literature, cinema or as prostitution, throughout the remainder of the nineteenth and into the twentieth century.[39]

It was in towns which housed garrisons that prostitution was most public. In 1860 an 'amazing influx of prostitutes' into Clonmel was attributed to the town 'becoming headquarters to a regiment of the line'.[40] During the nineteenth century a garrison force of about 26,000 troops was maintained in the country.[41] Indeed, every garrison town had its red-light district. At Swinford market a tout sat in a *suisteog* (a type of straw-woven armchair) and solicited on behalf of the ladies of 'The Lane'. Claremorris had its Bothar Garbh; Mullingar had 'Slap Arse Lane'.[42] Mason, in his parochial survey, noted the immorality which existed in the garrison town of Athlone and the Protestant rector commented that prostitutes,

infest the streets, as well as the hedges and ditches about the town, not only to the destruction of the moral[ity], of the present as well as the rising generation, but even in violation of common decency; to such a pitch is depravity risen, that vice does not hide its deeds in darkness, but boldly stalks abroad in open day.[43]

Isaac Weld, writing of Roscommon Town in 1832, noted,

that the evil [prostitution] was of far greater magnitude than it appeared at first view. In Castle Street, on the skirts of the town, there was actually a range of brothels, at the doors of which females stood, at noonday, to entice passengers, with gestures too plain to be misunderstood.[44]

He ascertained that the problem of prostitution was so evident because of the 'contiguity of Roscommon to the great military establishment maintained at Athlone'. Roscommon, being the county town, was also the place where army pensioners received their pensions through the paymasters of the police. In 1830 at least 1,120 men received their money there and these were thought to be easy prey for the prostitutes of the area. A witness to the poor law inquiry of the 1830s stated that prostitutes 'follow the barracks while they are well looking and are obliged to beg when they have lost their good looks'.[45] In 1847, at the height of the famine, a Colonel More, writing from Newbridge, which he claimed was 'infested with prostitutes', sought advice on how to punish these women who 'climb over the barracks wall'.[46] Dundalk, another garrison town, also had its share of prostitution. At least seventeen women were arrested in that town between July 1859 and January 1861 for 'loitering in a public street . . . for the purposes of prostitution'.[47]

The problem of prostitution in Ennis became significantly worse after the establishment of the militia barracks on Military Road in the middle of the 1850s. In December 1858 it was noted that 'whole families' in the town were said to be living off the 'wages of prostitution'.[48] In 1884 there were complaints of prostitutes and soldiers from Clare Castle conducting business in the graveyard at Clare Abbey.[49] But prostitution was not confined solely to the garrison towns of the country. The Rev. Anthony McIntyre who visited the poor in Belfast in the 1850s observed that 'off North Street we entered several of the worst houses in this place, houses full of unfortunate females . . . called at no 13 Long Lane . . . I learned that there are two very bad houses in this place.' Worse was to come when he visited several houses about Smithfield. 'This', he noted, 'is a filthy place in every sense . . . I learned that there are from 16 to 20 houses of ill fame in the area, and that on average there are from 4 to 7 unfortunate females in every house.'[50] On another visit to the Suffern's Entry, he observed,

This is a very bad place. I did not go into any of the houses but stood without; asked some of the wretched women who were standing about whether they approved of the life they were leading. Some asked me what I would have them do. Some asked me for money. Some talked the language of their profession.[51]

The Rev. William O'Hanlon reinforced McIntyre's account of the misery that was evident in the back streets and alleys of Belfast. He described Plunkett's Court in the city as 'the resort of miserable women and pickpockets, who find a fit asylum in its dark and filthy receptacles'.[52] Likewise, a report from the *Ballymena Observer* of 1866 noted that Sydney Lane, behind High Street, was the most notorious of the town's back lanes. It was, according to the paper, a

pestilent plague spot – a pandemonium of contaminating vice and every species of criminality. Successive gangs of thieves, swindlers and harlots have haunted or had their habitations in it during a considerable portion of the present century. And most disreputable scenes of riot, drunkenness and immorality are of almost daily occurrence amongst its denizens.[53]

The newspaper noted that the tenements were let on a weekly basis, and suggested that the area be cleared of every 'householder of questionable character', and the place should then be renamed 'The Arcade'.

Renaming streets associated with prostitution was a relatively common occurrence. Anderson's Row in Belfast, noted as an area of immorality, was renamed Millfield Place in December 1860, although this did not reduce its infamous links.[54] In 1885 Lower Temple Street in Dublin was renamed Hill Street in consequence of a memorial to the corporation from a number of inhabitants who 'had suffered serious deterioration in the value of [their] property' as certain houses in the lower end of the street were occupied by 'immoral characters'.[55] In 1888 Dublin Corporation renamed Mecklenburgh Street Tyrone Street, to please the respectable working-class residents of the area. The memorial of the inhabitants noted that the female members of the 'humble residents' found it difficult to 'obtain employment as domestic servants owing to their residence in a locality to the name of which such bad odour attaches'.[56] Writing to Archbishop Walsh in February 1889, a resident warned of the possibility of 'infamous contamination'. He observed that in this street,

there stands a block of five houses. On one side of these houses are the catholic schools with about 300 pupils. Opposite are tenement houses whose rooms are occupied by respectable tradesmen and their families who live here owing to their proximity to the factories, etc. These five houses of ill fame stand out in bold relief, their outward respectability being of itself an attraction. By day you will see these handsome balconied windows all open and young women of abandoned life, fashionably attired, smoking cigarettes and cracking audibly their obscene jests. At night these houses are illuminated and cars conveying tipsy young gentlemen rolling to the doors which are thrown open no privacy being observed. The children and their teachers cannot avoid these sights.[57]

Though the street name had been changed the area remained notorious as the red-light district of Dublin until the mid-1920s.[58]

Prostitution and the police

A manual for the DMP noted in 1889 that 'prostitutes cannot legally be taken into custody for being prostitutes; to justify their apprehension they must commit some specific act that which is an offence against law'. It was also noted that

the police have no power to interfere with men and women talking together in the streets, so long as they behave themselves properly, and are not assembled together in such numbers as actually to cause obstruction; but if it is absolutely necessary to interfere, then it is to be done civilly and firmly, without offensive language or manner.[59]

By 1910 the official Royal Irish Constabulary (RIC) manual informed the ordinary constable that his duty in respect of 'prostitutes loitering to the annoyance of the inhabitants or passengers on his beat' was to caution them.[60] Police were also told that if they observed 'a prostitute decoying a tipsy person into any back place, [they] should follow and warn such person of his danger'.[61] They were not always encouraged to arrest these women. Police activity was often a pretence of vigilance. While the police had many legal codes to help them deal with prostitutes, there was no legal definition of what constituted a prostitute and prostitution itself was not outlawed.

Throughout the nineteenth century the Vagrancy Act of 1824[62] was the one most commonly used to arrest women who were deemed prostitutes. Under the Police Clauses Acts of 1847 a woman believed to be 'a common prostitute or night walker loitering or importuning passengers for the purpose of prostitution', could be arrested. This provision was extended under the Towns Improvements Acts of 1854, which did not apply to Dublin, Cork or Limerick, to include women being 'otherwise offensive', thus providing the police with broad discretionary powers of arrest.[63] Prostitutes, together with other kinds of individuals trying to earn a living, such as fortune-tellers, performers and beggars, were targeted under the Act as potential threats to public order. There were also laws against keeping bawdy houses or brothels, although as we have seen none of these laws was enforced consistently. Even where these laws were enforced they did not result in the decline of prostitution. The laws appeared to indicate that legislation could clear the streets of prostitution, but did more to reassure middle-class reformers of that possibility than to realise it. As we shall see it was under the CDAs legislation of the 1860s[64] that the police were given their broadest powers with regard to prostitution. The role of the state in monitoring sexual behaviour was virtually confined to arrests for public prostitution and solicitation, and hence singled out one lowly class of prostitutes, those who peddled their wares in the streets, for arrest throughout the period under review. It was these 'public' women who were subject to the most thorough scrutiny by the police, the reformers and the state.

There is some evidence that police vigilance with regard to prostitution was undermined by corruption. Between January 1838 and 1858 at least 122 police officers of the DMP were either fined, demoted or dismissed for engaging with prostitutes. John Landy, for instance, was fined £2 for being in a brothel, with a woman, while off duty. Another policeman was dismissed, being caught in bed in a brothel with his uniform on. Yet another was fined 5 shillings for being in a brothel in plain clothes and talking obscenely with a prostitute.[65] Police officers found in houses of ill repute could always claim, of course, to be there to look for stolen property or to be engaged in other police work.[66] The information provided about the police in brothels also allows us to note the geography of Dublin's brothels in these decades. The streets most often named were Sycamore Alley, Thomas Street, Long Lane, Exchequer Street, Lees Lane, Temple Bar, Dame Street, Bow Lane, Phoenix Street, Reddy's Court, Stirrup Lane and Bay View. How extensive corruption was is unclear and there appears to be no concrete evidence that police took

money from prostitutes to leave them alone. However, given the proximity of many police to prostitutes it would be highly unlikely that over two
centuries some police did not seek money, or services, from prostitutes to
prevent arrest. The fact that brothels were allowed to operate almost
unhindered is indicative of some level of corruption.

Clearing the streets

But if the police response to prostitution was more often characterised by
inactivity than activity, periodic efforts were made to clear certain streets
or areas of prostitutes. These clearance attempts were often less than successful. For example, the *Freeman's Journal* reported in 1855 that a magistrate complained that DMP efforts to clear prostitutes from French
Street were of dubious value since they merely had the effect of dispersing
the women into 'respectable locales'.[67] Two years later the paper reported
that on becoming aware of the existence of a brothel above a cigar shop in
Duke Street, the DMP, rather than shutting it down, simply warned
'respectable persons' of the nature of the establishment.[68] In the 1870s
anxiety about prostitution in Dublin becomes much more evident. It was
frequently claimed that the leading streets of Dublin were 'disgraced at all
hours of the day and night by bevies not of soiled doves but of rampant,
impudent thieves who deserve no quarter from society'.[69] A leader in the
Freeman's Journal contended that 'from the Rotundo to Stephens Green
in a line is not peaceably passable at night. Something needs to be done.'[70]
Sackville Street was considered impassable at night after 8 pm.[71] The
1870s was also one decade in which the DMP appeared to make some
efforts to tackle the visible extent of prostitution. Rawton McNamara, the
senior surgeon of the Westmoreland lock hospital, reported to a committee of inquiry into the CDAs of the methods used by the police at this
time:

Almost all the houses of ill fame were in a street called French Street, and another
street called Clarendon Street; French Street is very close to the square in which I
live . . . St Stephens's Green Park, and we did not like to have such people near us,
and we were anxious to close it. Clarendon Street is the locale of a very beautiful
chapel, and the priests did not like to have them there. The result was that police
were put at the doors and took down the names of every one who came; these were
what we would call the upper class . . . and the police took down the names of all
gentlemen going to enter, and that at once drove them out of that, and then they
went to the banks of the canal. But they were removed from there, and the result is
that they are scattered in different outlying parts.

McNamara did not believe that this action by the police made any impact
upon the extent of prostitution.[72] These attempts in the 1870s may have

been occasioned by the CDAs legislation and were often instigated and supported by the public and by the clergy. In a letter published in the *Freeman's Journal* in 1877, a priest lamented that in Dublin 'the social evil' was everywhere and was

spreading to a most alarming extent, and that the purity that was once the proudest boast of our country threatens to be its no longer. Not more than a week ago I passed along Stephen's Green and through Grafton Street at about eight o'clock at night, and sights met my eyes which were enough to shock the most hardened. Dozens upon dozens of females belonging to that class truly designated unfortunate, the majority of them not eighteen years of age, with faces fair enough to people heaven, passed me, using language and openly flaunting a shame the very mention of which is enough to bring a blush to the cheek of virtue.[73]

The cleric's letter exposed a number of concerns which were then, in the first decade of the CDAs legislation, clearly emerging about prostitution in the country: the belief that Ireland was rapidly losing its reputation for purity, the changing geography of sexual display in Dublin, the youth of prostitutes, the contamination of public space with lewd behaviour and abusive language, and the assault on respectability. Individual policeman sometimes undertook efforts to clear the streets of prostitutes. In 1864 the closure of brothels in Godsil's Lane, Cork, was attributed to the 'persevering exertions' of Head Constable Mills.[74] The women who had lived in the houses, however, merely relocated.[75] Likewise in May 1880 the *Freeman's Journal* noted that the suppression of seventeen brothels by the police in Bull Lane in Dublin had led merely to the dispersal of the women rather than the suppression of prostitution.[76]

Sometimes the public took matters into its own hands. In 1851 a riot erupted in Susan Lee's brothel in Talbot Street, Belfast, due to the 'conduct of some inmates'. It was reported that

the persons in the house commenced the affray by beating one another and breaking the windows . . . a mob then collected, and commenced wrecking the house, in order to rid the street of such disagreeable neighbours, and would speedily have 'turned it inside out' but for the interference of the police.[77]

An association to 'discountenance vice' was formed in the Robert Street and Talbot Street area of Belfast in August 1856 in a failed attempt to close down brothels in the area.[78] Some businessmen complained about the lack of police activity in Belfast in 1872 noting that Distillery Street was never patrolled by a police constable, 'which should be done frequently, as this street, leading to the fields . . . is a great resort for night walkers of both sexes, (especially in the summer time) and now it is not safe to walk the street at night'.[79] The Rev. Maguire, a priest in Cork City, explained his attitude to prostitution to the CDAs commission of 1871.

He observed that the Catholic clergy in Cork would not allow prostitutes to operate, directing their activities very much at encouraging these women to enter the Magdalen asylums. However, the clergy also tried to contain the problem as much as possible. Indeed, clerics such as Maguire appear to have been more concerned with containment than the eradication of prostitution. Voicing contemporary beliefs about prostitution, which saw women as temptresses and as sites of contagion, he declared to the commission:

I would not allow a woman at all in the streets. I would compel them to reside inside such localities as those I have named. I would say that knowing our people, and knowing, generally speaking, the virtue that is in them, that half our married men and half our youths would be preserved from misfortune if they did not meet these unfortunate women in the streets . . . It is the looseness and freedom of these women who can walk the streets at night that, generally speaking, have tended to the immorality of our youth and advanced men for years more than anything I know of.[80]

From the 1850s the Catholic clergy became more prominent in trying to rid certain areas of prostitution. In 1850 a newspaper reported on the efforts of some of the local clergy to rid Nenagh of 'the unfortunate outcast women with which it has been infested for a long period much to the detriment of public morality'. The article also noted that the 'magistracy do not interfere in this matter'.[81] In 1851 a priest pursued a prostitute named Anne Miles through the streets of Ennis in an attempt to cut her hair off. In her efforts to escape, Miles ran, through an open side door, into the kitchen of a Mr Leech. She was cornered inside by the priest and a servant boy present volunteered to complete the hair cut while the priest held the woman down. The servant boy was summonsed by the magistrates and fined for his offence; the magistrates, after some debate, decided not to summons the priest.[82] Again in Ennis, in April 1853 Fr Quinlivan summonsed a man named Grady for keeping a brothel.[83] In the 1855 Kilkee petty sessions court a local priest, Fr McMahon, was prosecuted for assaulting two notorious 'young *ladies* from Kilrush'. The priest, despite having been previously warned by the court, apparently tore at the prostitutes' clothes and beat them. In his defence, according to the *Clare Freeman*, McMahon asserted that 'he had spiritual and temporal jurisdiction, which he may exercise at [his] discretion'. Not entirely accepting his authority the court punished him with a small fine.[84] A number of days later one of the women involved, Bridget Cavanagh, was back in court, claiming that, because she had sworn against Fr McMahon, she had been thrown down the stairs by a local man.[85] In 1855 the *Limerick Chronicle* reported that in Kilkee, a 'place infested by a number of unfortunate women', the parish priest had 'publicly warned from the chapel altar' the harbourers of these women.[86] In 1864 one Ennis priest tore the clothes 'off two bad girls in College Road', and carried the 'toggeries' to the house of the parish priest as a 'trophy'.[87] Likewise, Fr David Humphreys of Tipperary Town, noted for his political efforts on behalf of the Land League, constantly harassed soldiers and 'fallen women' lurking in the side streets and alleys of the town.[88] In 1871 one Catholic cleric described the actions taken to remove 'camp followers' from Cobh. His comments also reveal a fear of the single woman:

In Queenstown [Cobh] . . . there is not a bad woman in any house there. It is a seaport town: there are bad women there, but they are in the bush. The clergy would not allow any single woman to remain in the town; they are all in the bush. They live on the brake, the portion of land not built on, which consists of trees and furze, and they go and live there, and come up to Cork very often to get rest for the next time; they remain in the bush and sleep in the bush, but not a woman dares to be received into the town.[89]

Activity by the clergy seemed to depend very much on the character of the clergyman himself and the level of activity by prostitutes. In 1876 one clergyman determined to close down a number of brothels in Cork City. Fr Michael Shinkwin of St Finbarre's parish was said to have achieved what was 'humanly impossible'.[90] He went to Cuthbert's Lane 'armed with . . . the invisible power of prayer' and managed to convince the local inhabitants to give up their way of life. In this area he found '20 miserable filthy hovels', occupied by about 120 'unfortunate women'. The women were sent either to the workhouse, the Magdalen asylum or reunited with friends. Rev. Shinkwin continued his work in Phoenix Street and by August was working his way through North Street.[91] Michael McCarthy, who had been brought up in Cork, was later to recall 'that there was a great deal of ostentatious formality . . . about the proceeding, such as religious processions through the street, [and the] blessing of the houses from which the women had been evicted'.[92] The adult McCarthy living in Dublin attended Mass regularly in the pro-cathedral in Marlborough Street, close to an area of brothels, and claimed that he had never heard a sermon preached against prostitution.[93] The Rev. Thomas O'Reilly, giving evidence to a CDAs committee, observed that before the Acts came into force women in brothels could never be visited by clergymen. 'No clergyman', he stated, 'would attempt to visit the women in those brothels which were dens of infamy and shame; it would be absolutely dangerous for him to [do] so notwithstanding that he is a priest.'[94] Another witness related that a Catholic priest called to a dying prostitute in Bracken's Lane in Dublin refused to attend her 'in consequence of a most indecent assault on the last priest' who had gone into the area 'for the purpose of the administration of his religion'.[95] Though it was rare for a woman to assault a cleric, it was not unprecedented. A Protestant clergyman, the Rev. Charles Ward, found himself the victim of the 'most filthy . . . and abusive language' from an 'unfortunate'.[96] Priests also needed to exert some discretion over any accusations they made against women they deemed immoral. In 1857 Ellen Noonan, from Mitchelstown, wrote to the diocesan bishop, William Keane, after her local priest denounced her from the altar for keeping an 'improper house'. Noonan claimed to be a respectable lodging-house keeper and demanded that she be allowed to defend herself.[97] Similarly in the same year, Elizabeth Hayes, who sometimes kept a lodging-house in Queenstown, wrote to Bishop Keane complaining that the local priest had denounced her as an immoral woman. Viewing this as a result of envy and spite on the part of her neighbours, Hayes demanded that the bishop investigate the matter and restore or 'set right' her character.[98] While apparently successful, these sporadic attempts by the police, by clergy and by active individuals appear to have made little real impact on levels of prostitution.[99]

The complacency evident in police attitudes to prostitution was echoed in the inaction of the military establishment in the matter. In an editorial addressed to the local military authorities the *Kilkenny Moderator* asked, without success, that action be taken against 'exhibitions of a very disgraceful nature made by soldiers and women of infamous character on the Hebron Road, where public decency is greatly outraged in the open day'.[100] A number of town commissioners in those towns which housed garrisons attempted to have the local military authorities take responsibility for the problem of prostitution. However, while requesting the assistance of the military authorities in reducing the incidence of prostitution, town commissioners were also wary of being too forceful in case the business brought to the town by the resident garrison should dissipate.[101] In 1886 the urban district council in Fermoy corresponded with the district inspector of the RIC to put 'a stop to what threatens to become a grave scandal within the township'.[102] Little was to change. By 1890 things had deteriorated further and the urban district council noted that 'some of the soldiers of the garrison are guilty night after night of gross immoral and violent conduct in the unfrequented lanes and streets of the town'. They requested the military authorities to censure the soldiers, but again nothing happened.[103] Further complaints were made when it was discovered that the new graveyard which was attached to the barracks had become 'the resort of prostitutes and soldiers'. Such complaints continued until after the First World War but received almost no attention from either the police or the military authorities.[104]

However, as the nineteenth century progressed prostitution in Dublin, at least, became more geographically confined. After the police activities of the 1870s brothels began to emerge, as women began to move into the cheaper accommodation of the Lower Mecklenburgh Street area. The evidence of the Rev. Robert Conlan to a commission on housing in 1885 revealed that brothels were extending into the district. While admitting that 'improper characters and houses occupied by people of that sort in Dublin are not nearly so bad as they are in other cities', he stated that 'whether from want of power on the part of the police, or from other causes, they [were] allowed considerable immunity'.[105] He also noted that the poor would not go to the authorities to have these individuals arrested.[106] He observed that some of the houses were regular bad houses; but that in the case of tenement houses 'bad people who would carry on the same trade would take a flat',[107] so that brothels in this area were now to be found in tenement houses which also contained respectable families. As early as 1837 this area was noted for its 'great number of destitute poor, [and] dissolute and depraved characters' of both sexes.[108] The Mecklenburgh/Montgomery district of the city, north-east of the Custom House, marked the infamous Monto district. In 1886 the residents of Upper Mecklenburgh Street, who described themselves as of the 'respectable working classes', tried to disassociate themselves from the residents in the lower part of the street where 'many of the houses were used for improper purposes and inhabited by persons of the worst character'. Although they succeeded in having the upper part of the street renamed Tyrone Street in 1887, unfortunately for the inhabitants the lower part of the street was known as Lower Tyrone Street. However, in 1911 the upper part became Waterford Street, and the lower part, still notorious, was renamed Railway Street.[109] The nearby Mabbot Street was also notorious because many houses there were brothels.[110] Dublin Corporation undertook some slum clearance in Montgomery Street and by 1905 the former tenements of numbers 51 to 70 had been demolished. New buildings and a new name, Foley Street, did not however, remove the notorious reputation for infamy the street had acquired under its previous name.[111] While Tyrone Street was the most infamous street in the area with a considerable number of brothels, the adjoining streets, Montgomery Street, Mabbot Street, Beaver Street, Purdon Street, Elliott Place, Faithful Place, Uxbridge and Nickleby were almost as disreputable (see map 1).[112] In this area was located the famous Becky Cooper's (immortalised as Bella Cohen's in the 'Circe' episode of Joyce's *Ulysses*) and Mrs Mack's was located at 85 Tyrone Street.[113] Halliday Sutherland recalled that in 1904, as a medical student in Dublin, he had walked one evening down Tyrone Street. He observed that 'in no other capital of Europe have I seen its equal. It was a street of Georgian houses and each one was a brothel. On the steps of every house

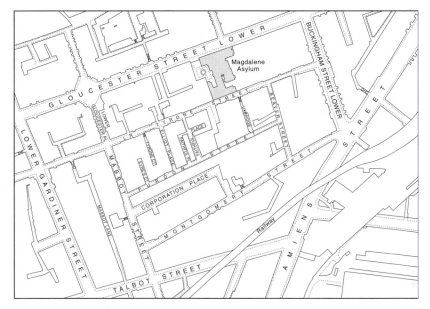

Map 1. The 'Monto' district of Dublin *c.* 1910–14. Courtesy of the Valuations Office, Dublin.

women and girls dressed in everything from evening dress to a nightdress stood or sat.'[114] This was an impoverished area of the city. In 1914 a report of the work of the St Vincent de Paul Society noted the poverty that existed in the district of Lower Gardiner Street, Gloucester Street, Railway Street and Corporation Street. They instituted free breakfasts on Sunday morning in an attempt to stop the poor from going to a local pros-elytising charity.[115]

It was to this area that prostitutes had been gradually confined from the 1880s by the prospect of cheap accommodation and lack of police harass-ment. However, this did not mean that prostitution did not exist or was less obvious in other parts of the city. Sackville Street (now O'Connell Street) was a principal promenading ground for prostitutes, and many women working as prostitutes were also to be found in St Stephen's Green and around the dock area. A police commissioner reported that prior to 1922 prostitution was mainly confined to a particular area stretching from Summerhill to Talbot Street and from Marlborough Street to the Five Lamps at the junction of Amiens Street and Portland Row. Soliciting went on in the public streets and a police report of the period noted prostitutes were always able to bring their 'unfortunate clients to the brothels which existed quite openly without much particular let or hindrance on the part of police authorities'.[116]

Containment and contagion

Containment and visibility were the key issues which surfaced in attempts to deal with prostitution. While the DMP were not terribly successful in closing down brothels they remarked in 1886 that 'considerable progress . . . [had] been made in narrowing the area within which such houses are situated'.[117] What the public most often wanted was for prostitutes to be kept out of public sight. The cry was that they be confined to a place beyond the view of the general public. 'It is strange', one commentator of Cork noted, 'that nothing is done to expel them from places in which their appearance is a profanation and to confine them to haunts where neither eye nor ear will be offended by their deeds.'[118] But not everyone believed that Dublin was as immoral as the papers declared. In 1886 Count Plunkett had alerted Archbishop Walsh to the deplorable state of Dublin's thoroughfares. In response the archbishop walked from Earlsfort Terrace to Rutland Square to judge for himself. 'I did not see anywhere the slightest indication that would lead anyone to suspect anything wrong.'[119] If the archbishop picked a quiet night for his stroll, Major Reynolds of the Salvation Army had a different story to tell. Reynolds, who had finished an Irish tour in 1894, was greatly moved by the 'terrible sights of the Irish capital'. He reported that

in the slum district where the poorest women live we went through the streets . . . I have never seen . . . such brazen immorality. There were literally hundreds of the women sitting about on the pavements and doorsteps. Their first floor windows – curtainless – were wide open, and the ground floor rooms were similar, so that passers-by could see the whole interior, with a bed.[120]

Throughout the nineteenth and early twentieth centuries moments of panic about prostitution found public expression most consistently through the newspapers of the period. The letters columns of the national press offered a public forum to individuals and groups to voice their concerns about prostitution. Through these letters correspondents detailed their own public encounters with the mass of prostitutes who seemed to have taken over the streets of the capital, voiced their horror at the display of immorality, discussed the causes of prostitution and suggested remedies for it. Despite public concern and calls for action to eliminate prostitution from the streets and alleys of Irish towns and cities, the perception that it remained a considerable problem lasted until the 1920s.

It is significant that on the three occasions when prostitution received widespread newspaper coverage in the period from 1850 to 1900, issues of health were also predominant. A series of letters appeared in the *Freeman's Journal* in September 1866 complaining about the 'public nuisance' in Dublin. Attention was drawn to the 'fearful sights' of Grafton Street, which 'during each afternoon literally swarmed with women of loose character'. It was, one writer declared, 'a nuisance . . . so debasing to all classes of society, and so demoralising and contagious to all who come in contact with its promoters'.[121] It is not, I think, coincidental that at the same time, in the same paper, numerous reports were published about the presence of cholera in the country. Words, such as 'fearful', 'dreadful', 'contagion', 'contagious', the same words used about prostitution, appear in these letters revealing a fear of bodily violation, contamination and even the fear of death. The connection with contagion became even more explicit in Cork City in the 1870s. Here a powerful link was made between squalid living conditions, disease and prostitution. The streets associated with prostitution in Cork included Furze's Alley, Godsil's Lane, North Street, Barrack Street, Evergreen Street, Cuthberts Lane, Carey's Lane and Half-Moon Street. In 1876 it was reported that 'in a very short space of time the visitor [to Barrack Street] necessarily becomes corrupted by evil association and carry with them to other parts of the city, the infection of this horrid plague spot'.[122] In 1876, as we have seen above, the clergy of St Finbarre's parish made a concerted effort to clear the district of brothels. When in July Cork Corporation began sanitary work in the areas believed to be 'amongst the most vile and noxious dens in the city, dreadful for their inhabitants and pestilent to the surrounding community',[123] it was reported that both the clergy and the corporation were contributing to 'sweeping away a foul plague spot and changing almost in an instant a street of sinners, the vilest and most hardened to a street of penitents'.[124] This area of the city was, in fact, unhealthy and prone to typhus, smallpox and cholera. A local doctor described the lanes from Barrack Street to Evergreen Street as an 'abominable pesthole'.[125] The slum clearance tackled both prostitution and unhealthy living conditions, again equating one with the other. The third occasion when prostitution was discussed widely in the papers was in 1877–8 when the CDAs informed the discussion. The much publicised annual meeting of the Association for the Repeal of the Contagious Diseases Acts was held in Dublin in 1878 and provoked considerable discussion on the subject of prostitution.[126] In the twentieth century the issue of prostitution again became a topic for the letter pages of the press, particularly in the context of debates on 'white slavery' and the equating of the British garrison in Ireland with immorality.[127] Prostitution was, of course, also associated with the spread of venereal disease, the subject of a later chapter.

Not only was prostitution viewed as a source of physical disease but prostitutes were themselves regarded as sites of moral infection. In 1809 the women prisoners confined for debt in the Four Courts Marshalsea, fearing moral and physical contagion, complained about having to mix with 'women of the town (some from the very flags [streets])'.[128] A witness to a hospital commission noted that 'if we allowed these swell ladies from Mecklenburgh Street to flit about in pink wrappers and so on, it would be a distinct inducement to others less hardened to persevere in that life in the hope that probably they would arrive at similar distinction'.[129] One commentator reported on the case of a maid who was caught, by her mistress, looking out the window at 'one of our most notable courtesans, gaily attired, and on horseback'. The mistress warned the maid of the 'vicious practices by which such indulgences were procured'. The maid apparently took on board what was being said but returned to her work 'with a sigh'. Within a few months she had been 'seduced', the author noting that 'her mind had been polluted from that very day' she had witnessed the courtesan. She fell pregnant, emigrated to America, went on the streets, fell pregnant again and in a fit of 'agony, shame, misery and despair', killed herself and her unborn child.[130] In 1898 a young girl, Mary Thomas, was up before the Dublin police court for residing with prostitutes. The judge decided that the best place for her was Lakelands industrial school in Sandymount, run by the Sisters of Charity. However, they refused to take her 'as from experience she [the Superior] can say that one such child is capable of corrupting hundreds of the other inmates'.[131] Consternation was caused by the judicial confinement for a month of a young striker in the High Park Reformatory in 1913. The case, used by James Connolly and James Larkin during the 1913 lock-out as a means to attack the government, Church and employers also revealed the danger of contamination. By being in close proximity to the 'fallen women' of the adjacent Magdalen asylum it was feared that the girl would be defiled.[132] Young women were not the only individuals who could be corrupted by an association with prostitution. In 1839 a twelve-year-old boy was in court for assaulting his mother and using violent and indecent language. He was her only child, and, the court was told, had been associating with the boys of bad character who frequented Mecklenburgh Street. He was in the 'habit of visiting houses of bad character, and to such an extent had his disposition been contaminated that there was no act of wickedness of which he was not then capable'.[133]

For many commentators the solution to the problem of prostitution was to encourage more refuges to rescue these women. From the 1860s Magdalen asylums were identified by many as the way to reduce the incidence of prostitution. One priest, noting the great work of the Magdalen asylums, observed: 'what is to become of them when this institution will not allow their being admitted – the imagination can only picture and God alone can tell'.[134] The first attempts to target sexual vice in itself came from individuals who were concerned with moral reform. Rescue work became an important arena of public philanthropy among women in the nineteenth century.[135] The first involvement of women in collective efforts to reform prostitutes and discourage young women from being drawn into a life of prostitution appears to have the Magdalen asylum established by Arbella Denny in 1765. Between 1765 and 1914 at least forty refuges or asylums were formed in Ireland for the rescue of 'fallen women' and many of these survived in the Republic until the 1990s.[136] Greater interest in the problem of prostitution can be seen from the 1870s. There is no doubt that the CDAs legislation, and the campaign to repeal the Acts, had a public impact in Ireland which raised awareness about the problem of prostitution.[137] Some of this interest developed from the government's attempts to change the marriage laws and raise the age of consent at marriage to twenty-one. One commentator at the time observed that if twenty-one was to be the marriage age, and the consent of parents was needed for that, then there should also be a law rescuing girls under twenty-one from prostitution.[138]

Prostitution and prostitutes were the targets of the vigilance associations and purity organisations that emerged from the 1880s. The Church of Ireland-linked White Cross Vigilance Association (WCVA), which made its appearance in Dublin in 1885, organised patrols to combat the evils of prostitution. The WCVA, which had an entirely male membership, pledged, among other things, to 'maintain the laws of purity as equally binding on men and women'.[139] Besides attending lectures members of the association engaged in 'patrol work'. In effect this meant keeping watch outside known 'evil houses' and through such harassment forcing them to close. By 1887 the association claimed that through the strict application of section 13 of the 1885 Criminal Law Amendment Act, which allowed for the closure of brothels, the 'greatest possible change' was now evident in Dublin 'compared to former times'.[140] In 1888 one brothel-owner, it was reported, offered a bribe of £1,000 to the members of a patrol if they would desist from watching his premises.[141] In 1891 the association claimed to have fourteen branches in Dublin with 530 members.[142] Through the activities of this movement thirty-five brothels were claimed to have been closed down and Mecklenburgh Street cleared of prostitutes in the 1890s.[143] Without doubt the WCVA exaggerated its successes, although its claim that it had forced brothel-keepers to confine their business to a 'few streets almost wholly given up to vicious inhabitants' where even the police had no control may have helped to configure the Monto district.[144]

What is evident from this overview of prostitution in Ireland in the nineteenth and early twentieth centuries is that there was no consistent way in which prostitutes were treated. Police activity against prostitutes and brothels was most often motivated by public complaint, and police dealings with prostitutes were sporadic and targeted streetwalkers, who were the most vulnerable of the prostitute community. Clerics and neighbours took vigilante action against brothels and prostitutes when they became frustrated with police inactivity and when these women became too visible in their streets. Through police and public action the municipal space in which prostitutes could operate, where they could live or congregate, became more limited. However, prostitution, particularly in the cities, appeared to thrive for most of the nineteenth century. Visibility and containment remained the concerns of the authorities and the general public throughout the period. But who were these women who were so prevalent in Irish society as to threaten its reputation for purity?

2 'Looking for my living': women, community and prostitution in Ireland

Commentators on prostitutes portrayed them as women whose lives had been destroyed by sexual experience. It was rarely accepted that they might choose prostitution as a viable means of earning or supplementing an income in a country which offered few employment opportunities for women. While we may never know the personal reasons why Irish women engaged in prostitution there are some sources which help us reconstruct, to some extent, the common experiences of women who engaged in this occupation. We have most information about the women who walked the streets: these were the most vulnerable, public and impoverished of those who engaged in prostitution. While this chapter will focus on those women, particular attention will be paid to a 'community' of women known as the 'wrens of the Curragh' about whom we have a substantial amount of information. A general portrait of Irish prostitutes can be reconstructed from the available information. Prostitution was most often an occupation engaged in by women between the ages of twenty and thirty years, although girls as young as fourteen and women as old as seventy do appear. Child prostitution does not seem to have been a significant problem in Ireland at any period between 1800 and 1940. In Dublin in 1844 for instance, seven girls under the age of fifteen were summarily convicted of loitering for the purposes of solicitation. In 1855 the figure was six; by 1900 the figure was one.[1] Illiteracy among those arrested for soliciting averaged about 97 per cent.[2] Married women, along with single and widowed women, found their way into prostitution. These appear to be the bald facts about the women who engaged in prostitution in Ireland throughout the period 1800–1940. From the available sources, mediated as they are, we can construct a fuller picture of who these women actually were and the difficulties they faced in their lives.

Prostitution, as we have seen, existed publicly in the streets, and less openly in the brothels and pubs of the towns and cities of Ireland. As with the rest of society, a social hierarchy operated among prostitutes. The Rev. Maguire, in evidence given to a commission on the CDAs in 1871, noted the class distinctions which existed. In Furze's Alley in Cork he described women 'of the most abandoned and low class' who generally went with soldiers and sailors. There also existed three brothels in North Street which were filled with what he called 'the upper class of that portion of the community, the class who do not go after the ordinary men'.[3] We get a brief glimpse of an upmarket brothel from a court case conducted in Belfast in 1851. The *Belfast Newsletter* noted that a huge crowd turned out in the court to hear the tale of a 'fast' young gentleman of family and fortune, who had prosecuted 'a fashionable female' for robbing him of 50 sovereigns. The woman called herself Mrs Elizabeth Smith, and she was charged with keeping a house of improper resort, in Queen Street, which the paper noted was 'formerly one of the most quietly respectable thoroughfares in Belfast, but which already, in cause of the nuisance complained of, has been deserted by some of its late inhabitants'. The report observed that Smith was a woman of ambiguous age, between thirty-five and forty, and spoke with an English accent, although in a previous trial she had been declared as a native of Ballynahinch. A number of the 'young ladies' of her establishment were also in court. The prosecutor had expected to bring a number of witnesses but was advised that 'as many of those parties moved in [a] highly respectable sphere, the course would give rise to much unpleasantness and disgrace in families'. Much of the detailed evidence the gentleman gave to the court to support his case, the *Newsletter* noted, was 'of course, altogether unfit for publication'. The gentleman had visited the place at least twenty to thirty times, and had been there several times within the last six months, sometimes in company with other gentlemen. Wine was sold there, champagne was £1 a bottle, he paid £7 one night for wine alone.[4] One of the interesting features of this case is that the brothel-keeper, Elizabeth Smith, was clearly able to conceal her true identity, change her accent and manage a group of 'young ladies' in an unhindered fashion for over a year before being forced, following this court case, to close her establishment.

For the poorer prostitutes conditions could be miserable. The 'Bush' was a wooded place near Cobh where '20 to 25 to 30 women . . . lived . . . all the year round under the furze . . . like animals'. Many prostitutes also followed soldiers around from one depot to another. The surgeon, James Curtis, who gave evidence to a select committee on the operation of the CDAs, stated that 'they [the prostitutes] are always moving about from Fermoy to Kinsale, and the garrison towns . . . and sleeping under forts, and behind the barracks'.[5] Similarly the women known as 'the wrens of the Curragh' lived in ditches around the Curragh army camp in County Kildare (fig. 1 is a picture of the camp).[6]

The fact that prostitution was relatively common in industrial Belfast suggests that many women were either unable to support themselves on

Fig. 1. A view of the Curragh army camp, County Kildare, c. 1878. Courtesy of the Irish Architectural Archive.

industrial wages, wanted more in terms of wages or were without employment.[7] Indeed, women workers, particularly factory workers, were often associated with immorality. Many contemporaries viewed spinners as immoral and shameless women. In 1864, for instance, the chief factory inspector saw factories as a hotbed of vice and corruption, where the unsupervised congregation of women and men could only lead to depravity.[8] In the 1890s lady inspectors still feared sexual immorality in the factories. It was on issues of sanitation that such matters came to the fore. Water closets were often shared by men and women and the doors were sometimes broken, and without latches, and the implication was that these closets were scenes of sexual activity.[9] Even in the early twentieth century women's waged work in Belfast was often not enough to adequately sustain them. One commentator observed the consequence of low wages:

A weekly wage that at its best only about allows to provide for lodgings and breakfast must be supplemented at any cost. The old class of nymphs of the pavement, we have still with us, scattered through their habitations over the length and breath of the city, but there are others who behave with more decorum to be met with everywhere.[10]

For some women prostitution was a way of life, but for others it was a casual occupation. The poor law inquiry of 1836 provides some evidence on prostitution in Ireland in the 1830s. It was observed that in a number of parishes an unmarried mother who could not get the putative father to support her and the child was 'in some instances driven . . . to prostitution as a mode of support'.[11] In 1901 one woman in Belfast noted she had been occasionally obliged to frequent a 'house of ill fame . . . looking for my living'.[12] In Dublin in 1911 May Madden was in the courts for smashing the windows of Eliza Byrne, and was sentenced to nine months. She told the court that she had been in despair, 'that her husband had wanted her to support him by going on the streets'.[13] Ellen Doran had a complex view of her relationship to prostitution. When giving evidence in a burglary case she was cross-examined regarding her occupation and while admitting to being a prostitute noted 'I do sometimes be out at all hours of the night . . . I do not sell myself to prostitution.' When asked to swear she was not a common prostitute she said 'I do swear that I am not a common person such as you mean; I am not out on the streets like other unfortunate girls.'[14] There is evidence to suggest that a long spell working as a prostitute did not mean that women could not leave the work behind them when their circumstances changed. For instance in 1913 a Mrs Reid suffered a number of attacks on her house in Leadbetter Street, Belfast, which was 'notoriously a street of brothels and . . . nearly all the women in the neighbourhood were prostitutes'. Reid, a woman of fifty, admitted that she had been a prostitute all her life until she married 'a few months ago'. Besides her husband and herself, another woman, Minie Woods, resided in the house; she too was a prostitute and had a string of convictions for drunkenness, disorderly conduct and 'other offences common to their class'.[15]

Looking at the 1901 census returns for Montgomery Street, the street that gave Monto its name, we can get some indication of the circumstances of a number of women who may have worked as prostitutes. There were thirty-five inhabited houses in the area containing 130 separate families. The 'notorious' dwellings were the tenements from numbers 56 to 62. In these seven buildings there resided thirty-eight distinct families, thirty of whom lived in one room, with a total of eighty-one persons residing in the seven buildings. The majority of the families, twenty-eight, consisted of groups of between one and five unmarried women with occupations ranging from domestic servants (the majority) to housekeepers and milliners. In one room in number 59 lived three women, two single and one widowed, aged between twenty-six and forty whose occupations were given as domestic servants. In number 60, two rooms were occupied by six women, one of whom was married while another had her illegitimate four-year-old daughter with her. Again all the adult women were listed as domestic servants or housekeepers.[16] One of the most disreputable districts within the area of Monto was Elliott Place. In 1904 it consisted almost entirely of tenements.[17] The 1901 census reveals that eleven women, within an age range of twenty to forty-five, living in Elliott Place, were unmarried and enumerated as having no occupation. It is likely that these women, one of whom was illiterate, worked as prostitutes. In what may have been a brothel run by two sisters, listed as room keepers, four women aged between twenty-three and forty-two, described as boarders, were included as having no occupation. The house run by Catherine Gordon may also have been a brothel, containing as it did three boarders aged between twenty-six and forty-three years, who were all listed as housekeepers. Many of the women living in this area worked as domestic servants and housekeepers, occupations which were very poorly paid.[18] It is also unlikely that a domestic servant providing an address within this area would have been acceptable to any 'respectable' household. In 1911 of the sixteen households enumerated for Elliott Place, nine were headed by women. The general profile evident in the 1901 census of unmarried, unemployed women was still strong at this time.[19] The infamous brothel-keeper Eliza Mack ran her business from 85 Lower Tyrone Street and in 1901 she had five 'lodgers' ranging in age from twenty-one to twenty-seven. These women were listed as having occupations such as dressmaker, housekeeper, waitress, milliner and lace-maker, and the household also contained a servant, a widow aged thirty-two, who probably looked after the women. The 'lodgers' were all literate and unmarried and two were from England, while the rest came from areas outside Dublin. Eliza Mack herself was fifty at this time, a widow and had been born in Cork City.[20] She was described by Oliver St John Gogarty as having 'a brick-red face, on which avarice was written like a hieroglyphic, and a laugh like a guffaw in hell'.[21] It is difficult to state with any certainty which buildings in the area were brothels. Many of the houses and tenements contained women who either lived on their own or shared their accommodation with other women. Large numbers of women in the area appear to have been unmarried and in the age group between twenty and fifty. Purdon Street, for instance, also contained a number of young, single women living alone or sharing rooms, who were unemployed or worked as dealers or domestic servants.[22] Only two women from the 1911 census returns were listed as prostitutes: both were twenty-eight, one a Maggie Boylan, who lived in Faithful Place, and the other Maud Hamilton, from Elliott Place, who had listed an occupation (which is illegible) but the enumerator had added prostitute to the form.[23] What seems evident from the census material is that these women, whether engaged in prostitution as a full-time occupation or not, were earning precarious livings as dealers, huxters and domestic servants.

Before the courts

Prostitutes are most evident to the historian through their court appearances. Women who worked as prostitutes and who found themselves in court were most often charged with theft, being drunk and disorderly, vagrancy and sometimes murder. When convicted of soliciting the general sentence was a fine, or in default of payment two weeks or longer in prison. Over the nineteenth century in particular, hundreds of women, from all over the country, are named as prostitutes when they appear before the courts whether accused of soliciting or not. One young man who encountered Margaret Brown at the Donnybrook Fair in 1834 stayed with her for the evening in a brothel and woke to find his clothes taken. Brown suggested that if he paid a night's lodgings he would have his clothing returned.[24] In Clonmel Margaret Ryan, 'one of the pave', pleaded guilty to a charge of receiving money and goods stolen from an army captain stationed in the town.[25] In Kilkenny a prostitute who stole £200 from a farmer got six months with hard labour in 1871. The judge had little sympathy for the victim observing that married men should not be 'going about drinking with abandoned females'.[26] One woman confined to Grangegorman prison for five years for larceny in 1885 was recorded in the register as a prostitute, and at the age of forty-four had accumulated 93 previous convictions.[27] It is also evident that many newspaper reporters used some of these court cases as a way to amuse their readers. For instance, two women who lived in a hovel in Ennis were charged with not paying their landlord rent. In evidence it emerged that both women, Fanny Crowe and Bridget Hogan, were 'prostitutes of the most infamous character' and considered a nuisance to the entire neighbourhood. Fanny Crowe was described as 'a masculine looking woman with a Connaught accent'. Crowe, when asked by a solicitor if she were not a 'quiet, mild and respectable woman', answered to the delight of the court, 'I think it would be very hard for you to find a woman that you'd get the three in.'[28]

Even if convicted of criminal offences it is clear that many women's primary occupation was prostitution. A number of women transported from Ireland had clearly worked as prostitutes.[29] Susanna Price took to prostitution and crime to support herself when her soldier husband was overseas. In 1840 she was sentenced to seven years' transportation for larceny.[30] Mary Ann McCrystal, from Armagh, was sentenced to transportation in 1841 for stealing clothes from a man named Fox. Her father, who pleaded on her behalf, said he had been absent for three months during which time his daughter had 'fallen into bad company'.[31] Catherine Grady, 'a notoriously improper character and public nuisance' pleaded guilty to theft in Kilkenny in 1846 and was transported for seven years. The reporter commented that it was a 'happy riddance for the city'.[32] Margaret Shelly, aged fifty-four and from King's County, was tried and transported for stealing a pair of shoes. To the court she 'appeared to be a person of the most abandoned character, having for a series of years kept a house of ill repute in the town of Birr'.[33] Bridget Hayes, who was transported for larceny in 1848, pleaded in her petition that she had been seduced by a young man who cast her off and that she 'had to pursue a wicked life to keep herself from starvation'. This claim had no impact on the judge who declared her a 'notorious' bad character, a thief and a prostitute.[34] Margaret Mack, aged sixty, from Waterford, was transported for receiving stolen goods in 1851. The witnesses who gave evidence against her, showing her little loyalty, were 'street walkers who rendezvous[ed] at her home'.[35]

Particular areas of cities were prone to scenes of disorderly conduct, especially at the weekends. Walker's Lane and Anderson's Row in Belfast were two such areas. The residents of Walker's Lane were constantly before the courts on charges of robbery, and of being drunk and disorderly. In 1852 it was reported that an old 'Hecate, named Anne Watt, who presides at the usual Saturday night revels of Walker's Lane, was charged by one of the constabulary, as a principal in the customary nocturnal jubilee'.[36] Prostitutes often fought among themselves.[37] Murders were also committed. In 1824 Honora Concannon of Corofin was executed for the murder of William Higgins. She had been in service in the Galway area 'until seduced into a course of vice'.[38] In Belfast in 1912 Mary Jane Bailie and Mary Maguire were accused of the murder of Mary Ann McMullan. Bailie had kept a brothel where Maguire had acted as her 'lieutenant'. McMullan was a prostitute who sometimes resided with Bailie.[39] Evidently there was some jealousy between the women and it was reported that 'one of the accused apparently is supposed to have made a statement that she out of revenge for some infidelity imagined or actual between the dead woman and the living woman's husband had taken her blood'.[40]

At times women who worked as prostitutes received a sympathetic hearing in the courts, though this is much less frequent than has recently been alleged by Caroline Conley.[41] In Kilkenny in 1856 Catherine Walsh, a 'female of infamous character', prosecuted Patrick Hartigan for assault. He was found guilty and sentenced to six months' hard labour.[42] Mary Lackey, a prostitute, gave corroborative evidence in a case where a 'mulatto' had been raped. Patrick Crogan, who had committed the offence, was sentenced to be executed for the assault.[43] Likewise James Kennedy got one month and a fine of 10 shillings for assaulting Eliza Watson in a house of ill fame in Walker's Lane, Belfast.[44] A very violent assault committed by John Cahill on Fanny Helsham in 1856 saw the accused sentenced to seven years' transportation. However, the judge had to reduce the sentence, realising that his original imposition was not allowed in law. The prisoner instead got four years' penal servitude.[45] In Galway in 1881 a magistrate suggested to one young woman that he would deal with her more leniently if she agreed to enter a Magdalen asylum. The woman, who had previously been in the asylum, had attempted to rob a sailor she had picked up. On agreeing to re-enter the asylum she was given a sentence of one month's hard labour.[46] Similarly in Cork an 'unfortunate' girl of fifteen was sent to a Magdalen asylum rather than to prison for theft. In this case the judge ascertained that 'she had received a good education at a convent school' and she was not 'wholly depraved'.[47] Prostitutes were not shy in using the petty sessions to secure justice. When Bridget McInerheny summoned a soldier from a regiment stationed at Clare Castle for assault and rape in November 1844, the bench declared that even though she was a 'cyprian of the most degraded class' she should not be subjected to wanton abuse.[48] Mary Flanagan, an 'exceedingly juvenile cyprian' appeared before the court in Ennis in October 1845. She alleged that a client, Francis Kelly, had enticed her into a field, and raped her at knifepoint over a period of three hours.[49] Another prostitute had alerted the police and when discovered, according to one of the policemen, Flanagan was in a faint and exhausted state, and 'as cold as death'. Kelly was later acquitted when Flanagan refused to identify him.[50] Ellen Doran gave evidence against two men accused of breaking into a chapel. The men greatly resented being charged on the word of a prostitute. The prosecution argued that even if she were a prostitute this would 'not render her incompetent'. Doran was later violently assaulted for giving the evidence she gave.[51] In Limerick Mary Carmody, who admitted she had been a prostitute for four years, accused a young man of raping her. Her assailant, who said she was 'a prostitute and she was bound to go with him', told police she had taken a shilling and then told him to go to hell. Despite his claim he was convicted, as was a soldier whose excuse for raping a prostitute was that he had no money. A constable rescued Margaret Ryan when three men were trying to rape her. Surprisingly perhaps, given the fact that she was drunk at the time and made her living as a prostitute, her attackers were convicted.[52]

In 1890 an unusual complaint was made by the visiting committee of the women's prison in Waterford. They made an official complaint to the

Chief Secretary's Office regarding what they believed was 'a dispropor-
tionate severity with which female offenders are sentenced for the offence
termed loitering. We are of the opinion that sentences of one month, or
two months simply for walking the streets form an amount of punishment
hardly warranted by the offence.'[53] The response noted that women were
never arrested merely for loitering but only 'when it was accompanied by
importuning for prostitution or other disorderly conduct'. However,
prostitutes were not always treated leniently by the courts, as witnessed in
the many rape and assault cases dismissed by courts in Kildare.[54] When
Margaret O'Brien complained against Robert McGrath, a policeman,
for grievous assault in Tipperary Town the charge was thrown out of
court, and the woman noted as 'a common prostitute . . . of the worst
character'.[55] Likewise when Kathleen Dolan, 'a grey-haired woman of the
unfortunate class' was charged with drunkenness and using 'abominable
language' in Galway in 1912, the magistrate gave her a heavier fine than
usual, influenced perhaps by his knowledge that her convictions went
back to 1880.[56]

Whatever their treatment by the courts or the public, prostitutes were
not without some forms of resistance. It was a common practice for
women to change their names to confuse the authorities. They formed a
generally mobile population, migrating to towns and cities. With some
groups of prostitutes there was also solidarity, seen particularly in the case
of the wrens of the Curragh. It was noted by a number of magistrates that
when arrested the women were often 'very violent, and threw themselves
down and refuse[d] to walk'.[57] At the Roscommon sessions two 'unfortunate women' were about to be sentenced as vagrants when one of them
stated that her fellow prisoner had a large stone concealed, which she
intended to fling at the barrister, after the sentence should be passed. She
was seized, became furious and vowed the most terrible vengeance upon
her companion.[58] Sometimes the women committed crimes in order to
go to jail. Margaret Scanlan admitted to breaking the windows of a solicitor's office in Ennis in October 1843, stating that her purpose was to 'get
into gaol in order to procure medical treatment'.[59] Another woman who
broke a pawnbroker's windows told police that she did so 'for the purpose
of being with her companions, then in the police barracks'.[60] In 1846
Mary Murphy pleaded guilty to breaking the windows of the mayor's
office in Kilkenny in order to be imprisoned.[61] In Ennis the magistrates
observed that in one case that 'the object of the unfortunate persons who
committed these outrages was evident. They become diseased, would not
be taken into the county infirmary, and they sought refuge in the jail.
Such a state of things was most deplorable, but no suitable remedy had
yet been devised.'[62]

Women who worked as prostitutes left themselves open to violence and abuse. They were raped and attacked. Three men, for instance, attempted to drown a prostitute by throwing her off Pope's Quay in Cork in 1839.[63] They constantly appear before the courts on charges of drunkenness.[64] When they made themselves too public they were prone to abuse and violence from the general population. A number attempted suicide. Kathleen Dolan did so by jumping into the river in Galway stating she 'would not put up with all the warrants and imprisonments'. She received six months for her attempt.[65] A small number appear to have been committed to lunatic asylums. 'B. B.', a 19-year-old prostitute, was imprisoned for attempting to commit suicide and later confined to Ballinasloe asylum suffering from 'mania'. Likewise, another prostitute, 'K. D.', was also confined to Ballinasloe asylum with 'dementia' having been imprisoned for attempting suicide.[66] 'M. H.', aged twenty-five, and confined to Limerick jail for six months, was sent to the lunatic asylum in the city with dementia a month after her imprisonment.[67] Ellen Byrne, a 26-year-old prostitute from Dublin, committed infanticide having been refused entry to the workhouse. She was found guilty but insane and sent to Dundrum mental hospital in 1893 where she died within the year.[68]

As we have seen, by the end of the nineteenth century geographical limits were placed on where brothels and prostitutes might operate unhindered. Prostitutes, however, still roamed much more freely than the public or authorities wished. The growing presence of middle-class women in Irish public life witnessed in the suffrage campaign, the campaigns to improve women's legal standing and their employment and educational opportunities, paralleled the attempted narrowing of the public presence of prostitutes.[69] The formation of the Ladies' Land League in 1881 and its condemnation by Archbishop McCabe, who warned his flock not to 'tolerate in your sodalities the woman who so far disavows her birthright of modesty as to parade herself before the public gaze',[70] marked the distaste many felt about women's political involvement. When women of the Ladies' Land League were imprisoned it was under a statute from Edward III designed to keep prostitutes off the streets.[71] The outrage was noted in an editorial in the *Nation* which declared that 'some time ago a stipendiary magistrate designated the members of the Ladies' Land League by the worst name that can be applied to a woman'.[72] For many figures in authority women who engaged in public life were akin to prostitutes.

In 1890 the chairman of the General Prisons Board, C. F. Bourke, became involved in a spat with the police in Athlone when he complained that he had encountered cases 'which were . . . most serious instances of oppression and persecution on the part of the local authorities, whose instructions to the police are . . . to arrest any woman of the town who was seen in the streets'. Bourke believed that the intention was 'to drive them from the locality and by persecution to expel them from the jurisdiction of these local authorities'.[73] The RIC district inspector responded that he did 'not consider that the sentences passed on women of this class in Athlone [were] at all unduly severe'. Bourke was also to note that 'some of the police reports give as a reason for the arrest of these unfortunate creatures, that the clergy of the districts have complained of their conduct . . . this is entirely in accordance with what I have gathered from many years' observation in regard to these prisoners'. How strong the collusion was between police and clergy is open to debate. It may have been more common in rural Ireland, but certainly in Dublin the clergy made no headway in having the police deal with prostitution until the 1920s. Bourke insisted that these women's rights should be protected and they 'should not be driven by persecution into the class of heinous criminals or be deprived, on account of being prostitutes, of the protection and liberty accorded to other of her majesty's subjects'.[74] There is no evidence to suggest that Bourke's intervention had any impact on police activity or sentencing by magistrates. His was one of the few voices which argued for the rights of these women in society and before the law.

There is some evidence to suggest that women's work in prostitution was an essential form of support, not just for the women themselves, but for others in the locality. A community of prostitutes and brothels in Cuthbert's Lane in Cork City was reported to support a whole range of individuals.[75] However, 'fallen women' did not always support each other. In 1861 the board of guardians in the Westport workhouse ordered that the women in 'class 2' be deprived of one-third of their bread allowance until they identified the woman or women who had broken a recently erected toilet. Three women were quickly handed over and jailed for two weeks.[76] One woman convicted of larceny and sentenced to three years in Grangegorman prison had had 4 previous convictions for larceny and 112 convictions for petty offences. It was recorded by the governor of Galway jail that she had been known as a prostitute in the city for up to twenty years but had reformed in 1888 and stayed out of prison for three years. During that time she had supported herself through the sale of fruit. In 1891 she was arrested for stealing a watch taken from a man 'in whose company she was thought to be for immoral purposes'. The police were convinced she had now returned to prostitution, having 'taken to the drink and returned to her former life of prostitution, but not so openly as the other common prostitutes of the town with whom she did not associate'.[77] This woman may have thought her chances of staying out of jail were improved by her not consorting with other prostitutes in the city. Many women who were prostitutes had no interest in reforming. Betty Mackay, an 'emaciated, wasted-looking woman', was charged in Belfast with having been drunk and disorderly. It was noted that 'the prisoner is a woman of ill fame [and] has been a habitual frequenter of the court during the last thirty-five years. In the course of her vicious career she has undergone many imprisonments and refused all attempts at rehabilitation.'[78]

Though often considered 'vicious' the women who worked as prostitutes displayed their humanity in many ways. Elizabeth Finnegan, a 26-year-old single mother and prostitute from Clones, was convicted on 5 July 1883 at the County Monaghan assizes for stealing £110. She was sentenced to five years' penal servitude in Mountjoy from where she corresponded regularly with the master of the Monaghan workhouse to ensure the care of her child while she served her sentence.[79] Many women who worked as prostitutes appear to have been homeless.[80] In 1811 Betty McCartney, a prostitute in Belfast, had been lying in a dunghill in Joy's Entry for several weeks before being moved to the poor house. The local population had put 'victuals within her reach' but only sought her entry to the poor house when it was evident she could eat no longer.[81] The body of Bessy Lyons was found near a brothel in the village of Corofin. She died, according to the coroner's inquest, from 'exposure to the night air and the use of spirituous liquor'.[82] Another prostitute, whose name was unknown, was found dead in a field near Athlone covered only in a few 'tattered garments'.[83] Likewise, in March 1876, the body of Catherine Byrne was found drowned in the canal at Carrickmacross. It was noted that she had, from 'early in life acquired habits of intemperance which led to a course of infamy. She became a prostitute years ago and went under the nickname "The Gawk".'[84] Some women appeared to make a good life for themselves through prostitution, particularly those women who managed to become the mistresses of wealthy and influential men. Laura Bell, born in Glenavy in County Antrim in 1829 or 1832, was one of these. She worked in London as a shop girl and apparently supplemented her income with prostitution. She returned to Dublin in the late 1840s and worked as a prostitute there, with William Wilde reputedly being one of her regular visitors. Eventually she returned to London and became the mistress of the very wealthy Jung Bahador of Nepal, later to become prime minister of his country. By twenty-one she had become rich through her association with this man. Within three months the affair was over and a sum in the region of a quarter of a million pounds had been spent on her. She later married a wealthy man named Thistlethwayte and was widowed in 1887. She afterwards became a friend of the Gladstones and moved in high society. She died in 1894.[85] But Bell was unusual and few Irish women seem to have done as well as she did in this occupation.[86]

There was some recognition that poverty played a role in driving women to prostitution. In the poor law inquiry of the 1830s it was frequently noted that poverty brought many women on to the streets. One priest in Longford stated he knew of 'nine or ten cases where girls gave themselves up to prostitution from downright necessity, after they had struggled a year or two to support themselves and children, and in many cases had resisted tempting offers'.[87] Another witness reported that the

unfortunate creatures . . . are first driven from their cabins; they then rear a wretched hovel of sods against some ditch, which as soon as it is discovered by the farmer on whose ground it is, is immediately pulled down to prevent the corruption of his children and his servants: she then goes to another place and finds the whole neighbourhood leagued against her; she is then compelled to lead a wretched and vagabond life, and, gradually rendered reckless by her suffering and by a consciousness of her degradation, she instructs her children in every kind of vice, and ultimately takes refuge in a town, where she soon terminates her miserable existence.[88]

A correspondent to the *Cork Constitution* wrote that the public needed to recognise that

none are all evil . . . to remember that they have been sorely tried by poverty; to remember that in all probability their lives have been one long uninterrupted struggle against temptation, which when assisted by poverty is very hard to resist; to remember that for many of them before they have fallen 'hope has fallen and mercy sighed farewell'.[89]

Thomas Haslam analysed the causes of prostitution as lying in some degree in the lack of occupations open to women and the poor pay of some men, which did not allow them to marry. Drink was also an added factor and society's attitudes to women who were 'the victims of seduction' further complicated the matter. But he maintained, as did a number of suffragists like him, that 'it is men's unchastity and men's injustice which are mainly responsible for prostitution'.[90] Many, however, were less understanding and had little sympathy for the women. In Cork an outraged citizen described the local prostitutes in Barrack Street as 'frowsy, shameless women, unkempt and in foul apparel of all ages from the mere girl to the hoary hag'.[91]

The robberies constantly associated with brothels and with prostitution were attempts to make some extra money. Women earned from a few pence to a shilling or more in a night. In 1824 Mary Flynn, in giving evidence against brothel-keepers James and Margaret McNally of Athlone, stated 'there used men come every evening; upstairs in the house the men and the women used to retire; there was a bed in the room – for the accommodation of a bed McNally charged one shilling'.[92] In the early twentieth century a Belfast court was informed that a farmer was charged about 1 shilling and 6 pence, while 5 shillings could be had from a ship's fireman or as much as a pound from a sailor.[93] The most common way for a woman to approach a man was to ask him 'to stand her a drink'. In 1860 two 'nymphs of the pave' were found guilty of stealing 5 shillings and 6 pence from a rather 'green looking country lad' in Kilkenny. The women had approached him in the street and asked him to 'take a treat at a public house'. Once he succumbed he was robbed.[94] While the women often brought the man back to their lodgings or to a brothel, many also resorted to the fields.[95] There are a few references to pimps or bully boys. In 1877 Thomas Kelly of 10 Bull Lane, Dublin, was prosecuted for having assaulted a prostitute named Margaret Genter. The magistrate remarked 'that it was extraordinary that in all cases of brutality that occurred among the lower classes in Dublin the worst of them appeared to be committed on poor unfortunate women, who were brutally beaten by the men who actually lived on their prostitution'.[96] Patrick Dougherty was identified as 'a hanger-on and gentleman lacquey at some of the Long Lane schools of vice' and had been arrested for 'practicing his bruising powers on two little boys'.[97] Matthew Considine told the Ennis magistrates that he saw Michael Grady with a 'brace of cyprians' near the stables in Jail Street. The dispute between the two men however, revealed another truth; from the evidence of one of the women, Catherine Campbell, it was clear that 'Matty was the real Paphian guardian'.[98] The dangers for men of associating with prostitutes were clearly expressed in two extant street ballads from the nineteenth century (see appendix 5). Both ballads come from the 1860s and warn young men of the dangers of robbery and violence when associating with these women. Other dangers, such as the contraction of a venereal disease, are notably not highlighted. It is not clear how many such ballads survive but these two offer an amusing sidelight on the popular understanding of prostitution in the mid-nineteenth century.

Prostitution and workhouses

As early as 1802 we find a number of prostitutes confined to the Belfast poor house in the care of the Belfast Charitable Society. The committee of the society totally disapproved of the women's occupation and considered that 'the confinement of the eight women is not a sufficient punishment [and] desire that they shall be kept as low with respect to diet as is consistent with health'.[99] While this was an obviously punitive regime, poverty was such a significant force in the lives of many prostitutes that the poor house, the house of industry and later the workhouse, were the few public institutions which offered them shelter.[100] After 1838 prostitutes made their way in large numbers to the workhouses of Ireland, though they also entered Magdalen asylums in considerable numbers.[101] The workhouse had a number of advantages over the Magdalen asylum as a place of refuge. Women who entered the workhouse, and those labelled prostitutes, often had children with them and children were not allowed into a Magdalen asylum.[102] It was often easier to gain access to a workhouse ward than to an asylum, and the women who entered the workhouse had a greater degree of control over their lives than those who entered the Magdalen asylum. Nevertheless workhouses were the resort of the truly desperate and the fact that large numbers of prostitutes entered these institutions is an indication of how economically precarious life as a prostitute actually was. Many boards of guardians were concerned about the numbers of prostitutes who used their facilities. Within the confines of the workhouse the contagious nature of prostitution, whether physical or moral, was seen as a real problem. It was within the workhouses that prostitutes were considered truly infectious, to young girls, to the smooth management of the house, to the detriment of the ratepayers. Boards of guardians could not, by law, restrict entry as any woman who was destitute and presented herself to the board had to be admitted, if there was room in the house for her, and if not then she was eligible for outdoor relief.[103]

From the very beginning of the workhouse system guardians and clergy were concerned about the presence of prostitutes. It was commonly believed that women came into the workhouse to procure.[104] A strict classification system was expected to operate in all workhouses. While inmates were categorised and separated according to sex, health and age, considerable concern was also expressed about the need for moral classification. Prostitutes and women of bad character were expected to be separated from the respectable poor. The classification system was supposed to be rigid but in practice was as flexible as the workhouse system itself. In the Cork workhouse the classification system introduced in 1840 did not separate prostitutes from other women inmates.[105] The workhouse chaplains claimed that 'immoral women' came into that workhouse solely to tempt girls into a life of prostitution. They suggested that the 'deprived and virtuous' should be isolated so that the '*notoriously immoral*' could not influence innocent girls.[106] In 1841 Elisa McGrath, whose occupation was given as a servant, stated that she lived in a brothel in Cork. She was brought before the magistrates and charged with attempting to 'seduce' a fellow inmate in the workhouse into a life of prostitution. She admitted that she had been sent to the workhouse by the owner of the brothel in which she lived in order to procure.[107] In 1850 a young woman who attempted to gain entry to the Athlone workhouse informed the guardians that while previously in the house she came under the influence of 'an abandoned female' who had been, 'with some others of the same class, promiscuously placed in the wards with the moral and well-conducted'. In consequence she left the workhouse to become 'another member of the wretched class of outcasts'.[108] In 1861 Catherine Harvey swore a deposition to the effect that when she had entered the North Dublin union[109] she had been approached by a young girl who assured her that if she left the workhouse she would provide her with work in the country. On leaving the workhouse Harvey found herself in a brothel in Bull Lane, which she immediately left, and made her way back to the workhouse.[110]

By the beginning of 1843 prostitutes in the Cork workhouse were confined to wards of their own. However, the workhouse officials were always faced with problems when large numbers of women entered the workhouse. This was a common occurrence when military detachments came to the city. In early February 1843 there were twenty-two prostitutes aged between seventeen and twenty-three in the penitentiary ward of the workhouse and a few weeks later the place was 'crowded to suffocation' with forty-one women. Many, it was noted, were 'lying ill, in a most filthy manner on straw pallets without bedsteads, in a room not half sufficient for that number'.[111] It was soon observed that the women were conversing with men outside the building and in consequence the windows were boarded up. Workhouse officials disliked prostitutes entering their houses as they were disruptive and often not amenable to discipline. In 1845 the master of the Killarney workhouse warned the guardians about the admission of prostitutes noting that there were then ten of them in the workhouse and they seemed to 'defy all authority'.[112] The master of the Wexford workhouse informed the board of guardians that some prostitutes were in the habit of coming into the workhouse three or four nights a week. They would come in at night and leave the next morning. The master believed they were sent in by the police and magistrates and thought it a terrible thing 'to keep a lodging house for such people'.[113] Guardians who visited the Belfast workhouse in 1900 were embarrassed by the conduct of the women. 'The filthy language of the men was not nice', a newspaper reported, but 'that of the separation women[114] was revolting. They laughed, they clapped, the atmosphere was redolent of the language of the bagnio.'[115]

Many women were labelled prostitutes in the workhouse registers, though it is not always clear how this appellation was decided. Women who had no obvious occupation and who had illegitimate children were often so labelled. Sometimes it was their appearance or the company they kept that allowed them to be termed prostitutes. One commentator observed that, 'those among the inhabitants who are not actually included in the predatory class seem to be so intimately connected with that class in their social relations that it is very hard to say where the line of demarcation is to be drawn'.[116] Living in a particular area was often sufficient to label a woman a prostitute, whether she was one or not. From about 20,000 entrants to the Cork workhouse between December 1869 and May 1872, in the region of 563 women were labelled prostitutes. Many of these women entered the workhouse on numerous occasions. Catherine Cleary, for instance, was fifty years old and between December 1869 and January 1871 entered the workhouse at least fifteen times.[117] Sometimes she stayed a day, on other occasions she remained in the house for months. Mary Johnston, aged thirty, appeared in the workhouse on 11 January 1870 and entered eight more times to July 1872. Her address was given as either Peacocks Lane, the site of a Magdalen asylum, or Barrack Street, a noted haunt of prostitutes. Johnston may well have been moving between the workhouse and the Magdalen asylum in order to secure relief. Of all the women labelled as prostitutes who entered this workhouse in this period, 80 per cent were aged thirty years and younger. The youngest girl labelled a prostitute was aged fourteen.[118] A number had young children with them, including Hannah Dalton, aged twenty, who had a two-year-old son Robert. Mary McCarthy entered the workhouse on 23 March 1870 with her two-week-old daughter. Mary Kiely, aged forty, brought her two children aged thirteen and nine with her into the house in September 1870. While Mary remained in the house until March 1872, her eldest son left it in August 1871. A majority of the women were single, and some were pregnant when they entered the house. Those who brought their children with them saw them labelled as bastards. The residential addresses given by the women were those already noted above as being associated with prostitution in Cork City, Cuthbert's Lane, Furze Alley, Evergreen Street, Barrack Street, and from outside the city the Bush in Queenstown (Cobh).

Similar information can be gleaned from the indoor registers of the Belfast workhouse. Out of 5,000 entrants between October 1892 and February 1893, 214 women were labelled prostitutes. Lizzie McKeever, aged twenty-eight, entered the workhouse on four occasions between November 1892 and February 1893. On one occasion she took her five-year-old son with her, but on the other occasions he was either already in the house or being taken care of outside the workhouse.[119] Approximately 52 per cent of the women were aged thirty years and younger, suggesting that the Belfast workhouse was the resort of a slightly older woman than the Cork workhouse. Again, women in the Belfast workhouse brought their children with them, including Margaret McCrudden, aged thirty, who had three of her 'bastard' children with her. Nineteen of the women had come to the workhouse straight from jail, suggesting that they had no resources to fall back on when they left that institution. The most prominent places of residence for those women labelled prostitutes were again those commonly associated with vice in the city – Millfield, Carrick Hill, Marshall Court and York Street. While much more research needs to be completed on the numbers of women labelled prostitutes who entered Ireland's workhouses one thing is obvious from these two small samples: only about 3 per cent of the inmates of the Cork workhouse in the three-year sample were prostitutes and about 4 per cent of the one-year sample of the Belfast inmates were labelled as such. Whether this is true for other workhouses, or true for different time periods, still requires investigation, but the belief, widely held, that workhouses contained numerous prostitutes who were disruptive and the cause of immorality seems exaggerated. Whatever might be the reality of the numbers of prostitutes who utilised workhouses it is clear that the issue of moral contagion and hence classification formed a central role in the attempted control of immorality.

The issue of classification plagued the workhouse system throughout the nineteenth century. In response to a criticism made in 1854 that workhouses were dens of immorality the Irish Poor Law Commissioners requested that poor law inspectors investigate the issue of classification in Irish workhouses. All the responses from the inspectors indicated that prostitutes were kept separate, where possible, from other inmates, though the South Dublin union was noted as having only a partial separation. Mr Hall, the inspector of the workhouses in the county of Cork, noted that even where no separation arrangements existed 'any close intimacy with prostitutes is generally avoided by other female inmates . . . they are generally left, by a sort of tacit understanding to associate with each other'.[120] All of the inspectors agreed that the issue of women entering the workhouse to procure was exaggerated and no solid evidence had been presented to any inspector to prove the case. Further details about the classification system in the workhouses were published in 1855. Responding to a request for information from the Poor Law Commissioners regarding the arrangements they made for 'moral classification', of the 133 workhouses only a handful claimed they did not have any prostitutes using their workhouse. In the Belfast union it was noted that 'a separation ward has been established in which are placed all females labouring under venereal diseases, and all women who give birth to two or more illegitimate children'. Belmullet union declared itself to be without prostitutes. The Clogher union observed that 'those notoriously bad are separated from the rest'. But many unions had no separation system in operation.[121] Depending on the accommodation available in the workhouse unmarried mothers and prostitutes were sometimes placed together, particularly if a woman had more than one illegitimate child. This conflation of prostitutes with unmarried mothers was to last well into the twentieth century. For her 'improved conduct' Celia Hoban was moved from the 'dissolute females ward' to the ward occupied by unmarried mothers 'who were not common prostitutes' in the Westport workhouse.[122] Often it was marriage, and hence respectability, that allowed women to move from the separation ward into an ordinary ward. In the Westport union, for example, a woman with three illegitimate children was originally placed in the separation ward when she entered the workhouse. She then married and entered the workhouse again. The guardians allowed her to remain in the 'respectable class' while she conducted herself properly.[123] Further details on classification were published by the Commissioners in 1862. Again, there was no standard system in operation, and of the 163 unions then in existence different arrangements were in operation. In the Ballinasloe union, for instance, the women, it was noted, were divided into three groups: (1) married women and young women of proper character; (2) women who had had one or more illegitimate children; and (3) common prostitutes and women of profligate character who may have had one or more illegitimate children.[124] Tellingly, Boyle union had a ward divided in two, one for lunatic women and the other for prostitutes. In 1883 the local government board (LGB) asked the guardians in the Glenties union what provisions they made for classification. The guardians informed the board that for years there had been no prostitutes admitted to the house 'save casuals'. The 'casuals' were declared to be ballad singers who 'frequent fairs, and who may be prostitutes'. But as they only stayed a night they were kept in the probationary ward. About twelve such women were admitted each year.[125]

The question of moral contagion remained a constant theme for boards of guardians in the workhouse system. It was a stick often used by Catholic clerics and philanthropists to condemn the workhouse system. Accusations of the contaminating influence of the workhouse on young girls reached its height in 1861 when reformers and the Catholic Church pressured the government to hold an inquiry into the Irish poor law system. It was widely believed that young women who entered the workhouse, or were brought up in that institution, would end up as prostitutes. One commentator noted,

daughters after living a few years of squalid misery in the poorhouse, will leave the place and become prostitutes. They will lead the lives of prostitutes and die the death of prostitutes: they will drown their wretchedness in drunkenness . . . they will die of an unnamed disease in some splendid hospital. Such has been the fate of almost all the female children in the Irish poor houses.[126]

Ellen Woodlock, a philanthropist who gave evidence to the 1861 poor law inquiry, was particularly interested in the care of children in workhouses, and the archbishop of Dublin, Paul Cullen, gave evidence to the inquiry regarding classification. Woodlock advocated 'minute classification' in workhouses to prevent moral contagion.[127] Cullen suggested that 'women of notorious profligate character' should be removed from the workhouse and placed in appropriate institutions, such as Magdalen asylums.[128] The issue of classification was not resolved by the 1861 select committee and remained a source of debate into the first decades of the twentieth century.[129] Cullen's objective was largely achieved in independent Ireland where homes for unmarried mothers and Magdalen asylums became the primary means of containing 'immoral' women.

Unlike in Magdalen asylums, within the workhouse system women had rights, and were quick to assert them if they felt they were not being treated properly. In 1896 the guardians of the Drogheda union asked the LGB if they could cut the hair of women who were being placed in the separation ward. Hair cutting was a common occurrence in the Magdalen asylums. Long hair was believed to be a sign of vanity and in convent-run asylums the hair was kept cut to discourage the women from leaving.[130] Having shorn hair was an obvious sign of outcast status. The LGB, however, informed the guardians that they had no legal authority to cut the hair of women deemed 'bad characters' and that any attempt to do so would leave the workhouse officers open to legal proceedings and charges of assault.[131] Indeed, the Poor Law Commissioners noted that no one had any right to give the order for cutting of a female patient's hair, unless a doctor ordered it cut. If a medical doctor wished to have a woman's hair cut then he was obliged to give a reason for the direction. It was also noted that if a patient was conscious her hair ought not to be cut off without her consent.[132] In matters of discipline the LGB believed that the regulations of the poor law system allowed enough leeway for boards of guardians without their resorting to extreme measures. Likewise, guardians could not stop women entering the house. Women who were prostitutes were notorious for entering and leaving the workhouse at short notice, often to attend a local fair and ply their trade. The guardians at the Edenderry union asked if they could refuse admission to these women. The LGB responded by noting that if the women were destitute when they applied for admission to the workhouse, then they must receive relief.[133] At a meeting of the Galway board in 1881 a guardian who was attempting to have an old man, who was not destitute, admitted to the workhouse complained that 'it was unfair that a man such as the applicant should be refused admission when "strumpets" of girls who should not be allowed in were never refused'.[134]

The 'wrens' of the Curragh

Prostitutes were a common feature in all garrison towns, and for one group of such women, the 'wrens' of the Curragh, we have a substantial amount of information. In November 1879 the commandant of the Curragh brigade observed the presence of prostitutes within a few hundred yards of the Curragh camp. As a result the officers were complaining bitterly because 'in addition to their men breaking out of barracks, these prostitutes invade the camp nightly'.[135] Camp followers at the Curragh were not a new phenomenon. Since a permanent military base had been established there in 1855 camp followers lived primitively in makeshift huts on its perimeter.[136] The women were called 'wrens' because they 'live[d] in holes in the banks [ditches]'[137] around the army camp. While the military authorities constantly insisted that they did not permit or encourage prostitution in their camps or the surrounding districts, it is clear from the evidence available that while the military may have publicly denounced prostitution they also allowed it, in many instances, to flourish. The existence of camp followers on the Curragh is surprisingly well documented. Through an examination of contemporary accounts on how the 'wrens' lived, together with official and local reactions to their situations, it will become clear that there was a tacit acceptance of prostitution in this military camp and its locality. The material available on the 'wrens' provides us with a unique insight into a community of women who worked as prostitutes in a military encampment for almost seventy years. While there was a tacit acceptance of prostitution in the vicinity of the camp boundaries were created around these women to separate them from 'respectable' society. These boundaries were enforced by the police, the military authorities and the local civilian population.

For the local population and the military authorities the very presence of these women on the Curragh 'defiled' it,[138] and they are often recorded as 'infesting' the camp with their presence.[139] As with prostitution elsewhere in Ireland, the issue of containment and visibility was also relevant to the 'wrens'. As one army officer was to note, 'when all the vice is out of doors wandering shamelessly and defiant through the streets of Newbridge, the by-lanes of Cahir, and the purlieus of Limerick, Buttevant, Athlone and Templemore, it becomes far more mischievous than it can be in the cellars and courts of the back streets in Dublin'.[140] These women were sexually immodest, often drunk and used foul language; while they were named as individuals when appearing before a magistrate or in death, they were viewed as a collective mass of licentiousness. It was their collective existence that was the threat rather than their individual selves. The military authorities, the police and the local civilian population attempted, often without success, to limit the movements of these women and to confine them to particular geographical areas. However, while the authorities attempted to regulate the behaviour of these women it is clear that the 'wrens' often successfully resisted such regulation. These women provoked fear and fascination and were the polarised opposite to society's expectations of how women should behave and how they should appear in public.

The problem of the 'wrens' was brought to public attention through letters in local and national newspapers. In October 1855 one irate Kildare cesspayer observed that the camp followers were not only causing moral corruption but, possibly more importantly, were an extra expense on the cesspayers. Their presence around the camp had necessitated a resident magistrate residing there who had the women imprisoned in Naas jail for trespass on military lands and for vagrancy. The jail soon became overcrowded and a correspondent to the local press observed that in one week nine women had been jailed bringing to nineteen the total number of unfortunate women imprisoned there, half the prison population. Here they mixed with young women incarcerated for larceny and were considered a moral danger to them.[141] In 1857 the Presbyterian chaplain of the camp brought further attention to the wrens in a letter to *The Times*.[142] However, the most extensive information on these women comes from the journalist, James Greenwood, who visited the area in the 1860s and published a series of articles, between 15 and 19 October 1867, on the women in the *Pall Mall Gazette*. Greenwood was a journalist, writer and novelist, a social explorer of Victorian society. The piece that made his reputation was written about a night spent in disguise in the casual ward of a workhouse. The resulting series of articles, 'A night in a workhouse' caused a sensation when it appeared in the *Pall Mall Gazette* in 1866, and was reprinted in *The Times* and issued as a pamphlet.[143] Greenwood capitalised on the fame of his workhouse article and explicitly linked it directly in the reader's mind with his writings on the 'wrens' when he discussed the women's experiences in the Naas workhouse.[144] His work on the 'wrens' was reprinted as a pamphlet and appeared in a collection of his writings.[145] Greenwood has little new to say on the causes of prostitution but his journalistic efforts in recording the life of the 'wrens' revealed much about his own attitudes to prostitution and reinforced commonly held views about how these women lived.

On first becoming aware of the 'nests' Greenwood observed

heaps of furze [which] are built and furnished for human occupation; and here and there outside them were squatted groups of those who dwelt therein . . . Not one or two, but several groups – half naked, flagrant – indicating a considerable colony . . . Altogether there are ten bushes, with about sixty inhabitants. In them they sleep, cook, eat, drink, receive visits, and perform all the various offices of life. If they are sick, there they lie. Brothers, mothers and fathers go to see them there. There sometimes – such occurrences do happen – they lie in child-bed; and there sometimes they die.[146]

He then moves on to describe the physical space in which the women lived:

the nests have an interior space of about nine feet long by seven feet broad; and the roof is not more than four and a half feet from the ground. You crouch into them, as beasts crouch into cover; and there is no standing upright until you crawl out again. They are rough, misshapen domes of furze . . . the walls are some twenty inches thick . . . There is no chimney – not even a hole in the roof, which generally slopes forward . . . The door is a narrow opening nearly the height of the structure – a slit in it, kept open by two rude posts, which also serve to support the roof. To keep it down, and secure from the winds that drive over the Curragh so furiously, sods of earth are placed on top, here and there, with a piece of corrugated iron . . . as an additional protection from the rain. Flooring there is none of any kind whatever, nor any attempt to make the den snugger by burrowing down into the bosom of the earth . . . the nest is nothing but a furzy hole, such as, for comfort, any wild beast may match anywhere, leaving cleanliness out of the question.[147]

The number of women living in these conditions fluctuated between sixty and one hundred, depending on troop movements and also the season. One source claimed that up to five hundred women were to be found in the vicinity in the summer months.[148] Like other women who worked as prostitutes, for some of the 'wrens' at least prostitution was a seasonal occupation. Harvesters, for example, were known to join the band of women when they were not working, and the numbers of women at the Curragh declined during the winter when many of them returned to the city.[149] The ages of the women living at the Curragh varied, from young women under twenty to women in their fifties and sixties.[150] This age range is typical of that of women who worked as prostitutes in nineteenth-century Ireland.

While these women lived under terrible conditions, Greenwood noted a certain bond of solidarity among those who occupied the nests. The women pooled their limited financial resources and collectively lived off any earnings they made. 'None of the women have any money of their own', Greenwood observed, 'what each company get is thrown into a common purse, and the nest is provisioned out of it . . . It is an understanding that they take it in turns to do the marketing, and to keep the house when the rest go wandering at night.'[151] The 'colony' was also 'open to any poor wretch who imagines that there she can find comfort'. With some degree of sentimentalisation Greenwood wrote that the poor women who followed soldiers to the camp were 'made as welcome amongst the wrens as if they did not bring with them certain trouble and an inevitable increase to the common poverty'.[152]

The response of the local community to the 'wrens' centred on complaints to the authorities when the prostitutes appeared too public. In 1865 the *Leinster Express* reported an attempt to set up a 'mission to the fallen' at Newbridge and the Curragh. John LaTouche, who had spent some time in rescue work in London and was the president of a rescue home in Dublin, organised a meeting to initiate rescue work around the Curragh. It was reported later that a missionary lady had been employed to undertake this rescue work but nothing further was heard of the venture.[153] The 'wrens' represented depravity to the local community and because of the nature of their occupation were often shunned by the local population and in many instances treated quite badly. One individual writing of the 1840s when he had served at the camp, stated that it was 'quite common for the priest, when he met one of them [wrens] to seize her and cut her hair off close'.[154] Not surprisingly the clergy had little time for these women. The same soldier recalled the priest coming into the barracks at Newbridge to request a fatigue party of soldiers, who, with the permission of their commanding officer and the priest at their head, 'went out and burned down the shelter these unfortunates [wrens] had built'.[155] One of the women was believed to have indulged in 'extravagant behaviour . . . in the presence of a lady (related to a general officer) who was riding on the Curragh', in consequence they 'were all driven from the common, and their hovels destroyed'.[156] At the Curragh many local shopkeepers would not serve the women in their shops. The Ranger of the Curragh, writing a report of their situation in 1860, noted that:

Were I to attempt to describe the wretched unparalleled state of misery in which the women alluded to exist, I would fail to approach its character or extent. They are continually subjected to very brutal assaults, and robbery of their scanty clothing; a variety of causes prevent their following up complaints brought before magistrates as to what they suffer in those respects.[157]

In the 1880s the parish priest of the district would not allow any of his parishioners to give shelter to the women.[158] In order to curb the activities of the wrens, the Lord Lieutenant issued an order in council in 1873 establishing a byelaw that made it illegal 'for any night walker or common prostitute to locate herself or trespass on or resort to the Curragh of Kildare for the purpose of prostitution'.[159] When the authorities attempted to enforce the byelaws the women dispersed 'to the vicinity of the Curragh' and towards Kilcullen.

A report on the condition of the 'wrens' written in April 1878 noted:

at present the prostitutes are scattered about, some residing in a lane near the Curragh in the direction of Kilcullen. These frequent the edge of the Curragh at Athgarvan and are a great source of annoyance as they remain on the roads and give money to the soldiers to purchase spirits for them . . . They used to live in French Furze. When there it was noted that they were, with few exceptions, all in one place, and were more easily kept under control, without harassing the police as is now the case, and gave but little annoyance to the public.[160]

This correspondent noted that in the summer between 5 pm and 10 pm the police were constantly obliged to keep order on these roads or the road to Kilcullen would be impassable. The dispersal of the women from the Curragh in consequence of the 1873 byelaws meant they relocated to the nearby towns and villages where they were considered a nuisance by the local population. The magistrates at Kilcullen petty sessions ordered that the women were to be prosecuted, which resulted in them making their way back to the Curragh.[161] In 1879 the commander at the Curragh noted the return of the wrens to French Furze and observed that in consequence the 'men [were] breaking out of [the] barracks, these prostitutes invade the camp nightly, and persecuting them for trespass does little or no good'.[162] By 1880 the Lord Lieutenant insisted that the 1873 byelaws be 'rigorously enforced'.[163] An officer at the camp explained that the byelaws of 1873 were not enforced because it appeared 'that the Curragh is the best place on which these unfortunate women can be located'. He was convinced:

that it is impossible to banish the women from the neighbourhood of a camp . . . ever since the bye-laws have been passed they live in ditches, in lanes and in byways in the vicinity of the Curragh and chiefly in the direction of Kilcullen where they have been a grievous nuisance to all persons living there.[164]

By the 1880s the Ministry of Defence believed that 'public decency and morality are better served by allowing the women to remain on the Curragh, rather than in the vicinity'.[165] As long as the women did not create public scandal the army authorities were willing to let the women reside on the Curragh, believing that public decency and morality were better served by allowing them to remain.[166] The commander at the camp wrote to the War Office in 1880 to say 'that the women are warned to be quiet, so as not to be pursued, if they are not, that they will be hard pressed. The poorer inhabitants of the Curragh borders now are harbouring them – which is the best thing that can happen and will give the priest the chance of reclaiming them.'[167]

Not all the women who were camp followers lived as the wrens did. A number of women rented cottages in the locality and others worked in brothels. For instance, in one row of cottages in Brownstown, bordering the Curragh camp, Henry Hart was described as keeping 'a very bad house'.[168] It was reported that 'every kind of immorality [was] going on there. Some of the lodgers who frequent it are at times inmates of the Kildare Lock Hospital.'[169] Hart's wife and daughter were declared to be 'bad characters'. Catherine Mahon, a neighbour of Hart's, was said to keep an 'irregular house' and to admit lodgers of the worst character.[170] The other two cottages in the row, however, were said to be tenanted by 'respectable people'.[171]

The double standard of sexual morality which operated in the nineteenth century allowed men to excuse bad behaviour towards women who worked as prostitutes. Although there is evidence of some camaraderie between prostitutes and their soldier customers, sexual commerce often degenerated into violence. Harassing the 'wrens' was a common form of amusement for the soldiers. The miserable condition of the women was brought to the attention of the Lord Lieutenant in 1859 'after the occurrence of very deplorable outrages' against them. The letter writer requested that something be done for 'these unhappy women without delay', believing that 'delay will probably in the case of many of them be equivalent to a sentence of death'.[172] A correspondent to the *Pall Mall Gazette* in 1867 wrote of 'nesting':

Hunger and cold are sad assailants, but they [the wrens] suffer even more from the brutality and recklessness of the soldiers. To be knocked down and kicked by fellows half mad with drink is an everyday occurrence . . . Nesting was not the only amusement with which the miserable sisterhood furnished Privates Ramrod, Bit, Spur . . . 'Driving the wrens', as the phrase went ten to twelve years ago, was no unusual pastime. Gentlemen fresh from the hospital, with others who had been jilted or robbed, were always ready to organise parties for this purpose . . . Generally speaking the 'fun of the thing' was irresistible. After evening stables – half past seven to eight o'clock – the gang, usually a pretty large one, mustered and well armed with pieces of turf, cabbage stalks, and similar missiles, marched to the scene of action. That attained, supposing the evening to be a wet one, a general rush of the mob would tumble the frail edifices about the ears of the occupants, who received an unmerciful pelting as they bolted from the ruins. A dry summer or autumn evening, however, was preferred for perpetrating these acts of wantonness. Of course at these times the huts would be flammable, as so much tinder, and the application of a match would in a very few moments wrap the whole structure in flames. When this happened those inside would dash not only through the door, but through the sides of the burning nest, and plunge along among the mocking cheers and ready missiles of their tormentors, carry with them in their hair and clothes burning fragments of the wreck. What loss or injury they sustained by these amusements nobody cared.[173]

Individual women were also assaulted by soldiers. Mary Costelloe, for example, accused two privates of indecently assaulting her in December of 1886. The case was later dismissed at the assizes in 1887 when Costelloe was declared to have been drunk while in the camp.[174] Not only were the charges dismissed but the presiding chairman, who observed that 'statements from women like the prosecutrix required corroboration', wanted Costelloe to be charged with trespassing in the barracks. Hannah Dixon, another 'unfortunate' had been admitted to the Kildare infirmary in August 1860 having been attacked and wounded by a soldier, who was forced to pay the 2 shillings for car hire to remove her to the infirmary.[175] A soldier charged with the rape of Anne Cullen was discharged, but later re-arrested and tried for assaulting her.[176] Another serious assault had been perpetrated on Maryanne Williams.[177] Anne Nevin was acquitted of stealing from Private John Thomas of the Curragh while he was in the company of 'unfortunate girls'.[178] Bessie Hynes, named as an 'unfortunate', was sentenced to a month in Naas jail having been convicted of stealing a bath rug from the camp, valued at 4 shillings and a penny.[179]

A number of cases appear in the local press of soldiers accused of sexual assault. In the spring assizes of 1865, for example, four privates were accused of rape.[180] Unfortunately, few details of these cases were published in the papers. Even the physical setting of assault, such as that which was alleged to have taken place against Mary Costelloe, mentioned above, could determine the outcome of any court appearance. For soldiers sexual reputation was fluid and unlikely to be damaged by accusations of assaults on prostitutes. Prostitution was the most visible transgression of the sexual code, and prostitutes had lost their right to 'respectability' as a result of their occupation. In studies of the history of rape it is clear that the 'character' and 'reputation' of the victim was an important element in bringing about convictions.[181] The women were also arrested for offences committed in public. Anne Lennon, Bridget Ryan and Bridget Manning were fined 10 shillings each or seven days in jail for having 'obstructed the public footpath [in Newbridge] by crowding them'.[182] Again, Anne Lennon, along with three other 'unfortunates', was summoned before the magistrates at Kilcullen petty sessions on the charge of 'living in the open air' and having no visible means of support.[183] Mary Higgins was summoned for being drunk and disorderly in Naas and the police had to 'bring her nearly half naked through the streets'.[184] Bridget Doolan, another of the 'unfortunate class', was charged with three offences of drunkenness and ended up in jail for one month.[185]

The women who lived on the Curragh were viewed as less than human. Greenwood, for example, equated them with animals. The 'wrens' as women were recognisably different to 'real' women. Among the 'wrens' Greenwood observed that there

was a common look, so shocking to see, of hard depravity – the look of hopeless, miserable, but determined and defiant wickedness. Fine faces, and young ones too, were marred into something quite terrible by this look, and the spirit of it seemed to move in the lazy swing of their limbs, and was certainly heard in their voices.[186]

The demeanour of the 'wrens' signified their wantonness, just as their dress did. Describing their clothing Greenwood observed,

they are dressed alike. All day they lounge in a half-naked state, clothed simply in the one frieze petticoat, and another equally foul cast loosely over their shoulders, though towards evening they put on . . . decent attire. These bettermost clothes are kept clean and bright enough . . . these observations apply to the cotton gown, the stockings, the white petticoat alone – frieze and flannel never know anything of soap and water at all apparently. The 'Curragh petticoat' is familiarly known for miles and miles around: its peculiarity seems to be that it is starched, not ironed. The difference in the appearance of these poor wretches when the gown and petticoat are donned and when they are taken off again (that is to say, the moment they come back from the 'hunting grounds') answers precisely to their language and demeanour when sober and when tipsy. In the one condition they are generally as well behaved and civil as any decent peasant women need be; in the other they are like raging savages, with more than a savage's *vileness*.[187]

The supposed lack of humanity of the women is also evident from other comments Greenwood recorded. One 'gentleman', for example, remarked to him with apparent amazement, that the women 'used cups and saucers just like ordinary people'.[188] Greenwood also observed that a market was held near the camp once a week and that 'a certain number of the wrens are then allowed to approach and make purchases, just like ordinary people'. Similarly, Greenwood cites the crockery evident in the nests as more human than the women themselves:

I declare I was most thankful for the cups and saucers; and as for the teapot, it looked like an ark of redemption in crockery-ware. If they were not – as I told myself when my eyes first rested on them – the only human-looking things in the place, they did give one a comfortable assurance that these wretched and desperate outcasts had not absolutely broken with the common forms and habits of civilised life.[189]

The appearance of the women when drunk was also animalistic: 'their flushed faces, their embruted eyes, their wildly flowing hair, their reckless gestures, and, above all, their strong voices competing in the use of the most hideous language depravity ever invented', negated their femininity and their enforced remoteness from 'respectable' women.[190] In this state these women were no longer civilised but savage. Some of Greenwood's writings had been on colonial adventures where civilisation and savagery clashed. The 'otherness' of the women is constantly evoked through comparison with animals: Greenwood refers to their 'savage' behaviour, while another source equates their 'otherness' directly in racial terms with that of the 'uncivilized' tribes of Africa.[191]

While commentators such as Greenwood saw these women as less than human, the 'wrens' offered a support system to each other which was rarely to be found in the local community. Greenwood observed that 'in sickness the wrens administer to themselves or each other such remedies as they happen to believe in, or are able to procure . . . the communistic principle governs each nest, and in hard times one family readily helps another, or several help one'.[192] That the women were pragmatic in their attitudes to their occupation is evident from a number of comments. Greenwood remarked that it was the younger, better looking and better dressed women who sought out the soldiers at the camp, while the older women looked after the 'nests'. He noted also that the women 'put off their decent clothes immediately they have no further use for them as *ornaments*'.[193]

In the 1860s generally there was considerable discussion as to why women became prostitutes. Books such as William Acton's *Prostitution Considered*, first published in 1857, with a second edition appearing in 1869, and Henry Mayhew's *London Labour and the London Poor*, 1861–2, brought considerable attention to the causes of prostitution.[194] Greenwood too, was anxious to know how a woman came to 'be turned into a "wren"'. The story he was given in one instance is typical of the seduction stories which feature in the case histories of women who presented themselves as worthy objects for redemption at Magdalen asylums. For one of the 'wrens',

The story began with no father nor mother, an aunt who kept a whiskey store in Cork, an artilleryman who came to the whiskey store, and saw and seduced the girl. By-and-by his regiment was ordered to the Curragh. The girl followed him, being then with child. 'He blamed me for following him', said she. 'He'd have nothing to do with me. He told me to come here and do like other women did. And what could I do? My child was born here, in this very place, and glad I was of the shelter, and glad I was when the child died – thank the Blessed Mary! What could I do with a child? His father was sent away from here and a good riddance. He used me very bad!'[195]

It was commonly believed that women were frivolous creatures whose virtue was easily lost. One commentator declared that it was the glamour of the soldiers that attracted the women to prostitution. The 'dress of the soldiers, the gilding of the uniforms, the regular step, and the martial bearing of the men, are as if specifically contrived to carry the feelings and good wishes of spectators away captive'.[196]

Prostitution was an intrinsic part of army life. A soldier noted in his diary in 1815 that when his unit was sent to India only seven women were allowed to accompany them, though about thirty women were then living with men in the unit. Lots were drawn by all the soldiers and spaces were auctioned to those who wished to bring someone with them. One married man sold his lot to an unattached man, to enable him to bring a prostitute, whom they could all use, with the unit.[197] In 1857 there were 5,137 non-commissioned officers and men at the Curragh of whom only 7.74 per cent (398) were married, with 386 wives living with their husbands in the barracks.[198] The marriage of soldiers was restricted on the grounds of efficiency and cost.[199] Soldiers were believed to be promiscuous so that limits placed on marriage implied that their sexual needs must be met elsewhere. Prostitution offered the army authorities, who feared homosexuality, a way of reinforcing male heterosexuality. Commercial sex assisted the army to maintain the 'masculinity' of its troops and also allowed it to keep men single. The behaviour of the soldiers, particularly in their dealings with the 'wrens', distanced them from feminine weakness and even emotional attachments and, of course, bonded them with their fellow soldiers.

The three major problems facing the army authorities with regard to prostitution were the health and discipline of the troops, and public relations. For the public the problem with the 'wrens' was again one of visibility. In the late 1850s there was a long correspondence between the inhabitants of the Curragh and the army authorities on this issue. The main problem concerned a group of women who frequented the area between French Furze and the army camp. The inhabitants were not concerned with getting rid of the women but rather in removing them to 'some more remote place'. Once that was done the locality could be traversed by the inhabitants without witnessing the 'disgusting scenes daily presented'.[200]

Throughout the 1850s and 1860s there was much confusion within the local population as to who should police these women, the military authorities or the local magistrates. Sometimes when the magistrates tried to have the women moved they found the military authorities to be uncooperative.[201] The military authorities could call on the police to deal with prostitution, and when it suited them they did so. One suggestion, made by an army officer, proposed that the police should be encouraged to 'follow the prostitutes about . . . when parading in public'.[202] The police had, as previously noted, many legal codes to help them deal with prostitutes, though it was under vagrancy laws and laws of trespass that the women of the Curragh were most frequently taken up. Between 16 May and 17 November 1879, for example, 2,900 prostitutes were prosecuted for trespassing on the Curragh camp. In the same period 119 soldiers were confined to barracks for talking to the women.[203] Whether the law was enforced rigorously or not depended very much on complaints made by the public.

The 'wrens' and the workhouse

'At the first fall of snow I'll go to the workhouse' declared one of the women to Greenwood.[204] For the 'wrens' of the Curragh the workhouse proved to be one of the few institutions that offered them relief. In 1860 the board of guardians of the Naas union noted that the average number of 'unfortunate' women entering the workhouse every year was eighty. In common with boards of guardians elsewhere the Naas guardians disliked the burden of looking after these women, observing that they 'had no natural claim in this Union, being strangers, attracted solely by the presence of the military at the camp'. Arguing for the contagious nature of immorality the guardians believed that the admission of these women in such numbers to the workhouse, 'must inevitably tend to lower the character and impair the morality of its inmates'. They lobbied the government to provide a general hospital in the area where these women could be treated and 'so avoid the association with persons of unblemished character'. According to the guardians it cost the union £40 per annum to provide medical care for these women, a burden that should, in their eyes, be borne by the state.[205] The government allowed £100 per annum to the board of guardians towards the expense of maintaining and treating the prostitutes from the Curragh camp.[206] As a condition of the grant the military authorities were expected to inspect the workhouse each year.[207]

On 19 November 1862 the master of the workhouse reported that there were twenty-seven girls from the Curragh camp in the auxiliary workhouse.[208] During the year to March 1863, 163 out of 422 applicants for relief at the workhouse were women from the Curragh.[209] The workhouse doctor noted that several of the women were in danger of dying if they were not properly housed, observing that 'in order to protect themselves from snow and rain they lie on their faces'.[210] The women were quite capable of making use of the workhouse for their own ends. In 1864 it was noted that a number of women in the auxiliary workhouse were in the habit of obtaining their discharge on the 'eve of every fair day and public festival and returning the following day to the House'. Notices were put up in the house stating that inmates who left were not likely, unless the circumstances were 'most pressing', to regain access to the workhouse for thirty days after leaving.[211] In 1880 the board of guardians asked the LGB if they could limit the number of 'unfortunate women' entering the workhouse 'who take their discharge nearly every second or third day for improper purposes, and who remain out for the day and part of the night, taking discharge the next day in the same manner'.[212] However, poor law regulations were inflexible in this regard.

Greenwood was not impressed by the conditions that prevailed in the Naas workhouse. On his visit there he observed:

The workhouse itself was half empty; but these [wrens] were not allowed to enter it and share such comforts as it might easily have given them. The whole fifty, with four children, were turned into a range of low hovels separated from the main building by a high wall, and so ruinous as to be totally unfit for human habitation: and this was in the Winter. The beds were bags of foul straw, and two or three women slept on each of them – huddled, sick and sound together, without any attempt at separation; and more that one fourth of them were not sound. The measurement of one of these hovels was as follows: length 28 feet; breath 14 feet; height 9 feet. Imagine a room, a broken hovel, of these dimensions; imagine twelve such beds in it as we have described; imagine those twelve beds occupied by twenty-three women and two children; and ask whether you would not rather have lain out in the common. That is a fearful picture, nor indeed need anything be added to it, except that these despised and certainly very wicked women were not even allowed to worship with the other paupers; they had to thank God by themselves, and listen to the exhortations of his minister in their hovels apart.[213]

It was the state of this part of the workhouse that assistant commissioner, Henry Robinson, complained of in 1863, when he informed the board of guardians of the 'very unsatisfactory state of the auxiliary building occupied by women of bad character chiefly from the Curragh camp'.[214] In response the board of guardians, seizing an opportunity to extract more money from the government, sought an increase on the £100 allowed to care for the women, stating that the actual costs were in the region of £350 per annum. The Poor Law Commissioners did not agree with this request, noting 'it appears to them that all necessary provision for the relief of all the destitute within the Union, whatever cause may exist for their being within it, can be made, and ought to be made by the Board of Guardians and legally chargeable on the Poor Rate'.[215]

Although the workhouse was in theory available to all who needed it, in practice this was not always the case, as the death of Rosanna Doyle testifies. A local police sergeant had informed the relieving officer that Doyle, a prostitute, was lying in a ditch in a bad way. Doyle was left to lie in the ditch for two nights before being carried to the workhouse at Naas, where she died within ten minutes. When found she was described as being in a very poor state; 'she was all wet, and lying in the place on her side; there was no covering overhead . . . she had on a cotton frock, a petticoat, and some inside covering; she had no stockings; she was very much exhausted . . . [there were] spots on her face, and her eyes were swollen'. On being asked how she came to be so bad, she replied that she had slept out. When brought into the workhouse it was noted that she 'had got a beating, as her side and arm were black'.[216] Patrick Cosgrave, the relieving officer of the Naas poor law union, was charged with accelerating or occasioning the death of Doyle by not providing her with prompt relief, and he was charged with manslaughter. It was the first case of its kind in Ireland and attracted considerable press attention. At Cosgrave's first hearing the prosecuting barrister made much of the alleged significance of the case suggesting that:

First, it will show the public that all persons, no matter how humble their station, or vile their occupation, are entitled to the protection of the law, and that their persons and property will be protected quite as much as if they filled the highest positions or stations in the land. Second, it appears to me that it will have the effect of producing some amendment in the relief of unfortunate persons in the position of the deceased. Third, we are all familiar with the unfortunate state of things in the neighbourhood of the Curragh Camp, and it may have the effect of calling the attention of parties with the view to their mitigation, for all are agreed that something should be done in this respect.[217]

From the point of view of the Poor Law Commissioners, the case had important practical ramifications. Since 1850 the Poor Law Commissioners had removed forty-one relieving officers 'making . . . between 3 and 4 public examples annually'.[218] The Doyle case allowed them to assert their authority on all boards of guardians in Ireland by insisting that relieving officers must actively discharge their duties, and that the character of those seeking relief was irrelevant.[219] The Naas board of guardians did not want to dismiss Cosgrave, and accepted his explanation that Doyle, and many of the Curragh women, often refused relief in the workhouse when it was offered to them. The Poor Law Commissioners, however, insisted that Cosgrave lose his position.[220]

The high numbers of women seeking relief led the Poor Law Commissioners to suggest that an extra relieving officer, appointed in December 1863, should visit the Curragh three times a week and reside in Newbridge, which was deemed more accessible to the women who lived on the Curragh.[221] In November 1865 another 'unfortunate', Mary McCarthy, died in Newbridge in similar circumstances to those of Rosanna Doyle. An inquiry was held under the direction of the assistant Poor Law Commissioner, Henry Robinson, and informed that McCarthy had no place of residence, and for the previous four months had slept in a ditch in a lane at the back of Newbridge barracks.[222] Again it was noted that the area was too large for even two relieving officers. Robinson demanded that a third relieving officer be appointed, a proposal the board of guardians refused to implement because of the expense.[223] Shocked to read of another inquest in Kildare from exposure and misery, a woman correspondent to the *Leinster Express* wondered whether 'this [was] a civilised country, or are we lapsing into barbarism? Treating women, Irish females, as wild beasts and allowing them to die like rotten sheep, lying about in mid-winter, forbidding anyone to shelter them, is infinitely worse, it is slow murder.'[224]

The material context of these women's lives was one of deprivation and extreme poverty. Alcohol addiction was a common problem. Greenwood noted that the women also used tobacco but not as a 'luxury merely. That weed is a well known stifler of hunger – a fact which the wren discovers for herself before long.'[225] Thieving was probably a vital survival strategy for these women and provided a direct method of getting money. Women constantly appeared before the Naas petty sessions charged with trespassing, vagrancy, drunkenness or theft from their clients.

Like other women who worked as prostitutes the 'wrens' were not, however, without some forms of resistance and exercised their own forms of rebellion. They changed their names to confuse the authorities. They were mobile, often in an attempt to frustrate legal constraints placed on their activities. They constantly violated the boundaries set for them. The solidarity expressed by the 'wrens' offered some companionship and sharing of difficulties. The women could also act in their own defence. For example, the Ranger of the Curragh summonsed forty women to appear before Newbridge petty sessions in 1859 charged with trespassing. A deputation of the women presented themselves to him and told him that 'the military authorities informed them that if they went to the French Furze . . . on the Curragh they would not be molested'.[226] The papers also reported that on 'that understanding about one hundred immediately located themselves there'. On another occasion when the women were apprehended for trespassing they stated that 'they would go to any private corner of the Curragh which might be named but if this was not granted they declared they would take up their abodes in the adjoining ditches, haggards and farm yards of the farmers'.[227] The women, it was claimed, had threatened to involve themselves in crime if driven from the Curragh.[228] Once arrested, many women failed to make their court appearance. Of the forty women arrested for trespassing on the Curragh in 1859 only nine turned up in court.[229] Attempts at confinement by the authorities sought to limit the mobility of the women. Greater control could be exerted over their behaviour if their boundaries were fixed and of course, the public would not be offended by their behaviour. A local farmer observed that he had driven a number of the women from one of his fields, broken up their furniture and their pots and delph. One of his sheep was killed the same night. He allowed them to remain in his field because 'it would be more than my farm is worth to turn them off. I would rather have them in my fields than to have them looking at me through the windows.'[230]

The 'wrens' survived on the Curragh from the 1850s to at least the early years of the twentieth century.[231] They were a recognisable community

who did assist each other in times of need. While they were not typical of
the general run of prostitutes they shared common characteristics with
them. All women who worked as prostitutes were exposed to a rhetoric of
condemnation, from the police, from the local community and from the
clergy, though society was relatively at ease ignoring the problem as long as
it was hidden from public view. The 'wrens', like the majority of prostitutes, had no social or economic advantages and no standing in society
generally. Like other women who worked as prostitutes they were harassed
by the clergy, assaulted and attacked by individuals and were just as poor
and impoverished. Within the community of the wrens existed some of
the most destitute prostitutes, women like Rosanna Doyle and Mary
McCarthy, who did not have the material or physical resources to survive
their lives on the Curragh. As we have seen many prostitutes in the rest of
Ireland were also destitute, homeless and died from exposure. The existence of the 'wrens' provides us with insight into a particular group of
women who worked as prostitutes, adding to the complexity of our understanding of prostitution in Ireland in this period. In one respect they are
significantly different from prostitutes working in other parts of Ireland.
From the late eighteenth century many philanthropists took an interest in
rescue work and saving fallen women. None was successful in maintaining
a refuge at the Curragh. Even for rescue workers, these women were the
true outcasts of nineteenth-century Irish society.

3   'Behaved very ill': rescue work and Magdalen
     asylums in the nineteenth and twentieth
     centuries

Magdalen asylums appear to have entered Irish public consciousness sud-
denly in September 1993. At that time about a hundred bodies buried
within the grounds of the Convent of Our Lady of Charity of Refuge at High
Park in Drumcondra, Dublin, were exhumed and later reburied, having
been cremated, in Glasnevin cemetery. Considerable media attention
focused on this removal and reburial and there was a degree of public
protest about the fate of these women who had resided in Magdalen
asylums.[1] Later in 1993, BBC Northern Ireland broadcast a documentary
entitled *Washing Away the Stain*. Through interviews with women who had
been inmates, this told the history of these asylums in Scotland and Ireland
from the mid-twentieth century. One of the striking differences between the
systems in the two countries was that a riot by the inmates of the Scottish
lay-run asylum in 1958 prompted an inquiry into the management of the
institution as a consequence of which it was closed. Such an event would
have been unimaginable in Ireland in the 1950s.[2] Little more was heard of
the Magdalen asylums until an article appeared in the *Irish Times* in
September 1996 marking the closure of the Sisters of Our Lady of Charity
of Refuge Magdalen laundry in October of that year. The public's interest in
Magdalen asylums again surfaced in 1998 with the broadcast of a Channel
Four documentary entitled *Sex in a Cold Climate* which again relied on the
evidence of a number of women who had been incarcerated in the
Magdalen asylums in Ireland in the 1940s and 1950s. Since 1993 there have
been television documentaries, a film, television dramas, plays, songs and
poetry, art installations, and one work of history created around the subject
of Magdalen asylums.[3] But while interest in Magdalen asylums is a very
recent phenomenon, it is important to realise that their history in Ireland
goes back to 1765. This chapter explores the establishment and operation
of Magdalen asylums in Ireland, and pays particular attention to the women
who used these institutions. It relates how these institutions evolved over
the nineteenth century and, though the sources are limited, analyses the
ways in which these asylums were perceived and used in the twentieth
century. Care must be taken when generalising about how these institutions

operated from the 1920s onwards. The general popular understanding is that Magdalen asylums became institutions of confinement; however, until we gain access to the records this is a view that must be treated with caution.

The earlier asylums

From the eighteenth century at least forty-one asylums or refuges were established to rescue and reclaim 'fallen women' (see table 3.1). Of these at least eighteen operated in Dublin and Dun Laoghaire and five in Belfast. Ten of the asylums were eventually attached to convents, notably those of the Good Shepherd Sisters, the Sisters of Charity and the Sisters of Mercy.

Throughout the period there was a direct link between institutional religion and the asylums, strongest in those refuges run by female religious congregations. While there were certain similarities between the organisation of lay and religious asylums the differences were important and they will be treated separately here.

Lay asylums

The earliest refuge established was the Magdalen asylum in Leeson Street, Dublin which took in its first inmate in 1767. Lady Arbella Denny, who founded this home, had become interested in rescue work while involved in the reform of the Dublin foundling hospital. There she came across unmarried mothers who were forced to give up their children. The plight of these women, abandoned by their families, moved her to action. She opened a fund and received many contributions from her wealthy friends and on 17 August 1767 the first inmate was received.[4] The patroness, vice-patroness and governesses of this asylum were 'fully invested with the internal government of the house, without control of the president, vice president, guardians or any of them'.[5] A committee of fifteen ladies was chosen annually to act as visitors and in 1796 a governess or guardian paid £1 a year for the privilege of being associated with the institution.[6] In the eighteenth century it was decided that the 'penitents', as the inmates were called, should spend between eighteen months and two years in the asylum and that they were to leave only if their future could be guaranteed in some way, either through acquiring a position or returning home. It appears that these policies were also in force in the nineteenth century. Within this asylum women would be sheltered from 'Shame, from Reproach, from Disease, from Want, from the base Society that has either drawn you into vice, or prevailed upon you to continue in it, to the utmost hazard of your eternal happiness'.[7]

Table 3.1 Magdalen asylums in Ireland, 1765–1993[a]

Institution	Address	Denomination	Date founded	Other information
Magdalen asylum	Leeson St, Dublin	CI[b]	1767	11 inmates in 1911
Asylum for Penitent Females			1785	
Lock Penitentiary	Dorset St, Dublin	CI	1794	Founded by John Walker to employ and reform destitute women leaving the lock hospital
St Mary Magdalen Asylum for Female Penitents	Donnybrook	RC[c]	1798	Originally established at 91 Townsend St, Dublin; taken over by the Sisters of Charity in 1833 and moved to Donnybrook in 1837; 99 inmates in 1911
St Patrick's Refuge	Crofton Rd, Dun Laoghaire	RC	1786? 1798	Founded in Bow St, later moved to Dominick St, Dublin; Sisters of Mercy took the women from this asylum into a convent in Glasthule in 1856; moved to Dun Laoghaire in 1880; closed 1963; 44 inmates in 1901
Magdalen asylum	Waterford City	?	1799	May have survived to 1810
Magdalen asylum	Peacock Lane, Cork City	RC	1809	Founded by a Mr Terry; taken over by the Sisters of Charity, 1846; 97 inmates in 1911

Table 3.1 (*cont.*)

Institution	Address	Denomination	Date founded	Other information
Magdalen asylum	Sawmill St, Cork City	CI	1810	14 inmates in 1911
Dublin Female Penitentiary	Berkeley Place, North Circular Rd, Dublin	CI	1812	40 inmates in 1901
Richmond General Penitentiary	Grangegorman Lane, Dublin	CI	1812	
Ulster Female Penitentiary/later known as the Edgar Home (1892)	Belfast	Presbyterian	Opened in 1820/22	The original asylum closed and a new one was opened *c.* 1831; Originally in York Lane, new building erected on Brunswick St in 1839, when taken over by Rev. John Edgar; 47 inmates in 1911; closed 1926
St Mary's Penitents' Retreat	104 Lower Gloucester St, Dublin	RC	1822	In 1873 the asylum was taken over by the Sisters of Mercy and in 1887 handed over to the Sisters of Charity of Refuge; 79 inmates in 1901
Magdalen asylum	Carlow		*c.* 1824	No information
Magdalen asylum	Galway City	RC	1824	Sisters of Mercy assisted in the care of the women from 1840 and took over the asylum between 1845 and 1847; 64 inmates in 1901; laundry closed in 1984

Table 3.1 (*cont.*)

Institution	Address	Denomination	Date founded	Other information
Magdalen asylum	Limerick City	RC	1826	Taken over by the Good Shepherd nuns in 1848; 95 inmates in 1911; closed 1984
Female Penitents' Retreat	Marlborough St, Dublin	RC	1826	Originally founded in Chancery Lane, and then moved to James' St, in Marlborough St by 1850
Ulster Female Penitentiary	Derry city	?	1829	Originally known as the Londonderry Penitentiary; 17 inmates in 1901
Penitent asylum	Brown St South, Dublin	CI	1830	
Asylum for Penitent Females	South Circular Rd, Dublin	CI	1830	
St Mary's asylum	Drumcondra, Dublin	RC	1833	Taken over by the Sisters of Charity of Refuge in 1853; Moved to High Park, Drumcondra in 1858; room for 200
Asylum for Penitent Females	Upper Baggot St, Dublin	Episcopalian	1835	35 inmates in 1911
Magdalen asylum	82 Marlborough St, Dublin	RC	1839	'Lapsed' soon after 1839
Ulster Magdalen asylum	Donegal Pass, Belfast	CI	1842/49?	Closed in 1916
Magdalen asylum	Waterford City	RC	1842	Originally established by two priests and handed over to the Good Shepherd sisters

Table 3.1 (*cont.*)

Institution	Address	Denomination	Date founded	Other information
				in 1858; 121 inmates in 1911; closed in 1994
Magdalen asylum	Blackmill St, Kilkenny	RC	1843	Had closed by 1847
Olivemount Institution of the Good Samaritan	Dundrum, Co. Dublin	RC	1843	Had closed by 1857
Magdalen asylum	Belfast	RC	*c.* 1840s?	Originally managed by the Sisters of Mercy; taken over by the Good Shepherd nuns in 1867; 132 inmates in 1911; laundry closed 1977
Ulster Magdalen asylum	Donegal Pass, Belfast	CI	1849	Replaced an earlier asylum which had closed in the 1830s; 29 inmates 1911
Cork Midnight Mission and Temporary Refuge	Cork City	CI	*c.* 1850s	
Dublin by Lamplight	Ballsbridge, Dublin	CI	1855	20 inmates in 1911
Magdalen asylum	Tralee, County Kerry	RC	1858	Run by the Sisters of Mercy; asylum closed in 1910
The Rescue Home or the Home for Fallen Women	2 Northcote Avenue, Dun Laoghaire	CI	1860	15 inmates in 1898
Good Shepherd Magdalen asylum	New Ross, Co. Wexford	RC	1860	Closed 1967
Dublin Midnight Mission and Home	31 Marlborough St, Dublin	CI	1862	17 inmates in 1901

Table 3.1 (*cont.*)

Institution	Address	Denomination	Date founded	Other information
Belfast Midnight Mission	Malone Place, Belfast		*c.* 1862	
Derry Women's Penitentiary	Hawkins St		1862	
Rosevale Home, Lisburn	Co. Antrim	CI	1862	30 inmates in 1911; closed *c.* 1917
House of Refuge	Ballynafeigh Rd, Castlereagh, Co. Down		1869	
Good Shepherd Magdalen asylum	Cork City	RC	1872	167 inmates in 1911
The Rescue Mission Home	33 Lower Gardiner St, Dublin	CI	1875	19 women admitted in the year 1899–1900
Magdalen Cottage Home	Roches Street, Cork		1890	Room for 24

Notes:

[a] This is not intended to be a definitive list of asylums. The information on some asylums is so sparse that it is difficult to know whether they survived or not, or even if they were Magdalen asylums. Some of these listed may be the same asylum under a different name.

[b] CI = Church of Ireland.

[c] RC = Roman Catholic.

This refuge was based on a similar asylum which had been established in London a number of years previously. Writing in 1794 one observer declared that such an institution 'was greatly wanted for Dublin, where our sight was constantly struck by objects disgraceful to human nature; with wretched strumpets, tricked out in tawdry apparel, or covered with tattered weeds; where our ears were constantly assaulted with vociferations that would startle deafness, and appal blasphemy'.[8] The organisation and ethos of the Magdalen asylum was taken up by other refuges which appeared in Ireland later on in the eighteenth and nineteenth centuries. The title 'Magdalen asylum', used by many refuges, reveals the influence of religious symbolism using Mary Magdalen as the model of repentance and also of spiritual regeneration.

A Catholic Magdalen asylum was opened in Lombard Street, Galway, in November 1824, and managed by two women. There was a fund-raising committee of ladies and, as with other lay-run asylums, a penitent wishing to gain entry had to show that her desire to 'return to the bosom of society' was genuine. Given the regulations regarding entry to this asylum women appear to have been practically 'saved' before they went in:

That no female shall be received until she has been three months reclaimed from the crimes – that it is absolutely necessary that she shall have been under the care of a clergyman during that period – and that, after having given such proof of her sincerity, that she obtains a certificate of same from such clergyman, & that such certificate only be granted *not on hearsay*, but accurate observation – that during such time of probation, that the penitent must not have been seen ever in one instance to have held intercourse with her former companions; and that she shall have lodged in the house, and under the consideration of, some unobjectionable and honest housekeeper, who may give testimony of her mildness, repentance, sobriety, and regularity as to hours, and strict propriety – that during such period of probation, such extern penitent receive her daily support of the simplest kind from Miss Lynch, at the hour she should come to receive instruction; as also that she be supplied with some materials of industry, the produce of which to go towards defraying the expenses of her lodging.[9]

The asylum was small and had ten residents in 1826. An annual charity sermon seems to have the main means of support.[10] Women stayed for a number of years and were instructed in 'useful and practical industry'. Once it was felt that they had acquired 'regular and pious habits' they were placed in situations, usually as servants.[11]

In order to gain entry to an asylum, particularly the earlier ones, women had to be recommended by a subscriber. For the Dublin Female Penitentiary a petition had to be signed, which read

that your petitioner is an unfortunate female sensible of the offence which has plunged her into guilt and misery, and deprived her of every means of getting an honest livelihood; and being desirous of quitting her vicious courses . . . prays admittance.[12]

The use of petitions was soon abandoned and may initially have been a means of gaining subscribers to the charity with a personal interest in the homes, thus ensuring sympathy and funds for its purpose. Penitents most often gained entry by making their own way to the refuge. One reason given for rejecting penitents was the lack of room available in the institution, and many of the homes certainly catered for small numbers and had limited funds. However, judging from some of the reports it appears that a number of asylums also operated on a discriminatory basis. In those institutions under lay control penitents were more acceptable if they were 'young, unskilled . . . and not hardened in the ways of vice'.[13] The

Magdalen asylum in Leeson Street took in Protestant women who were most often under twenty years of age, or were expectant mothers, and the stated aim of the home was to afford protection to young women after a 'first fall'.[14] The Ulster Magdalen asylum in Belfast also wished only to take in women under twenty.[15] Between 1849 and 1916 that asylum had taken in more then 3,000 women.[16] The Ulster Female Penitentiary, also in Belfast, seemed more flexible in its approach. The Presbyterian Minister, Dr Edgar, was particularly active in rescue work and when he became involved with the penitentiary he took it upon himself to visit every 'den of iniquity' in Belfast, together with two policemen, in the process uncovering fifty-nine brothels and 236 prostitutes residing in them.[17] Many of these women entered up in the penitentiary.[18] The attitude of the committee of the Dublin Midnight Mission and Home towards prostitutes was very open. Its members, who appear to have been male, went onto the streets to gather in prostitutes, usually after midnight meetings. They accepted all 'penitents' and if there was not enough room in their own establishment they found other places of refuge or lodgings for the women immediately.[19] The majority of asylums did not discriminate on a religious basis and accepted penitents of all religious persuasions; in practice, however, Catholic women tended to go to the religious-run asylums and Protestants to the lay homes.

It is clear that lay Magdalen philanthropists generally excluded the admission of hardened prostitutes. From the case histories provided in some of the annual reports, many of the women appear not to have been prostitutes at all – or at least their lives were constructed in a particular way to appeal to subscribers. Many were described as 'seduced' women who on abandonment by their seducers and families turned to the asylums for protection. It was also probably easier to reclaim young and 'seduced' women than hardened prostitutes. And the greater the success rate claimed by the asylums in the reform of penitents the more justification they had for their existence and the greater their claim on public support, on which the lay asylums depended, particularly in their earlier years. The reports of these asylums included case histories of young, vulnerable females in an attempt to engage public sympathy. These case histories humanise the women, make them 'worthy' of care and encourage the public to subscribe to the refuges. The only requirement common to all these institutions in allowing entry was the expressed desire on the part of the penitent to reform. After that, asylums selected penitents to suit their own facilities. Some of the lay homes were more flexible in their attitudes to those they sought to help. The Belfast Midnight Mission employed a male agent who visited houses where prostitutes might reside. By the 1870s this agent was accompanied by 'some ladies of the committee . . . resulting in the drawing of several young women from the haunts of iniquity'.[20] The Mission held four midnight meetings in the year 1874, and 312 women passed through their rescue home in 1874–5.[21] A different model of assistance was provided by the Belfast Female Mission. Though the Mission did not manage a rescue home it found housing and employment for the women, and where possible reunited them with their families. This model of welfare, which did not involve some form of institutional stay, was a rare phenomenon in nineteenth- and even twentieth-century Ireland.[22] Almost no public opposition to the establishment of these refuges is evident, though some objections were raised in 1813 regarding the opening of the Dublin Female Penitentiary, on the basis that a public asylum could only encourage prostitution by providing the vice with publicity, and that there were sufficient refuges within Dublin already to cater for reform.[23]

Organisation and funding

What was life like for the women who entered these institutions? Once within the walls of a refuge the penitents were generally issued with a uniform, one outfit for Sundays and another for everyday wear. In some institutions the women were separated into different classes. In the Dublin Female Penitentiary the classification was carried out with reference 'to their [the inmates'] former education and habits of life',[24] suggesting a social rather than moral classification. The institutions were 'designed to comfort and relieve the distressed soul who has happily perceived the error of her ways and loathes her former vileness'.[25] While that statement appears benign there was a seemingly contradictory attitude towards the women accepted. In many of the reports the belief is expressed that the women, in themselves, were not evil; rather it was the keeping of bad company or other harmful influences which had led them astray. The Female Penitent Refuge in Summerhill wished to remove the young female 'from the contagious influence of her former associates'.[26] Inmates of the Ulster Female Penitentiary were removed from 'the common jails, and the low dens of infamy and crime'.[27] In the reports available for the Dublin Female Penitentiary the blame for the fall into vice was laid at abuse by seducers.[28] A pamphlet published in 1805 warned the male reader not to 'disdain to look for a moment into the awful distress which many of them have contributed to produce and encrease [sic] . . . they shall know that those who act the part of fiends in thus marring the good creation of God, shall, without repentance, share the fate of fiends for ever'.[29] It was one of the few acknowledgements publicly made of men's role in 'ruining' women.

Within the institutions, however, responsibility for their actions was laid firmly on the shoulders of the penitents themselves. A strict regime was followed in the asylums which stripped the women of their former identity and moulded a new one for them. Penitents were forbidden to use their own names or to speak of their past. In the Magdalen asylum in Leeson Street the penitents were given a number and known as Mrs One, Mrs Two, etc. In religious-run asylums they were given the name of a saint. But even in rejecting their past the penitents were never allowed to forget that they had sinned. Their daily life was made up of prayer, labour, recreation and silence. This programme of reform and discipline made no allowance for maternal feeling. The children of penitents were not allowed into these asylums, and it is unclear what became of them.[30] An attempt by the trustees of the Asylum for Penitent Females to allow infants to remain with their mothers was unanimously rejected by the committee in 1858.[31] Within all the asylums there was an exaggerated rejection of the penitent's past. 'Until the penitents forget the past', as one report stated, 'nothing solid can be done towards their permanent conversion.'[32] All contacts with their past life were broken. They could not write or receive letters without the matron first reading them. They were rarely allowed visitors and if they were they had to meet them with the matron present. The control these institutions attempted to exert over the women even extended to selecting topics of conversation among the inmates: 'all occasions which might give rise to improper mental associations are . . . carefully guarded against . . . all light and trifling conversation is strictly inhibited'.[33]

Within the asylums the inmates had to do a certain amount of work. A programme of religious instruction coupled with laundry work was normally followed. To effect reform and rehabilitation the homes inculcated a sense of guilt in the penitents and united this with lessons in sobriety and industry. The conversion of the inmates depended on their being constantly employed; an idle life was considered to be prejudicial to their good. The inmates, it was stressed, were changed by work; industry allowed 'the mind to be tranquillised and made the penitents more amenable to religious instruction'.[34] The aim was not only to keep the inmates busy but also to train them for new occupations once they had left the asylum. In the female penitent asylum the women were taught

to weep incessantly over their sins, and pray without intermission for their pious benefactors, their time being usefully filled up in washing and working for the public, and no opportunity was lost to refit them, to fill, at some future date, their proper station in society.[35]

All the asylums engaged in needle- and laundry work. Although the main reason given was the desire to discipline the penitents and to give them a trade, such work was also a vital source of financial support for the institutions. Generally, these charitable efforts were well supported by the public initially, but interest usually waned after the first years of an institution's existence. These charities raised funds through annual charity sermons, subscriptions, donations and legacies.[36] On occasions, when building work was required to extend an asylum, appeals for funding took different forms. When the nuns at High Park wished to extend their asylum a committee, led by the mayor, was organised to raise the necessary funds. In a number of public meetings it was made clear that the inmates of this establishment, 'would not be idlers, they would be given useful and to a large extent self supporting work'.[37] In providing work for the women in the asylums the managers were constructing them as members of the 'deserving' poor, entitled to the support of the public.

The Magdalen asylum in Leeson Street opened a chapel in January 1768. Existing as it did in the wealthiest part of Dublin, and attended by Lady Arbella Denny it became a fashionable and lucrative social outlet. The Ulster Female Penitentiary, established on a non-denominational basis in Belfast in 1820, owed much of its original success to the work of the Presbyterian minister John Edgar. In 1839 he saved the penitentiary from financial difficulty by raising over £2,000 from the public in the space of a few weeks.[38] The Dublin Female Penitentiary earned 11 per cent of its annual income from needle- and laundry work in 1815, compared to 27 per cent from subscriptions and donations. By 1824 the income derived from subscriptions and donations had dropped to 9 per cent while that from laundry work had increased to 55 per cent.[39] The pattern of becoming almost self-supporting through laundry work occurred in all of the larger asylums. Generally, subscriptions dropped after the first few years of an institution's existence and it had to rely on the laundry for financial support. Penitents did receive some money for their work, usually when they left the refuge. In the Magdalen asylum in Leeson Street this was determined by the length of time and conduct of the woman while she resided in the refuge and ranged from a few shillings to £7 or £8. In these lay-run establishments women stayed, generally, for a period of up to three years. When leaving after this time they were usually placed in domestic service if they did not return to their families. By the middle of the nineteenth century the Dublin by Lamplight institution also provided some women with the funds to emigrate; they also set aside a proportion of the women's earnings in the laundry and this was given to them when they left the refuge.[40] However, if a penitent left of her own accord, as many of them did, or was dismissed for any reason, she was not helped by the committee.

Only one register for an asylum that remained in lay hands appears to have survived from the nineteenth century. This, the register of the

Magdalen asylum in Leeson Street, Dublin, gives us some indication of how lay asylums dealt with their inmates. As we can see from table 3.2, the total number of entrants from 1809–28 numbered 384. Unlike many of the religious-run asylums the re-entrance of individuals was not a common phenomenon within this asylum. One individual, Mrs 689, had resided in the refuge for two years before returning home to her mother 'against the wish and remonstrance of the vice patroness'. When the woman sought re-admission less than two months later it was granted only after she brought a 'certificate from her mother of her not having left her roof and behaving well and also of her quiet and good behaviour to that day'.[41] It may be an indication of the refuge's success in placing its inmates that so few sought re-admittance. There was also a much higher rate of entry through recommendations from employers or guardians and governesses than is found in the religious-run homes. The age range of the entrants also tended to be much lower than that for religious-run homes. The youngest individual to enter Leeson Street was aged eight and the governesses do not seem to have taken in anyone older than twenty-five.[42] Mrs 649 was only fourteen when she entered the asylum but was 'put out' shortly afterwards for 'refractory behaviour'.[43] It appears that the 'success' rate of this institution was quite high. A much higher proportion of the inmates ended up in situations than is evident for the religious-run homes (see table 3.3). Mrs 677, for example, who had entered the asylum aged sixteen, was taken out by a resident of Grafton Street as 'children's maid to her family'.[44] A number of women were also returned to their families once they were considered to be 'rehabilitated'. Quite a few of the women also 'eloped' or escaped from the refuge. Some of these women had spent time in the refuge while others escaped after a few days, usually taking their asylum clothes with them.

Time spent in the refuge varied from a single day to just over seven years for one inmate. The average length of stay was about two years, again in contrast to the religious-run refuges where individuals could spend up to forty years in the home. The governesses also expelled almost 12 per cent of the inmates in this period. Mrs 753, for example, 'behaved very ill, after repeated remonstrances has obliged to be put out and sent to the House of Industry'. Mrs 770 was not re-admitted after being sent to hospital 'where she did not behave well'. Mrs 825, aged twenty, lived in the asylum two years, three months but 'after repeated trials occasioned by a warm temper and impatience [was] put out'. Mrs 105 and 183 were expelled for 'looking out of the street window . . . and speaking to a woman in the street of suspected ill character'. Two other inmates, one a Catholic, 'eloped, June 15, 1827', both taking the Magdalen clothes.[45] Many of the individuals who returned home were sent there because the governesses could not discipline them in the refuge.[46]

Table 3.2 Entries to lay asylums, 1796–1843

	Total no. entrants	Total no. re-entrants (%)	Sources of entry					
			Voluntary (%)	Religious referrals (%)	Family (%)	Police/prison (%)	Other (%)	Unaccounted (%)
Magdalen Asylum Townsend Street, Dublin December 1796–December 1832	130	Unknown	0	35 (26.92)	0	0	82 (63.07)	13 (10)
Magdalen Asylum Leeson Street, Dublin 1809–28	384	6 (1.56)	34 (8.85)	39 (10.15)	90 (23.44)	0	203 (52.86)	12 (3.13)
Magdalen Asylum Limerick May 1828–June 1843			0	170 (77.98)	0	0	48 (22.02)	0

Table 3.3 Departures from lay asylums, 1796–1843

	Left voluntarily (%)	Expelled (%)	Situation (%)	Emigrated (%)	Hospital (%)	Died (%)	Escaped (%)	Home/ friends (%)	House of industry (%)	Lunatic asylum (%)	Unaccounted (%)	To work (%)
						Reasons for leaving						
Magdalen Asylum Townsend Street, Dublin December 1796–December 1832	10 (10.42)	9 (9.37)	27 (28.12)	2 (2.08)	4 (4.16)	2 (2.08)	11 (11.46)	19 (19.79)	4 (4.16)	0	6 (6.25)	2 (2.08)
Magdalen Asylum Leeson Street, Dublin 1809–28	15 (3.09)	45 (11.71)	59 (15.36)	5 (1.30)	36 (9.38)	7 (1.82)	47 (12.24)	149 (38.80)	5 (1.30)	1 (0.26)	15 (3.90)	0
Magdalen Asylum Limerick May 1824–June 1843	42 (19.27)	39 (17.89)	47 (21.56)	0	15 (6.88)	5 (2.90)	0	34 (15.59)	0	0	34 (15.59)	0

It is difficult to assess how successful these institutions were in reforming or rescuing their inmates. Clearly claims made regarding the rehabilitation of the penitents in such annual reports as have survived should be treated with caution. In the Magdalen asylum, Leeson Street, the total number of inmates from 1767 to 1784 was 251. The committee claimed a reform rate of 52 per cent or 130 of the women and a failure rate of 32 per cent or 90 inmates.[47] The remaining 18 per cent were resident in the home when these figures were compiled. The Magdalen asylum in Limerick was run by a Miss Reddan until the Good Shepherd sisters took it over in 1848. It is one of the few lay-run refuges for which a complete list of penitents can be found. From May 1828 to June 1843 the total number of penitents admitted was 218 (see table 3.2); of these, 47 were placed in situations, and 34 were restored to friends or returned home. All of these penitents would have been seen as reclaimed and if we include the five deaths which occurred in the home, the ultimate redemption, 39 per cent of the women were rescued. Some homes claimed a high success rate. The Rescue Mission Home in Dublin, for example, pronounced a success rate of 65 per cent in 1899.[48] This home was very selective in choosing its inmates and the figure may indeed be accurate. Other institutions seem to have admitted high rates of failure. The Dublin by Lamplight institution appears to have, in 1899, a failure rate of about 70 per cent and a success rate of 13 per cent, the remaining 17 per cent being resident in the home when the figures were compiled.[49] Although these samples are too small to make any generalisation about the successes of the asylums, a study of prostitution in York suggests that many penitents placed in situations usually slipped back into their old lifestyles.[50] Many women also left or ran away from the refuges before their allotted release date. About 2 per cent of the inmates of the Limerick Magdalen asylum, for example, did so. It seems likely that many of the women used these homes as a temporary refuge and had no intention of reforming, an aspect which will be looked at later.

Lay women played an important role in running these establishments. All of the lay homes had male governors, patrons or committee members and they all had ladies' committees or lady visitors. The ladies' committees effectively took charge of the running of the institutions. Even when men made policy decisions, they were influenced by the women who did the routine work of ensuring that the homes ran smoothly. All the employees of the homes were female, usually with the exception of a male porter or carter who brought in the washing. In the institution founded by Lady Arbella Denny the women's committee ran the home completely and rarely sought advice from the male governors. The work these women did for the refuges covered three areas; first, the administration of the day-to-day running of the home; second, the instruction of the inmates in religion, reading and needlework; and third, the raising of funds. Groups of women generally visited the home a number of times during the week and recommended policy changes to the male governors. In the raising of funds the women mainly sought financial aid from other women. The committee of the Dublin female penitentiary sought money 'from all . . . but chiefly [looked] to their own sex, whose bosoms must beat with corresponding sentiments of anxiety to become instrumental in rescuing an unhappy fellow creature, a sister, from temporal and possibly, from spiritual destruction'.[51] Over the first ten years of its operation women averaged 52 per cent of subscribers to the Dublin female penitentiary.[52] In the Dublin by Lamplight institution they generally made up 40 per cent of subscribers.[53] Most of the lay asylums ran repositories where needlework or articles donated to the home were sold. Women organised bazaars where substantial amounts of money were often raised. The asylums also depended on a regular supply of laundry to ensure financial viability and it was women in charge of households who kept them supplied with such work. Without the voluntary and financial support of women it is certain that many of these refuges could not have functioned.

All the asylums were extremely conservative in their approach to the problem of prostitution.[54] They concentrated all their energies on saving the penitent. In the earlier part of the nineteenth century prostitution was an evil because it was 'injurious in its effects on society'.[55] If left unreclaimed a prostitute could not 'fill with credit the character of child, wife, mother, friend'.[56] The principal aim of the homes was to give back to society a virtuous being. Through discipline and work the prostitute learned self-control. A prostitute could be a corrupter of female innocence and could corrupt others. Not only was her temporal life a misery but if she continued on her way she would also lose eternal life and endanger the souls of others. These philanthropists believed that the causes of prostitution lay with the individual; if the woman could be reclaimed then the vice would be eliminated. Religious salvation was even more important to them than temporal salvation. These refuges were established in response to social demands, the alarming number of prostitutes who operated openly in the city generally being given as the reason for their existence. Women were not expected to be sexual beings – hence the pretence in these homes that prostitutes had no past life. The prostitute, by her 'unwomanly' behaviour in displaying her availability for sexual acts, was seen as an affront to 'respectable' women who were supposedly sexually ignorant. The function of such homes was not to question the existence of a sexual double standard. Rescuers wished to elevate the 'fallen woman' to an acceptable level of womanhood, to carry out her dutiful role in society without acknowledging her sexuality.

Convent institutions

The institutions run by nuns are of especial interest in regard to the idealised picture of women common in Ireland in the nineteenth century. In these refuges the 'purest' women looked after the most 'impure'. As in other charitable endeavours in which they became involved, female religious provided an extensive, organised network of refuges which operated throughout the country. The Good Shepherd nuns ran homes in Belfast, Cork, Limerick, New Ross and Waterford. The Sisters of Mercy ran a refuge in Galway and Tralee and an institution in Dun Laoghaire. The Sisters of Our Lady of Charity of Refuge operated the largest asylum in the country in Drumcondra and a branch of that order ran a home from Gloucester Street in Dublin. The Sisters of Charity also operated a home in Cork and one in Dublin. After 1845, no lay Catholic asylum was established to look after prostitutes and those begun earlier in the century were all taken over by religious congregations. The Good Shepherd asylum in Cork appears to have been the only religious-run asylum established to meet the demand for a refuge resulting from the implementation of the CDAs in the 1860s.[57]

In 1853 the Order of Our Lady of Charity of Refuge was invited from France to run a home established by the Rev. John Smith in 1833. When this home was begun it had only seven penitents and the laundry brought in £7 per week.[58] The nuns had considerable difficulty wresting control of the asylum from Fr Smith, who had expected to manage the asylum and the nuns in it. When he was unable to do so he went and organised a rival asylum which he was forced to close by Archbishop Cullen in 1857. Nuns generally took over institutions which were already in existence but which through both managerial and financial considerations had run into difficulties. It was a very practical move to bring nuns in because they had the personnel, commitment, organisation and financial support which many of the Catholic lay asylums lacked. It is clear that the Catholic hierarchy felt that the only worthwhile impact to be made on Magdalens could come from nuns.[59]

The Limerick asylum was established by a local priest as a shelter in Newgate Lane, near the city gaol, about 1826. Its everyday affairs were managed by women. The convent annals record that, at that time, penitents had to go out to get the laundry, and that they were dressed in blue petticoats and blue wrappers. When the Good Shepherd nuns took over the asylum in 1848 the number of penitents there was about twenty-eight. The annals noted that the sisters had to contend with many difficulties regarding the penitents who had 'to do without the petting, coaxing and familiar ways to which they had been accustomed, and which are so contrary to what is prescribed for us in our management of this class of persons and which we consider is ideally perspicuous for them'.[60] The asylums in the cities survived longer than those in the smaller towns. Carlow and Kilkenny asylums did not survive beyond a few years. The asylum managed by the Sisters of Mercy in Tralee, and established from a legacy left for that purpose, survived until 1910 but always had few inmates. A necessary part of the survival of the Magdalen asylum was numbers and location: the larger the institution the more chance it had of financial stability, in terms of earnings from laundry work. Small-town Ireland was not a fertile ground for Magdalens. The Good Shepherd asylum in New Ross never attracted a large number of penitents.[61]

The Sisters of Charity took over a Magdalen asylum in Cork in 1846 which had been established in 1809. A letter from the reverence mother to Mary Aikenhead records that when the sisters took over there was 'not a sound bit of timber in the place . . . rusty locks . . . no cutlery . . . very dirty . . . nothing in the house . . . the wash[room] is low and dark, when the water is taken from the troughs they [the penitents] are up to the ankles in it . . . the women are there without shoes'.[62] The nuns had to build a new washroom and with thirteen penitents in the home refused to take in any more until they could be adequately looked after. All the religious congregations insisted on having complete control over the asylums and, once they had gained this control, ran efficient homes.[63] Though the nuns had immediate day-to-day control over its refuges they were still ultimately answerable to the clergy. The Magdalen asylum operated by the Sisters of Charity in Donnybrook in Dublin, for example, sent regular reports of its work, along with detailed financial accounts, to the bishop.[64] The power which could be exerted by clerics is shown clearly in a number of letters emanating from St Mary's Penitent Retreat, the asylum which was operated by the Sisters of Mercy. Sister Gertrude Howell had the temerity to write directly to the secretary of charitable donations and bequests to ask when a legacy of £500, which had been left to Archbishop Cullen for the refuge, would be paid to them. Cullen was obviously informed of the letter and within two days the same nun was writing to him, with the most abject apologies, for daring to presume to interfere in this matter.[65]

Overall convent asylums were larger and catered for more individuals than the lay-run establishments. Though many of the lay asylums put sometimes hundreds of women through their homes annually, they had residential space for up to forty penitents at the most. Some of those refuges run by religious could house between one and two hundred inmates at a time. None of the religious-run asylums published annual reports but the majority did keep registers of their inmates. These documents provide fascinating details about the women who entered these refuges and it is worth looking at them in some depth.

The organisation of convent asylums

The general impression gained from reading any of the contemporary literature published about the asylums is that they were virtual prisons and that the women who entered them were unlikely ever to leave.[66] The evidence of the registers disproves this. Tables 3.4 and 3.5 provide a detailed breakdown of the inmates of seven asylums run by religious congregations during the nineteenth century. Overall these asylums catered for a total of 10,674 women during the period covered. Of this number approximately 2,219 entered an asylum more than once. This is an underestimate as not all the registers account for repeats. The majority of women who entered these refuges, approximately 7,110, or just over 66 per cent, did so voluntarily and a number of women entered up to ten times.[67] Thus entering a refuge was, for the majority of women, a matter of choice. While it is true that many such women had only the workhouse or the Magdalen asylum to turn to in times of utter distress, it would appear that the second was the favoured option of many. The length of stay in the asylums varied from one day for some women to an entire lifetime, of thirty or forty years, for others. It was generally women who entered in their teens or who were in their thirties or older, who remained in the homes. One woman, in the Donnybrook asylum, died in 1881 after spending nearly fifty-one years in the home. The decision to stay was made by the women themselves and although the nuns certainly did not encourage women to leave, they had little choice in the matter if the woman was determined to go. It would seem from the number of re-entries that some women may have used the asylums as a temporary shelter and once they thought it possible to return to the outside world they did so. It is obvious also that the diet within the homes was of a higher standard than that to be obtained elsewhere, and this may have encouraged some women to stay. The stability of life within a refuge, the order and discipline imposed may have given a sense of security to others and made remaining an attractive option.

The second largest source of referral, after voluntary entries, came from religious, either priests and in some cases bishops, or nuns in other convents. Lay referrals concern either parents sending their daughters to a refuge, or matrons from hospitals or employers sending women to a home. It appears likely that those women who were unaccounted for entered the homes of their own choice. The homes in Dublin appear to have catered almost exclusively for women from the Dublin area. In the

Fig. 2. The maintenance of penitents in the Magdalen asylum, Donnybrook, 1840

The expenses of each penitent's support in detail:

Each penitent for 1840	£9	−16	−1
Each penitent for one week	0	−3	−9¼
Each penitent for one day	0	−0	−6½

£323 − 11 − 7 for 33 penitents.

allowing them bread, butter, tea, sugar for breakfast. Sunday, Monday, Tuesday, Thursday beef soup and potatoes. Wednesday and Friday potatoes, butter and milk. Saturday rice, butter, eggs, tea, sugar for dinner and also an extra allowance of mutton, bacon, flour, tea, sugar on all the holy days of the Church and on all the usual festival days of the Blessed Virgin or the different seasons of the year. The expenses of the invalids and all other casual sickness is included in this item.

Description of penitent diet
The best black tea, second best sugar, second best bread, second best potatoes, apples, second best butter, rounds and laps of prime beef on holy and festival days. A hindquarter of muton and twenty four bacon and 1 (half) stone of flour with 1/2 lb. of tea, − 1/4 lb. stone of sugar.

Description of Penitent Clothing
One stiff gown for Sunday and Holy days. with suitable caps and handkerchiefs to compound. Two blue working wrappers. Two blue serge petticoats. Two linen chemise. Two neck handkerchiefs. One pocket handkerchief. One large shawl. One pair woollen and pair cotton stocking. Two pair shoes. Two fine linen caps.

Bedding
Each subject has: One iron bedstead, one hair mattress, one straw ticken, one feather bolster, two plain sheets, one plain blanket, two quilts.
Source: Murray Papers, File 31/9/30 (1841–2) DDA

Good Shepherd asylum in Cork the majority of women, or 91 per cent, came from the city, 4 per cent came from the county and the remaining 5 per cent from places as far away as Dublin, Liverpool and even Scotland.[68] The asylum in Limerick received women from the Limerick, Clare and Tipperary area generally, but took in women from other parts of the country as well. The majority of women who left the asylums did so of their own wish. Over the period of the registers (up to 1899) 5,527 or approximately 52 per cent of the women did this. It appears that some form of permission to leave had to be granted by the nuns and a small number of women, about 1 per cent, ran away or escaped from the homes. One woman who left the asylum in Donnybrook at her own request, after spending four years there, was intriguingly noted in the information column of the register as 'having Protestant tendencies', coupled with a bad temper.[69] Another woman in the same refuge asked and was granted

Table 3.4 Entries to religious-run Magdalen asylums in Ireland, 1833–99

Asylum	Dates	Total no. entrants	Total no. re-entrants (%)	Sources of entry					
				Voluntary (%)	Religious referrals (%)	Family (%)	Police/ prison (%)	Other (%)	Unaccounted (%)
GSB	April 1851– December 1899	894	266 (29.75)	294 (32.89)	130 (14.54)	37 (4.13)	0	27 (3.02)	406 (45.41)
GSC	July 1872– December 1899	1,749	592 (33.84)	902 (51.57)	569 (32.53)	74 (4.23)	103 (5.89)	93 (5.32)	8 (0.46)
GSL	1848–December 1899	2,039	873 (42.82)	675 (33.10)	902 (44.24)	29 (1.42)	27 (1.32)	81 (3.97)	325 (15.94)
GSW	July 1842– December 1899	705	54 (7.66)	350 (49.65)	250 (35.50)	34 (4.28)	11 (1.56)	53 (7.52)	7 (0.99)
SCC	June 1846– December 1899		Unknown						
SCD	January 1833– December 1899	1,387	Unknown	568 (40.49)	520 (37.49)	16 (1.15)	35 (2.52)	186 (13.41)	62 (4.47)
OLCR	May 1839– December 1899	2,633	434 (16.48)	Unknown	211 (8.01)	22 (0.84)	37 (1.41)	117 (4.44)	2,246 (85.30)

Notes:

GSB, Good Shepherd Asylum, Belfast
GSC, Good Shepherd Asylum, Cork
GSL, Good Shepherd Asylum, Limerick
GSW, Good Shepherd Asylum, Waterford
SCC, Sisters of Charity Asylum, Cork
SCD, Sisters of Charity Asylum, Dublin
OLCR, Our Lady of Charity of Refuge Asylum, Dublin

Table 3.5 Departures from religious-run Magdalen asylums in Ireland, 1833–99

Asylum	Dates	Reasons for leaving					
		Left voluntarily (%)	Expelled (%)	Situation (%)	Emigrated (%)	Magdalen class (%)	Hospital (%)
GSB	April 1851–December 1899	412 (46.09)	69 (7.72)	31 (3.47)	17 (1.90)	14 (1.57)	40 (4.47)
GSC	July 1872–December 1899	808 (46.20)	206 (11.78)	76 (4.35)	112 (6.40)	23 (1.32)	178 (10.18)
GSL	1848–December 1899	907 (44.48)	384 (18.83)	81 (3.97)	37 (1.81)	9 (0.44)	199 (9.76)
GSW	July 1842–December 1899	359 (50.92)	50 (7.09)	5 (0.71)	4 (0.57)	16 (2.27)	27 (3.83)
SCC	June 1846–December 1899	1,005 (79.32)	23 (1.81)	5 (0.39)	6 (0.47)	0	24 (1.89)
SCD	January 1833–December 1899	633 (44.48)	345 (24.24)	26 (1.83)	9 (0.63)	0	106 (7.45)
OLCR	May 1839–December 1899	1,403 (53.29)	232 (8.80)	16 (0.61)	21 (0.80)	0	211 (8.00)

Notes:
GSB, Good Shepherd Asylum, Belfast
GSC, Good Shepherd Asylum, Cork
GSL, Good Shepherd Asylum, Limerick
GSW, Good Shepherd Asylum, Waterford
SCC, Sisters of Charity Asylum, Cork
SCD, Sisters of Charity Asylum, Dublin
OLCR, Our Lady of Charity of Refuge Asylum, Dublin

permission to leave after a few weeks stating she could not survive a life in the home without smoking.[70]

Discipline and regulation

Surveillance was the main tool in maintaining discipline in the asylums. It is significant that the Good Shepherd nuns who worked directly with the

				Reasons for leaving				
Died (%)	Escaped (%)	Home/ friends (%)	Other convents (%)	Work houses (%)	Lunatic asylum (%)	Un accounted (%)	To marry (%)	To work (%)
49 (5.48)	11 (1.23)	95 (10.63)	14 (1.56)	4 (0.45)	3 (0.34)	116 (12.96)	0	19 (2.13)
44 (2.52)	23 (1.32)	136 (7.78)	27 (1.54)	3 (0.17)	15 (0.86)	91 (5.20)	7 (0.40)	0
88 (4.32)	47 (2.31)	142 (6.96)	13 (0.64)	12 (0.59)	7 (0.34)	113 (5.54)	0	0
48 (6.81)	3 (0.43)	45 (6.38)	5 (0.71)	2 (0.28)	5 (0.71)	136 (19.29)	0	0
119 (9.39)	1 (0.08)	27 (2.13)	10 (0.78)	0	6 (0.47)	41 (3.23)	0	0
128 (8.99)	4 (0.28)	115 (8.08)	34 (2.38)	10 (0.70)	0	11 (0.77)	0	0
147 (5.58)	1 (0.04)	103 (3.90)	3 (0.10)	3 (0.10)	4 (0.15)	489 (18.75)	0	0

women were called 'surveillantes'.[71] The Good Shepherd sisters were advised that

in the church, at their work, and especially during the recreation hours and in the dormitory, be watchful over our dear children . . . a lamp should burn all night in their dormitory . . . let your watchfulness extend itself to every one . . . if you . . . leave them to themselves you may be the cause of the loss of their souls.[72]

The sisters were further warned that 'we should not, at recreation nor elsewhere, allow two children to be alone . . . there should be no corners in which some could hide from the eyes of the Mistress. It is in such places that the demon lies in wait.'[73] The women within these asylums were watched twenty-four hours a day but that did not prevent them from being disruptive. About 14 per cent or 1,309 were expelled from the refuges. Insubordination, violence, madness or a refusal to attend to religious duties or ceremonies were the reasons usually given for dismissal. Women resisted the regimes in the asylums by escaping, refusing to take part in religious rituals and refusing to work. One penitent in Donnybrook was dismissed after ten years' residence. She was described as 'extremely slothful, irreligious and [having] a shocking tongue'.[74] Another woman in Limerick was expelled in 1891 after a month in the home. It was her sixth time in the refuge and the record of her dismissal states 'not to be admitted again . . . a very bad spirit'.[75] A number of women 'eloped' or escaped from the asylums, usually with the clothing that had been provided to them. These women were often arrested for stealing. Such was the case of Mary Ellen Hynes who had 'eloped' from the Magdalen asylum in Galway with 'a pair of petticoats, a jacket, an apron, a pair of boots, and a pair of stockings which did not belong to her'. The magistrates suggested that they would deal leniently with her if she returned to the asylum. Her response was to stamp her foot and declare 'No, I will never go back there.' She ended up with three months' hard labour.[76] A number of penitents were also dismissed for engaging in 'particular friendships' with other women in the home. This may refer to lesbianism but whether it involved actual sexual activity or not remains unrecorded. Nuns themselves were warned against forming 'particular' attachments to other nuns because they had to devote all their energies to serving God and the community. They may have seen intense friendships between the women under their care as dangerous because it could distract them from the purpose of their stay in the home – total self-abnegation, the suppression of their own desires and repentance.

Being disruptive was one way in which the penitents could express dissatisfaction with the institution; it was also a way for them to assert individuality and personality. One woman in the Good Shepherd asylum in Waterford was expelled in 1897 'for rebellion'. Another, in the same community, was expelled because of her 'troublesome disposition'. Yet another was sent away as she was 'very easily led into mischief'.[77] In the Good Shepherd asylum in Belfast a number of women were expelled for 'striking', or refusing to work.[78] Those who were most disruptive were the ones excluded by the sisters. Expulsion did not mean that a penitent would not be taken back into the refuge again at a later stage. Indeed, the nuns did not operate on any discriminatory basis and seem to have taken in any women who came to their doors. It is interesting to note that the small number of Protestants who entered the Good Shepherd asylum in Belfast were converted to Catholicism, much to the joy of the nuns, before they departed again.

The issue of the regulation of laundries, particularly Magdalen laundries, became a subject of concern in the 1890s.[79] Convents which ran laundries wished to be exempt from government inspection declaring that the nature of their charitable work meant that they could not be viewed in the same way as ordinary commercial enterprises. From 1895 considerable pressure was brought to bear on the government to include laundries in factory inspection legislation, although many of the convents lobbied strongly against this. Under an 1895 Act convent laundries were exempt from inspection, a fact much criticised by factory inspectors and others. However, in 1901 the Factory and Workshop Bill allowed for the inspection of convent laundries. This was condemned by John Redmond of the Irish Parliamentary Party, who stated that while the 'nuns were not afraid of inspection . . . [they] did not want unnecessary interference which would weaken their authority and so impede the work of rehabilitation'. They 'are unanimously of [the] opinion', Redmond continued, 'that the introduction into their institutions of an outside authority in the shape of government inspectors would completely destroy the discipline of their institutions'.[80] This was an attitude the nuns were to maintain right throughout the twentieth century. All convent laundries were inspected in 1905 and in Ireland the inspectors noted that in these laundries, while they were greeted with 'great civility', they were seldom met with 'complete frankness'.[81] The factory inspectors queried how useful laundry work was in the rehabilitation of 'fallen women' and suggested that commercial considerations often took precedence over the physical health of the penitents.[82] Between 1907 and 1914 many convent laundries were inspected, and although some were found wanting, the majority came out well from the inspections.[83] Significantly, inspections do not appear to have continued in independent Ireland.

By the end of the nineteenth century it is evident that many of the convent-run Magdalen asylums had a large number of inmates. Table 3.1 gives the numbers of penitents resident in some of these asylums at the turn of the twentieth century. While most of the lay-run asylums catered for small numbers, many of those run by convents were holding in the region of a hundred plus inmates each. The evidence of the available registers also reveals that in the 1890s, the last decade for which we have information, women were still entering and leaving the asylums of their own free will (see table 3.6). In the Good Shepherd asylum in Belfast, for instance, 85 per cent of those women who entered between 1890 and 1899 left the asylum. About 60 per cent left the Good Shepherd asylum in Waterford during the same period, as did 82 per cent of those who entered the Sisters of Charity asylum in Cork in the same decade. However, it is also clear that these asylums had a substantial number of residents by the end of the 1890s, even if turnover was high. There were still enough residents to ensure that the laundry work was continued by the penitents. It is certainly the case that for the most of the women who

Table 3.6 Asylum admission by year, 1846–99

	SC Cork	GS Cork	GS Belfast	GS Waterford	OLCRD
1846	7				
1847	9				
1848	17				
1849	14				
1850	25				
1851	26				
1852	12				
1853	16				
1854	28				27
1855	25				29
1856	24				21
1857	21				45
1858	23			10	64
1859	19			9	68
1860	24			18	51
1861	21			18	39
1862	24			8	46
1863	18			17	56
1864	20			17	28
1865	19			7	32
1866	14			12	30
1867	26			22	20
1868	19			13	13
1869	25			14	16
1870	17		5	22	17
1871	28		3	13	21
1872	20	27	5	15	42
1873	33	33	8	26	61
1874	20	40	16	23	87
1875	16	38	23	14	81
1876	32	97	29	17	55
1877	27	73	30	22	90
1878	36	90	31	16	80
1879	35	72	31	19	65
1880	27	98	30	19	21
1881	26	66	31	9	52
1882	40	71	11	9	78
1883	24	48	9	5	64
1884	32	70	24	2	71
1885	34	74	27	1	66
1886	28	81	28	9	127
1887	24	95	28	8	121
1888	34	86	25	14	56
1889	30	62	18	3	70
1890	26	40	15	13	96
1891	17	48	16	23	93

Table 3.6 (*cont.*)

	SCC Cork	GS Cork	GS Belfast	GS Waterford	OLCRD
1892	21	51	25	7	71
1893	20	71	67	7	91
1894	27	82	76	13	68
1895	17	53	43	31	74
1896	17	52	44	19	54
1897	25	23	56	38	63
1898	33	31	69	45	50
1899	22	76	35	55	47

Note:
SC, Sisters of Charity asylum, Cork
GS, Good Shepherd
OLCRD, Our Lady of Charity of Refuge asylum, High Park, Dublin.

entered these asylums in the nineteenth century, right up to the end of 1899, the majority were also able to leave if they wished to do so. The census evidence available for the Good Shepherd asylum in Limerick for 1911 shows that it contained eighty women but, as far as can be ascertained, only thirteen of these women had been in the asylum when the census was taken in April 1901. Again, this suggests that turnover was still very high in the first decade of the twentieth century.[84] Somewhere between 1912 and the 1920s these asylums appear to have become much less flexible institutions, or at least acquired this reputation.

Refuge or reformatory?

What is also obvious from the sources of information available is that most of the women had migrated to large centres of population from country areas. A large percentage of the inmates of the Magdalen asylums had been born outside large towns or cities. These women had therefore migrated to large towns and cities seeking occupations or indeed with the intention of going on the street. Some appear to have been illiterate. For instance, of the 165 women in the High Park refuge in 1901 about 15 per cent were illiterate. Of the 109 women in the Sisters of Mercy asylum in Galway in 1911, 28 per cent were illiterate.[85] (The Dublin Metropolitan District arrest statistics for 1911 showed that of the 578 convictions made for prostitution 35 women were illiterate and the remainder could only read only, or 'read and write imperfectly'.)[86] Few employment options were open to them. As we have seen, many of those women who worked as prostitutes in Dublin enumerated their occupations as servants, dealers and huxters, occupations that were precarious.[87] Manufacturing industry offered few opportunities in Ireland and where women found work in factories it normally proved to be a tedious, harsh and badly paid means of earning a livelihood. The largest opening for women would, of course, have been some form of service, and contemporary opinion believed that many prostitutes came from the ranks of the servant.

As we have already seen, many women had given up prostitution by the time they had reached forty and were most active in their twenties and thirties. Of the women who entered, and remained, in the refuges the majority had either entered very young, at sixteen, or were in their late thirties. It would seem then that the latter group had given up their life on the streets and purposely entered the refuges with the intention of 'retiring'. Unless they had saved enough money to establish a business, or had married, there was very little choice for them other than the workhouse. Many of the women who entered and left the refuges on a regular basis were in their twenties and thirties and were obviously using the homes as a temporary refuge from their occupation. One other fact that emerges from the evidence of the registers is that the majority of women involved were without an immediate family. Most often both parents were dead, and in some few instances parents had emigrated without taking their children with them. The home was often also disrupted by the death of one parent with the surviving parent remarrying, and in a number of cases it seems that the children of the first marriage were not welcome in the new home. The disruption of the family and migration to large centres of population would have removed the woman from the constraints of family life and expectations. The need to support herself, and perhaps the desire to be independent, may have made prostitution a viable option in a world where there was little else a woman could do to maintain an existence. Even if prostitution was a chosen career it was, as we have seen, also, a hazardous one.[88]

In terms of rehabilitation it is easier to judge the success rate of the religious-run asylums than their lay counterparts. If we take the women who were provided with situations, emigrated, entered a Magdalen class (see discussion on p. 108), returned home or entered another Magdalen asylum, and those who died (the deaths recorded in the tables refers to those women who died while in the home) 1,926 or 18 per cent of the women would be deemed reclaimed by the nuns. This percentage is probably much more accurate than that claimed by the lay asylums. Contact with the penitents was not maintained once they had left the asylums and neither lay nor religious refuges provided any after-care services for the women.

Life in the religious run homes was similar to that in the lay-run establishments. Like their counterparts in the lay asylums the penitents were well looked after physically. Their diet especially was better than anything they could have managed outside the refuges. In the Sisters of Mercy manual very specific instructions were laid down about how asylums were to be conducted. It was declared that:

the more secluded and quiet the asylum the better, as all means of intercourse between the penitents and their former companions must be entirely cut off; even a glance at them through a window, or the sound of their voices through a gate, wall, etc., is sometimes sufficient to shake the resolutions of those whose conversion is still incomplete; therefore great vigilance is necessary.[89]

Restrictions were also placed on their physical space within these institutions. Surveillance played a major roll in the control of the penitents. In the dormitory for example it was expected that:

A Sister's or Matron's room should be so placed as to command a view of each dormitory; and it would be well that the beds of some real penitents should be placed amongst the rest. In some asylum dormitories a lamp burns all night before the statue of the Blessed Virgin. The dormitories should be locked when the penitents have retired to them, and the key be kept by the Sister: They should be prevented from having any access to them during the day. They should be required to rise and dress modestly and promptly when the signal is given.[90]

Clear directions were also laid down regarding how the penitents spent their time. The Mercy manual again stated that:

The penitents should never be allowed to be idle; even on Sundays some suitable occupation should be provided, as devotions, religious instruction, learning to read &c. Labour should form part of their penance; it should be proportioned to their strength and capacity. They will generally be found disposed to idleness. On the judicious employment of their time their conversion greatly depends, but they ought not to be over-worked or harassed, lest it may deject them. Laundry-work is well suited to the generality of them. Should penitents be admitted very different from the ordinary class, it would be very desirable that they could be separated from these, and employed in a suitable manner; but constant occupation is necessary for all.[91]

There was, of course, no room for vanity and the most public aspect of vanity, the women's hair, was to be cut on entrance to the asylum. This, it was believed, was a means of

bringing grace, which the willing sacrifice of their hair – on which they usually set such value – generally brings them . . . As Magdalen began the evidence of her conversion by consecrating her hair to her Redeemer, so do they, and thus give reason to hope that they really intend to imitate her in her penance as they have done in her sins. As a check to the wild sallies of passion and temptation; under these violent impulses, some, who would not yield to better motives, have been known to defer leaving the Asylum until their hair should be sufficiently grown, in whom in the mean time grace grew and passion subsided, and they became good penitents. It is therefore, very advisable to encourage them from time to time, during their fits of fervour, to make a renewed offering of their hair to God in imitation of Magdalen. They should all be carefully prevented from oiling or greasing, or otherwise bestowing any unnecessary care on it, to which they are generally much inclined.[92]

Cutting their hair was also a test for their motivation on entering as the nuns believed that some women entered for the purpose of procuring.

The penitents' days were made up of work, prayer, silence and recreation. In the refuge run by the Sisters of Our Lady of Charity of Refuge, the penitents rose at 5 am in the summer, and half an hour later in the winter. The emphasis on keeping the penitents active and their minds engaged at all times is evident from the daily routine in this asylum. Once the signal for rising has been given,

they dress promptly; and in order that their first thought may be directed to God, one of them, appointed for the week, immediately commences the prayers, which are continued while they are dressing. When dressed all proceed to the lavatory, from which they descend to the classroom, where the image of Mary, the model of spotless innocence, welcomes them to a new day of labour and prayer. When the morning prayers are ended a chapter from a pious book is read. After an interval of work they go to the church for Mass, at which they daily assist. Mass is followed by breakfast, after which they kneel to recite some prayers. Then comes recreation for a short time; work is resumed again, and is continued without interruption until six o'clock in the evening with the exception of the interval for dinner and the hour's recreation after. At stated times during the day short prayers are said, and in this manner the day is filled up between labour and prayer. They sup at 6.30 and have recreation again for an hour. Instructions are given at 8. Night prayers follow, and all are in bed at 9.30.[93]

The penitents in convent asylums also worked in the laundry. Financial records for these laundries do exist but are not available for consultation. However, it is likely that many of these laundries made at least a small profit for the convent and it must be remembered that the inmates were not paid for their work. In 1841 the Sisters of Charity managed asylum in Donnybrook in Dublin made a net profit of £384/11 shillings and 9 pence from the work of the penitents.[94] The same congregation's asylum in Cork had an income of £12,863 and a halfpenny between October 1858 and October 1864. The money was derived from donations, bequests and the industry of the penitents. In the same period a total of £11,918/4 shillings and 1 penny was spent on furniture, clothing, food, repairs and other items such as soap, coal and starch to run the asylum.[95]

The current view of these asylums is that the regimes within them were punitive and that inmates were not allowed to leave. However, this was not the intention when these asylums were first created. In 1864 the Sisters of Mercy manual for instance noted that:

Establishing an asylum on the condition that the inmates should be confined in it for life, or else leave it destitute and unprovided for, prevents many from entering who though they desire to withdraw from their sinful life, shrink from perpetual enclosure; it peoples Protestant asylums with Catholic unfortunates, because those hold out hopes of future character and situations. This may be seen in our cities where the Catholic asylums are well established on the above principle. Many would not enter, or having entered, would not persevere at first without hope of being restored to society at a future time, will, when grace has achieved victory, choose to stay for life, in which they ought to be encouraged, but not constrained. Besides, providing for penitents leaves places for others to enter and receive the means of conversion; whereas many must be refused where all are expected to remain for life; unless the funds and accommodation are unlimited.[96]

Visitors to Magdalen asylums were not unknown in the late nineteenth or early twentieth centuries. Mary Hayden, who visited the High Park asylum in 1882, noted about a hundred penitents there ranging in age from sixteen to seventy. She recorded in her diary that she 'went over the whole house, it is very clean and tidy and large and cold and comfortless and maddening I think'.[97] Mary Costello, visiting a number of asylums fifteen years later, termed them 'spiritual hospitals'. She wrote of her experiences in a series of articles, entitled 'The Sisters of Sorrow', for *The Lady of the House*, a magazine intended for the well-heeled ladies of Dublin. Figure 3 is a photograph of a group of women from the Dublin Female Penitentiary which appeared in the magazine. Costello observed that the nuns had no 'power to keep anyone in restraint', but also remarked that the expectation was that women who entered this institution would remain there for life.[98] As we have noted, there was still a considerable amount of movement in and out of these asylums in the late 1890s, and it was not until the 1940s that there was any query about the legality of retaining women in these institutions.[99] For Costello these women were not the seduced, vulnerable victims so often presented in the annual reports of Magdalen asylums. She believed the asylum inmates to be

gathered in considerable majority from the lowest fields of licence; women of weak wills but strong appetites, initially, it may be assumed. Of wayward, emotional, pleasure-craving temperaments, a great many of whom in an effort to make bearable the degradation into which they had fallen, have contracted habits of drink.[100]

In the High Park asylum the penitents addressed the nuns as mother and were referred to privately as children. In public, and when being instructed, the title penitent was always used in order to make the inmates realise its true meaning.[101] The penitent was not treated as an adult and had no control over her life in the refuge. The nuns organised her day and took away all the responsibility of decision making. Within this refuge also

Fig. 3. A group of women from the Dublin Female Penitentiary, from *The Lady of the House*, 15 April 1897. Reproduced by permission of the British Library.

the women were never allowed to be left alone for a moment. Penitents in some of the religious-run homes could join a Magdalen class.[102] Within these homes, penitents were categorised in three groups, the ordinary penitents, Children of Mary and the 'consecrated', the latter also being called the 'class of perseverance'. Women could move from one class to another by displaying piety and discipline. The highest class was that of the 'consecrated' or class of perseverance. Women who entered this class took a form of religious vow similar to that taken by the nuns themselves. If consecrated the penitents were expected to remain in the home for life and were given special privileges within the community. They also wore a habit similar to that worn by the lay sisters.[103] The nuns' own ideal of austerity and holiness was offered as the ideal for the rescued penitents, but they could never become 'real' nuns or be totally integrated into the community. Those 'consecrated' remained part of the penitent community and were, by their example of piety, thought to influence other penitents for good. Although treated as children these women could never be full members of a religious family; the nuns kept their distance from their charges. The nuns were reminded that they 'must inspire the children [penitents] who are generally headstrong and obstinate, with confidence, without familiarising themselves with them in the slightest degree'.[104]

The popular novelist, Canon Sheehan, provided an idealised picture of an Irish Magdalen asylum in his novel *Luke Delmege*, published in 1901,[105] and any popular knowledge of these asylums in this period was likely to have come from Sheehan's book.[106] In one scene he has Luke conduct a profession ceremony for a penitent who is allowed to become a nun. In a scenario that was totally misleading he writes of how 'that little chapel . . . was filled that morning with a curious, happy, loving, eager throng of penitents; and the very idea that one of their number was about to be raised to the glory of the white habit, and a place of honour in the choir stalls, filled all with a kind of personal pride and exultation'.[107] In reality penitents could never become nuns.

The nuns reached out to more penitents, numerically speaking, than did the lay asylums. In the annals of those convents to which asylums were attached there are many stories related of women who led a holy and penitent life within the refuges. Great satisfaction was expressed by the nuns in the saving of these souls. The annals are full of anecdotes about the relationship between the nuns and the penitents. They generally refer to requests by penitents to leave and it is only the superior wit of the nun in charge which tricks them into remaining.

The social world of these refuges reproduced the patriarchal and class order of society in general. Women in the nineteenth century had a carefully defined sphere of action and this can be seen clearly in the operation of the Magdalen asylums. The women who ran these refuges played out their maternal role creating homes for the penitent 'child'. They sought to inculcate in the penitent the correct attitudes and behaviour expected of women in that age. Penitents were trained in deference and subordination in isolated refuges which shielded them from the world, the source of possible temptation. The importance of personal guilt was continually stressed and the fact that only personal discipline could lead to salvation. Any individual expression of personality or sexuality was denied to the women in these refuges and this was in keeping with what was considered correct behaviour for all women at this time. Judging from the large numbers of women who left these refuges voluntarily, it is obvious that these standards were unacceptable for many.

The Catholic discourse on prostitution was informed by the virginal and spiritual nature attributed to female religious. For society, both groups epitomised the extremes of womanhood. The sexual identity of nuns and of prostitutes rested on their opposition and their difference. A contemporary description of the arrival of a penitent at the gates of a religious-run Magdalen asylum shows clearly this opposition:

with the tears of a penitent upon her young and sinful face, she turns to the portals of the church and there . . . she finds the very ideal of purity – the highest, the grandest, the noblest of the Church's children. The woman who has never known the pollution of a single wicked thought – the woman whose virgin bosom has never been crossed by the shadow of a thought of sin! The woman breathing purity, innocence and grace receives the woman whose breath is the pestilence of hell![108]

Another description, written more than twenty-five years later, reiterates this oppositional comparison:

innocence and guilt face to face . . . the bright cheerfulness of unsullied virtue so near to the most abject wretchedness of multiplied sinfulness! The spotless lily side by side with the foul smelling weed! The consecrated nun speaking to the polluted outcast.[109]

Sheehan's hero Luke Delmege experiences what is probably expected to be a natural reaction to Magdalens. On visiting a Magdalen asylum he is shown into a workroom where he was

face to face with the Magdalens. The shudder that touches every pure and fastidious soul at the very name crept over him as he saw the realities. The awful dread that the sight of soiled womanhood created in the Catholic mind, so used to that sweet symbol of all womanly perfection – Our Blessed Lady – made him tremble.[110]

There is a dramatic confrontation between purity and impurity within these asylums and the battle between vice and virtue was often lost by the forces of respectability.

Nuns and prostitutes would appear to be worlds apart but as women they were connected in a number of ways. A woman's place in Irish society was defined according to her sexual activity. There were four stereotypes: the nun, the mother, the spinster and the 'fallen' woman. Although the nun was the ideal, held out as a beacon by the Catholic hierarchy, there are unexpected parallels between the lives of nuns and prostitutes. Both were removed from 'normal' society. Nuns voluntarily removed themselves and were also physically isolated by the limits placed upon public access to their convents. Similarly 'fallen women' were often voluntary, and sometimes involuntary, outcasts in society and were removed from the wider community. For example, prostitutes used to congregate in particular areas of towns and cities where they created their own community networks. There was almost no public access to the women in the Magdalen asylums and they did not receive visitors. Indeed, in some cases, even when they went to church, the women were not visible to the general congregation. In the Tralee asylum, for instance, the convent church was also used by the public but the penitents were kept in the gallery at the back of the church sealed off by wooden screens. The behaviour of both nuns and prostitutes was governed by men. Ultimate authority in convent life, and hence in Magdalen asylums, rested with priests and bishops. For prostitutes on the streets, authority in the shape of police officers governed their lives. There is a further similarity in the position of nuns and prostitutes within the Magdalen asylums. Both were denied individual expression of personality and sexuality, particularly in each other's company: nuns because of their strict vows of obedience and celibacy, prostitutes as a condition of their penitence.

Generally within both lay- and religious-run asylums and refuges, no serious consideration was given as to the causes of prostitution. Exceptionally, the lay-run Belfast Midnight Mission attempted to put some pressure on the authorities to deal with prostitution, suggesting that property owners should ensure that their properties did not house brothels, and urging the police to be more active in clearing the streets at night.[111] But for most rescue workers the only cure seemed to be to attempt to rescue the fallen. It is clear from the available evidence that more and more women entered religious-run asylums as the century progressed. Table 3.6 shows the entrance pattern for five of these convent refuges. But at the same time the majority of these women did not stay within the asylums which were still the flexible asylums they had been since the beginning of the nineteenth century.

Magdalen asylums in the twentieth century

All of the lay Magdalen asylums altered their function and purpose in the twentieth century. A number closed and those that continued in rescue work essentially became homes for unmarried mothers. Although we have little information on the running of these lay homes for much of the twentieth century we do have some information about the Edgar Home in Belfast. In 1907 the committee employed someone to work 'amongst the women in their homes and elsewhere'.[112] By 1909 a new woman was employed to visit 'all the parts of the city where our dishonoured sisters congregate'.[113] In contrast to the religious-run asylums admissions to lay-run Magdalen asylums appear to have been declining by the end of the nineteenth century, a problem that became more marked after the First World War. The hard labour involved in laundry work was recognised by the managing committee of the Edgar Home as a possible cause for the reduction in numbers and in consequence they introduced steam power in 1910. It was believed that this would ensure that 'suitable girls would no longer be deterred from entering the Home for fear of drudgery'.[114] Between 1900 and 1926, when it closed, there were 2,786 admissions,

Fig. 4. Interior of a Magdalen laundry, Dublin, from *The Lady of the House*, 15 February 1897. Reproduced by permission of the British Library.

including readmissions, to the Edgar Home. Of these women 437 were placed in service, 189 were restored to family and friends, and 140 were placed in domestic service. The vast majority of the women, 1,009, left the institution of their own accord.[115] It was also noted that a number of the women went back to their former lives 'until their case becomes hopeless'.[116] The matron of the Edgar Home often commented on the bad conduct of the women under her care, citing them as 'self-willed' and 'lacking in restraint' in a number of the home's annual reports.[117] We also have some figures for the numbers of inmates in these asylums in the rest of Ireland. The lay asylum run in Sawmill Street in Cork city had fourteen inmates in 1911, while the Magdalen asylum in Leeson Street had only twelve inmates, all aged between eighteen and twenty-three. The Dublin by Lamplight institution had twenty inmates. Larger numbers were to be found in the religious-run asylums. In 1911 the Good Shepherd asylum in New Ross had fifty-four inmates, over 80 per cent of them in the age range twenty to fifty, while their asylum in Cork held 166 women. The youngest of these was aged fourteen, and 60 per cent were aged between fourteen and thirty-nine. The Good Shepherd asylum in Limerick had

Fig. 5. Interior of a Magdalen laundry, Dublin, from *The Lady of the House*, 15 March 1897. Reproduced by permission of the British Library.

eighty inmates, the youngest being sixteen and again the majority, 55 per cent, were in the age range sixteen to thirty-nine. The Gloucester Street asylum in Dublin had fifty inmates, with 56 per cent in the age range of eighteen to thirty-nine. The Sisters of Mercy Magdalen asylum in Galway had 109 inmates, which had gone up considerably from the 65 resident in 1901. (Figure 6 shows a proposed new Magdalen asylum for the sisters of Mercy in Kingstown – a substantial building.) These women tended to be older than those in other asylums, with about 53 per cent aged between forty and eighty. Fifteen of these women, a higher total than in any other asylum, were married. From the information currently available it appears that the women in religious-run asylums generally tended to be under forty years of age, and that more women were resident in these institutions in 1911 than had been the case in 1901.[118] It is possible that the pool from which women entered religious-run Magdalen asylums was expanding by the early years of the twentieth century. While prostitutes still entered these institutions, it is likely that unmarried mothers now joined them in greater numbers. Until we have access to the relevant

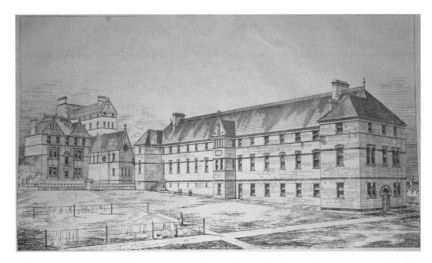

Fig. 6. Proposed new Magdalen asylum and laundry, Kingstown, for the Sisters of Mercy, from the *Irish Builder*, 1 June 1878. Courtesy of the Irish Architectural Archive.

archival sources it is difficult to make any accurate claims about the backgrounds of the women entering Magdalen asylums at this time, or the factors that brought them to these institutions.

The Belfast Midnight Mission, which had begun rescue work in 1862, had, by the early twentieth century, abandoned that work, and become principally a refuge for unmarried mothers.[119] The mission had an infirmary/hospital attached to the rescue home where 'those afflicted with diseases which are the result of vice', were treated.[120] From 1901 there was a room set aside in the home for unmarried mothers, whose babies were usually then given up for adoption.[121] At the annual general meeting of the mission in 1913 it was reported that there had been 38 fewer admissions to the rescue home, 339 as against 377 during the previous year. Many of the women left after staying one night. It was also noted that there was an increase in the numbers admitted to the maternity home, 113 confinements as compared to 100 in the previous year.[122] By the 1940s many of the women who used this refuge were prostitutes who were looking for a night's shelter but were not interested in being 'saved'.

The rise of preventative organisations

From the last decades of the nineteenth century women philanthropists became more interested in preventative work, particularly with unmarried mothers. The Dublin Hospital Girls' Aid Association, formed in 1880, by a group of Protestant women investigated the cases of young women about to become unmarried mothers. They offered them shelter, an occupation and tried to return them to their families.[123] In 1880 the Rotunda Girls' Aid Society, which had the same function, was also formed.[124] Such preventative organisations became more common in the first decades of the twentieth century with the establishment, for instance, in 1912 of the Church of Ireland Rescue League in Belfast. The aims of the league were to visit women in prisons and in their homes, to visit girls and women in the workhouse and do the 'outside rescue work of the Church of Ireland for those who have fallen'.[125] Similar organisations were established in Dublin, the most long lasting being the Catholic Protection and Rescue Society of Ireland, established in 1911.[126] By the 1920s charities such as St Joseph's Guild of Rescue assisted expectant mothers, nursing mothers and looked after young children; the Dublin maternity hostel, which was attached to Holles Street hospital, provided hostel accommodation to mothers. The Catholic Protection and Rescue Society of Ireland boarded out children, as did the Society for the Protection of Destitute Catholic Children, and St Patrick's Guild and St Patrick's infants' home.

The Magdalen asylum in Leeson Street catered for Protestant expectant mothers, as did the nursery rescue home in Templeogue in Dublin. By the 1930s the Magdalen asylum in Leeson Street took in girls before their confinement, and they were required to pay a small weekly fee where possible. The woman had her baby in a maternity hospital and returned to the home with her infant. She was then required to remain in the home for six or eight months, and unless physically incapable, had to nurse her child until it was old enough to be weaned. While in the home she was trained in domestic service, sewing, knitting, etc. and religious influence was brought to bear on her. When the child was weaned a situation was found for her and the infant given to the care of the nursery rescue which boarded out children to a foster mother while the girl contributed a sum per month in proportion to her wages.[127] Outside Dublin there was the Cork Open Air Association. In the private sphere and possibly for women whose families wished for, and could afford, anonymity there were a number of lodging houses in Dublin where women could reside until their confinements in Dublin.[128]

There was a strong belief that unmarried mothers could fall into prostitution. By the early years of the twentieth century then many rescue workers were moving, or had moved, into the arena of rescuing the unmarried mother. Many of the lay Magdalen asylums adapted themselves to meet this newly recognised client or had closed due to an absence of clients. While lay-run asylums were changing their function by the early years of the twentieth century, convent-run asylums continued taking in a variety of girls and women as Magdalens. For the historian it is very difficult to give any full account of the religious-run Magdalen asylums in twentieth-century Ireland. The records are closed to researchers and the kinds of questions that we might wish to ask of these sources remain currently unanswerable. However, there are some points that can be made about these institutions for the twentieth century.

Convent asylums in the twentieth century

In 1906 the author Nora Tynan O'Mahony wrote about a visit she had made to the High Park asylum in Drumcondra. She observed that she had never visited an institution of this kind before and did so 'with a feeling of something approaching depression'.[129] The visit occurred on the feast day of the St Mary Magdalen and the penitents had spent a week in retreat before celebrating. The nuns, she wrote, had spared no pains to make the occasion a pleasant one for 'their children'. Over two hundred women were present in the asylum and music was played in the hall to an audience of penitents, nuns and ladies and children. Tynan has nothing but praise for the nuns. 'All nuns are beautiful', she wrote, 'but these nuns of the penitent asylum had a new beauty for me, a kind of maternal tenderness, love and pity, half earthly, wholly divine.'[130] Michael McCarthy was much less benign in his view of these institutions observing in 1903 that these 'asylums do not decrease female immorality. They are devoted to lucrative laundry work, which must enhance the wealth of the religious. And they appear to draw only a sufficient supply of recruits from the immoral reservations to maintain their staffs!'[131] There are other published accounts of Magdalen asylums in twentieth-century Ireland but the majority come from the convents themselves and tend to celebrate anniversaries or centenaries.[132] These convent Magdalen asylums were, however, relatively well advertised in the Catholic directories available annually throughout the century. The Good Shepherds, if not other communities, also advertised their laundry services with brochures and price lists. Funds were collected for their asylums through the use of charity sermons and an annual collection appears to have been made in churches in Cork, Waterford, Belfast, New Ross and Limerick, at least until the 1960s.[133] There was no concealment about the actual work carried on in these asylums; what was more hidden were the circumstances of the women who did the work.

Many of the women who entered Magdalen asylums in the nineteenth century were prostitutes, but the population of these institutions also included unmarried mothers and on occasion women released from prison. This pattern continued into the twentieth century when it seems that unmarried mothers began to make up a greater proportion of those who entered these asylums. By the beginning of the twentieth century there was a growing conviction among rescue workers that Magdalen asylums were the best resort for the unmarried mother, particularly the mother who had more than one illegitimate child. It was thought to be a more appropriate resort for them than the workhouse. A substantial number of Irish witnesses to the Poor Law Reform Commission (1906) suggested that 'unfortunate women' instead of going to the workhouse, should 'go to a religious institution of reform'.[134] This echoed beliefs first expressed in the 1861 poor law inquiry that separate institutions should be made available, preferably staffed by nuns, to 'fallen women'. A large number of charitable institutions assisted unmarried, expectant mothers outside the establishment of the workhouse. Many of these rescue homes excluded girls who were pregnant outside marriage for a second time. Indeed, repeated pregnancy outside marriage was to become closely identified with mental deficiency.[135]

From 1922 religious communities of nuns established and staffed homes specifically targeted at unmarried mothers. The first of these was opened in Bessboro', Blackrock in Cork by the Sisters of the Sacred Heart of Jesus and Mary. They opened a second home at Sean Ross Abbey in County Tipperary in 1930, and later a third home in Castlepollard. By the early 1930s there were a range of establishments that dealt with unmarried mothers.[136] The government and local author-ities funded the county homes and maintained patients in the homes managed by nuns. They wanted the county homes to be the refuge of the 'respectable poor'. The presence of unmarried mothers in these institu-tions was felt to be an embarrassment and to reduce the willingness of the 'respectable poor' to enter such institutions. The government's keenness to remove unmarried mothers, particularly those with more than one child, from these institutions was part of the process of redefining work-houses, renaming them as county homes, and removing the stigma attached to entering them. By 1932 the government saw Magdalen asylums as the proper place for unmarried mothers. In an official, pub-lished report for 1931/2 it was observed that:

With regard to the more intractable problem presented by unmarried mothers of more than one child, the Sister-in-Charge of the Magdalen Asylum in Dublin and elsewhere throughout the country are willing to co-operate with local authorities by admitting them into their institutions. Many of these women appear to be feeble-minded and need supervision and guardianship. The Magdalen Asylum offers the only special provision at present for this class.[137]

The state and the Church identified unmarried mothers as belonging to one of the following categories: those who were redeemable and those who were not. Such distinctions are clearly reminiscent of the ethos of rescue homes. Attitudes to 'first' offenders were not necessarily harsh. They were depicted as unfortunate rather than immoral. This was someone who needed to be taken in hand immediately to ensure a successful recovery of virtue.[138] Both the state and the Church approved of the 'hopeful cases' being cared for in institutions set aside for that purpose and ideally these were to be managed by nuns. The fear expressed for these 'first' offenders was that they might fall into prostitution. Early intervention was the best way of rescuing them from such a fate.

These unmarried mothers' homes served a number of functions, in some ways similar to those of the Magdalen asylum. They offered 'respectable' society the promise of freedom from contamination, not only for the inmates but also for the wider community. They also offered secrecy and for the woman involved the possibility of regaining her reputation by returning to society with her 'secret' intact. Within these homes women, and often more importantly their families, could hide their shame. They shielded both the woman and her family from the gaze and scrutiny of the public. The homes also functioned in protecting social norms. Women entered these institutions voluntarily but once inside they were subjected to strict discipline and limitations as to their freedom of movement, and pressure was put on them to stay within the safe confines of the institution. The nuns at Bessboro', for instance, argued that since many of the girls were 'very weak willed' they had to be maintained in the home for a long period to secure them against 'a second lapse'.[139] The government continued to report favourably on these institutions seeing them as providing a valuable service to the country.[140]

In a society that viewed unmarried motherhood as a lapse from grace, humbly accepting the discipline and rigours of the homes would, it was believed, restore moral and spiritual values to these women's lives. The Good Shepherd asylum in Limerick City averaged forty admissions annually for unmarried mothers in the years between 1925 and 1930.[141] In 1922 the Galway Board of Health clarified its approach to unmarried mothers. It was ruled that

Women not entitled to admission to the Children's Home should be offered the opportunity of relief and retrievement in the Magdalen Asylum, Galway. Those who refuse to enter a Magdalen Asylum should not be allowed under any circumstances to become chargeable to the Public rates.[142]

By 1928 the board passed a resolution calling upon the government to introduce legislation, which was never drafted, allowing for 'second-offenders' to be committed to a Magdalen asylum.[143] It is likely that unmarried mothers, especially those with more than one child, were moved from mother and baby homes to the Magdalen asylum, though no government funding was provided for this removal or for the care of the women. While there was considerable discussion around, and support for, retaining unmarried mothers in Magdalen asylums, especially those who had more than one illegitimate child, no legislation was ever put in place to enact these objectives. We will not be sure how many such women entered Magdalen asylums, or of their route to that institution, until the asylum records become available for study.

There were other routes by which women entered these asylums in the twentieth century. The Westmoreland lock hospital sent, until 1922, between fifteen and twenty women a year to these asylums. From 1923 to 1931 the numbers sent from the hospital ranged between one and eight, but from 1925 the published reports of the hospital recorded these women as being sent to 'convents' rather than to Magdalen asylums, as if the phrase itself was no longer acceptable.[144] There were also other means of being sent to an asylum. Among the papers of Edward Byrne, who became Archbishop of Dublin in October 1920, are letters seeking financial assistance. One mother of fourteen wrote of her eldest, unmarried daughter, aged twenty, who was pregnant for the second time by a different man. Assuring the archbishop that her daughter 'is not bad only foolish' and a good Catholic, but that 'now she has not a friend in the world to give her a cup of tea', she asked for his assistance. As was usual in these cases the local priest investigated the family's circumstances. It was suggested the girl be sent to High Park convent, which she apparently agreed to, and her two children were sent to the Sacred Heart home in Dublin.[145] It is likely that other women in the same position also ended up in the Magdalen asylums. The report of the Carrigan Committee suggested that a number girls from the industrial schools system 'drift into evil ways' and that a large cohort fell into the 'hands of vicious associates and are ruined'.[146] Margaret McNeill, the Department of Education's inspector of industrial schools for girls, investigated and refuted the 'allegation made regarding girls trained in such schools'.[147] Over a period of nine months McNeill sought information from various Magdalen asylums, the lock hospital and other institutions about the numbers of former industrial school inmates they had in their systems. She discovered that of the 3,594 girls who left industrial schools between 1920 and 1930, fifty-five girls were known to be unmarried mothers.[148] Three other women were 'led into an immoral life' but McNeill claimed these had been rescued by their former schools. How accurate her figures are may be open to question considering industrial school managers were unlikely to concede that the girls who left their institutions turned to prostitution to earn a living. Also, there was no consistent follow-up for girls who left industrial schools. McNeill did admit, however, that some refuges took in 'for protection' girls of 'weak mentality'. Some of these 'weak mentality' girls were committed to industrial schools and were then placed in refuges for 'protection'.[149] Frank Duff, one of the founders of the Legion of Mary, noted in 1935 that in the penitents' section of the High Park asylum 'a class of girls [is] kept for preventive reasons',[150] suggesting that girls from the attached industrial school were contained there. Duff remarked that 'so far as I have heard there is no segregation from the penitents and I certainly do not think it fair to put any girl in that position. It would be fruitless for her in later life to say she was only in High Park because she was wild.'[151] In 1948 Duff believed that as many as 50 per cent of prostitutes came from industrial schools.[152]

The Legion of Mary also sent women into the Magdalen asylums, though Duff did not completely approve of their methods.[153] Of the 158 girls rescued from the brothels of Dublin in the 1920s the Legion placed eight of them in Magdalen asylums. The Legion noted that 'from our experience of the class of girls obtained, we are at a loss to define the class who of their own volition present themselves at the Magdalen Asylum. We think we can say that we have met no more than half a dozen who would do this.' In making such a statement, the Legion, was of course arguing for the value of its own rescue work.[154] Fr Creedon, who worked closely with the Legion, claimed in 1922 that most of the inmates in Magdalen asylums stayed for their life. 'These asylums', he wrote,

do not legislate for the ordinary run of women. Of the fifty women who came to us [at the Sancta Maria hostel] we found only 1 willing to enter permanently a Magdalen Asylum. The deprivation of their liberty and the fact they can't smoke, seems to fill nearly all with dread. The Magdalen Asylum is too much of a sacrifice for them.[155]

Between October 1930 and May 1932 the Legion placed forty women, who were originally resident in their Sancta Maria hostel, in Magdalen asylums. Twenty-four women who 'passed through' the hostel were also referred to Magdalen asylums.[156] That many women were unwilling to enter Magdalen asylums by the 1920s is evident in information provided by Fr Richard S. Devane, a keen commentator and campaigner on moral issues in the first decades after independence. He observed, in 1924, that many women refused to enter these institutions because of the harsh regimes and reputation for lifelong servitude. Devane also commented that a magistrate of 'very wide experience' had informed him that many offenders 'have in *many instances* . . . expressed to me in Court a desire to go, in *some* cases they have begged to be sent, to prison rather than a Home'.[157]

There was one other important source which supplied women to the convent-run Magdalen asylums. In the years between 1923 (the year from which figures are available) and 1940 the number of reported murders of infants below one year old, together with concealment of birth cases in the Irish Free State, was 738.[158] From 1926 to 1940 proceedings were taken against at least 375 women,[159] and 42 of these were found guilty and given suspended prison sentences on condition that they entered an institution other than a prison. Three of these women were placed in the Bethany Home in Dublin, a home for Protestant unmarried mothers. Their sentences ranged from one to three years. Seventeen women were placed in Our Lady's House, in Henrietta Street Dublin, with sentences ranging from three months to two years. Our Lady's House, which took in discharged female prisoners, was run by the Sisters of Charity of St Vincent de Paul.[160] One woman was placed in the Legion of Mary hostel in Limerick. Twenty-two of the women were placed in Magdalen asylums.[161] Of that twenty-two, seven were placed in the High Park asylum, one was sent to Waterford, two to the asylum in Galway, two to the asylum in Limerick, one to the Sisters of Charity asylum in Cork, and one to the Good Shepherds in Cork, one to the Good Shepherd in New Ross, six were sent to the Sisters of Charity asylum in Donnybrook, and one was sent to the Sisters of Mercy asylum in Dun Laoghaire. Their sentences ranged from one to three years. In 1936 a 22-year-old domestic servant had her one-year sentence for concealment suspended on condition that she enter a Magdalen asylum for two years.[162] There was absolutely no legal basis for allowing these women to spend their sentences in convents. The problem was only recognised in 1942 when legislation was proposed to amend the existing law in relation to the detention of young female offenders. In a memo it was observed that

at present some justices have adopted the practice, in cases where they think fit (usually infanticide cases), to sentence a female offender to a term of imprisonment not to be enforced if she undertakes to stay in a convent for a fixed period. This is, however, only a makeshift practice and there are no positive means of compelling the offender to remain in the convent, if at any time she chooses to leave.[163]

From the available records it appears that the women had to consent to enter the convent and abide by the rules operating in these asylums. It seems that a number of women stayed on after completing their sentences, and in some cases at least, the convents agreed to retain the women, particularly if they had no place else to go. Without access to the relevant archives it is impossible at present to ascertain how many of these women actually left the Magdalen asylums.[164] It is not yet clear what role was played by the probation officers involved in these cases. In 1941 one woman who had been convicted of the manslaughter of her newborn infant was given a three-year suspended sentence if she agreed to enter Our Lady's House in Henrietta Street. Having served a year she was allowed to return home as her father was terminally ill and had requested to see her. The probation officer involved played a key role ensuring the woman was allowed to return home.[165] The practice of placing such women in Magdalen asylums was particularly common in the 1940s, with at least thirty women being sent to these institutions. Some Magdalen asylums also took in women who had been given probationary sentences.[166] However, by the late 1940s it was noted that 'comparatively few girls are willing to accept probation with condition of residence in a convent'.[167] Although illegal, it appears that young women were sometimes transferred from reformatory schools to Magdalen asylums.[168] There were clearly women who were also sent by their families to these institutions in the twentieth century.[169]

There are many questions that can be raised about Magdalen asylums in Ireland in the twentieth century. Among the most important are the backgrounds of those who entered the asylums. How did they enter? Were they sent by the judiciary, their parents, priests, others? How long did they stay in these asylums? What were their class backgrounds? Were these institutions as inflexible as they are reported to have been? Did they become institutions of confinement rather than welfare in the twentieth century? If so, when did this happen? What was the public awareness of these institutions? There has been a general view that no one knew about these women, or about these asylums, yet middle-class Irish families had their washing done by them.

The perception of Magdalen asylums in twentieth-century Ireland is extremely negative. Undoubtedly, women were institutionalised and harshly treated. While they might have been places of welfare in the nineteenth century this may not be the case in the twentieth century. From some of the documentary evidence of government files, and the oral testimonies of women who were in these institutions, it appears that women were held against their will, that they engaged in unpaid labour and lost whatever rights both the law and the Constitution granted to them as Irish citizens. From the late nineteenth century it is evident that the asylums were beginning to be used by Catholic parents to hide the 'shame' visited on their families by wayward or pregnant daughters. It is also evident that some of the women being brought to these asylums were 'simple' and again were being hidden by their families. While the records of these institutions are closed to historians we can judge them only in the context of the oral histories that have been presented to us in documentaries. For much of the twentieth century the concern of the Church, the state and the general public with sexual immorality allowed these institutions to exist. Families hid their 'shame' and colluded with the Church and state and in doing so ensured that ultimately no one took responsibility, or was prepared to be accountable, for the care of these individuals.

4 'The black plague': venereal diseases in nineteenth-century Ireland

Robert McDonnell, a surgeon in Dr Steevens's hospital, Dublin, observed to a group of medical students in 1868 that the range of their studies offered 'few subjects at once so interesting and so perplexing' as venereal diseases.[1] For medical men of the period there was no clear understanding of these diseases or of the most effective treatment. The term venereal disease was used to describe a whole host of diseases, and it was only in 1797 that syphilis and gonorrhoea were recognised as different disorders, the distinction between them being confirmed in 1837. The third type of venereal disease, the soft chancre, was not recognised until 1852.[2] While the technical identification of the nature of the diseases and the medical understanding of effective treatment evolved slowly over the nineteenth and early twentieth centuries, one certainty remained constant within the medical profession regarding these diseases: that they were a social menace.

It is impossible to gauge the extent of venereal disease infection in nineteenth-century Ireland. There are no reliable statistics and the only widespread discussion of the diseases occurred in the medical journals of the period. However, these diseases were not as hidden as might be expected. In the press, advertisements appeared offering cures for 'the French disease'; doctors who specialised in the treatment of venereal diseases offered their services to those well-off sufferers who wished their illnesses to remain unknown; quacks offered private treatments and remedies for sale. The medical understanding of venereal diseases underwent considerable change in the nineteenth century and the professional development of the treatment for these diseases found an outlet in the medical journals of the period. However, the association of these diseases with women, and particularly with prostitutes, gained strength as the century progressed, and was seen particularly in the implementation of the CDAs. This chapter will explore the medical and public understandings of venereal disease in the nineteenth century, and examine state intervention in this field through the workings of the lock hospitals, particularly the Westmoreland lock hospital, and the implementation of the

CDAs. State intervention was directed at women. This was in many cases punitive and attempted to impose restrictions on their personal and geographic freedom. The social purity movement had its origin in the campaign to repeal the CDAs. This chapter will also explore the development of that campaign in Ireland and the discussions that were taking place around preventative work with young women.

Syphilis was a disease feared by both doctor and patient, and was of greater concern to the medical community than gonorrhoea. The treatment for syphilis relied heavily on mercury, administered either orally or as an ointment. Potassium iodine was also used in the early part of the nineteenth century.[3] Other treatments were available but mercury retained its primacy until the twentieth century. Within the Westmoreland lock hospital the dominant form of treatment in the early nineteenth century appears to have been 'salivation'. Mercury was applied, as an ointment or taken as a pill, and the patient was then confined and kept warm and in the process produced a significant amount of spit. This treatment could last from four to six weeks and the patient often suffered significant side effects, which included internal pain, intense nausea and permanent damage to the mouth, including loss of teeth, gum damage and the complete loss of the uvula.[4] In 1826, on a visit to the Westmoreland lock hospital, which he saw as a 'manufactory of Magdalens', 'Erinensis' caustically observed the treatment available in the institution and noted:

The treatment of the patients . . . is as fantastic as the opinions of their medical attendants are eccentric; every patient on her admission, being put on a course of mercury and the Bible, and having spit her pint a day, and perused her diurnal portion of chapters, she has a choice of stitching 'plain or fancy work' in the Dorset Asylum, or go out to 'catch cold' once more on Sackville Street.[5]

Given the nature of the treatment it is not surprising that many patients sought alternative means to deal with the disease. From the early decades of the nineteenth century advertisements appeared in the *Freeman's Journal* and other papers offering all kinds of remedies for these ailments. There was no mistaking what these advertisements were offering. Information and remedies took a number of forms. Books and pamphlets were advertised, visiting doctors proposed to see afflicted patients in private, and a range of pills and potions were offered for sale. In 1820 the *Freeman's Journal* advertised *Mr Abernethy's Surgical Works Complete*, in three volumes at £22 shillings. Readers were informed that Dr Abernethy was the author of works that included 'On diseases resembling syphilis, and on Diseases of the Urethra'.[6] Throughout the 1820s advertisements ran in the *Freeman's Journal* for 'The French Pills'. A number of important promises were made regarding these pills. It was declared that 'in every stage of the venereal disease, these pills are an immediate, safe and *radical cure*', but they also offered a much less harsh treatment than was available from the medical profession. In taking the pills the patient did not 'require any confinement or restraint in diet; but by uniform, mild, specific operation, neutralise and eradicate the virus; leaving the constitution unimpaired and the reputation unsullied'. The point of retaining one's reputation was possibly the most important selling feature. Not only did an individual not have to attend a practitioner, which might reveal the fact of his illness, but the physical signs of the disease would not be evident. The great advantage for purchasers was that individuals could 'cure themselves'. The 'pills' were available from Bull's patent medicine warehouse, 79 Dame Street, Dublin and priced at 2 shillings, 6 pence per box and came with 'full and direct instructions'.[7] As a means of ensuring the validity of the pills, the packages 'were labelled and signed by the proprietor'.[8] The 'Concentrated Detersive Essence' was advertised in 1846 as 'an anti-syphilitic remedy for searching out and purifying the diseased humours of secondary symptoms'.[9] Many of the advertisements did not confine themselves to 'gentlemen's eyes only' and many remedies were deemed suitable for 'persons of either sex'. These cures were often advertised as containing no mercury, a clear attraction to those who wished to use the treatment. In case readers were unaware of the side effects of treatment by mercury they were described in detail in some of the advertisements, which at the same time, condemned current medical practitioners for their use of mercury:

It is a melancholy fact that thousands fall victim to this horrid disease, owing to the unskillfullness of those who by the use of that deadly poison, Mercury, ruin the constitution, cause ulceration, blotches on the entire body, dimness of sight, noise in the ears, deafness, obstinate gleets, nodes on the shin bones, ulcerated and diseased nose, with nocturnal pains on the head and limbs, and only a melancholy death puts an end to their suffering.[10]

Visiting doctors also came to Dublin to treat patients. One such was Surgeon Goss, 'from London' who was in Dublin in 1839 'for a very short period, and may be consulted every day (Sunday excepted), personally or by letter, from nine in the morning until two; and on Monday, Wednesday and Friday, from seven in the evening until ten, at 38 Great Brunswick Street'.[11] Those from rural Ireland could also be treated by 'transmitting their report, which will be immediately answered; their letters must minutely describe the case, and contain a remittance for advice and medicine'. It was also noted that 'no difficulty can occur, as the medicines will be securely packed, and carefully protected from observation'. Issues of privacy were selling points for such remedies. The advertisements appearing for Dr E. Smith declared that he had 'twenty-five years most extensive practice, in the treatment of this class of disease, in London and

Paris', and he had come to Dublin for private consultations. He was available 'every day (or by letter, post free, and enclosing a bank note)'.[12] Smith's *Practical Observations on the Tabes Dorsalis, Or, Nervous Atrophy* described as 'that species of decline induced by early dissipation, the indiscretion of youth, or the excesses and intemperance of riper years; in which an approved remedy and the best mode of treatment are recommended', was available at 79 Dame Street. This particular volume was also made available to the ladies and gentlemen of Galway 'and by most respectable booksellers in Great Britain and Ireland'.[13]

By 1837 new 'remedies' were appearing such as 'Franke's Specific Solution of Copaiba' described as a 'certain and most speedy cure for all urethral discharges, gleets, spasmodic strictures, irritation of the kidneys, bladder, urethra, and prostate'. Appended to these advertisements were a number of testimonials from medical doctors.[14] Perry's Purifying Pills were available from 1838 and advertised in the centre of the front page of the *Freeman's Journal* (see figs. 7 and 8). Many of these advertisements fed into the ignorance and fears that surrounded these diseases. The desire for secrecy was acknowledged, and the acquisition of the disease was often expressed in the advertisements as a mishap, something 'frequently contracted in a moment of inebriety', an unfortunate and unlucky event for which the individual should not have to suffer.[15] As the decades passed the advertisements became more elaborate and included drawings. An advertisement for a treatise on venereal disease and Perry's Purifying Specific Pills took up almost a complete column on the front page of the *Freeman's Journal* for months between 1839 and 1841.

Such remedies were no doubt welcomed by those afflicted with venereal diseases. They guaranteed, falsely of course, a cure that appeared to be unavailable to those who attended the medical profession. They seemed to guarantee a return to full health without the horrors or side effects of mercury treatment. They also guaranteed privacy, whether through the post, or in entering an establishment for advice through a 'private door'. For those who suffered from venereal diseases these advertisements offered an alternative to the acknowledged painful treatment available through medical practitioners. And while quack treatments proliferated around venereal diseases, doctors had to compete against these quacks for the same patients, since only those wealthy enough could afford these quack remedies or seek the advice of a visiting 'surgeon'.

However, these were remedies that were available only to those who had money. For those who could not afford such treatments hospital attendance was one possibility, either in a charity or public hospital or after the establishment of the workhouse system in a workhouse infirmary.[16] The medical report of the dispensary in Dundalk revealed that in 1839

IN CASES OF SECRECY CONSULT THE
TREATISE
On every Stage and Symptom of the VENEREAL DISEASE, in its mild and most alarming forms, just published by
MESSRS. PERRY AND CO., SURGEONS,
4, Great Charles-street, Birmingham; 23, Slater-street, Liverpool; and 2, Bale-street, Manchester; and given *gratis*
with each Box of
PERRY'S PURIFYING SPECIFIC PILLS,
Price 2s. 9d. and 11s. per Box,

CONTAINING a full description of the above Complaint. ILLUSTRATED BY ENGRAVINGS, shewing the different stages of this deplorable and often fatal disease, as well as the dreadful effects arising from the use of Mercury, accompanied with plain and practical directions for an effectual and speedy cure with ease, secrecy, and safety, without the aid of medical assistance.

PERRY'S PURIFYING SPECIFIC PILLS, *price 2s. 9d., or Five Boxes in one for 11s.*, by which 2s. 9d. is saved, are well known throughout Europe and America, to be the most certain and effectual cure ever discovered for every stage and symptom of the Venereal Disease, in both Sexes, including Gonorrhœa, Gleets, Secondary Symptoms, Strictures, Seminal Weakness, Deficiency, and all Diseases of the Urinary Passages, without loss of time, confinement, or hindrance from business; they have effected the most surprising cures, not only in recent and severe cases, but when salivation and all other means have failed, and when an early application is made to these Pills for the cure of the Venereal Disease, frequently contracted in a moment of inebriety, the eradication is generally completed in a few days; and in the more advanced and inveterate stages of venereal infection, characterised by a variety of painful and distressing symptoms, a perseverance in the Specific Pills, and to the directions fully pointed out in the Treatise, will ensure to the patient a permanent and radical cure.

Fig. 7. Advertisement for a cure for venereal disease: 'Perry's Purifying Specific Pills', *Freeman's Journal*, 20 August 1838. Reproduced by permission of the National Library of Ireland.

seventeen people were treated for venereal diseases.[17] In 1833–4, 120 syphilis cases were admitted to the general hospital, Belfast. More than half the patients treated in the year 1839–40 were suffering from syphilis, and most of these were women who were 'kept by themselves in the lock ward'. Fifty-six cases of syphilis were admitted to the hospital and confined to the lock ward in 1843 'constituting nearly one-fourth of all the patients in [the] hospital'.[18] In 1859 Thomas Woods, the newly appointed medical officer to the Parsonstown workhouse infirmary, 'found patients of the worst character, and affected with syphilis, mixed up with other patients'. He proceeded to separate and classify the patients in an attempt to avoid 'moral and physical contagion'.[19] Many hospitals were unwilling to take patients suffering from venereal diseases and the Westmoreland lock hospital was the only government-funded hospital of its type in Ireland until the 1860s.

FRANKS'S SPECIFIC SOLUTION OF COPAIBA,
A CERTAIN and MOST SPEEDY CURE for all
Urethral Discharges, Gleets, Spasmodic Strictures,
Irritation of the Kidneys, Bladder, Urethra, and Prostate
Gland. TESTIMONIALS.

From Joseph Henry Green, Esq., F.R.S., one of the Coun-
cil of the Royal College of Surgeons, Surgeon to St.
Thomas's Hospital, and Professor of Surgery in King's
College, London.

"I have made trial of Mr. Franks's Solution of Copaiba,
at St. Thomas's Hospital, in a variety of cases of discharges
in the male and female, and the results warrant my stating,
that it is an efficacious remedy, and one which does not produce the usual unpleasant effects of Copaiba.

(Signed), "JOSEPH HENRY GREEN.
" 46, Lincoln's Inn Fields, April 25, 1835."

From Bransby Cooper, Esq., F.R.S., Surgeon to Guy's
Hospital, and Lecturer on Anatomy, &c &c.

" Mr. Bransby Cooper presents his compliments to Mr.
George Franks, and has great pleasure in bearing testimony
of the efficacy of his Solution of Copabia in Gonorrhœa, for
which disease Mr. Cooper has prescribed the Solution in ten
or twelve cases with perfect success.

" New street, Spring Gardens, April 13, 1835."

Fig. 8. Advertisement for a cure for venereal disease: 'Franks's Specific
Solution of Copaiba', *Freeman's Journal*, 14 March 1837. Reproduced
by permission of the National Library of Ireland.

The Westmoreland lock hospital

In the eighteenth century two lock hospitals were established in the country; the Westmoreland lock hospital in Dublin, opened in 1755 (fig. 9), and St John's fever and lock hospitals in Limerick, established in 1787, which had originated as a small three-bed facility funded by Lady Harstonge in 1780.[20] Between 1817 and 1836 this hospital admitted 2,999 venereal disease patients, of whom 2,968 were claimed to have been cured, while 31 had died. However, the reports published on this hospital appear almost embarrassed by the venereal element of its work and are generally given over to discussing the fever cases admitted.[21] It was not until the introduction of the CDAs that such hospitals were opened in Cork and the Curragh, though lock wards were available in workhouses and the Northern Infirmary in Cork had a ward of four to five beds for such patients.[22] The Westmoreland lock hospital opened originally in Rainsford Lane, Dublin.[23] By 1792 it had been relocated to Townsend Street and initially catered for both male and female patients who suffered from venereal diseases. A report on the hospital, published in 1809, attempted to address the difficulties the hospital experienced in treating patients and the question of the apparent prevalence of venereal disease in Dublin at the time. The authors suggested that the large numbers of troops and sailors quartered 'in every large town, nay in every small village' in the country had led to an 'increased prolificacy of manners amongst the lower order of females'.[24] The existence of the Westmoreland lock hospital had drawn individuals suffering from the disease to Dublin thus augmenting 'vice, misery and disease in the capital'. It was found difficult to maintain order in the hospital, and it was stated that since the surgeons only attended infrequently, patients were often discharged without being cured.[25]

From March 1820, after further inquiries had been made into the condition of the hospital and its clientele, it catered only for female patients.[26] The move to treat women only was occasioned by a number of scandals that had arisen in the hospital. These scandals were attributed to a range of factors: the presence of male and female patients; the absence of moral and religious instruction and employment in the hospital; a 'want of classification of patients'; and the admission of visitors.[27] In arguing against the necessity to provide treatment for men the governors of the hospital made treatment a moral issue. In the case of men, moral culpability seemed to deny them the possibility of treatment, while for women it was the excuse for their care. The governors argued that the existence of a male ward had deprived 'the venereal disease of many of its terrors by affording too great a facility of obtaining a cure'.[28] The institution, which had been

Fig. 9. Westmoreland lock hospital. Courtesy of the Irish Architectural Archive.

created for paupers, was used by 'men in comfortable circumstances' and the sons of wealthy tradesmen were to be found in the hospital, sent there as a punishment for contracting the disease by their fathers. Men, it was claimed, did not have the same entitlement to relief from the disease as women, as they most often contracted it 'merely in the indulgence of vicious propensities'. Women, however, were constructed as the 'melancholy victims of seduction, cast off by their parents for a single error, and are actually forced into prostitution, as affording them the only means of subsistence'.[29] The hospital remained open to women, as the governors noted, because 'every diseased woman is not only in herself the centre of a circle of infection, whose radius is indefinite, but an object of peculiar compassion, in every view that can be taken of her truly destitute and unhappy condition'.[30] They had constructed the female patient as a site of contagion, and also as an object of pity. The closure of the hospital to male patients resulted in the government funding a ward in Steevens's Hospital for their treatment. Generally, a powerful stigma was attached to those patients who suffered from venereal diseases and there was a great reluctance on the part of voluntary hospitals to admit such patients.[31] However, women were sometimes admitted to other hospitals suffering with these diseases. For instance, in 1854 a doctor from the Richmond Hospital noted that he 'on several occasions . . . admitted women of the town into my wards pressed by the entreaties of the unfortunates themselves'. However, this was not unproblematic and he reported that the women were 'generally treated with such contumely by the other patients, that a fierce spirit of resistance was excited in them, ending in violent and abusive language'.[32]

A large number, though not all, of the women admitted to the Westmoreland hospital were prostitutes and it was claimed that once 'cured' many of them remained in the hospital to entice other women into prostitution.[33] From 1819 the government insisted that the grant they provided for the running of the hospital was conditional on some form of moral reformation being attempted. The Westmoreland lock hospital thus became more than a place of physical treatment, it also became a site of moral reclamation. The reformative nature of the institution became a feature of inquiries and reports on the hospital from 1820 and the hospital was displayed to the various government inquiries as a disciplined and well-run institution. Rules were in place which attempted to control patients' movements and to manage how they spent their time. The patients rose at

seven o'clock in summer, and eight in winter; the hour of rest, nine o'clock in summer, eight o'clock in winter. The patients are to confine themselves to their respective wards, and to keep their persons and clothes clean and decent. No patient to remain in bed that is not expressly directed to do so by the surgeons . . . patients are, on no account whatever, to expose themselves by looking out the windows; this is a regulation which, independent of the decorum of the act, their own health is materially concerned in observing.[34]

Any messages for the patients had to come via the nurses. The greatest level of control over the patients was exerted in the form of classification. The issue of classification within the hospital was a matter of concern to the governors and the medical staff throughout the century. The classification of the patients was considered absolutely necessary in order to prevent contamination of innocent women by the prostitutes who used the hospital. In 1829 classification was designed to 'separate the novice in crime from the hardened offender, and the married woman who is the victim of her husband's profligacy, from those whose disease has proceeded from their own personal misconduct'.[35] However, there seems to have been no level of consistency in the use of classification. In 1842 it was reported that patients were classified according to their ages; the first class were women under twenty years of age, the second class were women above that age, and the third class of patient were married women who had contracted the disease from their husbands.[36] A different classification system was in operation up to 1854 when there appear to have been three classes of patient admitted; 'women of the streets, married women, [and] relapsed cases that came from the asylums'.[37]

Classification appears to have been in abeyance in the 1860s and 1870s but by the 1880s it was again in place and by 1885 there were four separate wards for admissions. One ward was for the treatment of two types of women, the young prostitute who had been diseased for the first time, and those 'women who are not prostitutes at all – that is whose livelihood is not earned by prostitution – servant girls and girls employed in shops . . . among this class is very often a girl who has been seduced and who really has not morally gone permanently astray before at all'.[38] There was another ward for Protestant women and the two remaining wards were for Catholic women, those who were married (all women who claimed to be married had to produce a marriage certificate) and those who were 'common prostitutes'.[39] Many women flouted these forms of separation and it was believed that numerous Catholic women, particularly those who were better off, went into the Protestant women's ward 'to avoid the common prostitutes and the priest'.[40]

The punitive nature of the lock hospital was also expressed in other ways. Patients were expelled from the hospital for bad behaviour and if they left before they were cured, that is without the permission of the surgeon, the governors insisted that they not be re-admitted to the hospital.[41] According to the rules of admission no patient was to be admitted 'that does not submit to the cutting off of her hair previous to being sent to her ward'. This practice appears to have ended before the 1880s.[42] While visits from friends and relatives were allowed, these were strictly supervised. The patients also wore a uniform. Not only was the type of clothing worn by women thought to signify their moral behaviour, but, as one doctor noted, 'some of the very lowest of our race come to us, and are in such rags and tatters that we are obliged to put uniforms on them'. Clothing could also signify a prostitute's occupation and it was observed that there would be considerable dissatisfaction in the hospital if 'one set of women [the prostitutes] were allowed to dress in their silk and satins'. This, it was feared, would act as a source of temptation for other women in the hospital who might consider prostitution the best means of being able to acquire such finery.[43] All the inmates, except for the married women, had their correspondence opened and read by the matron.[44] The reason given for this was that many brothel-owners offered employment to women once they were cured. This reading of the patients' mail was a point of contention between the members of the board of governors and some of the medical staff in the hospital. One doctor claimed that this acted as a deterrent to women who might otherwise have entered the hospital while being the cause of others leaving before they were cured.[45] The women who worked in the laundry were not allowed to have visitors without the permission of a governor of the hospital and it appears that, in general, visitors were not encouraged. The porter kept a record of all visitors and the doors of the hospital were locked at five each evening. Nurses, in case they might go on messages for inmates, were strictly timed regarding their absence and were fined and reprimanded if it was thought they had remained outside the hospital for an excessive length of time.[46]

In 1829 the governors argued that the hospital had an important moral role in saving women from becoming hardened prostitutes.[47] This moral aspect shadowed the work carried out in Magdalen asylums in Dublin at this time. The moral reformation of the inmates appears primarily to have involved learning how to do laundry work. The laundry, which was to contribute to the support of the hospital, was established in June 1821.[48] It was considered the same as a Magdalen asylum and was called the lock penitentiary and the 'reformed' females in it did the washing of the hospital. The existence of the laundry was noted to 'diminish the candidates by 13, who if not sheltered here, would probably be driven to prostitution'.[49] The establishment of the Lock penitentiary where women 'cured' in the hospital could work seems to have been motivated by financial considerations. The washing for the hospital cost £200 per annum, and a saving of £25 was expected to be made by employing these women to do that work. Although this amount may appear small, for the board of governors, constantly trying to save money, it was a not inconsiderable sum. The women were employed for four hours per day in the laundry but they were not paid for the work they did. Instead, they were allowed to do some sewing, in their own time, which the matron sold for them.[50] Originally eleven women worked in the laundry but by 1854 that number had been reduced to six and the penitentiary, though not the laundry, had been abandoned by the 1880s.[51]

Admissions to the hospital appear high with in excess of 60,491 patients being treated from 1792 to 1910 (see tables 4.1 to 4.4), and 99,982 outpatients being treated between 1792 and 1818.[52] It is difficult to assess whether venereal disease rates were rising or falling in any period. Many of those admitted were repeat cases so it is impossible to ascertain how many new cases of venereal disease were presented annually to the hospital. It must also be remembered that the figures from 1820 deal with women only. After 1887 it was noted that more servants, shop girls and factory girls were entering the hospital and by 1910 the chief surgeon observed that few women sought admission unless they were compelled by age or poverty.[53] While the Westmoreland lock hospital was the only one that dealt specifically with venereal diseases, such patients did find treatment in other hospitals. Elizabeth Malcolm has shown that some venereal disease patients were dealt with in dispensaries but that there was a general reluctance, given the sensitive nature of the

Table 4.1 Admissions to the Westmoreland lock hospital, Dublin, 1792–1818

From	To	Admitted	Discharged	Died
20 November 1792	24 March 1795	2,541	2,339	40
25 March 1795	1796	1,491	1,372	32
1796	1797	1,750	1,715	42
1797	1798	1,620	1,584	31
1798	1799	1,519	1,511	29
1799	1800	1,651	1,589	53
1800	31 December 1800	1,187	1,171	27
1 January 1800	5 January 1802	1,810	1,753	38
6 January 1802	1803	1,806	1,748	39
1803	1804	1,738	1,715	35
1804	1805	1,558	1,516	47
1805	1806	1,395	1,372	34
1806	1807	1,322	1,236	35
1807	1808	1,423	1,391	43
1808	1809	1,285	1,247	34
1809	1810	1,275	1,232	36
1810	1811	1,320	1,276	39
1811	1812	1,395	1,368	37
1812	1813	1,430	1,388	58
1813	1814	1,646	1,559	65
1814	1815	1,666	1,612	61
1815	1816	1,588	1,507	59
1816	1817	1,586	1,575	51
1817	1818	1,670	1,618	43
1818	1819	1,888	1,842	44
Total		39,558	38,226	

Source: Report on the Select Committee on the Irish Miscellaneous Estimates, HC 1829 (342) iv, 127, p. 176.

affliction, among country people and doctors to report on these cases.[54] Cormac Ó Gráda has revealed that admissions to the Lock hospital from women who came from outside Dublin increased considerably during the famine years. The annual intake of the hospital rose from an average of 744 in 1842–7 to 1,000 in 1848–52. At the same time the average age of the inmates was lower and there was a proportionate rise of very young women coming into the hospital.[55] Women came to the hospital to be treated from all parts of the country, and some had been born in Scotland and England. The number of beds declined from 150 to 40 by 1854 and this was blamed on the decline of government funding. The hospital was supported entirely by the government with a grant which averaged

Table 4.2 Admissions to the Westmoreland lock hospital, Dublin, 1828–41

Year	Inmates at close of 1827	Admitted yearly	Totals	Discharged: cured	Died	Inmates at close of each year	Totals
1828	150	740	890	724	16	150	890
1829	150	765	915	747	18	150	915
1830	150	677	827	665	12	150	827
1831	150	688	838	677	11	150	838
1832	150	757	907	741	16	150	907
1833	150	698	848	690	15	143	848
1834	143	781	924	758	16	150	924
1835	150	861	1,011	853	14	144	1,011
1836	144	832	976	820	18	138	976
1837	138	880	1,108	863	9	146	1,018
1838	146	878	1,024	874	9	141	1,024
1839	141	818	959	854	12	93	959
1840	93	732	825	709	5	111	825
1841	111	694	805	674	6	125	805
Total	1,966	10,801	12,767	10,649	177	1,941	12,767

Source: Report of the Commissioners Appointed by the Lord Lieutenant of Ireland to Inspect Charitable Institutions, Dublin, HC 1842 (337) xxxviii, p. 43.

Table 4.3 Admissions to the Westmoreland lock hospital, Dublin, 1847–54

Year	Admissions	Natives of Dublin	Rest of Ireland	Britain and the colonies	Deaths	Women reformed	Number of beds
1847	667	305	342	20	5	178	130
1848	729	294	400	35	11	213	130
1849	992	430	520	42	9	182	130
1850	1,128	364	730	34	9	236	100
1851	985	267	700	18	1	82	80
1852	1,027	245	754	28	5	61	60
1853	861	253	571	37	3	19	50
1854	575	130	405	40	1	5	50
Total	6,964	2,288	4,422	254	44	976	

Source: Report from the Select Committee on Dublin Hospitals, HC 1854 (338) xii, Appendix, p. 20.

Table 4.4 Admissions to the Westmoreland lock hospital, Dublin, 1860–1910

Years	Admissions	Natives of Dublin	Rest of Ireland	Outside Ireland
1860–70	1,748	877	342	119
1870–80	1,933	1,111	400	171
1880–90	1,668	981	520	147
1890–1900	1,375	798	400	119
1900–10	1,202	706	520	92

Source: G. Pugin Meldon, 'Some notes on the admissions to the Westmoreland Lock Hospital, Dublin, since the year 1860', *Dublin Journal of Medical Science*, 137 (1914), p. 116.

£2,500 per annum, though from 1899 to 1906 the War Office contributed another £1,125 per year. The all-male committee of the hospital never sought public support or subscriptions for their institution because it was thought that the function of the hospital was too delicate to bring to public attention.[56] Indeed, doctors at the Westmoreland lock hospital were conscious of the status of their hospital. One of them remarked to a select committee that the 'difference between the Coombe and Lying-in Hospital and ours is this – the one is innocence – the other guilt'.[57]

Patients clearly got some relief from their symptoms or they would not have entered the hospital in such numbers. However, in attempting to prevent the spread of venereal diseases the hospital was quite inefficient. For example, in 1867 alone, seventy patients had, on average, already been inmates on three previous occasions. In fact, one of these women, a Bridget Tutnell, aged twenty-six, had received treatment on fourteen previous occasions, while Kate Ryan had been in the hospital on eight previous occasions.[58] Women entered the hospital voluntarily and could not be detained against their will. They were often in the full throes of the disease by the time they entered and had ample opportunity to infect others before receiving treatment. Of the seventy women mentioned above the majority had become aware that they were infected at least three weeks before admission.[59] One doctor, reporting cases from the Westmoreland lock hospital, seems to have been making a moral judgement when he noted a particular venereal sore, which he associated with prostitution, that bore 'no relation to age, temperament whether robust or not', and 'most affects those who have for some time been dissipated'. In his case histories he refers to women who have been prostitutes for many years and noted when they were first infected: E. M., for instance, was admitted on 1 April 1868, aged thirty-four. He recorded that she had been 'first unvirtuous fourteen years ago. Got the sore first 13 years ago.' She was treated with mercury at that time and had no further symptoms. She was married and lived with her husband for eight years but had never been pregnant. Three years before her admission her husband died and she returned to her former life, and got a sore. During the subsequent four months before her admission she was 'living irregularly, pursuing an unvirtuous life . . . she is thin, looks much older than she states her age to be. Readmitted 18 December 1868. Was treated with arsenic. Eventually cured and discharged 26 November 1868.'[60] The treatment of syphilis and gonorrhoea was still in a primitive state and many women were released in the mistaken belief that they were cured. During the secondary stage of syphilis victims appear to have recovered as the disease is quiescent but the tertiary stage was always fatal. Because of the double standards relating to sexual behaviour that existed, no serious attempt was made to treat male suffers.[61] Soldiers were not treated in confinement as women were and yet obviously infected a large number of women. Of the 6,550 unmarried women admitted in 1850, half were believed to have been infected by soldiers.[62] Patients could be expelled from the hospital. Some were discharged for 'dirty habits', though it is not made explicit whether this refers to a sexual offence, or was related to personal hygiene. Some women created a disturbance in the hospital which got them expelled, or were put out for not taking their medicine, clearly a form of rebellion. Expelling patients for their poor behaviour was hardly conducive to assisting in their cure. It was believed that the establishment of lock hospitals for women in garrison towns was the best means of preventing the spread of venereal diseases among the soldiery.[63] The lock hospital had always been an institutional device, sanctioned by government, which sought short-term solutions to the diseases associated with prostitution. Both the government and the hospital authorities claimed that it was also a moral space which controlled and managed the behaviour of its patients.

Again and again in reports and inquiries into the hospital the medical staff and governors were keen to show that the hospital was a place of reformation. By 1842 one of the hospital governors stated that morally, the effects of the hospital were 'most manifest'. He observed that besides those who entered Magdalen asylums or were returned to parents or friends the majority of the rest of the patients had 'been able to turn to account the habits they have acquired, and preferred the paths of industry rather than the wages of prostitution'.[64] Many of the 'cured' patients were kept on as wardsmaids and to do the kitchen work of the hospital. Between 1820 and 1828, 154 inmates were sent to outside Magdalen asylums.[65] In the decade between March 1875 and 1885, from 7, 456 admissions, at least 417 women were sent to Magdalen asylums.[66] The claims made by the committee in terms of rescuing women were exaggerated; the majority of these 'reclaimed' women were actually sent to rescue homes.[67] Since patients spent, on average, thirty-one days in the hospital it is unlikely that the hospital authorities could claim the credit for any reform made in the characters or situation of the women. Protestant and Catholic clergymen were the only constant visitors allowed, though a Catholic clergyman was not given a salaried position at the hospital until after 1856.[68] These clerics may have persuaded some women from an immoral life. Women visitors, allowed into other hospitals, were not granted entrance to the lock hospital until 1889, when Protestant visitors were allowed visit their few co-religionists who were patients. The majority of the board of governors, when pressed at a hospital commissions' inquiry in 1887, declared they had no major objection to the suggestion that the Mercy nuns should nurse there. However, this seemed to be an attempt to appease the commission on a moral issue, rather than showing any great willingness to allow entrance, as the nuns were never asked to work there. Mr Edward Fottrell, a governor of the hospital in 1887, stated that the nuns could not improve the hospital any more than the lay staff.[69]

In cases of venereal infections it seemed important for doctors to know what 'kind' of woman was being treated. The belief that it was women who were spreading venereal diseases, and that prostitution was the principal source of infection, is evident in a story related by one doctor. Dr W. H. Porter, one time surgeon at the Westmoreland lock hospital in Dublin, wrote that:

Many years ago, while yet a student, several of my companions in College contracted the disease, and all attributed the infection to one courtesan; they had ulcers of different characters, and one of them in particular had one of the worst phagedenic chancres I ever saw. This female, after having wrought such variety of mischief, became a patient . . . in the old Lock Hospital, where I had an opportunity of seeing and attending her. Through curiosity on the subject, as I was acquainted with so many of her victims, I suggested she should be carefully examined . . .[70]

While it was acknowledged that it was possible for husbands to give the disease to their wives it was the body of the prostitute that became identified as the source of venereal disease.[71] Reports of cases from the Westmoreland lock hospital often described the patients as 'unvirtuous'.[72] Many believed that by treating women they were also preventing the spread of venereal infection among the soldiery. Doctors often made explicit reference to class when discussing venereal infection. John Morgan, a surgeon at the Westmoreland lock hospital, noted in 1869 that venereal diseases were spread by 'the characteristic recklessness of the working population, and of the higher classes of society when living a "fast" life'. The middle classes appear innocent in this formulation.[73] Similarly, Robert McDonnell peopled what he termed 'the syphilitic drama' with the lower classes.[74] By the 1860s the issue of the health of soldiers was to bring about a major policy change in the government's response to venereal disease and to prostitution, through the implementation of the CDAs.

Throughout the nineteenth century discussion on the understanding of venereal diseases and their treatment was carried on by the medical profession in the medical journals. Doctors who wrote in the medical journals were doing a number of things: they were developing their professional competence, marking themselves as the experts, disseminating information and knowledge, and adding to and creating a level of knowledge about the subject which they wished to share with their peers. They were also, of course, marking their territory and distinguishing themselves from the many quacks who were offering serious competition for the venereal-diseased patient. The medical journals were the principal means used by the medical profession to disseminate their ideas. Within the journals we find correspondence, case reports, articles and texts of lectures, reviews of the latest books and pamphlets, illustrations, and reviews not only of the medical issues associated with venereal diseases, but also of the moral and social implications of these diseases. The medical journals also offered medical men a forum in which to discuss and debate the subject of the CDAs.[75]

Contagious Diseases Acts

In 1864 Parliament passed the first of three statutes that permitted the compulsory inspection of prostitutes for venereal disease in certain military camps in both England and Ireland.[76] In Ireland the areas designated 'subjected districts' were Cork, Cobh and the Curragh camp, and the Acts were applicable to within a five-mile radius of each camp. In effect the Acts subjected women who were on the street to arbitrary and compulsory medical examination. Women who were arrested and summonsed were ordered to be examined at a certified hospital. If they refused to be examined they could be imprisoned for a month. If they were discovered to be suffering from a venereal disease they were forcibly detained in a lock hospital and treated for a period of up to three months. This was later extended to six months in 1866 and nine months in 1869. As a result of the introduction of the Acts a lock hospital was established in the Curragh (fig. 10) and in Cork in 1869.[77] The CDAs were concerned with keeping the troops free of venereal disease. The prostitute was identified as the

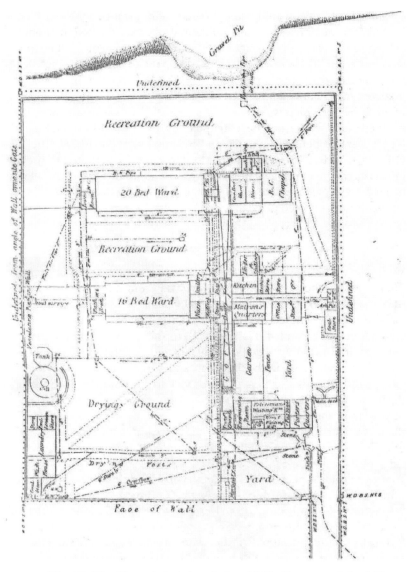

Fig. 10. The Curragh lock hospital, *c.* 1869. Courtesy of the Military Archives, Dublin.

source of infection and thus she had to be dealt with. Again the issue was one of confinement and policemen were appointed as special constables to carry out the provisions of the Act.[78] The function of these police was to 'to search out and carefully register all common prostitutes: – obtain their voluntary submission under the 17th section; arrange with the visiting surgeon for the times and places of their attendance for examination, and subsequent escort to hospitals for required treatment'.[79] The police who undertook these responsibilities were paid an extra allowance due to the 'unattractive nature of the duty'.[80] The RIC regulations stated that 'married men should be selected, whenever practicable, for the discharge of all duties in which women are concerned'.[81] It was also believed that married men would not be corrupted by the prostitutes. Though the CDAs were suspended in 1883 (and repealed in 1886) in 1884 the War Office received a request to retain a constable at the Curragh. The medical officer in charge of the lock hospital there believed that the constable was needed to provide information to the women since they 'are mostly strangers with no fixed place of abode'.

The army and the Contagious Diseases Acts

While, as we have seen, the army authorities showed some concern for public feeling, their major concern revolved around the health problems they associated with prostitution. As the *Dublin Quarterly Medical Journal of Medical Science* noted in August 1858 the 'staple disease of a military hospital in a garrison town is venereal'. In the first two years of the existence of the Curragh camp the average number of men there was 5,266. Of that number 2,142 in the first year, and 1,978 in the second year were admitted to hospital for treatment for venereal diseases.[82] The infirmary doctor in Kildare noted the increase and spread of syphilis and its effects on the labouring class in the area. He believed that the increase was due to the fact that there was no suitable place to treat the 'unfortunate females' infected with the disease on the Curragh, as they were not allowed by the rules of the infirmary to get attention there.[83] Again, noting the idea of contagion and respectability the doctor observed that 'these women can not come into the infirmary because their admission would inform the character of the institution as no decent woman would come into the hospital if they were admitted'.[84] A medical treatise written by Hamilton LaBatt contains accounts of his work among the soldiers of the Curragh. His case studies lack complete discretion as he names the soldiers treated. He did observe that 'all seemed to agree to speak of these abandoned women as a kind of dreadful and scandalous necessity, and as beings beyond the pale of human sympathy or help'.[85]

The idea of building a lock hospital at the Curragh camp was first discussed as early as 1859, though the possibility was deemed unfeasible as it 'would be impossible to have all the women referred to where the soldiers are quartered, examined and sent to the hospital if diseased'.[86] A number of other suggestions were made regarding the possible location of a lock hospital. The idea of placing the hospital at Athy was rejected because of the likelihood of strenuous objection from the local inhabitants. Similar plans to have the lock hospital as part of the County Kildare infirmary also floundered.[87] The provision of a lock hospital for the area came under considerable discussion in the 1860s. In 1865 there was a proposal that the hospital might be located in Kildare town, but a public meeting was held to oppose the plan.[88] A memorial was subsequently forwarded to the governors of the Kildare infirmary insisting that a 'hospital for discarded women . . . which would bring the vices of Newbridge and the Curragh to our doors' must not be located in the town.[89] The memorialists claimed that in summer and winter there were, on average, three hundred prostitutes in the district of the Curragh and Newbridge, while Kildare only had eight such women.[90] The governors of the Kildare infirmary had no objection to assisting in the management of a lock hospital but they suggested Newbridge as the most appropriate location. However, a lock hospital had to wait until the implementation of the CDAs and was opened at the Curragh in December 1869.

At the implementation of the CDAs at the Curragh it was reported that there were 101 'common women' known to the police in 1870. This had gone up to 104 in 1871, but had been reduced to 93 by 1878 and 76 by 1879.[91] Many of the women were admitted more than twice to the hospital. The hospital had 205 admittances in 1870, 217 in 1871, 240 in 1878 and 208 in 1879.[92] It was claimed that some of the worst cases came from Dublin, or other places outside the district, revealing, perhaps, a belief by the lock hospital doctor that the treatment received by local women was effective and that the Acts were beneficial to the Curragh. A number of the local doctors believed that the Acts had reduced the level of venereal disease in the area. According to statistics the rate of infection of primary syphilis per 1,000 among soldiers admitted to the hospital at the Curragh and at Newbridge in 1868 and 1869 was 85 and 88 respectively. The average per 1,000 fell to 56 in 1870 and 35 in 1871.[93] It was claimed that 'the disease is generally brought in from the outside' by regiments moving into the area from unprotected districts and the camp followers who came with them.[94] The benefits of the CDAs were believed not only to have reduced levels of venereal disease at the Curragh, but also to have been instrumental in saving many 'fallen women'.[95] Out of a group of 171 women who passed through the hospital the majority were deemed to have been reclaimed and returned to their friends, sent to reformatories, or other places. Only 29 women apparently returned to their former life.[96] Though the Acts were suspended in 1883 the hospital remained and there were 23 voluntary admissions between July and September 1884.[97] The evidence about whether the Acts diminished or had any impact on the extent of venereal disease is contradictory. Where the numbers of prostitutes were reduced it seems likely that women moved from subjected districts rather than be arrested or confined to a lock hospital. The continued problem with the 'wrens' evident in the 1870s and 1880s leads to the supposition that their numbers were not vastly reduced by the CDAs legislation.

It appears that the authorities at the Curragh had some difficulties with the women who were forced to enter the hospital. An account of the hospital published in 1872 records how arduous it was to retain and discipline the women there:

Obedience to rule, cleanliness, order, respectful behaviour, employment, all that is comprised by civilised habits, and especially in public institutions, was step by step fought against by these women. The Hospital itself was not built with any view to imprisonment, and the patients could climb walls and gates with the greatest facility. This power they availed themselves of at every favourable opportunity, by getting on the roofs or tops of walls, from whence they could hail the passers-by on the public roads, and by a hundred ingenious devices contrive to give annoyance to all within their reach.[98]

The author further outlines the behaviour of the women in the hospital and echoes Greenwood's account of their behaviour in the 'nests':

Any kind of work was felt to be a grievous hardship not to be borne . . . they would not take their meals at table; they would not attempt to keep their clothes or persons tidy; they would lie down and rise up almost as they pleased; they would address anyone, in or out of season, in their own language . . . all sense of respect for others, as well as shame for themselves, seemed dead in these unhappy beings. Unaccustomed above all to the presence of the respectable of their own sex, they were in turn abashed or insolent, sullen, or abusive.[99]

In this account it was the contact with 'proper' femininity in the form of matrons and nurses that helped alter the women's behaviour. The author makes clear that it was their confinement that had 'civilised' them. Through the kindness of the officials a 'thousand little traits of good feeling were quickly discovered; and above all, the slumbering embers of religious faith were seized on and nursed to the utmost'.[100] It was institutionalisation that saved the bodies and souls of the women. The value of confinement was exhorted for 'fallen women' for whom the best mode of redemption was believed to be the Magdalen asylum.

Under the conditions of the CDAs any woman discharged from the lock hospital could have her fare paid to her 'place of residence' and it was thought that a large number of the women availed themselves of this opportunity. The military authorities also tried to have the chaplains at Naas workhouse deal with the women. But the chaplains were reluctant to do so, having little faith in their possible moral redemption. While willing to be involved in acquiring money for the women to be returned home, John Nolan, the parish priest of Kildare, noted, 'I have no confidence in the means proposed to effect the object required and intended.'[101]

Evidence of the effects of the CDAs in Ireland is contradictory. Numerous commissions to judge the effects and effectiveness of the Acts were conducted from 1869 to 1882. Depending on the stance taken by the person giving the evidence, the Acts were reported to have reduced the numbers of prostitutes operating in the designated areas and led to the reclamation of many women, or they encouraged women to remain in the trade and merely drove the vice further underground, without reducing the number of people suffering from venereal diseases. Evidence to the commissions in Ireland came solely from men, mainly clerics, medical doctors or those who claimed to have an interest in the subject. It is impossible to gauge the accuracy of the information relating to either the decline or increase in prostitution put forward by the witnesses. In 1871 Henry Richardson, who was against the Acts, informed a commission of inquiry that they had done more harm than good, since women were now 'constantly' soliciting in the streets.[102] At the same inquiry the Catholic cleric, the Rev. Maguire, believed that the Acts had brought about a great improvement in the streets of Cork.[103] Yet the *Medical Enquirer* noted in 1876 that the number of prostitutes in Cork had increased from 90 in 1866 to 114 in 1875. It also stated that the incidence of venereal disease had risen in the city since the introduction of the Acts.[104] Dr Curtis, who was a visiting surgeon to Cork lock hospital, asserted that when the Acts came into force in the city,

nearly 400 phrynes of the lowest type nightly paraded the chief thoroughfares, so sunk in vice that one could hardly fancy them human beings. Of the large number of prostitutes there now remain in the district but 181 of which latter there are usually in hospital, prison and workhouses 104, leaving the actual number at present in Cork, Queenstown and district 10 miles but 77 at large.[105]

Between April 1872 and March 1881 the number of cases dealt with in the lock hospital in Cork was 2,310, made up of 693 individual women.[106] From June 1869 to June 1880 the number of women who were registered as prostitutes was 664. Of this number 248 were natives of Cork, 34 came from Cobh, with 382 coming from outside the subjected district.[107] It seems unlikely that the number of prostitutes diminished significantly with the introduction of the Acts. Prostitution resulted above all from poverty and was a means of earning a livelihood, and the conditions for the gainful employment of women had not improved in any dramatic way in the 1870s. Between 1869 and 1881 only eighteen women were jailed in Cork for 'neglecting to attend for periodic examination'.[108] The prostitutes in Cork were either keen to comply with the regulations or more probably found ways to subvert the process by moving out of the subjected district or being more secretive about their activities.

Prostitutes themselves also had some comments to make on the Acts. Henry Richardson, who engaged in rescue work in Cork, reported his discussions with prostitutes to the 1882 commission of inquiry. He spoke to two 'respectable women' at the door of a brothel in Cork who regarded the CDAs as 'shocking' and one observed that 'we are not quite so bad yet that we should not object to those examinations'.[109] Another woman stated that she underwent the examination and it was the most 'disgusting thing she ever knew'.[110] A 'superior class' prostitute to whom Richardson spoke maintained that the Acts were a good thing. 'We can', she noted, 'carry on our business now more correctly; it takes away the filth of it.'[111] Another stated that 'they had a great fight to get her on the [examining] table, and now that they had succeeded in that she did not care what end became of her'.[112] Richardson reported that he had heard several women declaring themselves to be 'Queen's women' and had been informed by a lady in Cork that she had heard a prostitute say to a young man 'come with me and I will guarantee you'.[113] Another woman claimed to have observed a soldier being closely followed by a prostitute in Cork City who 'recommended herself to the man's attention thus: "I am Mary Collins . . . in the employment of her Majesty"'.[114]

In 1867 a campaign was started to extend the Acts to other towns in the United Kingdom. A subcommittee of the Association for the Extension of the Contagious Diseases Acts was established in Dublin, Cork and Belfast in 1868, and it included a number of medical men among its members.[115] Charles Cameron, a professor of hygiene in the Royal College of Surgeons (who later became chief medical officer of Dublin in 1880), supported the Acts and called for their extension to Dublin.[116] By 1871 Cameron acknowledged the increase in opposition to the Acts but still favoured their extension. He wrote that in Dublin 'there is certainly a large amount of syphilitic poison present amongst the lowest class of unfortunates, and it can hardly be doubted but that the enforced surveillance of those persons would soon lessen the spread of the disease'.[117] A number of campaigners called for the extension of the Acts to Dublin, for as one commentator observed, 'no city has greater need of some means of checking the ravages of venereal disease'.[118] Another claimed that in Dublin 'with a large number of contagious centres [brothels] as are known to exist in this city the amount of mischief done to the health of the public is almost incalculable'.[119] The military authorities were particularly keen to have the Acts extended to Dublin and campaigned on the issue into the early 1880s.[120]

Opposition to the Acts arose for a number of reasons. Their implementation was seen, by some groups, as interference with civil liberties and by others as the recognition and support of vice by the state. In England a number of associations were established to campaign for the repeal of the CDAs. Among these were the National Association for the Repeal of the Contagious Diseases Acts (NARCDA) formed in 1869, and the Ladies' National Association (LNA), also formed in 1869. Both of these organisations had branches in Ireland. Members of the National Association in Ireland were to be found in Cork City, Derry, Dublin, Belfast, Cobh, Clonakilty, Waterford, Mallow and Dundalk.[121] The NARCDA held a number of meetings in Dublin, Cork and Belfast and appears to have been most active in the early 1870s. The majority of its meetings seem to have been for men only.[122] By 1877 it was reported that branches of the LNA and the National Vigilance Association were 'steadily' circulating suitable literature and canvassing for signatures for petitions. At this stage the NARCDA believed that there was no need for public meetings as 'all oppose' the Acts.[123] Mr Kingston, who gave evidence to the CDAs inquiry in 1871, was a member of the repeal association in Cork. He claimed that the meetings held in the city were well attended.[124] There is evidence also that posters and placards announcing meetings were visible in the city which suggests at least some form of public activity against the Acts in Cork.[125] In 1870 a 'splendid demonstration' against the Acts was organised in Belfast. The event had been widely publicised with 'thousands of small hand bills' being extensively circulated, as well as 'large posters and advertisements, employed to inform the inhabitants of the atrocities of the law, and the intended demonstrations against it'.[126] One of the speakers observed that the Acts were not appropriate for Ireland where 'it was a cause of happiness to every Irishman to know that the propriety, modesty and chastity of their countrywomen was not only an acknowledged fact at home, but had always been acknowledged as a fact in every civilised country where the Irish character was known'.[127] By 1871 three branches of the LNA had been established, in Belfast, Dublin and Cork. Both Isabella Tod and Anna Haslam, active suffragists and campaigners on a range of issues relating to women, were involved in the campaign from the beginning. Tod also served on the executive committee of the London-based LNA until 1889 when Haslam took her place.[128] They both also served on the general council of the NARCDA, although this society was run by men[129] and women council members had little impact on policy.

The LNA, in Ireland, was a very localised and small affair. Throughout its active period, from 1871 to 1885, it never had more than forty-nine subscribers, the majority of whom were residents of Dublin, Cork and

Waterford.[130] Although the association was small, its very existence marked a new departure for Irishwomen. For the first time they were willing to discuss openly matters pertaining to sexual morality, and to initiate a public campaign to question and alter the sexual double standard which existed. In England there was a certain degree of hostility towards women's activism in this area,[131] and although there is no direct evidence of such hostility towards women activists in Ireland, the size of the association indicates how few were willing to be associated with such a campaign. One witness before the select committee on the effects of the CDAs in 1871, a Catholic priest, when asked if women were involved in any way against the Acts stated that 'there are a great many ladies who exert themselves very much and we Catholic clergy do not approve of their putting placards before young females inviting them to read these acts of which women never heard before'.[132] The matter was a delicate one even for the women involved. Mrs Henry Wigham, who spoke at a drawing-room meeting in Dublin in 1880, sympathised 'with the natural repugnance felt by women in approaching so loathsome a subject', but she urged that women 'must lay aside our tastes and inclinations, and the veil of blissful ignorance in which we indolently shroud ourselves, and come face to face with the evil in its most repellent forms'.[133] That some women were either embarrassed or wary of working with men in this area can be seen in the fact that whereas the original committee of the NARCDA in Dublin was a mixed one, in 1878 a sub-committee for women only was established as 'some ladies', it was stated, 'are not yet prepared to join a mixed committee'.[134]

Many members of the medical profession supported the Acts. Within the Irish medical press doctors and surgeons used their professional expertise and knowledge as a means to bolster their support of the Acts and to denigrate those who opposed them. One commentator noted that the 'united opinion of the Surgical Society of Ireland that the acts are for the good of mankind, is sufficient to establish these acts against anything that silly people may say'.[135] The editors of the *Medical Press and Circular* believed that as the 'anti-vivisectionists and the anti-vaccinators, so are the pro-syphilis fanatics utterly impervious to reason, and incapable of any idea but their own craze'.[136] Thomas Grimshaw, the registrar-general for Ireland, also approved of the Acts, believing that they had

diminished prostitution, almost suppressed juvenile prostitution, rescued fallen women from a most frightful life of disease and immorality, and made them amenable to humanising and refining influences, and contributed to promote public order and decency, besides securing their hygienic advantages intended.[137]

But not all medical men supported the Acts, many seeing them as a licensing of vice and conducive to an increase in immorality.[138] Many also disapproved of women's involvement in the campaign. As one commentator noted:

Anti-contagionists are on the warpath; they are holding public and private meetings, they are circulating pamphlets and leaflets, and doing all in their power to contaminate the homes of the country, by talking about disease the names of which have been hitherto unknown to the majority of women of this country. It is very astonishing that a large number of women who are engaged in this campaign are either spinsters of uncertain age or wives who are childless . . . we would urge upon the well meaning, but mistaken women who are connected with this agitation, the harm they do by the indiscriminate dissemination of literature of this nature among young innocent girls . . . better for them to establish refuges, and above all to teach their fellow women to be kind to those who have fallen . . . women are very severe upon women – many an unfortunate has been made by the cruelty of her sisters. Turned out of situation after situation, for an offence committed perhaps, many years before, many a hapless girl has been thrown upon the streets.[139]

The function of the LNA in Ireland was to support the aims of the parent body in London. In practice this meant raising funds, organising petitions to Parliament against the Acts, attempting to alter public opinion by distributing pamphlets and papers on the subject, and holding meetings. The majority of meetings were held in the drawing-rooms of activists and were attended by women only. These meetings always began and ended with prayers.[140] A number of petitions, favouring repeal, were forwarded to London and between 1870 and 1881 these mustered 85,759 signatures. Of the eighty-eight petitions forwarded, repeal associations sent sixteen with 85 signatures and groups of unidentified Irishwomen sent in nine petitions with 8,770 signatures. It is likely that these were organised by the LNA. Four petitions, with 188 signatures, were sent in favour of the Acts.[141] In 1877 the Belfast branch of the LNA claimed that the enlargement of the lock hospital in that city, which patients entered voluntarily since the city was not one of the 'subjected districts', resulted from the committee's attempts to improve the treatment of women afflicted with venereal diseases. They were thus proving that individual action could prevent the spread of such diseases and that the CDAs were essentially unnecessary.[142] The Belfast branch of the LNA was active in trying to ensure that the Acts would not be extended to that city. They claimed that their efforts in bringing the operation of the Acts to the attention of the public had averted 'the terrible danger and degradation of being subjected to the direct operation of the Acts'.[143] They saw the implementation of the Acts as an affront 'to the decency and purity of society – the dignity and independence of every woman in the land'.[144]

The parent body in London was anxious to extend its range of activities in Ireland and sent a number of its agents and members to give public talks on the subject there. In 1874 Mr Burgess, an organising agent employed by the English LNA, visited Ireland and arranged meetings in Cork. Another agent, Mr Bligh, organised a meeting in Dublin and later travelled to Carlow, Wicklow, Wexford, Waterford and Limerick, where he put up posters against the Acts.[145] Bligh was in Ireland again in 1876 when he toured towns in Ulster where 'had it not been for the insufficiency of funds, which caused this important work to be suspended very substantial results in the influencing of Irish votes would . . . have accrued'.[146] It appears that the NARCDA may not have as much support as it claimed in Ireland.[147] In 1878 the annual general meeting of the Association was held in Dublin, and was attended by Josephine Butler. The anti-regulationists were reported to have found in Dublin,

a somewhat favourable scene for their operations, for there the general public is entirely and helplessly ignorant of the subject, has a vague idea that the Contagious Diseases Acts have something to say on foot-and-mouth disease in cows, and naturally expected that Mrs Josephine Butler would have expended her oratory in a denunciation of the traffic in pleuro-pneumonic beef, or on some kindred subject.[148]

A public conference was organised, for a mixed audience, in the Rotunda while the women held their own meeting in the Antient Concert Rooms. Among the speakers at the latter were Sir James Stansfield MP, one of the leading advocates for repeal, and Butler herself also spoke. When Stansfield rose to speak there were cries that the women in the audience should be put out and a number of young men began to disrupt the meeting; the police had to be called to clear the hall and the meeting had to be abandoned. A further meeting was held on the following day, again with a mixed audience.[149] The committee blamed the disruption on a group of disorderly students but it is clear that the campaign was unpopular in some quarters.

The women who were active in the movement in Ireland were predominantly Quakers. Anna Haslam, Mrs Henry Wigham, Mary Edmundson, Mrs Henry Allen and all the women in the Webb family were subscribers.[150] Isabella Tod was a Presbyterian, and it appears that very few, if any, of the women were Catholics. One of the characteristics of repeal activists was the involvement of members of the same family in the campaign. Thus, for example, Henry Wigham, Henry Allen, Alfred Webb and Thomas Haslam, all active in the NARCDA, were married, or related to, members of the LNA.[151] The degree of such family support probably encouraged activists to continue in their campaign. Indeed, Anna Haslam's husband, Thomas, published a pamphlet on the CDAs in Ireland. The CDAs were, he wrote, 'a dangerous piece of legislative bungling' and he called for their immediate repeal or radical amendment.[152] The opposition to the Acts came generally from non-conformist Churches which saw them as an acceptance of immorality and prostitution. There was lobbying from Irish non-conformists also. In February 1883 Josephine Butler wrote of the confrontation that had occurred between Isabella Tod and the chairman of the select committee on the CDAs, Richard O'Shaughnessy. Tod and two other Irish ladies 'set upon him, in the House, & left him pale & with his ears tingling! He won't forget it, *they say*'.[153] From 1871 until the repeal of the Acts in 1886, the Presbyterian Church discussed issues of sexual morality and prostitution at its general assemblies. It also presented a petition to Parliament each year after 1871 demanding the repeal of the Acts which 'were calculated to inflict such bodily and mental suffering on a helpless class of the community, to outrage their feelings, deaden their sensibilities and to infringe upon their constitutional rights; while the efficacy of these acts is, to say the least, extremely doubtful'.[154] In 1883 when the motion of James Stansfield calling for the suspension of the Acts was passed in the Commons all of the local Presbyterian MPs voted in favour.[155] Likewise the Conference of Irish Methodist Ministers also opposed the Acts and petitioned against them.[156] The Catholic Church, on the other hand, approved of the Acts; Canon James Hegarty believed that the Acts brought the greatest possible improvement to Cork City and claimed that 'the reformation in the habits and manners even of the fallen and degraded women is most wonderful'.[157] The Rev. Thomas O'Reilly also believed that the physical examination experienced by the women and their treatment within the lock hospital were an essential part of their moral reform. For him the physical treatment of the women was a means of punishment which would turn them away from prostitution.[158]

The LNA in Britain worked on the premise that one standard of sexual morality, for both men and women, should exist. The campaign against the CDAs itself was a moral rather than a social crusade. Like the philosophy espoused by rescue workers, self-discipline and a higher moral standard were advocated by the repeal associations. Recognition and articulation of the sexual double standard which operated were central to the campaign and a higher moral standard for men in particular was demanded. Women, it was believed, possessed this high standard naturally and men were expected to aspire to the same standard. Isabella Tod, in a speech to the Christian Women's Union, articulated the problem and proposed the solution:

the greatest and most consistent force at work, both in lowering the moral tone throughout all classes, and in bringing about not only individual acts of vice, but in degrading a number of women into a class where occupation is vice, is that unspeakably wicked idea that most men may be expected so to sin, and that in them it is a venial offence . . . We must utterly refuse . . . to acknowledge the existence of any such class of men, in any rank, as inevitable; or any class of women to meet their horrible demands . . . We owe a duty to men . . . to awaken their consciences to pull down the selfish screen which society has set up . . . We have the power of the newly awakened conscience of women, as to their duty to protect their poorer and weaker sisters, and to withstand and enlighten those who would seek to assail them.[159]

The work of the women in the LNA was also used by Tod to support women's claim for the vote. The success of the repeal movement, she maintained, had shown how effective women's activism could be: 'it was not only for the help which women must give to women, but even more, for the discharge of their special duty to the whole state – a duty which God has entrusted to them, and which no man can do – women are bound to demand their immediate admission within the electorate'.[160]

One important issue addressed by the LNA was the necessity to analyse why women became prostitutes. It accepted that prostitution was the result of poverty and Irish activists in the LNA, through their involvement in societies to improve the educational, work and political prospects of women, were hoping to improve conditions for all women. It is interesting to note that although the English branch of the LNA advocated that its members become involved in rescue work none of the Irish activists was so involved.[161] The impact of the repeal campaign on Irishwomen, in general, is impossible to gauge. The Acts were repealed in 1886 and in Ireland the membership of the LNA had steadily declined in the latter years of the campaign, with only ten subscribers from 1884.[162] Because of their religious affiliations and indeed their political and social activism, the women of the Irish branch of the LNA were unrepresentative of Irishwomen in general. They were part of a reform tradition rather than the more common benevolent tradition to which the majority of women philanthropists subscribed in the nineteenth century.[163] The final meeting of the LNA took place in Dublin in May 1886; a letter was read from Josephine Butler announcing a new organisation which would assist in the efforts to suppress state-regulated vice in the colonies and on the continent, and would also assist in the 'purification of the moral standard of society'.[164] The eventual success of the repeal campaign saw British activists direct their energies into new areas of concern and, as Walkowitz has noted, the 1880s saw the growth in 'clubs and armies to train the young and innocent in sexual repression'.[165] Concern for social purity was also evident in Ireland.

Social purity in Ireland

The LNA in England argued that it had set the pace for the social purity movement established by Ellice Hopkins in 1883 in an attempt to improve the sexual behaviour of men. This was the White Cross Army,[166] and only men were recruited to it, pledging, among other things, to 'treat all women with respect . . . to endeavour to put down all indecent language and jests . . . to maintain the laws of purity as equally binding on men and women'.[167] In the year 1885 William T. Stead shocked the British public with his 'Maiden tribute of Modern Babylon', a series of articles in the *Pall Mall Gazette* which focused on child prostitution and the so-called 'white slave trade'. Social purity groups in England had tried to have the government pass a Criminal Law Amendment Act which would, among other things, raise the age of consent for girls from thirteen to sixteen. By 1885 this attempt at legislation had ground to a halt and it was Stead's journalism, which led to the mass rallies and calls for government intervention, that eventually helped to provide the support that enabled the Criminal Law Amendment Act to pass. Stead later organised a conference on the 'Maiden Tribute' and from this conference a Vigilance Association was formed in London.[168] There is little available evidence on the impact of Stead's campaign in Ireland. The Chief Commissioner of the DMP reported that he was unaware of any traffic in young girls between Ireland and England. Such a traffic, he noted, could not 'be carried on without the knowledge of the detective department as there is no class with whom we are more frequently brought into contact in the discharge of our duties than female servants, brothel keepers and prostitutes'.[169]

Although the Criminal Law Amendment Act of 1885 was implemented in Ireland, it seems to have had little effect on streetwalking or the numbers of brothels that operated in the country.[170] However, the purity movement did make some headway in Ireland. The White Cross Army established by Hopkins quickly became associated with the Church of England. In 1885 the Church of Ireland Purity Society was established by the General Synod.[171] Hopkins herself visited Dublin in May of that year and spoke to separate audiences of men and women. Her rousing speeches were claimed to have initiated the formation of the Dublin White Cross Vigilance Association (WCVA).[172] Besides attending lectures, members of the association engaged in 'patrol work'. Patrol work was carried out between 9 pm and 1 or 2 am. The greatest opposition to patrol work was deemed to come from the married men who 'would not think of periling their reputation by entering a house of ill fame in daylight, but who come crawling up and creeping into them under cover of the darkness of night'.[173] The patrols often kept watch outside known 'evil houses' and through such harassment forced them to close. In 1886 the Dublin WCVA claimed to have closed nine brothels and four lodging-houses. It was noted that they had 'obliged five proprietresses to move their houses from respectable into disreputable streets'.[174] Also in 1888 the committee of the association brought a successful prosecution against one hotel owner for keeping a brothel in the city.[175] In 1891 the association claimed to have fourteen branches in Dublin with 530 members.[176] In another visit, in 1893, Hopkins revitalized the WCVA and a group of about twenty-four members accosted customers leaving the city's brothels.[177] Through the activities of this movement thirty-five brothels were claimed to have been closed down, and Mecklenburgh Street cleared of prostitutes in 1895.[178]

The committee of the Dublin WCVA believed that 'giving the least possible publicity to the facts that come to the knowledge of the committee . . . best tends to secure the results the committee look for'.[179] Its patrol members were not allowed to keep any record of those who entered houses of ill repute, the object of the patrol being not 'detection but prevention'.[180] In practice the Dublin patrols appear to have moved brothels from the 'respectable' to the disreputable streets of Dublin. In this way they were acting in concert with the DMP who were, by the 1890s, consigning prostitution to the Monto district of the city. It was the WCVA, however, which took the credit for the supposed improvement in the streets of the capital.[181] It is difficult to gauge how successful these vigilance associations were in reality. The Dublin WCVA noted in 1898 that it had not held meetings for the three previous years, although it had engaged in vigilance work. An attempt was made to revitalise the association at a meeting in Dublin in December 1897. Originally the idea had been to organise parochial branches of the association, but this was now abandoned (as it was in England). The funds of the association were also in a poor state by this stage.[182]

Attempts to inculcate purity among men were also carried out by Catholic agencies, particularly through confraternities. For example, the priests' campaign to close brothels in Cork City was carried through with the aid of men from a confraternity.[183] However, it is not until the first decades of the twentieth century that vigilance associations (which were similar to purity groups) were organised within the Catholic population and these were closely linked with nationalism and the idea of contagion through association with England.[184] The energies of Irishwomen generally in the control of sexual immorality centred almost completely on rescue work. This appears to have had little social impact save for the few women who were supposedly 'reclaimed'. Refuges in a sense reinforced the sexual double standard by concentrating all their energies on the victim rather than the seducer.

There was a campaign, from the 1870s, to establish clubs in Dublin to provide recreational facilities for working girls. The principal objective was to provide a room where such girls could meet for 'instruction or recreation', where they could pass their free time and be 'saved from the temptation of passing these hours in places and in a society which would be for them the high road to ruin and shame'.[185] The scheme was initiated by an unknown Protestant Englishwoman and Catholics were later urged to introduce a similar plan. The Catholic strategy was to go further than providing recreational facilities and the best proposal was thought to be to establish a residential home for such girls.[186] To this end, St Martha's Home was founded in 1880. This not only provided accommodation but also acted as a registry where young women could seek employment.[187] These kinds of homes were intended to be preventative. Young girls coming to the city were believed to be naive and in danger of getting into bad company. Homes and clubs offered shelter and companionship, thus saving the girls from the streets. As we have seen within the sphere of moral care, the establishment of societies to protect unmarried mothers began to emerge in the last decades of the nineteenth century. The philosophy behind such homes was to prevent the women from pursuing a life on the streets. Attitudes to unmarried mothers and prostitutes were similar and the connection made between unmarried motherhood and the possibility of becoming a prostitute was constantly highlighted in the annual reports of these societies. It is a conflation that became even more powerful in the twentieth century.

By the end of the nineteenth century, and as a consequence of the implementation of the CDAs, prostitutes were firmly associated with the spread of venereal diseases. By the end of the 1890s most brothels in Dublin were confined to an area on the north side of the city. In many of these brothels one individual had the responsibility of insisting that any of the women infected with venereal disease go to hospital. Also, by the end of the nineteenth century many of these brothels had their own medical attendant.[188] The punitive regime of the Westmoreland lock hospital was unappealing to a large number of women. The CDAs legislation did little to reduce the level of prostitution and it is unclear whether it had any considerable effect on the levels of venereal disease prevalent in Irish society. Those women who campaigned against the CDAs in Ireland used the figure of the prostitute, constructed as a vulnerable and seduced young woman, to argue for the political rights of primarily middle-class women. There is no evidence to show that any of the campaigners took a personal interest in the real lives of women who worked as prostitutes. The use of the prostitute to argue for political rights took on a new dimension in Ireland at the turn of the twentieth century.

5 'Soldier's totty': nationalists, suffragists and the surveillance of women, 1900–22

The late nineteenth and early twentieth century in Ireland was a period of great upheaval. In times of upheaval issues of sexual morality often become a focus of attention and anxiety. Concern about sexual morality often reflects fear and apprehension about change in society. It is this landscape of sexual morality, examined within the context of political change, that will be explored in this chapter. While the problems of prostitution, venereal disease and women's sexuality remained as much the focus of concern and debate in the early decades of the twentieth century as they had in the nineteenth century, there were considerable differences in the ways in which these issues were discussed and configured. Prostitution in the nineteenth century was a social and moral issue. It remained so in the twentieth century, but now a new dimension was added, that of the political. Prostitution in early twentieth-century Ireland became bound up with the cause of Irish independence. The prostitute became a symbol of British oppression and the means by which the British soldier infected the Irish nation with physical disease and immorality. In the early decades of the twentieth century there was more widespread discussion of issues relating to sexual morality, much of which came through the suffrage and labour press. The disruption of the First World War brought matters relating to venereal disease to greater public awareness and a new figure, that of the separation woman, the dependant of a British Army soldier, joined the prostitute as a figure of dissolution and immorality within nationalist Ireland.

Recent studies have considered the meanings of sexual immorality in Ireland in terms of identity formation. Ben Novick's *Conceiving Revolution*,[1] for instance, devotes a chapter to this subject. He argues that the importance of moral tone to Irish revolutionary discourse did not come about as a result of the war, but that the socio-cultural dislocations of war and the support of the Irish Parliamentary party for the British war effort gave advanced nationalist moral crusaders new impetus in their campaigns. The highlighting of moral dichotomies between Britain and Ireland was central to the construction of a new

Irish identity, particularly that of the Irish Free State.[2] Margaret O'Callaghan has asserted that the traditional conservatism of the Catholic hierarchy in relation to sexuality was intensified in the years after independence. It is argued here that the period between 1900 and 1922 saw sexuality politicised in Irish society as never before. Public discussion on issues of sexual morality in Ireland during these years and the prevalence of any resistance to the apparently dominating discourses is explored in this chapter. The process of Irish independence was disruptive in a number of ways: traditional ideas about gender were challenged to a greater extent than ever before by the advance of the suffrage campaign, new spaces for the discussion of sexuality and sexual morality opened up in the suffrage and labour press, women were demanding more inclusive social and political roles to an extent previously unseen in Ireland, the politicisation of prostitution and venereal disease embraced and gave voice to nationalist concerns of the dominance of English culture in Irish society. At the same time activists who opposed prostitution or were concerned with the public health issues of disease were influenced by international trends in 'social hygiene' movements, and the white slavery debates. While concerns with sexual immorality appear to be closely linked to Irish self-determination, that apparent insularity was shaped significantly by international debates on prostitution, immorality and public health.

What was the state of the nation's morals in the early twentieth century? Prostitution remained a considerable problem, particularly in Dublin, where it offered a springboard from which many commentators vented their concern with declining moral standards in the country. Prostitution was more immediately obvious in Dublin and Belfast than in the rest of the country, yet the apparent crisis in immorality was discussed much more forcefully in the Dublin press than in the northern press. Arrests for prostitution in Dublin went from 431 in 1900 to a high of 1,067 in 1912 and then decreased dramatically to 198 arrests in 1919 (see appendix 1). In Dublin the Monto district remained the centre of brothel activity in the city, although the number of complaints about the state of the streets reveals that prostitution was not confined or hidden from general public view.

There had been some grumblings about the condition of the streets in Dublin in 1901. Archbishop Walsh, in a letter to the *Freeman's Journal*, observed that while in Europe he had passed through a number of garrison towns in France, Austria and Germany but had seen nothing as bad as Dublin. He argued that in those countries soldiers would not have been allowed to congregate in public thoroughfares as they were in Dublin.[3] In response to the archbishop's letter a Dublin priest observed that a delegation had come to him to see if anything could be done about the soldiers and women congregating on Sackville Street.[4] In 1904 Maud Gonne McBride stated that she had received letters from parents complaining of the difficulties facing children attending Inghinidhe na hÉireann (Daughters of Ireland) language classes, in various parts of the city, 'because of the condition of the streets through the disgraceful conduct of the British military'. Gonne reported that she had occasion to go to the general post office at 10 pm in the evening and 'was intentionally jostled against by soldiers and screamed at by poor unfortunate girls, whom the soldiers seem to incite to insult any respectable woman who ventures, on what they consider, and what the police consider, their side of the street'. That this behaviour was tolerated in Dublin was for Gonne, 'one of the most humiliating evidences of foreign rule and the demoralising effect on men's characters of foreign rule'.[5] An article in the tenth edition of the *Encyclopaedia Britannica* (*c.* 1905) described Dublin as the worst city in Europe for streetwalking prostitutes, observing that the police, 'permit open brothels confined to one area, but carried on more openly than in the south of Europe or even Algiers'.[6] Noting the numbers of soldiers who had been treated for venereal disease in military barracks in Ireland, *Sinn Féin* argued in 1907 that 'all hopes of improving the health of the country are fruitless until this is dealt with'.[7] The following year a meeting of the Dublin County committee of Sinn Féin passed a resolution in 'protest against the continual monopolisation of the principal thoroughfare of our city by the soldiers of the British Army, and the disgraceful conduct nightly carried on by them'. Copies of the resolution were sent to Catholic and Protestant clerics and Dublin Corporation were urged to deal with the matter.[8]

It was not until 1910 that prostitution in Dublin became a major issue in the newspapers. In October of that year the Jesuit, Fr Gwynn, delivered a scathing attack on the immorality apparent on the Dublin streets to the Catholic Truth Society. Gwynn observed that Dublin was 'rapidly earning for itself the reputation of being one of the most immoral of cities'. He claimed that the streets of London and Brussels, and the cities of Germany and France, 'had by no means that air, whatever be the reality, of looseness and depravity which invaded our main thoroughfares at night'.[9] Gywnn's views led to a tidal wave of opinions being expressed in the newspapers. A special meeting was held by Dublin Corporation to consider his lecture. Those Corporation members who were reported were adamant that Dublin was one of the most moral of cities. If there was a problem with immorality then the responsibility lay with the police who were not doing their duty. It was claimed that Gwynn had exaggerated the situation. As one member commented, what gave a bad name to the city was the conduct of a few straggling persons. Statistics would prove that Dublin was not only not immoral, but a really moral city. Only a half per cent of the women of Dublin engaged in immoral traffic, although there were in the city 120,000 women without employment. The figures for Paris and London were as high as 10 to 12 per cent.[10]

If there was a 'certain amount of immorality' in Dublin there were, it was suggested, good reasons for it. These included the facts that it was a seaport and a garrison town. There were also a large number of constabulary and students and, it was claimed, about 15,000 unmarried men. Mr James, to shouts of 'hear, hear', declared he was 'proud to belong as a citizen of Dublin, to the most moral city in the world'. He insisted he had never seen any immorality on the post office side of Sackville Street at night. Boisterous youths and 'hysterical young girls who perambulated up and down the thoroughfare to the annoyance of the public' were, in his opinion, the cause of disturbance. When the police took charge and prosecutions followed, these young men were, he maintained, frightened away and the nuisance abated.[11] Mr Briscoe also emphatically rejected Gwynn's views. One of the real problems, he believed, was that Gwynn's 'statement would be circulated and broadcast all over the kingdom and be quoted against the people of Dublin'. He submitted it was a 'libel to say that Dublin was an immoral city' and proposed a resolution that Gwynn's statement was due to a total lack of knowledge. While approving of the Corporation's views on the morality of Dublin, Mr Hutchenson asked how they could call the attention of the authorities to a state that it was argued did not exist.[12]

Notwithstanding the Corporation's declaration there were further letters to the press in which correspondents complained of the impossibility of passing through Sackville Street in the evenings without coming across hordes of prostitutes. One correspondent observed that Dublin's reputation as a centre for vice and venereal disease was internationally known, commenting 'that the worst possible news which can reach those interested in the moral welfare of the military in India is that a regiment has been ordered to Dublin'.[13] The Dublin Citizens' Association and the suburban councils felt they were much more active in the matter of controlling vice than Dublin Corporation. Another correspondent observed that the 'scenes nightly in the neighbourhood of the Dodder banks and by the canals are far worse than along the quays or Metal Bridge'.[14] Another believed that Gwynn had understated the problem. A doctor maintained that venereal disease or, as he delicately put it 'the maladies associated with this life', were on the increase in Dublin. While members of the Corporation had argued that it was respectable servant girls and soldiers who crowded the streets of Dublin at night, another correspondent observed that there were two classes of girls known as servants in this city. There is a great army of respectable girl servants, who serve the gentry, are educated, and attend to religious duties. The other class of servant are those taken from the workhouses, orphanages, industrial schools to 'comfortable homes' by people who can ill afford to pay the rents of the houses they occupy, but for the sake of being respectable, are obliged to keep paying guests or lodgers, and of necessity a servant, but a cap and apron do not make a servant. These helpless girls are given more liberty at night than the genuine servant, to compensate for the poor wages, food, etc., and their employers who are morally responsible for them allow them to wander the streets alone.[15]

What was becoming evident in this debate was an understanding of the economic causes of prostitution. Poor wages, unemployment, poor working and living conditions were now clearly aired as the probable causes of prostitution. With '21,747 families in Dublin' living in one-roomed tenements, how, one correspondent asked, 'can the decencies of life be observed under these circumstances or anything but vice and crime be the result?'[16] Another noted that it was the 'filthy tenement system' that drove young people on to the streets 'leading them to perdition',[17] while another went so far as to suggest that the cause of the 'social evil' was 'hereditary feeblemindedness'.[18] The fear that prostitution might spread to other parts of the city was also apparent. The recent clearance of the tenements in Montgomery Street, which had occurred in 1905,[19] was said to have 'spread immorality, not alone along the Dodder banks but within close proximity to the leading squares and residential districts of our city'. Conflating prostitution with disease, this correspondent suggested that these prostitutes and 'bad characters' be isolated 'as one would leprosy or small-pox'.[20] A medical man observed that the prevalence of 'certain diseases' was not a sign of the level of immorality that existed: 'long study in this subject has convinced me that the abnormal abundance of disease of a certain class in Dublin is an indirect outcome of the abnormal purity of our country'. There were calls for greater action by the police on prostitution, and suggestions that there should be no tolerance for the geographical confinement of brothels and prostitution.[21]

The Rev. William Proctor, who had been engaged in rescue work in Dublin for twenty years, advocated that landlords and citizens spy on their neighbours and support the police in their efforts to tackle vice. In response a landlord noted that the vice was so secretive that he had not realised that some of his tenants were involved until he put a watch on the house. He suggested that every brothel should be branded 'as a plague spot with a red danger signal. Keep it in one locality, concentrate it, hide it from the gaze of our rising generation.'[22] Another suggested that the real issue was the immorality of men. Men had to improve their moral sense, and should have the same sexual moral standards as women. This correspondent observed that the 'churches of all denominations' had failed to deal with this problem. 'If men', it was declared, 'were made criminally responsible jointly with the mother (on infanticide for instance) by law, it would act as one of the greatest preventives of morality and prostitution.'[23] This was an argument that was to find much support within the ranks of suffragists. Mrs Agatha Richardson, a member of the Church of Ireland Nursery Rescue Home Committee, wrote that she was glad that the public were at last taking notice of the problem. For her, preventative work was the most important element in reducing vice. She was particularly concerned with the pregnant young girl who was hastily sent from the country to 'save the disgrace of their families (the chief and often the only thing families seem to think of)'. Some of these the rescue agencies could save, but there were others who had no choice but to 'stray around the streets not knowing where to go'. Some young women ended up in the workhouse 'there to associate with women polluted to the very soul with guilty knowledge. They go in, erring, faulty, foolish; they come out, knowing only too well how a living can be most certainly earned in Dublin.'[24] Richardson stressed some of the issues that were, by the beginning of the twentieth century, becoming familiar arguments within the arena of rescue work; the need to make distinctions between first and second offences, and the requirement that rescue homes 'should have a spiritual and religious feeling'.[25]

So why did prostitution become such an issue, even if only for a brief period, in 1910? By the early twentieth century what we have on the streets of the metropolis are apparently large numbers of women traversing the main thoroughfares and causing a nuisance to 'respectable' citizens. With the establishment of the Irish Women's Franchise League in 1908, the first decade of the twentieth century witnessed the growth of the Irish women's suffrage campaign which became more vocal and public in this period. In cultural, political and social life women were more conspicuous than ever before. It is no coincidence that concern with 'public' women, that is prostitutes, becomes more pronounced when 'respectable' women become more public. In the debate that occurs in 1910, the actors are members of the corporation and letter writers, some of whom are doctors, others rescue workers and a number are the 'concerned public'. What is different about the debate at this stage is the recognition of the economic and social causes of vice and prostitution. Such causes have not previously been enumerated in such a distinct and consistent manner. The arguments now were about who should deal with the problem of vice and the best means of doing so. In some ways the debate was more an argument about authority than about the practical means of ridding the city of its prostitutes. Suffragists and nationalists became enmeshed in this debate, but ultimately these groups had considerably different expectations of the outcome of their actions and debates. One group, the suffragists, were arguing for their right to political authority, the other, nationalists, for their right to political and cultural autonomy. Another force, vigilance societies, added to the complexity of views on vice, authority and control being expressed in this period.

Vigilance societies

In December 1911 the *Irish Worker* declared that

vigilance committees have broken out all over Ireland within the past two weeks. Like measles. Every newspaper we open informs us of the establishment of another . . . [they] declare their determination to do certain things – to wit, stamp out the circulation in Ireland of certain English weekly newspapers.[26]

The paper had suggestions about vigilance societies which it opined, might be more useful if they formed, for instance, 'a committee to be known as the Committee for the prevention of the exposure of dead children outside Glasnevin Cemetery gates'.[27] In the vigilance campaigns of this period the concern was with the sale of 'objectionable newspapers'. Immoral English newspapers were seized and destroyed, and pickets were placed on music halls and newsagents.[28] Newsagents in Dublin were asked to sign a pledge against stocking or selling 'immoral' papers. It was later noted that 'this campaign was only partially successful, for the lure of gain overcame their sense of righteousness and the "dirty" papers were sold *sub rosa*'.[29] Enormous efforts were made to rouse public opinion on the matter, demonstrations were organised, reports and letters appeared in the press, handbills were distributed, and booklets published and circulated. Deputations met with a major wholesale agent for these papers in the city and with the managers of 'certain Dublin journals who inserted advertisements on behalf of objectionable papers'. But for all this effort the results 'were not satisfactory'. Local vigilance committees were formed in different parts of the country but they again were not considered successful. The crusade was not solely Catholic and, as we have seen, vigilance societies which focused exclusively on sexual immorality were a feature of rescue work from 1885. However, the language in which these new vigilance societies expressed their concerns was, as Michael Wheatley has noted, strongly Catholic, nationalist and anti-English.[30] In some cases the language used was similar to that invoked in relation to prostitution and white slavery, especially when the police were urged to intervene in this 'immoral traffic' of English newspapers.[31] By 1913 these societies appear only to have been active in Dublin, Limerick and Queenstown, though this type of vigilance society was to remain functional on a lesser scale until the establishment of the Irish Free State when their ultimate aim, censorship, was granted.[32] New vigilance societies continued to be formed, again in Dublin, but these were very different from those organised to influence newspaper circulation. They were concerned with suppressing sexual immorality, particularly that evident on the streets of Dublin. The immediate catalyst was the panic raised by the 'white slave' scare.

White slavery

The agitation over the white slave issue brought the subject of prostitution to wider public attention in 1912. The issue of white slavery had, as we have seen, surfaced in the 1880s and continued to be of international concern throughout the first decades of the twentieth century. White slavery meant the selling of women's and girls' bodies for the purposes of prostitution. It was implied that force was used to bring a woman into prostitution and to keep her from leaving it. For the reading public the appeal of white slavery was its lurid and melodramatic stories of intrigue, crime, seduction and sex. Such tales provided virtually pornographic entertainment to the reading audience.[33] In Ireland the white slavery issue was pursued most vigorously by suffragists who appear to have believed that it was a real phenomenon. The existence of white slavery, and the dangers it posed to women and girls, was used by Irish suffragists to argue for women's political rights. The Irish authorities appear never to have taken allegations of white slavery seriously. Discussions of the issue that took place in papers like the *Irish Citizen* had little to do with the real problem of prostitution and more to do with the political agenda set by suffragists and nationalists in Ireland at this time. It was a way for suffragists to challenge male power, particularly their sexual power, and to argue for the necessity of change in the sexual relations between men and women.

The suffrage paper, the *Irish Citizen* used the lecture tour of Alice Abadam[34] in 1912 as the point of departure for a discussion of sexuality, white slavery and politics. Abadam, who was an organiser of the Catholic Women's Suffrage Society, made her first appearance in Dublin in October 1912 to talk about the 'white slave trade'.[35] It was Abadam's lecture tour in Ireland that brought the issue of white slavery to a wider public audience. She spoke in Belfast, and Lisburn, where 'extra seats had to be brought in to accommodate the audience, some of whom came from a long distance', Newry and Warrenpoint. At Abadam's Dublin meeting

Fig. 11. 'White Slavery in Dublin', *The Irish Worker*, 25 May 1912.

the audience was composed of over a thousand women.[36] After the Dublin meeting a 'committee of ladies' was appointed to form a vigilance association.[37] This association was considered suspect by the *Irish Catholic* which saw 'sinister motives of proselytism behind it'. In consequence the *Irish Citizen* had to reassure readers that Abadam was Catholic.[38] The large audiences, of women only, indicate a degree of fascination with this apparent sexual underworld, although there was some opposition to these lectures. In Waterford, for example, it was claimed 'that there was no such thing as this traffic . . . and, therefore, any plain speaking on the subject could only do harm by soiling the minds of the innocent'.[39] A correspondent to the *Irish Times* charged 'suffragists with distributing among young girls literature dealing with subjects with which it is not fitting that at their age they should become acquainted'. The suffragists denied this stating that any literature was carefully edited before distribution and that 'nothing is further from our intention than to sully the purity of a girl's mind'.[40]

Abadam was clear that economic considerations were a factor in prostitution. 'While we pay the good and modest woman 2s 6d a week for making army trousers', she declared, 'we allow men to pay the woman on the street £20 or £30 a week for selling herself. Is it any wonder that such a girl is driven to the streets?'[41] She also suggested that the high moral standard prevalent in Ireland meant that 'regulations and precautions against the evil' were less strict there. In consequence, she warned, in case anyone was feeling complacent, that 'the agents of this nefarious traffic find Dublin their happy hunting ground'.[42] Abadam noted that all previous efforts to ameliorate the social evil 'are practically useless, and have been useless in the past, owing to the political helplessness of women'.[43] An editorial in the *Irish Citizen* in 1913 stressed that

women's lack of political power leaves women a helpless prey to the sweating employer, and is therefore one of the causes of prostitution. Prostitution is the cause of venereal disease, the greatest scourge of our civilisation, and one that will finally sweep it away unless its ravages are checked. Therefore, suffragists, to awaken public conscience, and to show the urgent necessity of women's emancipation, are taking steps to enlighten women, and the public generally, on the subjects of Sweating, Prostitution, Venereal Disease, with the discreet causal relationship between the three.[44]

The issue of white slavery in Ireland also centred on the naivety of country girls. The Rev. G. Collins informed a meeting of the Girls Friendly Society in Belfast that 'it was appalling to think that girls might come up from country parts without knowing the dangers of a great city. They were placed within reach of unscrupulous men or women who would bring them to lodgings where they would soon fall into bad company.'[45] At the annual meeting of the Belfast Midnight Mission, Lady Dufferin observed, with regard to white slavery, that 'few had any idea of the widespread nature of this evil'.[46] The innocence of the country girl was threatened by life in the city. Within the discourse of white slavery there was a further demonisation of male sexuality. The threat posed by white slavery was a masculine threat. James Cousins was to remark in a lecture that, 'I declare with shame that it is the low and selfish character of many of my sex that make white slavery possible . . . in matters of sex, man is the natural aggressor . . . men have enslaved themselves to a part of themselves.'[47] For the labour press in Ireland, white slavery was a useful way to critique the factory system redefining it as 'wage slavery' and thus associated with the problems of sweated labour (fig. 11).[48] The connection with employment was made more explicit when it was revealed that many employment agencies were allegedly fronts for white slavers. During the war years the issue was linked with Irish emigration, particularly to England. A letter to the *Irish Times* reported that the National Vigilance Association in London looked after the welfare of more Irish girls than any other nationality, save Norwegians.[49] Even after the white slave panic had subsided, it was reported from Belfast in 1916 that 'white slave traffickers were rumoured to be trying to tempt girls to England under the pretence of finding war work there. The [women's] patrols investigated the matter but have not found any case, though a girl who had answered a questionable ad re [sic] nursing, was prevented by the patrols from going to London.'[50] What these commentators were doing was creating an image of a vulnerable girl, highlighting the 'dangers of ignorance, especially when so many gently bred girls must make their way unprotected in the world'.[51]

This vulnerable girl would become the object of close scrutiny when the issue of women police and women's patrols emerged in Ireland in 1914. It is interesting here, as in other material relating to the white slave traffic, that the foreigner, an international figure symbolic of the white slaver, was, in Irish terms, English. Departing for England was or could be tantamount to heading into white slavery. The white slavery victim in Ireland was always a girl, not a woman. In later years, in the 1920s and beyond, the danger of migrating to England for Irish women lay in the possibility of losing one's religion and falling into prostitution.[52]

By 1913 the *Irish Citizen* admitted that many of the stories circulating around white slavery 'were wild and unauthenticated'. What needed to be investigated in Ireland was the problem of immorality that 'incontrovertibly' existed.[53] The white slavery issue proved a versatile weapon for the suffragists. It allowed them a way to discuss sexuality and the problems associated with it, particularly the dominance of men in the private and public spheres. Suffragists used the campaign to discuss the victimisation of women in marriage, and to argue, as their nineteenth-century forebears had, for an equal standard of morality for men and women. They used the white slavery campaign to extend their authority in public. Gaining access to the courts was one aspect of this move into public life. As Walkowitz has shown, narratives of white slavery in the nineteenth century were taken up by different constituencies, including feminists, and used for their own particular purposes.[54] The campaign also allowed suffragists to challenge the traditional gender divide of the public sphere. The fact that more than a thousand women turned up in the Mansion House to hear Abadam speak suggests a very visible public presence of women.

The idea of white slavery served to deflect attention away from the very real social and economic factors that led women into prostitution. Instead, at least in the mainstream press, attention was focused on the threat of the 'foreigner'. In the Irish case, and even within the suffrage press, the foreigner was associated with England. Interestingly, women who debated the issue of white slavery in Ireland were not rescue workers themselves, nor did they seek to become involved in such work. Their involvement with white slavery was about arguing for women's right to the parliamentary franchise. They did not, as women did in other countries, initiate any investigations into the extent of white slavery or even the extent of prostitution in Ireland. The debate did, however, strengthen the efforts of rescue organisations and groups involved in preventative work, such as the Young Women's Christian Association and the Girls' Friendly Society who met travellers at railway stations and ports.

It was unsurprising that the white slave issue should become a concern of those who resided in Dublin and Belfast. Throughout the early years of the twentieth century fears were expressed about the presence of country girls in the city, about the vulnerability of working-class girls, and the necessity for middle-class women to step in to protect and save them. Much of the concern came about through the increasing opportunities for leisure which were available to the working girl. Urban amusements such as the cinema, the music hall and the dancehall were considered sites of danger to these young women. The establishment of hostels and clubs for these girls, discussed previously, was an attempt to keep them safe and under control.

The significance of legislative change and women's role in seeking such modification evolved from the white slavery crusade to a support for the introduction into Ireland of the Criminal Law Amendment Act of 1912. The Act, referred to as the 'White Slavery Act', gave the police increased powers to prosecute procurers and brothel-keepers. Landlords were expected to evict any tenants who used rented premises as a brothel, and judges could also impose a sentence of whipping on procurers and male brothel-keepers.[55] Irish activists argued for the extension of the Act to Ireland, and the publicity provided by Abadam on the white slave trade provided the context in which they could make their case. At each of the reported meetings held by Abadam it was noted that the Criminal Law Amendment Act must include Ireland. At the Mansion House meeting at which Abadam lectured, the suffragist and philanthropist Rosa M. Barrett alerted the meeting to a 'rumour . . . [that] . . . had spread that Ireland might be excluded from the Bill', and to the fact that a number of Irish MPs opposed it. Barrett had sent a telegram to Dublin Castle to ask if this was the case. She also remarked that the Lord Mayor of Dublin had 'gone to the bar at the House of Commons to plead the women's cause'.[56] The 1912 Criminal Law Amendment Bill was of interest to groups other than suffragists. Protestant Church organisations, especially those who had engaged in rescue work, supported the Bill. The White Cross League suggested a campaign of petitions and the establishment of a dedicated group to fight for the Bill.[57] It was noted that support for the Criminal Law Amendment Act was not forthcoming from the Catholic clergy in Ireland. A member of the White Cross Association urged the Catholic Church to do more since the campaign's success depended on its cooperation and by far the greatest number of those to be assisted belonged to that denomination.[58] For some the issues at stake in the Criminal Law Amendment Bill were more significant than the issue of home rule. As one commentator observed, 'saving our young women from being the prey of the pimp or procuress, may be of even greater importance than the method to be adopted for governing the country'.[59] The Irish Women's Reform League held a meeting on the issue of the Criminal Law Amendment Act in the Mansion House.[60] The social reform committee of the Presbyterian Church in Ireland lobbied the chief secretary and MPs, noting that the committee 'would strongly protest against any attempt to omit Ireland from the operation of the Bill'.[61] A resolution was also passed at the meeting of the South Dublin union board of guardians urging that the Bill include Ireland.[62]

The Bill was passed in December 1912 and Ireland was included in its operation. That the discussion of the Bill had some effect may be seen from the rise in the numbers of arrests for prostitution in Dublin, 1,067 as opposed to 650 and 689 in the preceding and following years.[63] With the passage of the Criminal Law Amendment Act the concern with white slavery abated, though it did not disappear totally. In March 1913 the *Irish Citizen* again warned its readers that Ireland was a 'particularly favourable field' for the 'traffickers in women's bodies'.[64] It was now being suggested that Irish women should be involved in organising a committee to investigate the moral condition of Dublin and 'seek the necessary remedy or remedies'. The passage of the Act might have ended women's concern about white slavery but they were now arguing for an extension of their activities into social investigation. Abadam returned to Dublin to engage in another lecture tour in 1913, and again linked the white slavery issue to women's oppression more generally. 'Where there was one slavery there were many', she argued; 'political slavery led to wage slavery, and this to immoral slavery.' By doing away with political slavery women would resolve all three kinds of slavery.[65] She suggested that the Criminal Law Amendment Act was ineffectual and that the issue would never be dealt with until 'the administration was responsible to women'.[66] In response to the implementation of the Act, a vigilance committee was formed by a group of women in Dublin whose principal aim was once again to protect girls. It was argued that the 'easiest prey of the white slavers is the country girl who, with little money and no experience, and no friends to welcome her, comes to Dublin or some other large city, in search of employment'.[67] This new society would safeguard these girls with notices in railway stations and elsewhere, and workers would meet the girls and direct them to lodgings.[68]

The streets of Dublin

The *Irish Times* reported in 1913 that

the condition of the streets of Dublin after sunset is a reproach to us all. The immorality in Dublin is more public than elsewhere . . . all through the evening and well into the small hours of the morning, the streets are occupied by groups of girls who cannot possibly have reached sixteen years of age.[69]

The paper suggested that this information was known to all but that the public were loath to discuss the issue. When the matter was raised in City Hall, the paper noted, 'it was always without result . . . some patriotic councillor emits a few fierce phrases about "the English soldiery and their female companions" and there the matter ends'. The paper called for a campaign 'for the purification of the streets'.[70] However, issues of sexual morality took on another tinge in the first decade of the twentieth century. The concept of moral regeneration for suffragists had involved the elimination of the sexual double standard and the elevations of men's sexual morality to the same level as that of women. This argument was still being expressed by suffragists in Ireland in the twentieth century. However, advanced nationalists transformed the idea of moral regeneration into a recognition that vice was to be found in the British soldier. Regenerating

Irish society thus involved demonising the British as amoral and the spreaders of disease among the Irish population. The state of the Dublin streets was thus an issue of concern not only for suffragists and vigilance campaigners, but also increasingly for advanced Irish nationalists.

In his valuable study of the views of advanced nationalists, Novick has shown how propagandists attempted to construct and develop an image of the ideal revolutionary, both male and female. In doing so constant comparison was drawn between the noble Gael and the debased Saxon. Ireland needed to get rid of its English garrison before it could become pure and wholesome again.[71] Novick argues that the image of Great Britain as an 'unclean and impure sink of perversion' reached its height in scare propaganda about venereal disease and the immoral sexual threat of English troops in Ireland during the First World War. However, the concern about immorality and the contagious nature of the British soldier, who had replaced the prostitute as the source of disease, is evident from the late nineteenth century. The construction of the British soldier as the enemy of Irish women and Irish purity was one in which nationalist men and women played a significant role. From the eighteenth century the army in Ireland had been used for internal security, national defence and was a reserve for the empire.[72] At times throughout the century its role in assisting the civil authorities in keeping the peace, in policing elections, evictions and performing other duties caused tensions within local communities.[73] In 1848, for instance, a Catholic priest worried about the morals of the young women in the neighbourhood of Adare, where he perceived 'outrages [were] committed on decency' and morality by the local soldiers.[74] The issue of Irish girls going out with soldiers had, on occasions, been problematic. In 1881 much bad feeling was noted in the town of Ennistymon against troops 'walking out' with local girls.[75] Similar feelings were expressed by Irish nationalists from the period of the Boer War, and were common in the early twentieth century when a consistent campaign against Irish girls 'going with' soldiers emerged (fig. 12). Helena Molony and others recalled that the women's nationalist organisation, Inghinidhe na hÉireann, carried on an anti-recruiting campaign from its foundation in 1900 until 1914. This basically consisted of distributing leaflets which 'were in all cases addressed to Irish girls appealing to them not to consort with the armed and uniformed enemies of their country'. She described how the soldiers in Dublin were:

confined to one side of O'Connell Street, i.e., the GPO side. No respectable person – man or woman – would dream of walking on that side of the street after twilight. But many thousands of innocent young country girls, up in Dublin, at domestic service mostly, were dazzled by these handsome and brilliant uniforms with polite young men with English accents inside them – and dazzled often with

1nʒ1n1ʋe nᴀ nℯ́1ℝℯᴧnn.

I R I S H   G I R L S !

Ireland has need of the loving service of all her children.   Irishwomen do not sufficiently realise the power they have to help or hinder the cause of Ireland's freedom.

If they did we should not see the sad sight of Irish girls walking through the streets with men wearing the uniform of Ireland's oppressor.

No man can serve two masters ; no man can honestly serve Ireland and serve England.   The Irishman who has chosen to wear the English uniform has chosen to serve the enemy of Ireland, and it is the duty of every Irishwoman, who believes in the freedom of Ireland, to show her disapproval of his conduct by shunning his company.

Irish girls who walk with Irishmen wearing England's uniform, remember you are walking with traitors.   Irish girls who walk with English soldiers, remember you are walking with your country's enemies, and with men who are unfit to be the companions of any girl, for it is well known that the English army is the most degraded and immoral army in Europe, chiefly recruited in the slums of English cities, among men of the lowest and most depraved characters.   You endanger your purity and honour by associating with such men and you insult your Motherland.   Hearken to the words of Father Kavanagh, the Irish Franciscan Patriot Priest, who pronounces it a heinous crime against Ireland, for Irishmen to join the forces of robber England.   Do you think it is less a crime for Irish girls to honour these men with their company.   Remember the history of your country.   Remember the women of Limerick and the glorious patriot women of the great rebellion of '98, and let us, who are their descendants try to be worthy of them.   What would those noble women think if they knew their daughters were associating with men belonging to that army, which has so often wrought ruin and havoc in Ireland, and murdered in cold blood thousands of Irishwomen and children.   What English soldiers have done in Ireland in the past they would do again if ordered to do so.   They would slaughter our kith and kin and murder women and children again as unhesitatingly as they hemmed in the helpless Boer women and children in those horrible concentration camps, where ten thousand little Boer children died from want and suffering.

Irish girls make a vow, not only that you will yourselves refuse to associate with any man who wears an English uniform, but that you will also try and induce your girl companions to do the same.

Women's influence is strong.   Let us see, fellow-countrywomen, that we use it to the fullest for the Glory of God and for the honour and freedom of Ireland.

1nʒ1n1ʋe nᴀ nℯ́1ℝℯᴧnn.

Fig. 12. Inghinidhe na hÉireann, 'Irish Girls', leaflet, early twentieth century. The Clark collection, courtesy of the Burns Library, Boston College.

disastrous results to themselves, but that is another side of the matter, and we were only concerned with the National political side. These young girls had not the faintest idea of the moral, social or political implications of their association with the 'red-coats'.[76]

Margaret Quinn, treasurer of Inghinidhe na hÉireann and later a member of Cumann na mBan (Irishwomen's Council), recorded that the women of Inghinidhe na hÉireann used to go into the public houses with our anti-recruiting leaflets and had things thrown at us and very vile language sometimes. We tried to get the soldiers off the streets. We did not succeed fully in this. We got them, however, confined to certain areas . . . Our main object was to save the young Irish girls from falling into their hands. A decent girl could not walk down the Post Office side without being molested. Then such girls got the name of 'soldier's totty'.[77]

It is telling that the problem here is with immorality as a political issue; there is no concern at all for the fate of the women involved, though Inghinidhe na hÉireann was a feminist leaning organisation. The evils of conscription were outlined for readers of the advanced nationalist journal *The Hibernian* in 1915, highlighting the dangers that barrack life presented to the young Irish recruit:

Conscription leads to immorality. The atmosphere of the average British barracks . . . does not help young men to preserve their morality. The great majority of young men in Ireland at present are honourable in their attitudes to women and fairly attentive to their religious duties. Many who have joined the army are shocked by the conduct and language and driven . . . to conclude that death on the battlefield would be much preferable to the risk to the soul entailed by a sojourn in the barracks . . . it has happened too often that decent young Irishmen, removed from the restraint of home life, and placed in the corrupting surroundings of a barrack, have taken to drink and got into the habit of keeping company with the unfortunate women, who are found wherever soldiers are stationed . . . conscription is the enemy of Ireland: at present women in Ireland are able to live free from molestation, but if their protectors are taken away and the country garrisoned by a licentious soldiery, all sense of security will be gone.[78]

Propagandists were adamant that the 'only way in which Irishmen could be brought to immoral sexual behaviour was to join the army'.[79] The advanced nationalist press reported cases of violence against women perpetrated by the British garrison in Ireland as further condemnation of their presence in the country. James Connolly, as Novick observes, was making a political rather than a moral point, when he suggested that 'if you want to make Dublin clean in its moral standards remove your garrison'.[80]

Women's patrols

The outbreak of the First World War brought the problem of girls and young women on the streets to the attention of the public and rescue workers. The matter of the moral condition of the Dublin streets was highlighted again at the Church of Ireland Synod in November 1915, when it was asserted that it was difficult for the police to deal with immorality due to the fact that 'there were hundreds of single women living in single rooms in Dublin'.[81] The contaminating influence of single women was the issue here and the assumption that all single women were clandestine prostitutes. It was observed that a single woman taking a room in a respectable house 'could contaminate the other respectable women living in the house'. The archbishop of Dublin believed that 'the vice in Dublin was more sordid and more degrading than it used to be, and it was more difficult to grapple with'.[82] Further reports and correspondence in the press remarked on the state of the streets in Dublin in 1915. A letter to one paper argued that regarding the

problem of sordid and squalid vice in our streets . . . so long as the demand exists the supply will somehow be found. We must set forces working to control the demand . . . we have to create the change in thinking which will make the moral system at present prevailing appear to the general public in its true light as shameful, cruel, wasteful, dangerous.[83]

The double standard of morality, it was argued, must be consigned to the past. Lady Fingall, in an address to the Catholic Truth Society, commented that the streets of Dublin were a disgrace to Catholic Ireland. She suggested that something needed to be done by offering people decent homes. It was no wonder she said, that those who lived in tenements 'seek the openness and brightness of the streets'.[84] A special meeting of Dublin Corporation was held where P. T. Daly 'drew a fearful picture of the immorality obtaining from the Customs House to the North Wall after nightfall', and spoke of the 'lewdness [that] stalks unblushingly through our principal streets when evening falls . . . young girls and foul mouthed soldiers startle the ears of passers by with their horrifying crosstalk'.[85] The Corporation's usual response was to ask the police to do something. The common cry at this stage was that some scheme was needed to 'protect our young girls from contact with debased soldiery'.[86]

The *Irish Citizen* claimed that it was suffragists who raised the problem of immorality on the streets and were adamant that the root cause of the problem 'was the state of the slums and the whole housing problem . . . so long as vice pays better wages than virtue, so long will the trade of the prostitute thrive'.[87] The suffragists used the state of the streets to broaden their political and social activity, and they called for the establishment of women's patrols. The Irish Women's Suffrage and Local Government Association had affiliated to the National Union of Women Workers of Great Britain and Ireland (NUWW), a philanthropic body that addressed issues of work, morality, education and public health that had a bearing on women. In 1914 the NUWW established women's patrols in England, and Anna Haslam and other suffragists were keen to have similar patrols in Ireland. In consequence of a letter that Haslam and her fellow suffragist Mary Hayden had published in the press on immorality in Dublin they were asked to attend for interview with Sir Matthew Nathan, the Under-Secretary for Ireland, to discuss the subject. The chief commissioner of police was also present. Nathan was adamant that the comments made by various individuals on the characters of women seeing soldiers off at the North Wall were exaggerated and that these women were in an emotional state, and not prostitutes. He also argued that much of the commentary about immorality in Dublin was an attempt to discredit the soldiery. Haslam and Hayden, in class if not in feminist solidarity, accepted that it was 'the women rather than the soldiers who were to blame and that there were extraordinarily few soldiers who were intoxicated in the streets'.[88] The women also informed him that there was a good deal of soliciting going on in Sackville Street in Dublin, a view confirmed by the police commissioner. The women suggested that soldiers should not be allowed out so late at night, and that women police should be appointed.

In January 1915 the *Freeman's Journal* reported on the formation of women patrols in Ireland.[89] The patrols had the approval of the Irish Under-Secretary and Lord Lieutenant and the support of a large number of women's organisations.[90] In an interview she gave on the patrols, Haslam stated clearly that the women were not engaged in rescue work. The work of the patrols was 'to be purely preventative'. The duties of the women were to 'patrol the beat assigned to them by the organiser, to make friends with the girls and gain their confidence, to warn girls behaving unsuitably, and to put them in touch with local societies, clubs, or classes'. The qualifications required of a patrol member were that 'she would be between 25 and 50 years of age, have tact and sympathy, some previous experience of work, good health and the ability to give not less than two hours at least twice a week to the work, also to write a brief daily report'.[91] The women did not wear a uniform. It was suggested that 'it might be desirable if there was a dark blue dress and a quiet hat, but each patrol would wear a distinctive armlet'. They would also have a small book of regulations and a card (signed by the district police inspector). Each patrol would be known to the authorities and would be able to call on their assistance and the women would always work in pairs.[92]

The *Irish Times* related the function of the patrols as 'patrolling the streets and warning young girls (and young men if necessary), of certain dangers'.[93] The NUWW was closely associated with controlling the behaviour of working-class women. In these patrols women monitored public places, separating couples thought to be embracing too closely, following those they expected might be about to embark on an unsavoury course of behaviour, and warning youngsters of the dangers of overly casual behaviour.[94] The labour press, recognising the class bias of this issue, remained wary of the patrols. The *Irish Worker* for instance, concluded:

That we are to be afflicted with a new form of inquisition. This is to take the form of an organisation to place upon the streets of Dublin women patrols whose function it will be to look after the morals and behaviour of Dublin women and girls . . . this project is simply an impertinent attempt of a number of ladies to interfere with the lives of the poor, to boss, to direct, to control and supervise, and regulate and order and rule and determine and discipline and arrange and keep in subjection as they would not admit to themselves the actions and the conduct of their poorer sisters.[95]

The *Irish Citizen* was also wary, and would have preferred to see a paid women police system in operation. The *Citizen* observed that conditions in Ireland were not as bad as in England and Ireland was not 'so directly under the influence of the militarist wave as in England, this country has not manifested any such scenes of pernicious "enthusiasm" for the troops on the part of the girls as seen in England'.[96] The *Citizen* urged that the patrols should not confine themselves to 'keeping numerous young women off the street', but should ensure that 'innocent women are not made the victims of unscrupulous, and sometimes brutal policemen and that guilty women are brought to the police station in a civilised way'.[97]

What impact did these women's patrols have on immorality? The experiences and work of patrols organised in Dublin and Belfast were reported on positively in the *Irish Citizen*, and a woman patrol recounted her involvement. She was generally on patrol between 9.30 and 11.30 pm and her beat was Sackville Street, Middle Abbey Street, Bachelor's Walk, Princes Street, along the quays to Alexandra Basin and 'through the many dirty laneways that run between the main thoroughfares'. She remarked on the youth of many of the girls on the street and claimed that many of them were drunk. These individuals, she noted, were 'too cute' for the police and she had 'witnessed scenes that I dare not describe in a weekly journal'.[98] In an unnamed street she noted that a room could be hired for 6 pence a night. She wrote, 'one can pick up vermin as easily as one can get one's boots muddy on a rainy day'.[99] There is no doubt that this woman enjoyed her work, which brought her into close and immediate contact with young women working as prostitutes in the city. The most sensational case to come to public attention was the Metal Bridge case. In December 1915 two of the women patrollers were accosted by a man who made 'an improper and insulting' suggestion to one of them as they attempted to cross the Ha'penny Bridge.[100] One of the women charged the man with assault and the case was widely reported in the papers in January 1916. The defendant was fined and the women were lauded by the judge who tried the case for showing 'great pluck and determination'.[101] The *Irish Citizen* reported the case a little differently, noting that the defendant, being male, could not be charged with soliciting and that he received a 'slight fine' with his solicitor apologising to the ladies 'on behalf of his client who did not realise that they were not the kind that are his lawful prey'.[102] By 1916 it was noted that the Belfast Patrol Committee had had many setbacks and there had been no report of any work being carried out there for some time, while in Dublin 'most excellent work has been carried out', and it was generally recognised that 'the patrols movement is responsible for much improvement in the Dublin Streets'.[103]

The patrols were still operating in 1919 when the presidents were Anna Haslam and Mary Hayden. The women patrols offered a form of sexual surveillance. Their rhetoric stressed their role in helping women, but it was also women who were their primary targets. They were attempting to claim the public streets for women and to transform those streets into the moral highways that would correspond with their own moral and social goals. The aim was to rid public spaces of any hint of sexual impropriety – but this was impossible for the women's patrols in Ireland. There simply were not enough of them to make any real impact. What they did achieve was to raise the public profile of suffragist women and use that profile to argue for more political power. Their attention focused on working-class girls and women. Church groups also became involved in this type of work. The Mothers' Union in Dublin, for instance, reported that in their vigilance work

they had accomplished a great deal at the North Wall, helping girls going to Municipal Works in England, arranging their passports where they were not in order, directing country girls who would otherwise have been lost in Dublin and helping in various ways girls who had run away from home. Miss D'Arcy mentioned the similar work done by the Belfast organisation, where they had some dreadful cases to deal with, many of which were traceable to the bad influence of (certain) cinema (films) [sic]. She thought members of the Council might endeavour to ensure a more efficient censorship of films.[104]

Irish suffragists also developed other forms of surveillance, all of them directed at the working classes. In April 1914, and under the auspices of the Irish Women's Reform League, a watching the courts committee was established.[105] By March 1915 the committee was well organised under the effective direction of Marion Duggan, who had a law degree.[106] The aims of the committee were described as follows:

1) to show by their presence in court that women demand, both as a right and a duty, to be admitted to the administration of justice, on equal terms with men, as police, jurors, solicitors, barristers, magistrates and judges 2) to collect evidence bearing on the above demands, and on any other legal or legislative reforms needed for the protection of women and children, together with accurate information as to moral conditions.[107]

In essence the committee were alerting their readers to sexual crimes and the often very lenient ways in which they were dealt with by the courts. They were also ensuring that these cases which were not generally reported in the press were made public. The women had difficulty in getting access to the courts and eventually were allowed attend all cases except incest cases which were held *in camera*. An editorial in the *Irish Citizen* remarked that 'one fails to grasp why, if public morality is such that these crimes take place, it can best be served by hushing them up and attempting to give the impression that such offences are unheard of in our Christian civilisation'.[108]

While advanced nationalist propaganda promulgated that the only way in which an Irish man could be brought to immoral sexual behaviour was to join the army, the suffragist and labour press attempted to alert the public to problems of immorality which were very much caused by Irish men. The *Irish Citizen* reported cases of sexual crime and emphasised the vulnerability of adolescent girls to sexual assault, and the inadequacy of the law to protect them. They highlighted the failure of the daily newspapers to report such cases and were critical of the promotion of a false and idealised view of Ireland. Through the pages of the *Irish Citizen*, the watching the courts committee brought to public attention sexual crimes committed against girls and women. The *Irish Worker* denounced a moral purity movement more anxious about contamination by the foreign press than about the evils around them, and castigated a 'quiescent public and a criminally silent press'. The paper condemned the Irish media for 'deluging its readers with boastings of the purity of our women and the inviolable honour of our men and with tales of the "days of Brian Boru" ', but ignoring the subject of sexual crime while 'filthy assaults upon children passed weekly through the courts'.[109]

Suffragists constructed a discourse around women's and children's vulnerability, even within the judicial system, which allowed them the moral authority to broaden their entrance into new areas of the public sphere, the courts. Suffragists were empowered by these narratives; working women were not. Restriction and control of working-class women's sexual activities expanded even further as the war continued. In January 1916 a Dublin Watch Committee was formed whose secretary was Miss Mosher, a member of the women's patrols. The committee consisted of a number of sub-committees which dealt with different forms of vice, drunkenness, immorality, lending, gambling, acts by and against children.[110] By early 1917 the sub-committee on immorality decided to 'take up the work of combating venereal disease', and actively sought to organise a branch of the Society for Combating Venereal Diseases in Dublin. The committee appears to have remained in existence until, at least, 1919.[111] Watching the courts, organising hostels and refuges for women workers and travellers brought middle-class women into direct contact with potential outcasts, a class they had a hand in constructing.

Separation women

From 1914 a new figure to the Irish scene became an odious symbol of British rule in Ireland, and a symbol that overtook the prostitute in the public understanding of immorality. This was the separation woman. Separation allowances were paid to the wives and other female relatives and dependants of soldiers and sailors who were away at, or killed in, the First World War. Money, the separation allowance, was paid to these women to compensate a family for the financial loss incurred in the enlistment and service of the man.[112] It is unclear how many women in Ireland were in receipt of separation allowances but the number was probably quite substantial. In the region of 140,460 Irish men enlisted in the British army during the war and the majority, if not all of these, would have had dependants.[113] From the very beginning women receiving these allowances were called separation women and they were all tainted with immorality, particularly with drunkenness. In December 1914 an inquiry was carried out in Ireland by the government in response to allegations that separation allowances had led to an increase in drunkenness among the wives of soldiers. The main findings rejected the accusation and noted that in many parts of the country, 'on the contrary the women and children are better clothed and fed and many are saving money'. A marked increase in drinking habits was noted in Clonmel, County Tipperary, 'among a certain class of women'. While there were complaints made about the women, the inquiring officer decided they arose 'out of personal squabbles and may frequently not be true'.[114] However, in Tralee in October 1914, after some violent incidents between the police and soldiers, the military authorities asked the local justices to take steps to restrict the sale of alcohol and in consequence the public houses of the town were closed every night from nine, from 16 October to 1 December.[115] The value of the separation allowance was made clear in a song from around 1918 which observed

> Now there's lino in the parlour
> And in the kitchen too;
> There's a glass-back cheffoneur
> That we got from Dicky Glue . . .[116]

However, over the remaining years of the war the reputation of separation women declined further. Instances of fraud appear to have been high and the government was keen that any attempt at deception would be prosecuted and reported in the press; this gave rise to a large number of separation women being arrested.[117]

With the mobilisation for war the problem of women and alcohol became one of major concern for the government and the vigilance societies. A women's vigilance committee carried out nightly patrols of public houses in Dublin. From 1915 this committee compiled information on the numbers of women drinking in public houses and their reports were published in the press. In one instance one of the women had disguised herself as 'a woman of the working class' and had investigated a number of public houses, only to find 'abhorrent scenes' within.[118] The women they were policing were, of course, women of the working classes who appear to have had a culture and tradition of public-house drinking, in Dublin at least.[119] Matthew Nathan received deputations, particularly from the Quakers, requesting that curtailments be placed on the drinking habits of soldiers and their wives and dependants.[120] Numerous reports of the bad behaviour of the separation women appeared regularly in the press. Women were often arrested for being drunk and disorderly, for neglecting their children and for engaging in violent activity. In those cases where women were accused of child neglect the National Society for the Prevention of Cruelty to Children (NSPCC) often brought the prosecutions. Indeed, it could be argued that the outbreak of the war provided a whole new group, women, rather than families, for the inspectors of the NSPCC to investigate.[121] Often women who were convicted of such behaviour had their separation allowances administered either by the NSPCC, or they were distributed by the local branch of the Soldiers and Sailors Families Association, or some reputable local person.[122] Separation women were open to constant surveillance, from the police, from vigilance committees, and from the local and central authorities. They appear to have been more tightly scrutinised than prostitutes were at this time.

Separation women also came under fire because they were seen to support the British government. It was noted in 1920 that these women were often 'surrounded by more or less hostile neighbours, [but] kept the old flag flying on the home front'.[123] They appear constantly to have disrupted Sinn Féin meetings and election campaigns, as in Waterford in 1918.[124] They also disrupted suffrage meetings. Máire Nic Shiúbhlaigh recalled that as the rising was starting in Dublin she was near Jacob's biscuit factory where 'a huge crowd of poorly dressed men and women, some of them shouting and screaming and waving fists, came into view . . . this was a mixed crowd of Jacob's factory employees and "separation allowance" women'.[125] When a number of women, who had taken part in the rising, were arrested and were being moved from Richmond barracks to Kilmainham jail an antagonistic crowd of separation women had gathered outside the gates. One of the captives noted that never had she seen 'such savage women'.[126] When the rebels of 1916 were being escorted to prison they were often assaulted by separation women. William O'Brien observed that when he was being transferred to Richmond barracks 'there was a considerable crowd assembled, made up mainly of separation allowance women who booed and hissed us vigorously'.[127] Rosamond Jacob noted in her diary that in Waterford Sinn Féin fund raisers 'wouldn't sell flags in the streets for fear of being attacked by the separation women, who are always damning them when they meet them'.[128]

The separation women were also associated with sexual immorality, particularly those who were unmarried mothers. One commentator remarked that the separation allowance 'legalised immorality'.[129] By 1916 the payment of separation allowances had been extended to unmarried women who were the dependants of soldiers for their support and that of any children resulting from the relationship. Many considered this an acceptance by the government of 'illegitimacy, or co-habitation between unmarried people of different sex!' While this might have been acceptable in England, it was considered an outrage in Ireland.[130] Unmarried motherhood also figured prominently in the contemporary discussions of immorality. A particularly voluble debate occurred in the boardroom of the Cork board of guardians on this issue. One board member suggested that the Cork union was little more than a brothel given the numbers of deserted and illegitimate children, and unmarried mothers, who sought relief there. It was alleged that many of the unmarried mothers were allowed wear their own clothes and were getting preferential treatment. Mr Dorgan moved a motion

that as we are of the opinion the abnormal number of girls about to become mothers is due to the delirium attendant on the present war fever, we consider it to be the duty of the government to provide for those sufferers by maintaining for a period of 12 months all mothers between the ages of 15 and 21 years, their babies, if they so wish, to be boarded out at the expense of the State and not have them thrown on the rates and detained in the poor house.

The motion was refused and Dorgan responded that the board was 'managing a brothel for Kitchener's army'.[131]

Separation women were a particular target of advanced nationalists on the basis of their drinking habits and their perceived sexual immorality.[132] In Boyle, County Roscommon, there were complaints that the local excise officer, who investigated claims for the allowance, insulted the women and made disparaging remarks about their sons and husbands who were serving in the army.[133] In Rochestown, post office staff were reported to 'insult the women who collect the separation allowance . . . [and] the British army is ridiculed and every class of scurrility is indulged in, in order to make the creatures who have lost a son or a husband in the war feel more keenly a labour in which they have no control'.[134] Supporters of the Irish Parliamentary Party candidate in the 1917 by-election in County Longford were depicted as separation women, and would easily have been recognised as such, being drunk, ragged and wearing a union jack (see fig. 13). The disdain felt for the recruit to the army had now been projected onto the separation woman. The odium attached to separation women remained strong. At a Blue Shirts meeting at Dunshaughlin, County Meath, in 1934, de Valera's supporters were ridiculed as being

the old women who . . . were shouting 'Up the Union Jack' [in 1918] when they were getting the 'Separation Allowance'. It was these who were following him in every town and every village – the Separation Allowance women or their descendants and if he could not get better than this then poor de Valera's cause was lost.[135]

While both nationalists and suffragists utilised the issue of immorality for their own ends, for suffragists the solution to prostitution and immorality lay in their acquiring the parliamentary franchise. As a correspondent to the *Northern Whig* noted it

is a woman's political disability that causes her to be to be regarded by the law as a chattel and a cipher, and that shapes legislation dealing with divorce, illegitimacy, the guardianship of children, and the responsibilities of parenthood to the disadvantage and detriment of women. How can we expect right living and an improvement in morals based upon such a foundation?[136]

Novick's concern is with the ways in which advanced nationalists constructed immorality and disease as propaganda tools against the British presence in Ireland.[137] Equally important, however, was the resistance offered by the feminist and labour press to these views as hiding reality, and their highlighting of the actual sexual crimes that were perpetrated by Irish men on women and children. Within the period 1900–22 there are complementary and competing discourses on the nature, causes and implications of sexual immorality in the country. In one discourse the problem lay with the English and the resolution was to achieve Irish independence from Britain, in the other women were both the source of the problem and its resolution. Both discourses were to run concurrently throughout the period but by the early 1920s the resolution of issues of immorality was vested in an anti-modernist stance that saw women as the single most important force in regenerating moral Irish society.[138]

One of the most prominent features of the women's suffrage campaign in twentieth-century Ireland was the use made of women's bodies for propaganda and political purposes. The new suffrage organisations, such as

Fig. 13. The Irish Party's Only Props in Longford (by-election poster, 1917). DK 17, folder 8, item 30, Department of Special Collections, Spencer Research Library, University of Kansas Libraries.

the Irish Women's Franchise League (IWFL) (1908), introduced a range of strategies that Irish women were able to use to develop their arguments for the franchise. More than ever Irish women now appeared on public platforms to argue their case. From 1912 the *Irish Citizen* became a central forum for the articulation of ideas about suffrage, citizenship, duties and rights, gender and sexuality in Irish society. *Tableaux vivants* became a significant feature of suffrage activity providing displays of feminine heroism. In November 1910 six IWFL members were imprisoned in England when they participated in protests organised by the WSPU.[139] In the summer of 1912 the IWFL decided to take militant action within Ireland, and on the morning of 13 June 1912 eight women threw stones through the windows of various government offices in Dublin and were arrested.[140] In prison many of the suffragettes went on hunger strike.[141] In December 1913, the Irish Women's Suffrage Federation sponsored a 'Suffrage Week' in Dublin.[142]

Irish women were physically present in the public consciousness in a way that had never before been witnessed by the Irish public. As O'Callaghan has argued, organisations such as the Gaelic League allowed a space for 'a new kind of socialising between men and women'.[143] In the early years of the twentieth century a cohort of intellectually powerful women 'operated in a variety of social and political networks'.[144] Women were publicly active in all the great movements of the period, including nationalism, labour politics and suffrage. Just as the courtroom became a key space, indeed a theatre, in which suffragettes made their cause public, so courts were, for many suffragists, the arena where crimes against the bodies of women and children remained unpunished, where men escaped justice. Women's oppression and sexual corruption went hand in hand. While discussions of sexuality in the suffrage press reveal an inherent fear of the abuse of women's bodies, suffragettes used their bodies through their willingness to be imprisoned and to hunger strike in ways that made them bodies of protest. In refusing to pay fines, by undergoing imprisonment, the Irish suffragettes used the court room as a space of protest and their bodies as a fundamental form of resistance to their lack of political recognition. At the same time women who went out with soldiers had traitorous bodies. They were individuals who needed to be warned away from the contaminating influence of these soldiers. Such warnings were given right throughout the period. Rosamond Jacob was to note in 1918 that, 'Mrs Phelan's daughter, Nan, was found to be going with a Navy man and was asked to explain it to Cumann na mBan or resign, so she resigned promptly with no explanation'.[145] 'Walking with soldiers' continued to be harshly treated by Irish republicans. Speaking to a friend in April 1919, Jacob was informed of the allegedly shocking state of the streets at night, and the suggested women's patrols and the bishops talking of course as if the girls did all the scandal by themselves . . . a man from Limerick boasted . . . how some young men there – Volunteers I think – caught 6 girls that had been walking with soldiers and cut their hair off for a punishment.[146]

From the early twentieth century soldiers now represented a major source of contamination. They could make Irish women disloyal and they were also a source of infection, venereal disease.

The black plague[147]

Venereal diseases remained a topic of debate and discussion in the medical journals of the early twentieth century. However, substantial advances had been made in their treatment. In 1906 the Wasserman test for syphilis was introduced. In 1909 the first successful specific for syphilis, Paul Ehrlich's Salvarsan ('606'), an arsenical preparation which caused several unpleasant side effects, was introduced.[148] Despite the advances made in the treatment of these diseases there was still very little public discussion of them in Ireland. The use of Salvarsan and its derivatives, and the knowledge available about the prevention of venereal diseases, did not lead to any great level of enlightenment on the issue; the 'scientific' camp still had to deal with the 'moral' camp.

In a lecture delivered to the Royal Academy of Medicine in Ireland in 1907 education, free dispensaries for men, notification and punishment were advocated as means to reduce the prevalence of the diseases.[149] Albina Brodrick, a staunch republican, read a paper at a nursing conference in Dublin in June, 1913, in which she argued that, 'here in Ireland we have the so-called National Health Association,[150] trying to get rid of TB, laudable in itself but it should be concerned equally with the Black Plague'. For Brodrick the only real protection against these diseases was knowledge. What was required was a course of instruction for young men and young women in the methods of defence against venereal diseases. What was needed in the 'first instance was clean living and clean mating, self-control and self-discipline'.[151] There were some reactions to Brodrick's paper from the medical profession in Ireland. Dr Ella Webb thought it a 'splendid thing' that the nursing profession should take up this issue. Susanne Day, suffragist and poor law guardian in Cork, stated that the cause of the disease rather than its effects needed fuller discussion. She observed that venereal disease was the result of prostitution, and this often originated in economic conditions. She argued that '80 per cent of women were on the streets through no wish of their own, but were driven there by grinding poverty'. She also noted that 95 per cent of the girls caught in the white slave traffic went into it innocently. 'Do not', Day said, 'issue red tickets to the woman who walks in the streets and let the man who pays her go free.'[152]

That the issue was one for suffragists to address became more evident with the publication of Christabel Pankhurst's work on the 'The Great Scourge'. A series of articles in the *Suffragette* accused promiscuous men of encouraging the spread of 'humanity's greatest scourge', infecting women knowingly, and thereby committing 'race suicide'. Pankhurst's solution was twofold: sexual abstinence until such time as the moral standards of the male changed, and women's suffrage: 'Votes for Women, Celibacy for Men'.[153] The most significant intervention in relation to venereal disease was to come from the Royal Commission on Venereal Disease which began its work on 19 November 1913, and produced its final report in February 1916.[154] By the time it reported, prostitution and venereal diseases had a very high public profile, due to the war. The terms of reference of the commission were:

to inquire into the prevalence of VD in the United Kingdom, their effects upon the health of the community, and the means by which these effects can be alleviated or prevented, it being understood that no return to the policy or provisions of the Contagious Diseases Acts of 1864, 1866, or 1869 is to be regarded as falling within the scope of the inquiry.[155]

A considerable amount of evidence was given to the commission regarding venereal diseases in Ireland. Dr Brian O'Brien, the chief medical inspector to the Irish local government board, stated that having visited various towns in Ireland he believed venereal disease had declined. In his opinion venereal disease, and he meant syphilis, was almost non-existent in rural Ireland, and uncommon in the smaller towns. When asked about the 'splendid result' of almost no syphilis being evident, O'Brien responded 'that there was very little immorality' in rural Ireland.[156] However, he remarked that gonorrhoea cases might not have declined.[157] He attributed the fact that syphilis had special prevalence in Dublin to poverty, bad housing, the tendency of 'girls who go wrong' to drift to the city and the fact that Dublin was a refuge for people 'who are doing no good for themselves'.[158] He also reported that there was some prevalence of the diseases in Belfast, and to a lesser extent in Cork.[159] Interestingly, he related how a doctor in Belfast had sixty-six consecutive women gynaecological patients attending the Ulster hospital for women and children tested for syphilis. Of the sixty-six, twenty-seven tested positive, which suggests that venereal disease rates might have been higher in Belfast than noted.[160] In O'Brien's view the treatment of the disease in Ireland was inadequate. He argued that the means for diagnosis and institutional treatment should be subsidised by the government and that outpatient departments in hospitals, where men might be treated, should stay open late in the evening. He doubted that women would be keen to seek treatment. Like many medical men he was opposed to the notification of the disease, believing that notification would put people off seeking treatment.[161] O'Brien also observed that many cases of syphilis were treated by chemists and that quack medicines were also available and advertised in the press. He believed that most of the quack medicines came from England and 'sold to a very considerable extent' in Ireland.[162] The sale of such items again puts a question mark over the perceived low incidence of venereal diseases in rural and urban Ireland and the value of O'Brien's views. Similarly, he observed that the great majority of women with venereal diseases were not treated in institutions and that some were not treated at all, particularly in the early stages of the disease.[163] It is possible then that many more women were infected with these diseases that turned up in the statistics.

Albinia Brodrick, representing the Irish Association and the National Council of Trained Nurses of Great Britain and Ireland, also gave evidence to the commission. She took the opportunity to reiterate her call for much greater public awareness of the disease and the necessity to 'treat the matter scientifically instead of as a mysterious something which cannot be talked about'. She also recommended sex education for children in schools, and condemned the practice of the medical profession of treating women without allowing them to know the nature of the disease. She believed that the disease should be notified.[164] The Registrar General of Ireland, Sir William Thompson, provided the commission with death rates for venereal disease in Dublin. He included deaths from syphilis, gonorrhoea and phagedema, but excluded deaths also associated with venereal diseases, such as those listed under locomotor staxy, genereal paralysis of the insane and aneurysm. The death rate per 10,000 was 0.76 for London, 0.51 for Belfast but 1.4 for Dublin.[165] Those giving evidence relating to Ireland argued that this level of infection was because Dublin was a seaport, had a large garrison, and a lock hospital which attracted women for treatment from outside the city. Another interesting statistic to emerge from the commission was that illegitimacy rates in Ulster, 3.5 per 1000 births, were much higher than for the rest of Ireland at 2.8. Among the reasons given for this was that there was a greater level of industrialisation in Ulster that attracted young women, and that it was the only province in Ireland where women outnumbered men.[166]

The report of the Royal Commission reflected official concern over venereal disease. The links between the consumption of alcohol, sexual activity and the spread of disease were noted, and it was estimated that not less than 10 per cent of the population in the larger cities, as many as 3 million people, were infected with the diseases. The report emphasised the need for education, but concluded that no practical legislation could prevent the spread of disease among single or sexually promiscuous people. It also noted that many victims were not infected through immoral means, in other words prostitution was not the only or even principal means by which the disease spread. In May 1917, Parliament, acting on one of the committee's recommendations, outlawed the treatment of vene-real disease by anyone except qualified medical personnel. Efforts to check the spread of venereal diseases became of 'paramount national impor-tance' in England as well as in Ireland.[167] The Royal Commission pro-posed, and the government later implemented, a number of measures considered necessary to halt the spread of venereal diseases. These propos-als included the extension of facilities for diagnosis by laboratory methods, a programme of instruction in secondary schools, and that the larger local authorities should, subject to the approval of the LGB, organise free treat-ment, if at all possible in general hospitals. Three-quarters of the expendi-ture incurred would be borne by the national exchequer. There was to be no element of compulsion to enter into treatment, except in the case of prisoners, poor law inmates, lunatics and servicemen. Notification was dis-missed for the time being as impractical because it might encourage the concealment of the disease. The immediate solution was medical, not moral or social. In Ireland the establishment of treatment centres, rather than education, became the preferred solution to the treatment of venereal disease. That solution was not, however, without controversy.[168]

The report of the Royal Commission was not widely publicised in Ireland but it was certainly referred to on a number of occasions. The *Irish Citizen*, noting the evidence of Sir William Thompson, observed that Dublin 'has attained an evil pre-eminence . . . we trust we shall hear no more of the suggestions that venereal disease is a subject not to be spoken about or written about in Ireland'.[169] It suggested that Christabel Pankhurst's book on venereal disease should 'be in the hands of every suffragist in Ireland'. The immediate consequence of the report was a campaign to implement its recommendations. A newspaper report on 'Cry of the children: the baby week campaign' discussed the death rates among children, particularly illegitimate children, and the president of the Royal College of Physicians in Ireland was quoted as saying that 'another factor intimately associated with the appalling death rate was venereal disease'.[170]

As early as December 1916, at a public meeting of the medical profes-sion of Belfast, a motion was passed calling on the LGB of Ireland to act on the recommendations of the Royal Commission,[171] and the following month a branch of the National Council for Combating Venereal Diseases was formed in that city. Present at the inaugural meeting was the Lord

Bishop of Down, and the Moderator of the General Assembly of the Presbyterian Church, both of whom supported the organisation of the branch in the city.[172] By February the committee were urging the LGB to implement the recommendations of the Royal Commission.[173] In March it was organising a course of lectures for teachers, social workers and nurses and arranging a conference for clergy on the issue of the moral impact of venereal diseases.[174] Not all Churches approved of these methods. In April 1917 a resolution from the non-subscribing Presbyterian Church of Ireland was forwarded to the British Medical Association noting:

We protest against members of the medical profession degrading their profession by providing men with information or appliances which may enable them to consort with immoral women without fear of contracting disease; or by teaching people of either sex the method of preventing conception. We implore medical men to assist the teachers of religion and morals in the campaign against vice and disease.[175]

In October 1917 the LGB for Ireland finally issued regulations which required local councils to submit proposals for treatment schemes.[176] There was, however, considerable opposition to these proposals. A correspondent to the *Irish Independent* warned that the government was going to set up a venereal disease treatment centre in Dublin to which they proposed to send over men from England suffering from all forms of the diseases. 'This', he emphasised, 'is more than we can be expected to tolerate without protest.'[177] At Easter ceremonies in the Derry diocese, a resolution was passed emphatically protesting against the establishment of hospitals 'for the treatment of a most degrading disease within the diocese', and called on the people to oppose the proposal. The idea of such an establishment was considered 'an insult to the fair face of the country'.[178] A campaign of publicity was instituted in the north of Ireland by the National Council for Combating VD in 1917. They distributed pamphlets and had a paid organiser who delivered lectures. It was later reported that the campaign received 'scanty support'. Open opposition was not evident until the organiser visited Derry where the Catholic bishop 'declared his objections to the carrying out of the National Council's propaganda in this manner in his diocese'. A subsequent proposal to transfer the lecturer's activities to other parts of the country was 'not encouraged' by the Irish LGB.[179] The bishop of Cork and his priests in conference in 1918 passed a resolution calling attention to the terrible evil of young girls going to Queenstown for 'purposes of vice', reminding parents to exercise vigilance over their daughters, appealing to the girls to esteem the 'fair name of Irish womanhood for purity', and warning them of the risk of contracting a 'loathsome' disease. Regarding a rumour that the government contemplated the establishment of a hospital for syphilis on Spike Island, the conference protested strongly against such a move and explained that 'it is nothing short of an outrage to establish in our midst an hospital for treating English and other patients afflicted with this loathsome and most dangerous disease of syphilis, caused by sexual vice'.[180]

On 11 December 1917 the Abbey Theatre in Dublin presented a three-act play by Oliver St John Gogarty entitled *Blight (the Tragedy of Dublin)*. This was one of the few plays to deal with tenement life and slum conditions in Dublin in the period. The play focuses on a family living in a one-room tenement, with the absent father fighting with the British army in France. The eldest daughter, Lily, is a prostitute, having given up poorly paid work in a laundry. A local social worker, Miss Maxwell-Knox, is in the room one evening as Lily prepares to go to 'work' and admonishes her for her occupation. Maxwell-Knox informs Lily that the 'wages of sin is death'. Lily retorts that 'the wages of sin is a month in the Locke'.[181] Gogarty, as a medical student and doctor, was familiar with the conditions in which the poorest of Dublin's residents lived. The play presents both prostitution and venereal disease as serious problems. Lily does not appear again until alluded to at the end of the play. She has ended up in the lock hospital and a number of medical students discuss how syphilis can be eradicated. 'Medical Dick' observes that the disease is not properly dealt with because 'of our imported hypocrisy and because we haven't the courage to face the facts; because we won't realise that prevention is better than cure, because charity must prey on suffering; because we mix morals even in our medicine'.[182] It was most often members of the medical profession who accepted the reality of venereal disease in Ireland; most others could not conceive of it as an Irish problem.

The medical profession could, nevertheless, be difficult about the attempts made by the various local councils to implement treatment schemes. Often this was merely an effort to ensure that members of the profession were instrumental in any decisions made about providing treatment, and that they were properly paid for any services carried out. In 1917 the Ulster Medical Society wrote to the secretary of Antrim County Council observing that 'it is inadvisable that any public health scheme for the treatment of venereal disease shall be adopted until it is first placed before the medical profession'.[183] Armagh, Antrim and the Borough of Belfast had schemes in place by February 1918. When councillors in County Tyrone declared that the disease was virtually unknown in the countryside, Dr Thompson informed them tartly that 'there is a great deal of this disease that you know nothing about, but I do'.[184] A poster prepared by Belfast Council to advertise treatment centres was, however, criticised by Thompson on the grounds that the design, in lurid blue and red, 'savoured of hysteria and the gutter and I think official language might be more restrained without losing in effect'.[185] Others predicted that if the poster were put up in public places it would be 'cut and disfigured, and probably pulled down'.[186] However, it appears that the posters were eventually displayed and by May 1918 the president of the Royal Irish Academy of Medicine, Sir William Thompson, who had given evidence to the Royal Commission, believed he could detect a substantial change in public opinion 'with regard to the treatment of patients' suffering from these diseases and hoped that this would lead to a great improvement in public health.[187]

The reluctance of local authorities to take action continued to hamper efforts to extend treatment schemes across the country. Noting that treatment centres in Ireland had 12,785 outpatient attendances and 15,791 inpatient days in 1919,[188] the annual report of the LGB highlighted the

undesirable prevalence which is manifested chiefly, but by no means confined to, the large centres of population. The areas served are broadly speaking along the east coast and some distance inland but in view of the dangers it is obviously desirable to extend the system elsewhere, particularly along the lines of traffic, and in large centres of population, especially seaports. The Board have exerted their efforts accordingly, but have not met with the desired success. This is partly due to the reluctance of County Infirmary authorities to afford the required facilities.[189]

By 1922 schemes had been initiated in Dublin, Louth, Kildare, Monaghan, Westmeath and Wicklow. There was still no scheme in Cork County Borough and schemes in Louth and Westmeath had fallen 'into abeyance'.[190]

Venereal disease as an issue was taken up by a number of suffragists, feminists and nationalists in Ireland. After the release of the Royal Commission's report but before the enactment of the legislation in 1917, a group of women in England launched a letter-writing campaign demanding official notification and compulsory treatment of both men and women.[191] In Ireland suffragists became involved in the issue, supporting calls for public education on the matter, and notification. The Dublin Watch Committee and Cumann na dTeachaire (the Association of Women Delegates, which was affiliated with Sinn Féin) held two meetings in Dublin in January and February 1918 to discuss the subject of venereal disease. Believing the issue to be one of immense seriousness for Ireland the groups organised a conference of Irish women's societies 'to discuss the best measures to be adopted to combat this evil'. The conference was held on 19 March 1918.[192] Representatives from the Irish Women's Franchise League, the Irish Women's Reform League, Cumann na mBan, the Dublin Watch Committee and the IWWU attended the meeting.[193] A committee was established to campaign on the issue of educating the Irish public about these diseases, and ensuring that county councils would implement the treatment schemes advocated by the Royal Commission. At a later meeting it was agreed that the educational element to combat venereal disease was the prime motivation of the committee. Miss Mosher, of the Dublin Watch Committee, urged 'that all should join the watch committee in its efforts to have established in Dublin a branch of the Society for Combating the spread of VD'. Instead, the committee reformed itself into the Irish Society for Combating the Spread of VD, which was, it declared, aware of the implications, not the result of 'any antagonism towards the English society but [the conviction] that the matter was urgent and could be more quickly dealt with by these means'.[194] A further discussion on syphilitic babies ensued and the committee resolved 'that syphilitic infants be removed from families boarded out and treated in hospitals under the Children's Act'.[195] From this discussion of syphilitic babies the idea for a special hospital to deal with such infants arose. Eventually a house was found in Charlemont Street in Dublin and opened in November 1918.[196]

By May 1918 the committee had tellingly renamed itself Cóiste Cosanta na hÉireann ó Áicid na hAinméine (Committee for the Preservation of Ireland from VD). Even more interestingly it had decided to use an abbreviated form of the name, Coiste Cosanta na hÉireann, which left out the reference to venereal disease. The aim of the organisation was declared to be to combat the spread of the diseases in Ireland which it was considered 'so likely to occur from the presence of troops coming back from the front';[197] a leafleting and lobbying campaign followed. In a pamphlet published by Sinn Féin, Dr Kathleen Lynn and Richard Hayes argued that the responsibility for the diseases lay with the British army, and demanded that every soldier returning to Ireland should be tested for them. They estimated that 15,000 of the returning 100,000 troops would have syphilis and that it would be 'a national sin' if the Irish people allowed these men to infect 'thousands of yet unborn Irish children . . . with the stigma of this foulest and most shameful of diseases'. They rejected the attempt to 'saddle the Irish public boards with the responsibility of coping with this evil'. It was instead the responsibility of the British state.[198] From about August 1918 the committee appears to have become inactive, except in the matter of opening the infant hospital.[199] Concern about venereal disease became muted after the crisis of 1918 passed.[200] It was a subject that could never garner much public support and was of interest to the public and of value to the propagandists only in a symbolic way. It was not until the mid-1920s that it became a problematic issue again in Ireland.

There were two other issues which caught the attention of feminists in Ireland by 1917 and which can be dealt with briefly here; the Criminal Law

Amendment Act, and Regulation 40D. The Criminal Law Amendment Bill was introduced into Parliament in February 1917. The Bill focused on regulating sexual behaviour with a particular emphasis on controlling venereal disease. Under this law it would have been illegal for any woman or man to knowingly infect an individual with a venereal disease. Many believed that clause 2, which suggested the measure would apply equally to men and women, was disingenuous and assumed that it would apply to women only. The Bill was objected to on many grounds and suggestions for amendments allowed it to get bogged down. Speaking on the second reading of the Bill, John Dillon, leader of the Irish Parliamentary Party, observed that it was a 'bad specimen of . . . legislation'.[201] In March 1918 regulation 40D made it a criminal offence for any woman with venereal disease to solicit or have sexual relations with a member of the armed forces. Writing about the regulation, Rosamond Jacob revealed how entwined her feminist and nationalist views had become:

I went to an IWFL meeting . . . concerned entirely with the introduction of a part of CD acts in the interests of soldiers. It appears that a woman can get six months now for communicating disease to a soldier or sailor, under regulation 40D of DORA and the soldiers' mere word is enough to convict her unless she is willing to be examined to prove that she is not diseased. Also her name is always published whether she is proved innocent or guilty and the soldier's name is never published. They say hundreds of innocent women have been victimised under this regulation in England let alone those who were not innocent, and a woman in Belfast got six months without apparently any further proof than the word of a profligate soldier. Mrs Connery spoke first, then Miss Cahalan, and then a rather objectionable woman with an English accent, and a Miss Moser of the Dublin Watch committee, who spoke of our England, which we always thought was such a land of liberty. I told Mrs Connery afterwards that she should warn her not to talk like that again, and she said she had been got to speak only because Mrs Wyse Power failed to turn up and they had tried to get a speaker from the Women Delegates too, but none was sent. Dorothy Evans also spoke, and was less offensive than Miss Moser.[202]

Almost immediately a huge range of organisations began to exert pressure on the government to revoke the regulation. The Association for Moral and Social Hygiene, cooperating with the [Belfast] Women's Political League,[203] the Irishwomen's Reform League and other groups protested strongly against the measure.[204] Sylvia Pankhurst argued that women would be victimised over false allegations of solicitation and the communication of venereal diseases.[205] The *Irish Citizen* maintained that the regulation 'largely increases the danger of disease by giving men a false sense of security, while it constitutes an outrage in the honour and self-respect of women and is the gravest possible menace to their individual liberty'.[206] John Dillon could not recall 'a more scandalous act of executive government . . . nobody who voted for the Defence of the Realm Act ever dreamed it would be perverted to such uses as that'.[207] The very effective protest campaign ensured that the regulation was rescinded and it was dropped in November 1918.

The issue of venereal disease was much used by advanced Irish nationalists to denigrate the British soldier in Ireland and the returning soldier from the front. Feminists and suffragists, many of whom were also nationalists, used the venereal disease scare to argue for the franchise and viewed the campaign over regulation 40D in similar terms to the CDAs campaign. While the prostitute figured to some extent in these debates and campaign, she was not the central figure. For advanced nationalists the central contaminating figure was the British soldier. For suffragists and feminists the central figure was an authoritarian and increasingly alien government. Prostitutes were still to be found on the streets of Ireland's larger towns and cities, but from the end of the First World War she was to be joined by a new figure who came to symbolise a more degraded form of sexual immorality, the amateur. An information leaflet on venereal disease published in Ireland in 1919, while it placed some responsibility on men for the contraction of the disease, stated that 'syphilis was common among prostitutes, and among girls and women who, while not chaste, cannot be called prostitutes'.[208] The Phoenix Park in Dublin had been for many years a notorious meeting place for prostitutes, but by 1920 the authorities were noting that 'very many acts of immorality, etc., . . . take place in the Park in which women, who are not professional prostitutes, are concerned and of whom neither police forces (RIC and DMP) would have any knowledge'.[209] An article in the *Dublin Journal of Medical Science* warned that disease would increase after the war mainly because of the 'amateur'.[210] The author claimed that two-thirds of all cases of venereal diseases were 'infected by women of the "amateur" class'.[211] The figure of the amateur was to become even more significant from the establishment of the Irish Free State, when issues of prostitution, disease and unmarried mothers shaped the ways in which women were perceived in the newly independent state.

6 'Hopeless cases': prostitution and sexual danger in the Irish Free State, 1922–40

Contrary to popular perception there is ample evidence to show that there was considerable discussion of sexuality in Ireland in the 1920s and 1930s. Within the sphere of government the printed, but unpublished *Report of the Interdepartmental Committee of Inquiry Regarding Venereal Disease* (1926), and the *Report of the Committee on the Criminal Law Amendment Acts (1880–85) and Juvenile Prostitution* (1931), known as the Carrigan Committee report, offer extensive and complex accounts of perceived sexual activity throughout the country and the fears raised by that activity. Other publications include *The Report of the Committee on Evil Literature* (1927) and the *Report of the Commission on the Relief of the Sick and Destitute Poor* (1927). The Inter-Departmental Ad-Hoc Committee on the Suppression of Prostitution (1947–8), whose findings were again unpublished, provides much information on the 1920s and 1930s.[1] Through these reports and investigative committees, concerns were raised about illegitimacy, unmarried mothers, the apparent spread of venereal diseases, prostitution, levels of sexual crime, deviancy and the dangers of sociability, the latter particularly reflected in dancehalls and the motor car, which appeared to offer possibilities for unrestricted mixing of the sexes. Throughout the period earthy newspaper accounts of sexual crime,[2] the extensive publication of clerical sermons and pamphlets about immorality and about the dangers of sex reinforced public concern about sexual morality. Despite the reticence of a number of Teachtaí Dála (Members of the Irish Parliament) and Senators some of these issues even found public expression in the Dáil and Seanad. Both the state and the Church emphatically presented women's place as being in the home and the ideal role of the Irish woman was as mother. The idealisation of motherhood was a significant feature of the rhetoric of politicians in the new Irish state; the female body and the maternal body, particularly in its unmarried condition, became a central focus of concern to the state and the Catholic Church.

Women's place in Irish society and politics in the 1920s and 1930s has received some attention from historians.[3] Maryann Valiulis, in a number of important articles, analyses the language of political debate in Ireland to explore how women were excluded from political life in the 1920s and 1930s. Among the strategies used by male politicians to prevent women from exercising certain rights of citizenship, were the limitations placed on their right to sit on juries. Valiulis argues that 'purity was primarily cast as a woman's responsibility' and was a primary characteristic of the ideal Irish woman.[4] The 'ideal' Irishwoman was the means by which the Catholic Church could limit the impact of modernisation, and save the 'traditional way of life'.[5] Valiulis creates a strong case to reveal the ideology of Catholicism and its views on gender in this period. Sandra McAvoy explores the regulation of sexuality in this period, and argues that 'as Ireland was in the process of adapting to independence, sexuality became a focus for a paternalistic Church and government in their efforts to construct a stable, Catholic society'.[6] The strength of the alliance between Church and state, and the attention paid to morality, has been ably studied by John Whyte. Whyte demonstrates how the interest in sexual morality was evident in the pre-World War I years but became a cause for major concern from the 1920s.[7] In this present study the focus is on how both the Church and the state constructed the sexuality of young women as dangerous, and conflated unmarried mothers, sexually active young women and prostitution as a way of controlling the sexuality of all women.

As we have seen the politicisation of sexual behaviour had been a feature of Irish nationalism from the late nineteenth century, evident most strongly in the equation of the British garrison with a source of moral and physical contagion for Irishwomen. Problems were to arise when, with the British garrison gone, levels of sexual immorality appeared to rise rather than decrease in the new state. Commenting on prostitution in 1924, Richard S. Devane, SJ, evangelical in his concern with sexual immorality, observed that as long as the British garrison was 'in Dublin it was impossible to deal with prostitution effectively. Now a new order has opened up, and things can be done with comparative ease, quite impossible before.'[8] However, what was to emerge from the early 1920s was a belief, strongly evident in the various reports mentioned above, and in clerical and public discussion of sexuality, that the real threat to chastity and sexual morality resided in the bodies of women. Thus moral regulation, by Church and state, attempted to impose standards of idealised conduct, particularly on women, that would return the nation to purity.

Sermons – many reprinted in the press – and pamphlets abounded with views on how women should express or repress their sexuality. The bishop of Limerick, Dr Denis Hallinan, in a 1919 letter to the press, noted that the Pope had recently dwelt on 'one of the great evils of the time – the immodest fashions in women's dress'.[9] It was noted with horror in 1930 that 'even in the heart of the Gaeltacht some concession had been made to foreign fashions in dress'.[10] A 1926 sermon by the Rev. Dr Gilmartin, archbishop of Tuam, declared that 'there was a time in Ireland when the prevailing type of woman was the sister of Mary Immaculate, but, unfortunately in recent times there has been a kind of falling off. There was a time in Ireland when the dress was modest. In recent times, however, there is a bordering on the indecent.' He was further to note that, 'the future of the country is bound up with the dignity and purity of the women of Ireland'. Gilmartin prayed for the return of 'a holy and Catholic Ireland – an Ireland of brave, manly boys, an Ireland of pure, modest girls – an Ireland of honest toil, an Ireland of happy marriages'.[11] Again in 1926 Justice O'Brien delivered a lecture on women at the Catholic Truth Society conference in which he noted that Irishwomen 'heretofore renowned for their virtue and honour, go about furnished with the paint pot, the lip-stick, and the rest of a meretricious armoury, and many of them had acquired the habit of intemperance, perhaps one of the sequels of their lately adopted vogue of smoking'.[12] The Jesuit Michael Garahy published, as a pamphlet, a series of Lenten lectures that he had delivered in the church of St Francis Xavier in Upper Gardiner Street Dublin in 1922. The title of his sermons was 'Idols of modern society', where he explored the 'menace of materialism', the 'collapse of chastity' and 'godless education', among other issues.[13] Where materialism triumphs, Garahy noted, 'sexual vice, with all the evils that follow in its train, is spreading like a prairie fire . . . in the great centres of progress the streets swarm with harlots'.[14] Expressions of concern about women's place in public life were also evident in this period. There was considerable anxiety about women's roles in the fight for independence. Cardinal Logue saw women's involvement in the civil war, 'this wild orgy of violence and destruction', as a sure means of reducing their reputation for modesty, innocence and piety.[15] Issues relating to women and work, and their role in politics caused uneasiness in government and Church circles. The *Irish Independent* noted in 1925 that there were 'mothers who preferred the fashionable and crowded thoroughfare to their own quiet home; there were mothers who preferred talking on a platform or in a crowded council chamber to chatting to their children in a nursery'.[16] It was a clear message that such pursuits were 'unnatural' and unsuited to the role of women as wives and mothers.

While there was much public discussion of sexual immorality in the press of the period the *Freeman's Journal* also initiated a 'crusade against vice'. It was concerned with the moral dangers faced by the youth of the country and particularly urged Irish mothers to take care of their daughters.[17] The paper also tried, unsuccessfully, to revive the 'white slavery'

scare[18] and declared that if the police could not control 'the menace to
public morals' then the community must 'take matters into its own
hands'.[19] While these concerns – particularly over clothing – might
appear trivial, what was evident from the early 1920s was a focus on
women, whose appearance and presence in public life was deemed to
have upset the moral order or had the potential to continue to upset that
order. The danger to Irish survival and renewal became centred on the
form of debased womanhood. Some women were debased through sexual
immorality, others through their desire to have public careers. The
redemption of chaste reproductive sexuality was prescribed as the anti-
dote to moral bankruptcy: women must return to the home, to the
domestic sphere. While England and its culture might be the source of
moral corruption, once independence was achieved the focus on women,
and their moral regenerative powers, became central to the idea of the
Irish nation.

Evidence of this concern was particularly clear in one aspect of
immorality that caused anxiety in the government and the Catholic
Church, the unmarried mother. Both the state and the Church emphatically presented women's place as being in the home and the ideal role of
the Irish woman who was not to become a nun was as a mother.
Throughout the 1920s, and later, conflicting representations of unmarried mothers abounded. They were seen as innocent victims or corrupting agents, they were 'poor girls' or potential blackmailers. They brought
'shame' to the nation and to their families. Uneasiness about the apparent
rise in the numbers of unmarried mothers forced the state and the
Catholic Church to implement policies to stem illegitimacy and attempt
to control behaviour. While the state and the Church chose to care for
unmarried mothers and their children, they consistently evoked the oblig-
ation of the mother to support her child.[20]

The issue of unmarried mothers, a problem for welfare workers from
the late nineteenth century, came to light primarily through levels of illegitimacy, although official statistics for illegitimate births were low
throughout the period of the Irish Free State. In 1922 the birth rate for
illegitimate children was officially described as 'less than that recorded for
most other countries'.[21] For 1921–3, such births amounted to 2.6 per
cent of all births in the twenty-six counties.[22] The average illegitimate
birth rate per annum between 1920 and 1930 was deemed to be 1,706.[23]
Between 1926 and 1929 the numbers of such births had risen from 1,716
to 1,853, revealing a gradual increase in each intervening year. The
members of the Committee on the Criminal Law Amendment Act,
reflecting the voices of 'concerned citizens' and some members of the
government, found this rise worrying and believed that illegitimacy was

increasing throughout the country at an 'unprecedented rate'.[24] In 1926 the secretary of the Committee for the Reform of the Laws Relating to the Protection of Women and Young Girls alerted the Minister for Justice to the fact that the rescue societies were almost overwhelmed 'so much has the number of unmarried mothers increased during the last few years'.[25] What was more worrying to the members of the Carrigan Committee was the fact that illegitimacy levels were rising in social conditions that had stabilised after a period of civil strife. There was also a strong belief that unregistered births of illegitimate children possibly exceeded those registered.

The rise in illegitimacy levels was attributed to a loss of parental control and responsibility during the period of the war of independence and civil war. That parental control, it was argued, had never been restored. Moral laxity was seen to be a result of the prevalence of 'commercialised dance-halls, picture houses . . . and the opportunities afforded by the misuse of motor cars for luring girls.'[26] From the mid-1920s and throughout the early 1930s there were constant references in the newspapers to the problems of dancehalls and motor cars. In 1931 Cardinal McRory combined the two and saw a growing evil in 'the parking of cars close to dancehalls in badly lighted village streets or on dark country roads. Cars so placed are used . . . by young people for sitting out in the intervals between dances.'[27] 'Joy-riding' had a very different connotation in that period than it does now. Reporting on a sermon by the bishop of Galway, in language reminiscent of the white slave debate, the *Irish Independent* noted that 'joy-riding' was conducted by

Evil men – demons in human form come from outside the parish and outside the city – to indulge in this practice. They lure girls from the town to go for motor drives into the country, and you know what happens . . . it is not for the benefit of the motor drive. It is for something infinitely worse.[28]

The Report of the Committee on the Criminal Law Amendment Acts (the Carrigan Committee report) noted that solicitation was an 'offence very rife in Dublin . . . being practiced by men in motor cars who patrol the streets, stopping here and there to invite young women to whom they are unknown to accompany them for a drive'.[29]

Dancehalls were clearly sites of corruption; dancing could be sexually charged, and the presence of alcohol made the possibilities more frightening. In 1924 in one of the many published sermons by various bishops, the bishop of Galway and Kilmacduagh warned that dances were 'importations from the vilest dens of London, Paris and New York – direct and unmistakeable incitements to evil thoughts, evil desires, and the grossest acts of impurity'.[30] In 1925 the Irish Catholic Hierarchy issued 'a grave and solemn warning to the people with regard to the spiritual dangers associated with dancing'.[31] According to the bishops' statement, the proliferation of dancehalls had caused 'many a good, innocent girl into sin, shame, and scandal, and set the unwary feet on the road that leads to perdition'[32]. The 'warning' appears to have had little effect.[33] One judge observed in 1931 that an unsupervised Saturday dance was 'little better than a saturnalia'.[34] Jazz dancing was particularly targeted. In 1935 Bishop James McNamee of Ardagh and Clonmacnoise warned young Irish men and women to avoid 'these Negroid importations, earthly, sensual, and devilish, which are and were intended to be direct incitements to sensuality and sinful passion'.[35] Just like the 'white slavery' issue the 'stranger' was the figure of fear lurking behind and within the dancehall. This was most often someone from an urban area who made his way into a rural dance to seduce the naive local girls. This idea of the predatory stranger survived after the implementation of the Dance Halls Act in 1935. A judge in County Meath told all applicants for dancehall licences that in future permits would be denied unless cars could be kept away from the halls and he also suggested that 'strangers', or men from outside the area, had to be sponsored by someone of standing in the community before they could attend a dance.[36] Dangers lurked in cars, in dancehalls, in country lanes, in city streets, even in newspaper reports themselves. Providing the full address of a 'refreshment house' in Dublin where 'women of loose character' were allowed to assemble, for example, might very well have been good for the proprietor's business.[37] The legal regulation of recreation and recreational spaces was deemed, together with supervisory vigilance, to be the means by which appropriate behaviour at such venues could be ensured. For the Church, the state and many welfare workers, the way forward was to introduce legislation that would raise the age of consent, or introduce harsher punishments for solicitation, or regulate the dancehalls in a stricter way.[38] After considerable pressure from the Catholic clergy, the public Dance Halls Act was passed in February 1935. The new law, however, was rather different from the one expected. It relied on the wisdom of local judges in licensing dancehalls and led to confusion about how to interpret the Act. The discretion allowed to local judges saw the Act implemented in very different ways around the country. Devane was less than pleased with the legislation and encouraged 'concerned citizens' to challenge the renewal of dancehall licences whenever they could.[39] The implementation of the legislation revealed that many judges were not willing to defer to the Catholic Church on legal matters. For instance, against the wishes of the local Catholic clergy, who were represented at a licensing case in Tramore, Judge McCabe allowed dances on Sundays.[40] The cinema, of course, offered another major problem for the policing of morality. Again, it was women who were deemed most vulnerable to the message of the films. For some clerics, films were more insidious than evil literature. Fr Mageean observed in 1930 that films presented 'vice in its most seductive form', and catered to all that was 'erotic and abnormal in life'.[41]

Much of the discussion around young women, and the sexual dangers they faced, was informed by new psychological theories of adolescence. The interwar years were a period when adolescence came to be viewed as a critical time in the development of young people, and it was seen as a particularly crucial stage in the development of young women.[42] Devane, who had clearly been reading some of this new literature on adolescence, described a girl's adolescence as 'the time when her inordinate and her uncontrollable desire for admiration leads her unconsciously into very grave danger, the significance of which she does not by any means appreciate'.[43] The behaviour of adolescent women needed to be managed and controlled if they were to successfully survive the passage into mature adulthood. Devane again observed that in dealing with adolescent girls he had

consulted several women who had, each, many years experience of dealing intimately with growing girls of different kinds, in orphanage, industrial school, secondary school, sodality and Good Shepherd Convent. All agreed that danger was greatest at 16 or thereabouts, when the girl was a seething mass of emotion.[44]

He observed that 'even educated and observant fathers . . . cannot appreciate the growing girl's emotional nature and as a consequence her instability and abnormality'. As we will see below, in the 1920s and 1930s there were calls to increase the age of consent. Individuals such as Devane, and many of the witnesses to the Carrigan Committee, used the idea of adolescent instability to strengthen their calls for greater protection for girls.[45]

Unmarried mothers

The state and the Church identified unmarried mothers as a particular danger to the moral condition of the nation. In 1922 Sagart,[46] writing in the *Irish Ecclesiastical Record*, remarked on the need to deal with this issue. 'This whole subject', he wrote, 'is of extreme importance, concerning as it does the preservation of a strict standard of moral life in the nation, and the saving from utter ruin of the faith and morality of so many Catholic girls.'[47] He called for the views of priests on this subject and even more significantly on the views of Catholic lawyers, suggesting that legal measures might be necessary to deal with the problem.[48] For some commentators the moral consideration was outweighed by the possibility of proselytism. There was a considerable concern that expectant, unmarried, Catholic mothers might take assistance from Protestant agencies. These agencies, seen as soupers, 'bribe her . . . to violate her conscience, and to commit what she knows is a heinous sin'.[49] The Rev. M. H. McInerny, who wrote on the issue of souperism (the use of food relief as a means of religious proselytisation), regarded Protestant visitors to workhouses as 'proselytising prowlers', and he saw the private maternity homes as 'the happy hunting grounds for proselytisers'.[50] The 1923 annual report of the Catholic Protection and Rescue Society remarked, again in language reminiscent of 'white slavery', that 'the extent of this vile traffic . . . in human souls is not realised by Catholics, as these enemies of the faith work in secret; but all good Catholic social workers know how widespread is the evil, and that constant vigilance is required to protect the Irish poor'.[51] The protection offered to unmarried mothers by Catholic organisations was required to save their souls, their morals and the reputation of the nation. This could only be carried through by the provision of Catholic services to these women.

From 1922, as we have seen, religious communities of nuns established and staffed homes specifically targeted at unmarried mothers.[52] There was still the obsession with classifying these 'immoral' women. Sometimes attitudes to 'first' offenders were not harsh. They were depicted as unfortunate rather than immoral. One enlightened commentator noted that

the problem of unmarried mothers should be dealt with from the stand-point that they are entitled to take their place in ordinary life without any disability attaching to them as a result of their offence: and any child should get every opportunity to understand and appreciate the family life.[53]

Another, noting the availability of birth control methods or 'scientific vices', suggested that it was only the 'frail, ignorant girl, often mentally deficient, and always weak-willed who finds herself pregnant'. The lack of sexual knowledge revealed by a woman who became pregnant showed that she was 'not bad'. This was someone who needed to be taken in hand immediately to ensure a successful recovery of virtue.[54] Both the state and the Church approved of the 'hopeful cases' being cared for in institutions set aside for that purpose and, ideally, these were to be managed by nuns. For this group treatment was to be

in the nature of moral upbringing and, while requiring firmness and discipline, must be characterised by and blended with a certain amount of individual charity and sympathy which can only be given when a true estimate of the character of each girl or young woman has been made by those in charge.[55]

The fear expressed for these 'first' offenders was that they might fall into prostitution. Devane argued that 'it is well known that the ranks of the unfortunates are largely filled from such as these who have become mothers, and afterwards have almost automatically drifted onto the streets'. They needed the protection of the law, as he saw them being unable to protect themselves.[56] Early intervention was the best way of rescuing them from such a fate. For some commentators this was also a class issue. Devane identified women from working-class backgrounds as being in particular danger. It was the 'ignorant, the innocent, or the silly girl, who is forced to go out to make a living in conditions dangerous to her virtue, whether she be a domestic, or farm hand, or shop assistant, [who] should be safeguarded against her own inexperience and the insinuating advances of dangerous men'.[57] With regard to unmarried mothers Hugh Kennedy observed in a Dáil debate on affiliation orders that there are 'mothers who themselves are illegitimate, who come of an illegitimate stock, and who observe no moral code whatever, but are bred in the art of blackmail'.[58]

How were the 'less hopeful cases' to be dealt with? Issues of classification were again paramount, as they had been in the nineteenth century. The authorities and experts in the field believed it essential to separate the 'first offenders' from the 'less hopeful cases'. The issue of the 'second' or 'third' fall posed particular difficulties for a sympathetic representation of unmarried motherhood. The Commission for the Relief of the Sick and Indigent Poor provided very clear recommendations about what was to happen to these 'intractable' girls, suggesting that, where an unmarried mother applied for relief during or after a first pregnancy, it should be possible to detain her for up to one year. If the woman was to be admitted on a second pregnancy, she should be retained for two years; if she was being admitted for a third or subsequent pregnancy, she should be detained until it was considered suitable for her to return to society.[59] Though such recommendations never became legal requirements, this stance allowed for the development of an attitude that accepted detention as a means of protecting society from these re-offending women. A type of 'moral punishment' was advocated by Devane who made explicit the necessity to impress on unmarried mothers the nature of their 'sin'. He suggested that unmarried mothers who had their babies in workhouses should have the opportunity to immediately go on retreat after the event. To ensure a reformation of character and to

help towards the reformation of the girl it is not only very desirable, but in a sense necessary, that she should be deeply impressed with her sin, so that . . . her sin should, in the future, be always before her. The merely natural shame and disgrace will soon pass away when the child is placed at nurse; the only real deterrent will be to bring the *spiritual side of her fall* before the girl, and impress her in no superficial way with the guilt of her sin, and leave her with an abiding memory and sorrow.[60]

Re-offenders were also deemed to be 'mentally defective'. The inspector of boarded out children noted in her annual report of 1932 that many of these re-offenders were

Of weak intellect and completely lacking in moral fibre . . . A grave wrong is done to their children by maintaining them in the county homes, but retention is the only means of securing their mothers from the danger which freedom spells upon them. It is a question of whether a graver social wrong is not committed by allowing these women their freedom, since freedom, to them, will undoubtedly mean the birth of another child whose chances of average health and intelligence are small. I have no solution to offer except one which is repugnant to me, that is, the power of detention in special cases, which would allow boarding out of the children and at the same time keeping their mothers under control and discipline.[61]

The less hopeful cases presented images of contagion. Those unmarried mothers who 'offended' more than once offered tangible evidence of sexual transgression. It seemed imperative to categorise these women according to their level of sexual experience or knowledge in order to protect more innocent girls from corruption. These were women whose sexuality had to be managed and contained. The Commission on the Relief of the Sick and Indigent Poor recommended detention for repeat 'offenders' as a way to 'regulate control according to individual requirements, or in the most degraded cases to segregate those who have become sources of evil, danger, and expense to the community'.[62] What appears to have happened is that some of these 'repeat offenders' found themselves admitted to Magdalen asylums which then proved difficult to leave. While much more could be said about unmarried motherhood in Ireland what we need to note here is that unmarried mothers were stigmatised. Unmarried mothers and illegitimate children were symbols of moral and particularly of sexual failure. Unmarried motherhood was considered contagious and unmarried mothers were themselves in danger of resorting to prostitution.

Venereal disease

One of the concerns to re-emerge in the 1920s was the incidence of venereal diseases. As we have seen this had been a significant issue in Ireland during the period of the First World War, especially with the ending of the war in 1918, when there was the prospect of thousands of allegedly syphilitic troops returning to Ireland. Concern with venereal disease became muted after the crisis of 1918 had passed. With the withdrawal of the British garrison it was believed that the danger to Irish survival, to the future of the race, had passed. But the subject of venereal disease was to become problematic in the Irish Free State in the early 1920s. Logically the sexual danger evident in the presence of the British soldier in Ireland should have disappeared in 1922. The immorality associated by nationalist propagandists with the British presence could no longer exist. How, then, was the state to acknowledge the rising rates of illegitimacy, venereal diseases and sexual assault in the first years of independence? If the contaminant had been eliminated had the new state essentially failed, since sexual immorality seemed to be rife in the country?

We have no complete figures for the extent of venereal diseases in Ireland in the 1920s and 1930s. Steeven's hospital, Sir Patrick Duns and the Westmoreland lock hospital were the main treatment centres in Dublin, and the fullest figures appear to be available only for Steevens and Sir Patrick Duns. We know that the number of women treated in Steevens's hospital women's clinic between 1919 and 1924 and suffering from a venereal disease was 864.[63] During the year ending 31 March 1925 the number of patients dealt with in all the available treatment centres was stated to be 3,174.[64] Waterford, which did not inaugurate a treatment scheme until 1929, had at least twenty-eight cases of venereal disease in 1926.[65] By 1935 treatment schemes were in operation in four county boroughs, Cork, Dublin, Limerick and Waterford, and in thirteen counties: Carlow, Cavan, Dublin, Kildare, Laois, Limerick, Louth, Monaghan, Offaly, Waterford, Westmeath, Wexford and Wicklow.[66] From 1 April 1922 county councils were invited by the Free State government to resume the administration of the treatment programme. There was 'considerable apathy' shown in making arrangements for the scheme and it was observed that there was also a decided lack of interest among the medical profession for it. It was reported that more men than women received treatment and that there was a very small demand for treatment in the counties.[67] Table 6.1 provides some indication of treatment levels in the two Dublin hospitals, Steevens's and Sir Patrick Duns, with some figures also for the Westmoreland lock hospital. It can be seen that the number of patients receiving treatment in Steeven's and Sir Patrick Duns decreased from a high of 3,156 in 1926/7 to 2,234 by March 1941.[68] In 1935 the total number of patients dealt with in treatment centres in the Free State was 2,589. Of this number 1,926 were men, and 663 were women.[69] There is no indication of the numbers of individuals who may have contracted a venereal disease and did not seek treatment. The main treatment centres in Northern Ireland were in Belfast, where patients attended the Royal Victoria hospital and the Mater hospital.[70]

The most significant investigation into venereal disease in the Free State was to take place with the Inter-Departmental Committee of Inquiry regarding Venereal Disease which was established in 1924.[71] The inquiry was initiated by the Minister for Local Government and Public

Table 6.1 Hospital treatment for venereal disease in Dublin 1921–40[a]

Year	Number of patients	Outpatient attendances	Inpatient days	Westmoreland lock hospital treated/outpatients
1921–2	na	14,361	8,182	247/na
1922–3	na	22,230	6,783	315/na
1923–4	2,693	25,220	7,022	235/na
1924–5	na	26,076	7,591	274/na
1925–6	na	29,315	7,993	146/na
1926–7	3,156	26,598	8,833	137/138
1927–8	2,636	31,427	9,257	101/na
1928–9	2,796	34,376	9,741	154/na
1929–30	2,625	34,193	10,253	109/811
1930–1	2,552	33,323	11,547	143/791
1931–2	2,403	34,882	8,995	150/na
1932–3	2,394	37,052	10,499	217/1,044
1933–4	2,567	38,189	10,306	na
1934–5	2,490	40,086	10,487	na
1935–6	2,403	35,441	10,758	201/na
1936–7	2,215	29,233	9,840	187/na
1937–8	2,022	26,679	8,495	184/na
1938–9	2,135	24,088	10,485	171/na
1939–40	2,046	22,210	11,777	198/na
1940–1	2,234	23,899	9,031	202/na

Source: Department of Local Government and Public Health reports 1927–41 (Dublin, 1927–41); *Board of Superintendence of Dublin Hospitals, 1920* (Dublin, 1921); Annual Reports of Dublin Hospitals, 1920–1932 (Dublin, 1921–32); 'Venereal Diseases', Department of Health, B135/12 and B135/13, NAI.
[a] There are discrepancies between the figures available for venereal disease treatment in Dublin between department of health files and those published in the reports of the Department of Local Government and Public Health. Table 6.1 lists the published figures.

Health, Ernest Blythe, and its aim was to 'make inquiries as to the steps necessary, if any, which are desirable to secure that the extent of venereal disease may be diminished'.[72] The committee held sixteen meetings, examined twenty-four witnesses and received written submissions from a number of hospitals, government agencies and social workers.[73] The report, which was not made public, revealed that 'venereal disease was widespread throughout the country, and that it was disseminated largely by a class of girl who could not be regarded as a prostitute'[74] (see fig. 14 and map 2). While much might be said on this inquiry within the wider context of contemporary anxiety regarding the politics of the Irish army and issues of civil and military authority, it is sufficient to note here that it

	Gonorrhoea	Syphilis	Chancroids, etc
Total admissions from Ireland	598	202	64
Total admissions from Dublin	323	125	42
Total admissions exclusive of Dublin	275	77	22
Total admissions, place of infection unknown	20	21	13

Grand totals of admission from 1/10/1923 to 31/12/1925 918

Map 2. Places of infection of cases of venereal disease admitted during 1 October 1923 to 31 December 1925, *Inter-Departmental Committee of Inquiry Regarding Venereal Diesease, Report* (Dublin, n.d., *c.* 1926).

was suggested that venereal diseases were a serious health problem in Ireland.[75] The soldiers who contracted such a disease were obliged to identify the place and source of infection and it was suggested that, rather than being confined to urban areas, venereal disease was to be found 'in every parish in Ireland'[76] (see fig. 14). The army had a very broad definition of the term 'prostitute'. For instance, women who received 'the smallest reward, even a bottle of stout' from a soldier were identified as such.[77] It was also noted that prostitutes constituted the source of infection in only 30 per cent of cases, but the source of all contagion was attributed to women. Major O'Carroll, the chief sanitary officer of the army, claimed that 'VD appears to be conveyed by apparently decent girls throughout the country . . . there is considerable danger to the innocent sections of the community, because these so-called amateurs mix with all sections and include nurses, maids and cooks, etc.'[78]

To some extent, it can be argued that the venereal disease inquiry was an evaluation of sexual behaviour and revealed an apparently promiscuous nation. What was now becoming evident was that all women, not only prostitutes, were possible sites of venereal infection. Disease and moral corruption had made their way, momentously, into the preserves of respectability. Women had the ability to destroy or re-create, to foster sterility or to make fertile, to be the agent of contamination. There was still a way out for those who believed that it was impossible for Irish women to have such varied power and argued that England was still to blame. Fr Devane suggested to the committee of inquiry that the original source of the disease was the British soldiers stationed in Ireland and, in particular, the black and tans who had travelled around the country. He wrote: 'In the past few years we have had wave after wave of men passing over the country . . . It will be found that, *in many cases*, the girls who acted as camp followers to Black and Tans, etc., were the same who pursued the Free State troops, conveying in not a few cases infection.'[79] The shadow of the prostitute looms large in discussions of unmarried mothers and venereal disease. The prostitute was seen as 'a force of moral pestilence to the public', and Devane noted that on the route to prostitution the unmarried mother was 'an intermediary place'.[80] Frank Duff, founder of the Legion of Mary, was to note that unmarried mothers formed a major recruiting group for prostitution.[81] For Devane other recruits to the ranks of the prostitute were the 'semi-imbecile and mentally deficient' woman; and the woman over twenty-one who was 'of normal mentality, who, through some perversity of nature, take[s] up this life by preference'.[82] The worst offender, however, was the 'amateur', identified as a young woman who engaged in sexual activity without looking for monetary gain. The 'amateur' was the figure acknowledged in

Places of Infection of Cases of Venereal Disease.

Admitted during period 1st October, 1923–30th September, 1925.

Place.	Gonorrhœa.	Syphilis.	Chancraids, etc.
Dublin	273	114	39
Ardee	4	—	—
Gorey	2	—	—
Mullingar	7	1	—
Sligo	7	1	—
Roscrea	3	—	—
Athlone	9	5	—
Ballina	1	—	—
Dundalk	7	3	3
Claremorris	3	1	—
Naas	12	1	—
Galway	4	2	—
Belfast	—	3	—
Cork	24	3	1
Limerick	5	6	—
Wexford	13	1	1
Fermoy	1	3	2
Bridgetown, Co. Wexford	—	1	—
Clonmel	7	2	—
Bruff	2	1	—
Charleville	2	3	—
Waterford	4	2	—
Dungarvan	2	1	1
Longford	12	2	—
Ferbane	1	—	—
Trim	5	3	—
Tipperary	4	4	—
Templemore	1	—	—
Kilkenny	11	—	1
Tralee	1	—	—
Killarney	1	1	1
Mallow	—	—	1
Cavan	4	—	—
Edenderry	4	—	1
Lucan	1	1	—
New Ross	3	—	—
Ballingarry, Co. Tipperary	1	—	—
Kenmare	2	—	—
Ballydehob, Co. Cork	1	—	—
Tullamore	3	—	1
Bundoran	—	1	—
Bailieboro', Co. Cavan	1	—	—
Bandon	4	1	1
Ballyknockan, Co. Dublin	1	—	—
Rockbarton	—	1	—
Abbeyleix	1	—	—
Carrick-on-Suir	1	—	—
Arva, Co. Cavan	1	—	—
Ballymahon	1	—	—
Strabane	—	1	—
Kells	1	—	—
Kilcurry	1	—	—
Balbriggan	1	—	—
Castleblayney	3	—	—
Kinsale	1	—	—
Tramore, Co. Waterford	—	1	—
Swords, Co. Dublin	3	1	—
Maryboro'	3	1	—
Millstreet, Co. Cork	—	1	—
Greystones, Co. Wicklow	2	—	—
Emly, Co. Tipperary	1	—	—
Dromore	—	—	1
Enniscrone	1	—	—
Crossmolina	—	—	1
Monaghan	—	—	1
Finner Camp	2	—	1
Mount Mellick	1	—	—
Newbridge	4	—	—
Roscommon	1	—	—
Bantry	1	—	—
Enniscorthy	1	—	—

Place.	Gonorrhœa.	Syphilis.	Chancroids, etc.
Ballinasloe	5	—	—
Gormanstown	—	—	1
Thurles	3	—	—
Portarlington	1	—	—
Curragh	1	1	—
Arklow	—	1	—
Kilcullen	1	—	—
Clare	1	—	—
Boyle	6	3	—
Armagh	1	—	—
Donegal	—	1	—
Tullow	1	—	—
Drogheda	1	—	—
Clones	7	—	—
Youghal	2	—	—
Coolnaborna, Co. Wexford	1	—	—
Castlebar	—	—	1
Ballybrophy	1	—	—
Pettigo	—	1	—
Tallaght	—	1	—
Cahir	1	—	—
Buncrana	4	—	—
Cobh	2	—	—
Carlow	2	—	—
Dunmore, Co. Waterford	1	—	—
Laytown, Co. Meath	1	—	—
Kildare	1	—	—
Killiney, Co. Dublin	1	—	—
Totals	**529**	**185**	**59**

	Gonorrhœa	Syphilis	Chancroids
Total admissions from Ireland	529	185	59
„ „ „ Dublin	273	114	39
Total admissions, exclusive of Dublin	256	71	20
Total admissions, place of Infection unknown	20	21	11

Grand total of admissions from Venereal Disease from 1st October, 1923–30th September, 1925 825

Fig. 14. Places of Infection of Cases of Venereal Disease from *Inter-Departmental Committee of Inquiry Regarding Venereal Disease, Report* (Dublin, 1926).

the Inter-Departmental Committee of Inquiry regarding Venereal Disease as the source of infection. Though named as a prostitute by the inquiry, the 'amateur' was clearly not a prostitute. But the focus on the 'amateur' allied the sexuality of young women with that of the stigmatised prostitute. 'Amateurs' could and did come from the 'respectable classes'. Discussing the sexual activity of young women in the context of venereal disease identified them as a threat to national health and morals.

Prostitution

A Fr Creedon, who began to be involved in rescue work in the Monto area from 1922, noted that women who worked there as prostitutes were 'not pariahs . . . they appear to penetrate freely into the homes of the respectable poor, and are on familiar terms with the growing boys and

Table 6.2 Return giving particulars of women arrested for soliciting by the Dublin Metropolitan Police from 1 September 1924 to 20 October 1924, with residences of prostitutes

Residences of prostitutes	
48 Newmarket Street	(5 live here)
25 Chancery Lane	4
6 Newmarket	2
11 Newmarket	
37 Francis St	
8 Catherine St	
2 Catherine St	(a veteran lives here)
32 Lr. Bridge St	
45 Lr. Kevin St	
8 Meath St	
8 Upper Dorset St	
27 Corporation St	
15 Ryders Row	
19 Upper Mercer St	
11 Sinnot Place	(2 live here)
135 Townsend St	
40 Purdon St	
38 Railway St	
12 Elliott Place	

Source: Army Chaplain's Correspondence from 1923–39, Byrne Papers, Box Government and Politics, DDA.

girls in the neighbourhood'.[83] What was even more significant was that these women seemed to be accepted within the community. Creedon observed that 'half the natural disgust and fear at the idea of a depraved life is gone if those who we know and like are leading it. The boys and young men are not the better enabled to be good by the fact that immorality is locally so easy and attractive, and the effect on the young girls may be as bad.'[84] What was evident to Creedon, and others, was the fact that female sexuality went unregulated in the area, and that this was a dangerous and disruptive force to society at large.

Some information exists on the women who worked as prostitutes in Dublin during the 1920s. Table 6.2 provides an indication of the geographical areas in which women resided or worked as prostitutes in Dublin in the early 1920s; overall, a rather broad geographical spread that moved beyond the notorious Monto district (fig. 15). Further information on these women tells us the age, previous occupation and number of prior arrests for each woman. In the same 'return giving particulars of women arrested for soliciting by the Dublin Metropolitan Police from 1

Fig. 15. Elliott Place, Dublin c. 1930s. Frank Murphy Collection, courtesy of the Old Dublin Society.

September 1924 to October 20 1924',[85] we can note that of the seventy-eight women arrested and imprisoned in that period, forty-eight had no fixed address. The women ranged in age from nineteen to fifty, a range that had altered little from the nineteenth century.[86] An examination of their earlier occupations suggests that a large number had been servants, and others were in low-paid work prior to their becoming prostitutes.[87] The majority of those detained had previously been arrested, one woman having thirty previous convictions.[88]

In the same report the army chaplain listed the women from whom soldiers had allegedly contracted venereal disease (see table 6.3). The interesting feature of this list is the number of women identified as amateurs, women who were essentially not prostitutes. The fact that they are listed in the company of prostitutes reinforces the idea that the authorities, and particularly members of the Catholic Church, saw little difference between the two categories.

Frank Duff was later to recall the way in which prostitution was organised in the Monto district. He observed that women often owned and managed the brothels, but in some cases hired managers to run the business. In the case of the latter the profits were divided between the owner,

Table 6.3 Return giving particulars of women reputed to be infected with venereal disease as supplied by infected soldiers

Name	Address	Particulars
Maggie Ryan	Parkgate St	Amateur
K. Ennis	Inchicore	Amateur, age 20 years, tall, dresses in white. Usually at Fete, Parkgate St, at night
Mary Walsh	Murphy's Hotel Clonmel	Prostitute, 2/- per time
Tipperary Kate	'Lynch's Engine'	Alley or Wards, Bridge St. prostitute, on the Quays
Molly Smith	Tullow Hill Tullow, Co. Carlow	
Miss K. Wall	75 Harcourt St	Amateur
Miss Brogan	Waterford	Amateur
Miss A. Meredith	8 Moyne Road, Ranelagh	Amateur (domestic) age 22 or 23 years height 5' 6", hair, d. brown
Teresa Tyrell	Parkgate St.	Amateur, known as 'Killiney Kate'
Kathleen English	Blackrock	Amateur

Source: Army Chaplain's Correspondence from 1923–39, Byrne Papers, Box Government and Politics, DDA.

manager and the prostitute. If the owner was the manager then the profits were divided in two. He noted that the proprietors often owned a number of establishments. Most of the women who worked in the area were 'attached' to a house, but Duff claimed there was also a large 'privateer' section; these were women who had their own rented rooms and 'were complete freelancers'.[89]

A report on the level of prostitution drawn up in 1925 suggests how the police authorities viewed the problem. General William Murphy, the commissioner of the DMP, noted that until 1925 brothels in the Monto area operated 'without much let or hindrance on the part of the police authorities'.[90] Many of the brothels were run as 'shebeens' and the police viewed them as 'centres of every vice and the resort of robbers and decadents'. 'Stout', he noted, was 'sold by these managers at 3/- per bottle and sheebened there at a profit.' It was extremely difficult for the police to gather any evidence against the pimps or 'bullies' who controlled the prostitutes and lived 'on the earnings of the unfortunate women whom they maltreat[ed] in a scandalous fashion'. Murphy related that 'in some cases these women are stripped naked and flogged by their managers on suspicion of not giving up all their money'.[91] Murphy was anxious that the range of laws which dealt piecemeal with prostitution and brothel-keeping should be codified into one Act. He was also strongly supportive

of whatever legislation might be introduced, making provision for reformatory homes for prostitutes, and homes for girls in trouble. He was of
the opinion that currently the law 'respects too much the liberty of the
subject, and makes it practically impossible to present a satisfactory case'.
He believed that the chief defect of the law as it stood was that the visitors
to houses of ill fame got off scot free. He argued that the fear of 'exposure
would cut off demand, and would make police raids a very efficient way of
dealing with this issue'. As we have noted there was a belief, expressed in
the earlier part of the century that single women living in rooms or lodgings were morally suspect.[92] Murphy went so far in his suggestions for
combating prostitution as to indicate that every woman in a single room
should have her dwelling defined as a brothel.[93] He was also opposed to
the system of fines used generally by the courts to deal with these women,
viewing it as a form of the licensing of prostitution. In 1924 he observed
that 490 prostitutes had been arrested for soliciting in Dublin, and virtually all had been fined. In consequence there were many women with
hundreds of convictions against them and very little good came of prosecution. He alleged that prostitutes frequented dances in respectable
places and there was nothing the police could do about this.

In common with nineteenth-century beliefs, prostitutes remained sites
of moral contagion. Devane, deliberately arguing against the view that
prostitutes 'protect the decent woman and are necessary for civilisation',
provided an account of prostitution in Limerick City. He had been a military chaplain there for ten years and

there were in the city only four or five public prostitutes, of the poorest and most
repellant, bedraggled kind, who spent their time between the lock ward of the
workhouse and the local prison . . . they were not approached by anybody but
people like themselves. Things were healthy in the city until some young and well
dressed prostitutes appeared and immediately men flocked from all sides. On one
occasion, a girl came to me for protection. She was from County Kerry, was suspected of being 'loose', and was followed by a number of men who solicited her
frequently *throughout the day*. Sometimes a band of young domestics broke
restraint and went 'on the streets', and immediately young and old men flocked to
them. When they were got away in one manner or another, then things went back
to normal. Men 'simply did without' and I never, except on a couple of occasions,
heard anything of any attempt at interference with decent women.[94]

What is noticeable in his account is the opinion that a demand for prostitution only comes about because there are prostitutes to fill the need. The
presence of prostitutes damages men's moral sense and contaminates
the space respectable women occupy. The existence of prostitution necessitated the protection of respectable women. The prostitute is the
temptress. This was a belief also voiced by Frank Duff. Duff saw prostitutes

as predators 'lying in wait in cities to tempt men' and as girls who 'go out on the street to seek their prey'.[95] In the 1940s Duff was to give evidence to an inquiry into prostitution in Dublin. At this stage he noted that before 1922 there were in 'the region of 1,400' prostitutes working in the city. He believed that

economics was not the reason which made women prostitutes; quite as poor girls and in fact much poorer girls were not on the streets. Prostitution was not a mental problem though of course the life did create mental trouble. Environment and company were the main predisposing causes.[96]

Both Devane and Duff discussed how women who became prostitutes might be dealt with. For Devane, who had classified women who became prostitutes into three categories, there were three different regimes that might be followed. He believed that 'mentally defective' girls who became prostitutes should be placed with the Good Shepherd nuns. Those women under twenty-one who fell into prostitution he argued needed protection. Again, a refuge provided by nuns was the means to deal 'with this type of girl, who may at that period be reformed by strong religious influences'.[97] However, it was the 'perverse' woman who had freely chosen prostitution who was to have the severest punishment. He suggested that this woman should be confined for three months on a first offence, six months for a second and a year for a third or subsequent offence, without the option of paying a fine. While this would be sufficient for punishment, in order to ensure her reformation she should be given the option of entering a Good Shepherd Magdalen asylum. 'In this way, the girl gets a chance to reform, and if she refuse she must take the consequences in punishment, and at the same time the public is being safeguarded.'[98] Duff was keen on classification or segregation in institutions such as workhouses and particularly the lock hospital, which dealt with prostitutes and married women.[99] He, together with Devane, both witnesses to the inter-departmental inquiry, agreed that it was the prostitute who was the primary source of venereal infection.[100] For them, the brothel system which both sustained, and was sustained by, prostitution was the main site of contamination. Devane noted that Dublin 'seems to me to be the G.H.Q. of venereal disease as it is of the prostitute and the brothel'.[101] Dublin's red-light district was the site of both physical and moral contagion. Something then needed to be done about the brothel system in that city.

The Legion of Mary and the end of Monto

In September 1921 a group of fifteen women met with Frank Duff and Fr Michael Toher to form the Association of Our Lady of Mercy. This organisation was renamed the Legion of Mary in 1925. Elizabeth Kirwan was elected as the first president of the organisation and Ruth Donnelly as secretary.[102] The group, very much informed by a devotion to Mary, the Mother of God, and primarily concerned with the spiritual lives of its members, began their charitable work by visiting the incurably ill in the South Dublin union. The society was wary of competing with other Catholic charities, particularly the St Vincent de Paul Society, and sought to involve themselves in social problems that others were less willing to tackle. The group soon turned its attention to prostitution. Prior to this Duff himself had engaged in 'going door-to-door' in certain areas of Dublin and one evening accidentally found himself in the notorious brothel, Mrs Slicker's lodging house in Chancery Lane. There were thirty women in the house 'more or less getting themselves ready to go out onto the streets'. Duff made a hasty retreat and related his tale to Fr Creedon.[103] According to Duff's account of events, in June 1922, Fr Creedon and another priest went to Slicker's, where they gathered the women together in the front room and whatever transpired, had the girls weeping over their lives and claiming there was none to help them. Fr Creedon then offered to pay the owner 'an agreed sum for her maintenance of the girls until further notice' and during that period the girls were not to go out on to the streets.[104] Creedon was thought to have a way with these women and apparently his opening approach to every woman he met was 'And what's your beautiful name, dearie?' An opening which, it was claimed, swept any woman off her feet.[105] After a meeting with Duff and a number of priests, including Richard Devane, and two women from the Legion, it was decided to hold a retreat for the women. A three-day enclosed retreat was organised for them in the convent of the Sisters of Charity in Baldoyle. In the meantime Duff, Devane, Creedon and Josephine Plunkett from the Legion visited Slicker's and spent an entire day persuading the women to attend the retreat. At this stage Devane had heard that Archbishop Byrne was not supportive of the scheme and Devane wanted to bring it to an end.[106] However, twenty-three women went on the first retreat. While the retreat was proceeding, Duff, Creedon and Devane met with W. T. Cosgrave, then Minister for Local Government and about to become President of the Executive Council of the Irish Free State, and persuaded him to put 76 Harcourt Street, a government property, at the disposal of the Legion.[107] This was named the Sancta Maria hostel.

The campaign to close down Monto began in earnest in 1923. In March Duff and Plunkett managed to persuade fifteen women to attend a retreat at the Sancta Maria hostel. By the end of 1924 Duff claimed that the work of the Legion had been so successful that the numbers of prostitutes working in the area were reduced from about 200 to 30.[108] In

February 1925 a Lenten mission was organised for the Pro-Cathedral in Dublin, and the priests referred, in their sermons, for the first time in public to the activities in the Monto. At the same time members of the Legion and the St Vincent de Paul society were despatched throughout the densely populated parish to ensure high attendance at the mission, and to pray for the end of a 'great local evil'.[109] During the mission, Duff organised what he termed a 'beat up on a big scale' in an attempt to close all the brothels in the area.[110] He recalled that

everyone concerned was interviewed, from over-landlords, brothel keepers, costumiers, and usurers, to the bullies and the prostitutes themselves. The appeal was on purely religious grounds. As a result, three fourths of the brothels shut down voluntarily and one half of the total number of girls entered the rescue home.

The remaining keepers proved 'intractable' and so he called on the police for assistance.[111] General William Murphy agreed to shut down what remained of the brothels in Monto. A raid was organised for 12 March 1925, and more than a hundred people were arrested,[112] including forty-five prostitutes, twelve pimps and fifty customers. Most of the women involved were subsequently released into the custody of the Legion of Mary and were placed in the Sancta Maria hostel. Further raids were led by the police. In a report dated 16 March 1925 to the Minister for Justice on the progress being made during the campaign, General Murphy stated that many of the women would not give evidence against the bullies. For Murphy, the existence of Monto was 'a blot on the reputation of a Catholic city'.[113] The 1926 report of the inter-departmental committee regarding venereal disease accepted that, as a result of the 1925 actions, the problem of the 'open brothel' no longer existed in Dublin.[114]

During the period 1922–5 Monto came under assault as an area where prostitution was rife, and also as an area where the forces of disorder – and particularly political disorder – reigned.[115] (It was believed to be the location of many irregulars.) Why was the assault on Monto apparently so successful? There were some practical reasons for this success. Since the withdrawal of British forces, the area had declined in terms of business. Once the women agreed to attend a religious retreat over a number of days, respectable poor families who were living in tenement accommodation were moved into the former brothel premises to ensure that they would not re-open, leaving the women little option but to take shelter in the hostel provided by the Legion of Mary.[116] The assault on the brothels also reshaped the relationships the women had with the brothel-keepers.[117] Exploitative as brothel life might be, it had provided these women with a stable environment. Once that relationship had been broken the Legion of Mary attempted to form new, more appropriate relationships for the women. The reform process in the hostel was intense: 'Every entrant is made the object of a special and individual attention, directed in the first place to the creation of moral fibre.' Many of the women were married off; between 1922 and 1923, sixty-one of the entrants were married.[118] Marrying off the women quickly provided them with another form of stability, replacing the brothel-keeper with a more respectable husband. Within the hostel the women were domesticated, given housework to do and trained in neatness, tidiness and cleanliness. They were being taught the same virtues of domesticity that were advocated for all Irish women at this time. Through routine and the assumption of domesticity the behaviour of the women was modified. The hostel and retreat work was declared a great success by the Legion. By 1930 fewer than a hundred women were classified as common prostitutes by the police, though it is likely that more than this number were working as prostitutes in the city at this time.[119]

The Legion itself also went from strength to strength though it was not until the end of the 1930s that it had the approval of the archbishop of Dublin.[120] By the end of 1922 four praesidia had been established, by 1925 there were five, with a total membership of about 150, most of whom were female. By 1934 there were about 2,250 members. The Legion also extended its work and in 1927 it opened the Morning Star hostel for homeless men. In October 1930 it set up the Regina Coeli hostel for unmarried mothers and later in the 1930s it also took on conversion work among Protestants. The Legion also expanded outside Ireland.[121]

In a 1924 report on the Legion's operation at 76 Harcourt Street to the archbishop of Dublin, it was noted that the hostel rather than being a long-stay rescue home was a 'clearing house only'. The aim was

to get the girls in, put them through a retreat, then subject them to a certain formation process in the hostel, based chiefly on the idea of teaching them to use liberty properly. The rules are proportionate to the weakness found. Smoking is permitted, cigarettes to the number of six being supplied daily to each girl. The girls must be present at meals and do not go out after 6 o'clock in the evening. They are encouraged to go to Mass daily, but they are not in any way forced.[122]

The regime in the hostel was much more benign than that experienced by women in convent-run Magdalen asylums and a much greater level of personal freedom was allowed to them. The rescue work brought considerable pleasure to Duff and the Legion. Duff was to observe in 1926 that they had, over two nights 'taken into the net' eleven women. It was, he noted 'a gratifying capture'.[123]

Another report provides an account of what happened to the first women who came into the hostel. Of the initial group of twenty-three who were taken from Slicker's in Chancery Lane, seven had returned to 'their old life'. Of the total 156 women dealt with, 57 had returned to their 'old lives of sin', 68 had 'never fallen away', and 31 were 'now living good lives'. Of this 31, 5 were considered to be of 'doubtful calibre, goodness being due to temporary residence in some institution'; 17 of the girls had been married. 'One of these marriages', it was noted, 'is of doubtful success, and one is an undoubted failure. In many of the cases, the men did the weekend retreat in Rathfarnham as a preliminary to marriage.' The report observed that that conversion was a part of the Legion's work and it recorded that 'eight conversions from Protestantism have been secured [and] in addition two perverts were received back into the church'. Eight of the girls were sent to Magdalen asylums. The Legion was clear that the women who had left prostitution had not been replaced and though some 'new comers had drifted in' they were few in number. After 1925 the Legion observed that

in the worst area, Elliott Place and Purdon Street district, there is a notable change. The Legion of Mary visitors now command the situation, go where they like, can give orders and on one recent occasion actually entered through the window of a house that had been barred against them and took away a girl, who shortly afterwards wept tears of joy on the occasion of her reception into the church . . .

In declaring the value of their work, the Legion argued that without the Harcourt Street hostel a lot of these women would still be working as prostitutes,

sinning themselves and being a temptation to multitudes of men, very many of whom would not have sinned but for the chance meeting and the occurrence of the temptation. To show the gravity of the latter, the admission of one of our girls may be quoted that she frequently sinned with 20 different men in a night.[124]

It was also noted that some of the women had children of whom, thirty-three, the children of thirty mothers, were placed in various orphanages and industrial schools in Dublin.[125] The reports of the work in the hostel were always very positive, though there is evidence to show that matters did not always run smoothly there.[126] In December 1926 Duff reported that 'things are bad at 76 at present. All authority has gone by the board.'[127] Apparently one of the women had broken windows and defied the committee to put her out of the hostel. There appears to have been little consistency within the managing committee of the hostel about how to deal with such matters. Duff's remedy was that the police be sent for and the woman ejected from the hostel.[128]

Some of the case histories of the women who first entered the hostel are also available (see appendix 4). What is most notable about these short histories is the necessity to declare the fact that the women were all somehow brought back to religion, or saved from Protestantism. The attitude expressed towards religion is similar to that expressed by rescue workers in the nineteenth century.

Between 1922 and 1930 it was claimed that 357 girls passed through the hostel. Of that number the Legion declared 243 to be successfully reformed, which leaves 114 failures. They placed 25 of their resident women in Magdalen asylums, and encouraged 45 others who sought advice at the hostel to enter these asylums. A number of complaints were made about the hostel and the Legion felt obliged to respond to these, and in the process both defend and justify its work. In an undated report it was noted that

criticism of the Hostel has been neither fair nor informed. Girls have not corrupted households into which they were sent as servants, not even one. Men have not been cajoled into marriages with these girls. There have been over 60 marriages, exhibiting an infinitely better success proportion than the ordinary community can show. Girls have not been let out on the streets to ply their trade and allowed to use the Hostel as their centre. Relapse cases are taken back, and more than once.[129]

The Legion also stressed that the hostel dealt with a 'much more difficult class of girl than the Magdalen Asylums'. There was, in their eyes, a huge difference between the girl 'who turns up at a convent and one that has to be sought out'. It was clear to the Legion that many of the girls who came to the hostel would never go to a Magdalen asylum. It was noted that if a girl left the Magdalen or was expelled for some reason, there was no follow-up, while the Legion did engage in follow-up work. The Legion workers were occupied in a comprehensive surveillance of each of their 'girls':

She is visited regularly and made to feel that she is an object of solicitude . . . every place frequented by these girls is visited at least weekly:- their lodging houses, the venereal hospitals, the women's casual wards in the Union, the prison, the Bridewell, the proselytising centres.[130]

Miss Shaw, a member of the Legion, accounted for the girls who had passed through the hostel in 1939. The number of girls dealt with was 534. Of these 297 were leading good lives, 58 had died, 87 had fallen 'on [the] wrong side', while the whereabouts of 92 women was unknown. It was noted that of the 58 girls who died, '55 died after varying periods of preparation and repentance'.[131]

Despite the assault on Monto, prostitution was still evident in Dublin in the late 1920s. A total of seventy-eight women, who were known prostitutes, were imprisoned in Mountjoy jail in 1929 (see table 6.4). The majority of the women, fifty-eight in all, were aged between eighteen and forty. Most of the women were imprisoned for soliciting with a usual term

Table 6.4 Prostitutes committed to Mountjoy Prison, 1929

Name of prisoner	Age	Offences	Sentences	If fine paid during period	No. of convictions during period	Total no. of previous convictions	When first under police supervision
Ellen Doran	58	soliciting (4 cases)	1 c.month 40/- (3 cases), 7 days 10/-		4	134	approx. over 20 years ago
Frances Devereaux	49	do. (5 cases)	1 c.month 40/- (5 like cases)		5	92	do.
Esther Malone	49	drunk (2 cases)	4 days 5/-	paid part fine	2	58	approx. over 15 years ago
Julia Donegan	49	drunk (3 cases), soliciting	1 c.month 40/- (2 like sentences), 14 days impt.		4	123	do.
Rosanna Quigley	48	soliciting (4 cases)	1 c.month 40/- (3 like sentences), 14 days 20/-	paid pt fine	4	68	do.
Kate Delahoid	47	soliciting (4 cases)	1 c.month 40/- (like sentence), 14 days 20/- (like sentence)	do	4	47	do.
Emily Fitzgerald	46	soliciting (5 cases), drunk	1 c.month 40/- (5 like sentences)		6	101	approx. over 20 years ago
Nellie Greeks	46	soliciting (4 cases), drunk & disly. (2 cases)	1 c.month 40/- (4 like sentences), 4 days 2/6	do	6	54	approx. over 15 years ago
Mary A. Bannon	46	soliciting (3 cases) drunk (3 cases)	1 c.month 40/- (2 like sentences), 7 days 10/-, 4 days 5/- (like sentence)		6	91	do.
Jane Cusack	45	drunk	7 days 10/-		1	21	approx. over 12 years ago
Minnie Mills	44	soliciting	1 c.month 40/-		1	9	approx. over 8 years ago
Margt. Stritch	44	do.	14 days 20/-		1	23	do.
Mary Gaynor	43	do. (3 cases)	1 c.month 40/- (like sentence), 14 days 20/-		3	24	approx. over 15 years ago

Name	Age	Offence	Sentence		Count	No.	Period
Delia Goodwin	43	do. (3 cases), drunkeness (2 cases)	1 c.month 40/- (like sentence), 7 days 10/- like sentence, 14 days 20/-		5	78	do.
Lily Traynor	43	soliciting (3 cases)	1 c.month 40/-, 2 like sentences		3	150	approx. over 20 years ago
Emily McDonald	43	do. Do.	1 c.month 40/-, 2 like sentences		3	37	approx. over 15 years ago
Elizabeth Brady	43	soliciting (2 cases), drunkenness (3 cases)	1 c.month 40/-, 2 like sentences, 14 days 20/-, 4 days 5/-		5	132	approx. over 20 years ago
Annie Brown	43	soliciting	1 c.month 40/-		1	65	approx. over 15 years ago
Jos Sherlock	39	do. (3 cases)	1 c.month 40/-, 2 like sentence		3	51	do.
Gladys Bolton	39	do. (2 cases)	1 c.month 40/-, like sentence	paid pt. Fine	3	15	Year 1920
Julia Brown	39	soliciting (3 cases), drunkenness (4 cases)	1 c.month 40/-, 4 like sentences, 7 days 10/-, 14 days 20/-		7	89	approx. over 15 years ago
Eileen Loftus	39	soliciting (3 cases), drunkenness (4 cases)	1 c.month 40/-, 3 like sentences, 7 days 10/-, 4 days 5/-, like sentence		7	149	approx. over 20 years ago
Nancy Leonard	39	soliciting (4 cases), drunk	1 c.month 40/-, 2 like sentences, 14 days 20/-, 14 days impt.		5	24	Year 1921
Molly Byrne	37	soliciting (3 cases), drunk (2 cases)	1 c.month 40/-, 2 like sentences, 4 days 5/-		4	77	approx. over 15 years ago
Mary A. Farrell	37	drunk (2 cases)	1 c.month 40/-, 4 days 5/-		2	66	do.
Alice Ryan	37	soliciting (2 cases),	1 c.month 40/-, 2 like sentences, 14 days 20/-		4	85	do.

Table 6.4 (cont.)

Name of prisoner	Age	Offences	Sentences	If fine paid during period	No. of convictions during period	Total no. of previous convictions	When first under police supervision
Delia Quigley	36	soliciting (3 cases), drunkenness (7 cases) drunkenness (2 cases)	1 c.month 40/-, 5 like sentences, 7 days 10/-, 4 days 5/-, 2 like sentences	paid pt fine	10	78	approx. over 20 years ago
Molly Bruen	36	soliciting (4 cases), drunkenness (2 cases)	1 c.month 40/-, 5 like sentences		6	58	approx. about 15 years ago
Julia McCarthy	36	soliciting (4 cases), drunkenness (2 cases)	1 c.month 40/- 2 like sentences, 14 days 20/-, like sentence, 4 days 5/-	paid part fine on 3 occasions	6	54	approx. over 18 years ago
Kathleen O'Brien	35	soliciting (7 cases)	1 c.month 40/-, 6 like sentences		7	64	do.
Annie Doyle	34	do. (2 cases)	1 c.month 40/-, like sentence	paid part fine	2	10	approx. about 10 years ago
Kathleen Whelan	34	attempted suicide	3 months H.L.		1	10	do.
Bridie Dunne	33	soliciting (4 cases)	1 c.month 40/-, 3 like sentences		4	82	approx. over 15 years ago
Cissy Jackson	33	soliciting	1 c.month 40/-	paid pt fine	1	5	in year 1922

Name	Age	Offence	Sentence	Payment	No.	Period
May Tierney	33	soliciting (2 cases)	do. Like sentence		2	approx. about 15 years ago
Lizzie Keating	33	do.	14 days 20/-		1	do.
Nellie McManus	32	do. (3 cases)	1 c.month 40/-, 2 like sentences	paid pt fine	3	in year 1920
Mary A. O'Hara	32	do. Do.	1 c.month 40/-, 2 like sentences	paid pt fine on each sentence	3	approx. about 12 years ago
Molly Kelly	32	do. (2 cases)	1 c.month 40/-, like sentence	paid pt fine	2	in year 1922
Molly Woods	31	do. (4 cases)	1 c.month 40/-, like sentence, 14 days 20/-, like sentence	do.	4	approx. about 14 years ago
Emily O'Donnell	31	drunkenness (8 cases)	7 days 10/-, like sentence, 4 days 5/-, 3 like sentences, 4 days 2/6, like sentence	do.	8	do.
Annie McCabe	31	soliciting (5 cases), drunkenness (3 cases)	1 c.month 40/-, 3 like sentences, 7 days 10/-, like sentence, 7 days 20/-, 4 days 5/-	paid pt fine on 2 occasions	8	approx. about 20 years ago
Lily Darcy	29	soliciting (2 cases)	1 c.month 40/-, like sentence	do.	2	about year 1923
Netty Jackson	28	soliciting (2 cases)	1 c.month 40/-, like sentence	do.	2	in year 1923
Cissy Scully	28	do. (3 cases)	1 c.month 40/-, 2 like sentences	paid pt fine on each sentence	3	in year 1925
Mary Nally	28	do. Do.	1 c.month 40/-, 2 like sentences	paid pt fine	3	in year 1924
Lily Gilsenan	28	do. Do.	do.		3	in year 1922
Mary Hoey	30	do. Do.	do.		3	in year 1925
Nellie English	28	soliciting (3 cases), drunk	1 c.month 40/-, like sentence, 7 days 10/-, like sentence	do.	4	in year 1927
Mary McHugh	28	drunkenness (4 cases)	1 c.month H.L., 14 days 20/-, like sentence, 4 days 5/-		4	approx. over 10 years ago

Table 6.4 (*cont.*)

Name of prisoner	Age	Offences	Sentences	If fine paid during period	No. of convictions during period	Total no. of previous convictions	When first under police supervision
Julia Gordon	28	soliciting (5 cases)	1 c.month 40/-, 3 like sentences, 14 days 20/-		4	4	in present year
Florrie Demerage	27	do. (3 cases), indecency	1 c.month 40/-, 2 like sentences, 1 c.month impt.		4	9	in yr. '25
Molly Smullen	27	soliciting (3 cases), drunkenness (2 cases)	1 c.month 40/-, 2 like sentences, 14 days 20/-, like sentence	paid pt fine	5	45	in yr. '23
Maureen Blake	27	soliciting (3 cases), drunk	1 c.month 40/-, like sentence, 14 days 20/-, 7 days 10/-	do.	4	2	in yr. '28
Kate Reilly	27	soliciting, profane & obs. Language	1 c.month 40/-, 7 days 10/-	do.	2	6	in yr. '25
Molly Smith	27	soliciting (2 cases)	14 days 20/-, like sentence		2	23	in yr. '21
Martha Brady	26	soliciting (7 cases), drunk	1 c.month 40/-, 6 like sentences, 14 days 20/-		8	24	in yr. '25
Peggy O'Neill	26	soliciting (4 cases)	1 c.month 40/-, 3 like sentences		4	9	in yr. '27
Mary Ryan	25	do.	1 c.month 40/-	paid pt fine	1	4	do.
Maggie Good	23	do. (2 cases), drunk	14 days 20/-, like sentence, 1 c.month H.L.	do.	3	3	in present year

Name	Age	Charge	Sentence				Year
Lena Sherlock	23	soliciting (2 cases)	14 days 20/-, 1 c.month, 40/-		2	1	do.
Lily McLoughlin	23	do. (3 cases)	allowed out on recog, do., 1 c.month 40/-		3	3	do.
Lily O'Shaughnessey	23	do.	1 c.month 40/-, committed several times since June		1	19	in year '23
Annie O'Rourke	23	drunk (2 cases)	7 days 10/-, like sentence	paid full fine	2	12	do.
Maureen Joyce	24	soliciting	1 c.month 40/-		1	9	in yr. '26
Margt. Little	23	do. (5 cases)	1 c.month 40/-, 4 like sentences	paid pt fine on 2 sentences	5	12	in yr. '24
Minnie Quigley	23	do. (3 cases)	1 c.month 40/-, like sentence, 14 days 20/-	paid pt fine	3	21	in yr. '23
Bella Dobson	23	do. (4 cases)	1 c.month 40/-, 2 like sentences, 14 days 20/-	do. On 3 sentences	4	12	in yr. '22
Molly Furlong	23	do. (8 cases)	1 c.month 40/-, 7 like sentences	do. On 1 sentence	8	22	in yr. '22
Kathleen Glyan	23	soliciting (3 cases)	1 c. month 40/- like sentence	like sentence, 14 days 20/-	3	3	in yr. '24
Molly Graham	23	Do. Do.	1 c.month 40/-, 2 like sentences		3	11	in yr. '25
Agnes Meehan	22	Do. Do. Drunk, profane & obs. Lang.	1 c.month 40/-, like sentence, 14 days 20/-, 4 days 6 /-, like sentence		5	22	do.
Nora Lawlor	18	soliciting (3 cases)	1 c.month 40/-, 2 like sentences, 14 days 20/-		4	1	in yr. '28
Jennie Tiernan	18	Do. (3 cases)	allowed out on probation, 1 c.month 40/-, like sentence		3	3	in present year

Source: Department of Justice, File H247/41A. NAI.

of one calendar month and a fine that ranged between 5 and 40 shillings. Eight of the women had been engaged in prostitution for over twenty years, while twenty-one had been prostitutes for more than fourteen years. For instance, Ellen Doran, aged fifty-eight, had been working as a prostitute for more than twenty years and had 134 previous convictions.[132] Clearly these women had avoided or escaped the rescue network. It is evident from the information available that some of the younger women were starting out as prostitutes. It is not known whether all or any of these women were ever 'rescued'. The justification for the rescue work of the Legion was that they were offering a service that no other institution made available to prostitutes. Their clientele seems to have remained much the same in the 1930s as it was in the 1920s suggesting that prostitution, while it might have diminished, still existed in Dublin to some extent. Frank Duff was considered an expert on the subject of this type of rescue work and was called to give evidence at a number of inquires, including the inter-departmental inquiry into venereal disease and the Carrigan Committee.

The 1920s also provided some literary representations of prostitutes and prostitution in Ireland. Liam O'Flaherty's *The Informer*, published in 1925, has its central character, Gypo Nolan, wandering through the Monto area with 'Connemara Maggie', a prostitute, as his only friend. Maggie betrays him once his money is gone. O'Flaherty's descriptions of the women of the area enhance the main character's isolation and desolation and his alienation from normal society. The women, Katie Fox, Maggie Casey and Louisa Cummins, are depicted as barely human. They are 'ravaged', and their clothing is 'ragged'. Louisa Cummins has a 'shrivelled' head, and her teeth are 'crooked, yellow fangs'.[133] The greatest controversy over a literary representation of prostitution occurred with the Abbey theatre's production of Séan O'Casey's *The Plough and the Stars*, which was first staged in February 1926. The play was intended as a critique of the 1916 Rising and on the fourth night of its first production the audience rioted.[134] The riot was orchestrated by the republican Frank Ryan, and led by a number of republican women. Hanna Sheehy Skeffington, as the most vocal opponent of the play, viewed it as besmirching the memory of those who had died in 1916.[135] One of the characters, Rosie Redmond, is a prostitute and the portrayal of an Irish woman as a prostitute caused outrage, the character using her sexuality to seduce Irish men away from nationalist rebellion. Ria Mooney, who played the part of Rosie, recalled later that she based her portrayal on the prostitutes who hung around in the lanes around the theatre.[136] She also stated that members of the Abbey Company, particularly the women, tried to frighten her out of playing the part 'because they felt that they would be besmirched by the fact of one among them playing such a role'.[137] The body of the prostitute, in this instance, allows for a critique by O'Casey of the Rising. On the night of the riot, as O'Casey was leaving the theatre, he was verbally abused by a number of nationalist women. Having declared him a traitor and a pro-British propagandist, one of the women said 'an' I'd like you to know that there isn't a prostitute in Ireland from one end of it to th'other'.[138] O'Casey's depiction of the slums of Dublin and the people who lived in them, including prostitutes, was perhaps too brutal a realism for the nationalist audience of the play. O'Flaherty and O'Casey, in doing so, brought their middle-class readers and playgoers into a direct confrontation with the slum-dwellers and prostitutes of Dublin, a confrontation that brought an uncomfortable degree of reality into their lives. They broke the conspiracy of silence that surrounded Monto and prostitution in 1920s Ireland. Even the closure of brothels in the area had gone almost unremarked in the press.

The Carrigan Committee

It is striking that it was a Catholic lay organisation, the Legion of Mary, which essentially closed down the open brothel system in Dublin. Although eventually assisted by the police, Monto appears very much to have escaped consistent police action until 1925. From the foundation of the state there were constant calls for the government to legislate for morality, reflecting a more general reluctance within government to take the initiative in such cases. In 1926 the Inter-Departmental Committee on Venereal Disease observed that 'the extent to which the State can interfere to promote morality is strictly limited',[139] and it was believed to be preferable to look to organisations concerned with moral welfare and the Churches to deal with such issues. In November 1923 the Civic Committee of the IWWU sent a resolution to the Minister for Home Affairs noting that it was of 'vital importance to the moral safety of the youth of the nation that the age of consent should be raised to 18 years, and urge the government to bring in an amendment to that effect in the Criminal Law Amendment Act'.[140] Similarly the Irish Women Citizens' Association lobbied the government in January 1924 to amend the Criminal Law Amendment Act to the same ends.[141] In April 1925 Deputy Corish asked a Dáil question, inquiring if the minister intended to amend the Criminal Law Amendment Act of 1885 and also introduce legislation which would raise the age of consent.[142] Further requests were made until Deputy Little introduced a private members' Bill[143] to amend the Criminal Law Amendment Acts (1880–85) and this Bill, from a member of the opposition, finally forced the government into action.

Reflecting the level of concern that was being expressed about sexual immorality in the state, the call for the implementation of a new Criminal Law Amendment Act came from diverse groups in society. Devane and Duff advocated changes, as did a number of civic groups and social welfare organisations. After considerable delay the Carrigan Committee was eventually established in June 1930;[144] its brief was to consider whether it was necessary to amend sections of the 1885 Criminal Law Amendment Act relating to brothel-keeping and abduction, and whether to introduce legislation to curb juvenile prostitution.[145] The committee included a Catholic and Protestant cleric, along with two women members, one a commissioner of the Dublin poor law union, and another the matron of the Coombe hospital. One surgeon also sat on the committee, and Carrigan himself represented the law interest.[146] There was considerable agreement and consensus among the committee members and it was noted that

no witness appearing before us has dissented from the view expressed by nearly every witness that the moral condition of the country has become gravely menaced by modern abuses, widespread and pernicious in their consequences, which cannot be counteracted unless the laws of the State are revised and consistently enforced to combat them.[147]

Oral evidence was received from twenty-nine witnesses; eighteen were women, an unprecedented engagement by any committee of inquiry with the views of women. There were also eight written submissions made to the Committee.[148] The Committee covered a substantial amount of ground relating to public indecency, birth control, censorship, illegitimacy, unmarried mothers, brothel-keeping, soliciting, industrial schools, maternity homes, affiliation orders, servant registries, and women police officers.

Richard Devane, SJ was a key witness. He believed that there was a general 'apathy found in this country towards the solution of moral social problems'. He was opposed to an acceptance of the double standard of morality which he declared 'was accepted in this country, *as in perhaps no other*, where the woman is always hounded down and the man deal with leniently'. He also believed that the fact that administration and legislation were so completely in the hands of men meant that there was no 'adequate appreciation of female psychology in matters involving morality'. Like General Murphy in 1925 Devane suggested that there should be a new definition of the brothel 'to include a single room occupied by a woman in order to receive men for the purpose of prostitution'. He also suggested that brothel-keeping be made a felony and not a misdemeanour, and argued that no 'common lodging house which usually accommodates prostitutes shall allow a girl under 21 to reside in the premises'. Like many other witnesses Devane wanted the age of consent raised to eighteen. Using recent developments in psychology and theories of adolescence, Devane proposed that 'the most dangerous age in a girl's life when sexual passion is most assertive and her will weakest, I am informed . . . is 16'.[149]

Among the various women giving evidence to the committee there was also a concentration on the age of consent and the fragile condition of young women. Mrs Margaret Gavan Duffy, a visitor at the lock hospital, again used the moral weakness apparent in adolescents to bolster her argument for raising the age of consent. She found 'girls between the ages of 16 and 18 physically, mentally and emotionally at (what one may call) a dangerous age. It is the time to guard them well, until they have found their feet. It is useless to compare the age of consent in other countries. Irish girls are far more ignorant and innocent than others.'[150] Like many rescue workers she believed that it was the 'first fall' that mattered. If it happened again then 'there is no sense of shame, it becomes a habit'. Girls were most likely to 'fall', in her opinion, 'at dance halls all over the country and in the park in Dublin', while the cinema threw a 'glamour over much that is false'. She also believed that there was great danger for any girl from 'premature sexual experience. Sex curiosity is aroused, and it is the first step on the downward path.'[151]

All of the women who gave evidence individually or who represented a group agreed that the age of consent should be raised from sixteen to eighteen, and that the 'reasonable cause to believe' defence, that is that a man who declared he believed a young woman to be above the age of consent when sexual relations took place, should be abolished.[152] It was argued that the 'reasonable cause section' was used as an excuse by many men and made conviction very difficult.[153] The evidence of two clerics offered some account of the situation they met on the ground. Rev. Fitzpatrick of Limerick suggested that the age of consent should be raised to nineteen, basing his proposal on the 'very large number of unmarried mothers under that age'. But the number of unmarried mothers, he argued, was

only a small fraction of those who are being constantly defiled as the result of their ignorance in this matter, and the fact that sex curiosity and sex impulses are very active – and in many cases violent – during those years. All this is added to lack of parental control, cinemas, theatre shows, books and papers, the reading of which is a direct incitement to lust.

Measures such as raising the age of consent, would, he believed, 'really deter lustful blackguards from exploiting the simplicity, the giddiness, or the poverty of our young girls'.[154] Another cleric again stressed the vulnerability of Irish girls, where the 'country climate, social habits, and principles retard the maturity of girls. They need such protection as the law can give them up to that age.'[155]

The Irish Women Workers' Union argued that prostitution, 'this degrading social evil', should not be tolerated in any way, but should be 'attacked from every side, legal, moral, spiritual, physical, economic'. They believed that the law on solicitation bore too heavily, and unfairly, on women, 'while men are free to torment or incite women as much as they please, short of actual assault'. They also equated unmarried mothers with mental deficiency and urged that in the 'County Homes, etc., girls with one baby should be kept apart from girls with several illegitimate children, as the influence of the latter is undesirable'.[156] Many of the women who gave evidence before the committee had backgrounds in welfare work. Their evidence was shaped by an involvement with unmarried mothers and their work as doctors among the poorer women of society. In their comments they constructed a young, vulnerable girl who needed the protection of the law to emerge safely into adulthood. While their views were, in many instances, enlightening and humane, for example their call for sex education, they advocated a system of moral management which saw the necessity of institutions where women and girls who had 'fallen' could be rehabilitated and reformed under religious guidance.

The evidence of Dermot Gleeson, a district justice in Clarecastle, County Clare ran to a twelve-page, closely typed memo. He noted that while the level of prostitution in rural Ireland was very low the

number of uninformed, silly, foolish, or merely wild and uncontrolled girls is very large. These are easy prey to men. Dance halls and cinemas and books also have evil effects by suggesting the attractions of sexual looseness without pointing out the inevitable evils. It is from this type of girl you get the majority of unmarried mothers.

However, there was also another type of girl to be found in rural Ireland. This was one who was well informed about sexual matters, but who had been brought up under evil conditions of housing and had been neglected, with no proper education. This 'type' of young woman was destined to become an unmarried mother. While none of these types were 'inherently bad', they all needed protection. Gleeson believed that

in every town or rural area there is not more than one, two or more abandoned prostitutes or thoroughly immoral men, and sexual irregularities are confined for the most part to those whom a particular circumstance or circumstances bring together without premeditated evil or intent . . . public opinion is also stronger against sexual offences than elsewhere. Legislation is needed to protect the foolish, easily led, uncontrolled, ignorant but not definitely immoral young people, especially females and it is far more likely as preventive legislation to be effective.

Gleeson gave his considered opinion on how these girls emerged. Many of the farm labourers' daughters, he claimed, became domestic servants and found it 'difficult to settle and have no skills'. Schools, he argued, needed to 'turn out a more capable and self dependent type of girl'. Late marriage, he believed resulted in the seduction of girls in service, and also 'resulted in incest cases'. He blamed the 'spread of dance halls, and the motor car menace' as causes for the loosening of morals in Ireland. Arguing that levels of sexual crime were greater than statistics allowed he observed that 'in many areas the facts never get to the police at all'. In these cases, he claimed, that pressure was exercised against witnesses and attempts were made to interfere with juries: 'the weapon of intimidation is in common use in some rural areas in Ireland for many years and the practice of it has been reduced to a fine art'. He was keen on the age of consent being raised to eighteen and advocated that a 'reasonable cause' defence be abolished as it was a cause of serious miscarriages of justice. Gleeson noted that brothels hardly existed outside the cities but that in their place what was available was 'one or two prostitutes who invite men into their houses. Some of these have young children and their daughters are usually brought up to the same business.' He suggested that the police be given powers to raid such houses. Gleeson thought that a lack of parental responsibility was the chief cause of juvenile prostitution. The fact that more girls did not 'come to shame' he saw as a reflection on the 'decency of the men'. Again, dancehalls, indecent conduct in public and what he called parental anxiety were 'at the root of nearly all the moral evil in rural areas, especially to young persons'.[157]

Patrick J. Little, a member of the Irish Parliament, who had attempted to introduce a private members' bill on the Criminal Law Amendment Acts, was the only Member to give evidence to the committee.[158] For him cars were the 'real nuisance'. He also raised the issue of homosexuality urging that the committee

request that the terms of reference . . . be widened so as to deal with the whole problem of sex crime and not merely to remain as at present it is, I understand, limited to the problem of the age of consent . . . I have also been reminded by certain people who had official experience in connection with recent prosecutions for sodomy that the law dealing with certain types of offences is not effective enough to check crime.[159]

The evidence provided by 'medical women' to the committee made the greatest use of psychological theory.[160] Again they desired the age of consent to be raised from sixteen to eighteen. They argued that a girl of sixteen is not finished growing and developing and was often at this stage very unstable, mentally and emotionally, and 'cannot appreciate the nature and the result of the act to which she consents'. They believed that girls in England were more mature than Irish girls and stressed the harm that might be done to a girl by premature sexual experience and also the serious risk of physical injury she incurred if motherhood should result. They argued, naively, that raising the age of consent would save many girls from prostitution by making the girls inaccessible to men. Like all of the women's organisations they urged the committee to support the introduction of women police. They also suggested that since large numbers of prostitutes were mentally defective, they should be provided with greater care. Miss Kathleen M. Sullivan, a probation officer, noted that girls who were mentally deficient, those who suffered emotional strain and wildness at the age of sixteen or thereabouts, and the girl who had an illegitimate child, were the ones who fell into prostitution because 'it is an easy way to make money'.[161]

The Garda Commissioner, Eoin O'Duffy, presented detailed and statistically rich evidence to the committee on levels of sexual crime in Ireland. He also provided a substantial commentary on dancehalls around the country.[162] O'Duffy, like Devane and Duff, called for a redefinition of the brothel which would criminalise women who resided alone. He saw this as a problem particularly associated with rural Ireland where women living alone took men into their dwellings 'for immoral purposes and for pecuniary gain', and created much 'public scandal' in so doing.[163] O'Duffy was keen for the age of consent to be raised to eighteen, and he suggested that girls under twenty-one who were convicted of soliciting should be detained in reformatories until they reached the age of twenty-one. O'Duffy recognised the 'amateur' as the real problem. The prostitute he declared 'was known for what she is and avoided by right-thinking men and women. She is not causing social disorder or moral degradation in the same insidious manner as the so-called amateur.'[164] He also referred to indecent conduct, evident in the roads, parks and at seaside resorts around the country. Conflating prostitution with public indecency, he claimed that such indecency was more common in Ireland than in London, or in the state-licensed 'houses' of Europe.[165]

It was the statistics on sexual crime that he provided to the committee that convinced them that such crime was a serious problem in the Irish Free State. O'Duffy provided figures on crimes such as the rape of girls, indecent assaults on girls, incest, sodomy, indecent assaults on boys and men for the period 1924–9. In those years there were 207 cases of defilement, carnal knowledge or rape against girls under the age of eighteen, with 79 cases for women above eighteen. In the same period there were 233 cases of indecent assault against girls under eighteen, with 140 against women over eighteen. At the same time there were 28 cases relating to incest.[166] O'Duffy also informed the committee that his statistics represented about 15 per cent of all sexual crimes committed annually in the country, and that most of these were discovered 'accidentally'. He also observed that parents were often unwilling to pursue cases 'in the interests of their children'. The evidence provided by O'Duffy offered the first comprehensive survey (though it was limited) of sexual crime in Ireland. The earlier attempts by the suffrage and labour press to bring such matters to public attention had had little effect. O'Duffy's figures were not made known to the public but according to Finnane they formed 'the framework around which the [Carrigan] report was built'.[167]

There was, as the committee itself noted, a great deal of consensus about the causes of juvenile prostitution and its remedy. Prostitution had now become a matter of young women falling into vice, through ignorance or the temptations offered in dancehalls, motor cars and the cinema. The 'amateur' is rarely mentioned in the evidence. Though she did feature in the material O'Duffy[168] provided to the committee, as a figure she had largely been discarded, to be replaced by the vulnerable juvenile, who ranged in age from under sixteen to under twenty-five. The factors which led girls to prostitution were apparent to all who gave evidence to the committee; dance halls, adolescent emotions and turbulence, employment, and a bad home environment. A girl's sexual appetites were deemed to be strongest during adolescence and this was the period of greatest concern for her moral well-being. The existence of adolescence as a critical period of life marked by instability and vulnerability had clearly become an acceptable way for these witnesses, many of them social workers, doctors and clerics, to argue for the greater control of young women in Irish society.

A distinction was also made by witnesses between rescue and prevention work, with prevention work being given the greater emphasis. Prevention work was synonymous with protection. In the committee's view common prostitutes were 'usually girls between 16 and 21 years of age who have been betrayed and in their fallen condition, helpless and desperate, are driven to the streets for a living'.[169] This is a view that had been common in the nineteenth century and creates a picture of victimhood, the fall into prostitution being outside the control of the girl who is a figure of pity and someone that welfare workers and increasingly social workers must help. The issue of feeble-mindedness, a factor that had emerged in discussions of prostitution in the pre-war years, now came to the fore in the Irish situation. It was considered an important element in explaining why young women turned to prostitution. It was also a useful way for rescue workers to understand the phenomenon of the unmarried mother, especially those who had more than one child.[170] However, the identification of women's sexual activity with mental deficiency allowed for the acceptance of some level of institutionalisation for these women.[171]

Much of the evidence provided by witnesses was accepted by the committee and incorporated into its report. The committee suggested that no one under the age of twenty-one should be charged as a 'common prostitute'.[172] It proposed that laws against soliciting should be broadened; that men found in brothels should be charged with 'aiding and abetting' and fines for keeping brothels substantially raised. The term brothel was to be broadened to allow action to be taken against individual women. The age of consent was to be raised to eighteen and the 'reasonable cause to believe' clause abolished. They proposed that borstals should be provided for girls aged between sixteen and twenty-one; and argued that the probation service should be extended to provide 'protection' to girls discharged from industrial schools at the age of sixteen.[173] The committee acknowledged that some of their proposals might appear to be 'innovations or too drastic',[174] but stressed the value of their recommendations by noting that they were the result of 'views deliberately expressed by the witnesses examined before us, who, we feel assured, from their varied knowledge, training and experience represent the sound and healthy opinion of the public on the subjects under consideration'.[175]

However, when reviewed within the Department of Justice the report was forcefully criticised. It should, the reviewer declared, 'be taken with reserve. It leaves the impression that the authors did not face their task in a judicial and impartial frame of mind.'[176] The review suggested that the report did not take a broad enough representation of views on the condition of the country, and that it overrepresented the stance of Catholics on moral issues, and 'adopted the views of the organisations of social workers'.[177] In other words the report was considered to provide a distorted picture of the moral condition of Ireland. The reviewer also expressed the opinion that the proposals made by the committee would leave men open to prosecution where they had sexual relations with women who were willing partners. It was noted that the committee's 'recommendations are invariably to increase penalties, create offences, and remove existing safeguards for persons charged. Their main concern seems to be to secure convictions: they do not consider the case of the man charged in the wrong.'[178] The critique also argued that legislation would not 'suppress all sexual intercourse by females between the ages of 16 and 18' and would, instead, create a new class of offender. This review, by the Department of Justice, was not prepared until November 1931 and nothing happened with the report between then and February 1932 when consideration was delayed by a general election. Fianna Fáil won the election and the new Minister for Justice was James Geoghegan, SC.

In October 1932 copies of the Carrigan report, and a memo critical of its content, were forwarded to members of the executive council.

Geoghegan, according to a memo, 'was not disposed to adopt the report' as it stood, and was anxious that any Bill which might be introduced on the subject should have the support of all parties so that it might be passed through the Oireachtas 'with as little discussion or criticism as possible'.[179] The bishop of Limerick, David Keane, wrote to the minister, and having seen the Carrigan report, met him on 1 December 1932. The Catholic hierarchy wanted the age of consent to be raised to eighteen, and made some other suggestions. Keane proposed that the report not be made public as it 'would give rise to a good deal of unsavoury correspondence in the press'.[180] In the light of all the advice on offer Geoghegan established an all-party committee to agree heads of bills for a Criminal Law Amendment Bill. This committee would avoid 'as far as possible public discussion of a necessarily unsavoury subject'.[181] Among the decisions made by the Geoghegan Committee were that the age of consent be raised to seventeen, and the 'reasonable cause to believe clause' be abolished. They agreed that in trying sexual offences judges could clear the court, as recommended in the Carrigan report.[182] There was some discussion in the Dáil and Seanad of the Bill where the issues of censorship and contraception were aired.[183] Section 17 of the Act prohibited the importation and sale of contraceptives. The Bill was finally passed in the Dáil in February 1935.

James Smith has argued that the Criminal Law Amendment Act 'not only sanitized state policy with respect to institutional provision but also disembodied sexual practice, concealing sexual crime while simultaneously sexualising . . . women and children'.[184] He further contends that the Carrigan Committee and the Criminal Law Amendment Act were the foundational structures in an 'architecture of containment' that witnessed the acceptance of incarceration for women who were perceived to deviate from acceptable sexual standards. However, this study has shown that for the period certainly between 1767 and at least 1912, Magdalen asylums were flexible institutions that women were able to leave. The Criminal Law Amendment Act did not provide for the incarceration of women. The ideas put forward by welfare workers to the committee were long-held attitudes which expressed a belief in the necessity for institutionalisation in order to 'protect' vulnerable women. It was a belief held since the mid-nineteenth century. No new institutions were created under this legislation. While the recommendations of the Carrigan Committee were radical in many respects, the state refused to engage with the preventive and after-care suggestions made by it. The state preferred to allow existing welfare and charitable organisations, which included those run by the Churches, to take their own steps in this regard. This had been a common policy also in the nineteenth century.

The true test and significance of the Criminal Law Amendment Act can only be judged in its implementation. It appears to have had little real impact on levels of prostitution, with arrests and convictions becoming greater by the mid-1940s.[185] By then another investigative committee suggested that the nature of prostitution in Dublin had changed and was now carried on clandestinely in late-night cafes and pubs. The women who became prostitutes appear to have been substantially 'young girls of the domestic servant type'.[186] The police seemed to have difficulty with certain sections of the Act, especially those that dealt with indecency.[187] The Dance Hall Act, which was a separate piece of legislation passed at the same time, was open to very broad interpretation by district justices and substantial leeway was given in many parts of the country to dance-hall owners.[188] However, the police did seem to pursue 'sexual offences' in a more rigorous manner and crimes such as sexual assault on children appear more frequently in the statistics.[189] The Act may have had some impact on the press reporting of crimes of a sexual nature, since judges could now clear the court for certain cases. In the 1940s levels of illegitimacy and venereal disease were again on the rise.[190] The Act did not legislate for the incarceration of young women in danger of becoming prostitutes, nor did it offer any measures, as suggested by the Carrigan Committee, to support preventative work. Also, for those who were able, particularly a large number of unmarried mothers, resistance to both Church and social dictates can be witnessed in their migration to England to have their illegitimate babies.[191]

Many women's groups were dissatisfied with the Act and in consequence a new organisation, the Joint Committee of Women's Societies and Social Workers, was formed in March 1935.[192] The joint committee's first meeting was called to consider

what action should be taken with regard to the rejection of those amendments to the Criminal Law Amendment Act, which had been for the better protection of children and young people, namely . . . that the laws regarding solicitation should be the same for men and women and . . . that all offences against children should be tried in camera.[193]

The joint committee, accepting the Minister's view that the Act 'was an experimental measure' and open to amendment, were disappointed when he refused to meet with a deputation from the committee.[194] Reminiscent of the work done by the watching the courts committee, the joint committee decided that it would also monitor the courts, particularly in relation to offences committed against women and children. For many feminists there was still a distrust of the ways in which women would be treated before the courts.

The Committee of Inquiry Regarding Venereal Disease, the Report of the Committee on the Criminal Law Amendment Acts (1880–5) and Juvenile Prostitution (1931), and the Inter-Departmental Ad-Hoc Committee on the Suppression of Prostitution (1947–8) provide key information on prostitution and sexual crime in the early decades of the state. None of these reports was published. While the government had considered publishing an edited version of the venereal disease inquiry, Archbishop Byrne, who was shown a copy of the report, suggested it be delayed until it became evident that the incidence of venereal disease had actually declined.[195] The Department of Justice opposed the publication of the Carrigan Committee report, noting that

it contains numerous sweeping charges against the State of morality in the Saorstát and even if these statements were true, there would be little point in giving them currency. The obvious conclusion to be drawn is that the ordinary feelings of decency and the influence of religion have failed in this country and that the only remedy is police action. It is clearly undesirable that such a view of conditions in the Saorstat should be given wide circulation.[196]

The gap between ideal and practice was too much for the state to bear. While much more can be said about all of these reports, and the nature of sexuality in the first decades of the Free State, it is enough to note that making these reports public would have created the suggestion that sexual chaos and sexual immorality were rife in the state. It is clear that unmarried mothers, venereal disease and prostitution formed a significant focus of concern in these various enquiries and reports. The need to control venereal disease was used as a rationale for moral regulation. Unmarried mothers and prostitutes were particularly targeted as sites of contagion. Women were central to understanding how both disease and immorality became so evident in society. Much of the moral legislation imposed, such as the Criminal Law Act of 1935, reveals an attempt by the state and Church to curtail sexual autonomy, particularly that of women. Clear also is an attempt to curtail any expression of sexuality, and to curb the consumption of sexuality. This can be seen through censorship, through the assault on the Monto district, and through the regulation of dancehalls. Moral judgement had social power in Ireland, as seen particularly in the condemnation of unmarried motherhood. Intervention into the lives of unmarried mothers saw the state and the Church cooperate in creating a system that kept these women incarcerated, at best in mother and baby homes, and, at worse, in Magdalen asylums. The policing of sexual activities was to become a feature of Irish life for much of the twentieth century. This, allied with familial and community surveillance, exerted its greatest force on women.

Conclusion

In June 1925 Elizabeth (Lily) O'Neill, known as Honour Bright, was found murdered at Ticknock crossroads in County Dublin. For four years she and another young woman, known as 'Bridie' (Madge Hopkins) had shared a room in Dublin. O'Neill, according to the newspaper reports 'was compelled to seek her livelihood on the streets at night'.[1] Dr Patrick Purcell, a medical doctor in County Wicklow, and Leopold J. Dillon, a former superintendent of the police, were tried for her murder. The state's case was led by William Carrigan, KC, later to chair the Carrigan Committee. Purcell had met O'Neill and Hopkins at about 12.30 a.m. on the 9 June at St Stephen's Green and went to find Dillon who had fallen asleep in the Shelbourne Hotel. Purcell went off with Hopkins, and Dillon went with O'Neill. Purcell was to claim that Hopkins had stolen money and a silver cigarette case from him. Later in the night the two men, on their way home, came across O'Neill again standing at Leonard's Corner in the South Circular Road. She was seen getting into the car with the men and found dead the next morning from a gunshot wound. The prosecution claimed that Purcell and Dillon 'were a pair of moral degenerates, vicious types, who quitted their families and responsibilities to come to Dublin to spend the night in debauchery'.[2] The defence suggested that O'Neill had been 'murdered by those sinister societies that had abrogated to themselves the power of life or death'.[3] Despite the evidence given in court, that Purcell owned two revolvers, that O'Neill had been seen to get into the car with the two men on the second occasion in the evening, the jury took only three minutes to reach a 'not guilty' verdict.[4] The newspapers noted that the case had elicited great excitement and that the courthouse was full during the trial.

The case aroused great public interest, not because it dealt with the murder of a prostitute, but because of the social standing of the accused men. Indeed the figure of the prostitute, as an individual, is partially hidden. We know her name, where she lived, that she shared her lodgings, at 48 Newmarket Street, with another woman who worked as a prostitute. In 1924 it was noted that five women worked as prostitutes from this building.[5] We have some idea of where she plied her trade. We do not know what circumstances brought her to prostitution, where she was from, or her family background. The refusal of O'Neill and Hopkins to use their own names in their work situation may indicate a desire for some privacy. In this murder trial it was the men who represented degeneracy, but no one seemed to care much about Elizabeth O'Neill.

Between 1800 and 1940 thousands of women worked as prostitutes in Ireland. While this study has made some attempt to reclaim this most neglected group of women, for the majority their individual stories are lost to us. Throughout the period women who worked as prostitutes were viewed as carriers of disease and immorality, but they were dealt with in an erratic manner with national attention focused upon them only in times of crisis. Sometimes the crisis was a consequence of their visibility, or it was provoked by political circumstances. The authorities appeared obsessive in their attempts to classify 'immoral' women, whether in judicial terms or as entrants to welfare institutions such as workhouses. Such categorisation was often based on subjective views about how women dressed or looked, or where they lived. From the beginnings of the workhouse system the need to classify women within that institution structured the discourse around women's sexuality, a discourse which was still evident in the twentieth century, particularly when it pertained to unmarried mothers.

Rescue homes and Magdalen asylums offered the most sustained and enduring institutional response to the needs of women who worked as prostitutes. At the very least, and particularly in the nineteenth century, these institutions offered shelter and respite for many destitute women. Catholic institutions, managed by nuns, survived well into the twentieth century but have become associated with abuse and incarceration. The context in which these institutions operated from the 1920s was considerably different from that which existed in the nineteenth century. By the 1920s there was an intolerance in Ireland of unmarried mothers and young women who were deemed to be sexually active, or in danger of becoming so. That intolerance was shaped over time by rescue workers and the newly evolving welfare and social worker appearing by the turn of the twentieth century. Discourses around women's sexuality took on a new hue after Irish independence. Political and religious imperatives dictated an understanding that women's place was in the home, removed from both public and political life. In this atmosphere the problems associated with prostitution and unmarried motherhood, and the discussions around these issues, saw the sexuality of all women as suspect and in need of restraint. All women, it seemed, were potential carriers of disease and immorality and were vulnerable to the temptations of leisure.

By the early years of the twentieth century Irish middle-class women were using prostitution as a means to advance their own political agenda of votes for women. The issue of 'white slavery' offered them opportunities to contextualise their demands within the language of protection, a language that was to remain the central plank of their political repertoire until at least the 1940s. Middle-class women's public visibility increased substantially in the early twentieth century, much of that presence enhanced by their discussions of sexuality in campaigns around 'white slavery', the Criminal Law Amendment Act (1917) and the danger posed by venereal disease. Irish nationalists also made use of sexual immorality to fight their cause. For them, the immorality evident in Dublin in particular was a consequence of the presence of the British garrison in the city. Once independence was achieved Ireland would be returned to purity.

The various pieces of legislation passed to suppress prostitution or to control the spread of venereal diseases did little to effect their ends. Under these laws women were essentially defined by their sexual activity. As long as the conditions that gave rise to women becoming prostitutes persisted then the law was always going to be inadequate. Laws that attempted to enforce morality, especially in the area of prostitution, were again dealing with the symptoms rather than recognising the conditions that gave rise to exploitation in the first place. If prostitution was a result of immorality, or personal weakness, then there was no reason either to investigate or alter the social and economic conditions that gave rise to it. The causes of social problems were thus disregarded and the structural ways in which, for instance, poverty fed prostitution were not dealt with.

There is no doubt that the majority of women who entered prostitution did so out of economic need. For most of the women looked at in this study prostitution offered little opportunity to make a decent amount of money or to become financially independent. Some of the most wretched of these women were the camp followers who lived on the Curragh. However, in spite of their poverty they managed some form of communal life and offered a degree of support to each other.

It is difficult to generalise about prostitution in this period. There are no examples of a typical 'prostitute'. We do not have access to the voices of those who engaged in sexual commerce at this time. Eradicating prostitution was never on the agenda for either state or Church authorities in nineteenth- or twentieth-century Ireland. Even the closure of the brothel system in Dublin did not lead to the end of prostitution. For most members of Irish society a tolerance for prostitution was evident. But it was a tolerance based on hypocrisy; as long as the women did not reside, work or show their presence in middle-class areas then it was acceptable. It was the institutions of the period, workhouses, rescue homes and

Magdalen asylums, that offered practical aid to these women, but showed little concern for the social or economic conditions that brought them there.

Exploring the history of prostitution in Ireland not only throws light on a group of previously hidden women workers, but it also provides us with an insight into attitudes to sexuality generally. It offers us a way of understanding how sexuality can become linked with politics, whether within the fields of medicine, suffrage, or independence. A study of prostitution allows us some insight into attitudes to Irish masculinity. While advanced Irish nationalists were eager to blame the British soldier, and suffragists the 'white slaver', again generally of British origin, for exploiting Irish women little blame was placed on Irish men for their sexual use of women. 'Bullies' or pimps become more evident within Irish prostitution by the end of the nineteenth century. Men were certainly supported by women who worked as prostitutes and some earned their living protecting brothels. An exploration of the construction of Irish masculinity would throw further light on the how men who worked with, controlled or used prostitutes were viewed by society.

Prostitution offered women a hard and difficult life. Many were addicted to alcohol, and by the 1920s methylated spirits seems to have been commonly used by the women working in the Monto district. Death from violence and disease were common. Respectable society often refused to employ these women who left prostitution or desired to leave it. The sexual ideology of the period announced that once fallen, a woman could not be redeemed unless she spent the remainder of her life in an institution. Most reformers' accounts of prostitutes, and even that of some historians, present them as passive.[6] However difficult their lives, these were women who survived in often inhospitable surroundings. Their personalities mark the reporting of numerous court cases in the nineteenth and twentieth centuries. They were very rarely treated as individuals, as real human beings. While men used them in sexual transactions, both women and men used them in a symbolic way to argue for political and legal rights. Rights which they, as prostitutes, as women and as citizens, were often denied.

Appendix 1 Arrests for prostitution in Ireland, 1863–1940

Year	Persons proceeded against	Dismissed	Convicted	Fined	Imprisoned	Otherwise disposed of
1863	3,318	203	3,115	1,868	485	762
1864	3,768	117	3,651	2,081	412	1,091
1865	4,427	106	4,321	2,600	364	1,232
1866	4,242	160	4,082	2,608	220	1,179
1867	3,693	81	3,612	2,330	381	877
1868	4,393	215	4,178	2,810	317	1,051
1869	3,790	87	3,703	2,387	440	851
1870	3,673	68	3,605	2,431	327	818
1871	2,494	36	2,458	1,730	279	440
1872	2,181	32	2,149	1,507	336	301
1873	2,405	28	2,377	1,558	526	293
1874	1,778	28	1,750	1,090	70	239
1875	1,839	33	1,806	1,096	484	225
1876	2,382	35	2,347	1,642	528	174
1877	2,097	32	2,065	1,376	570	118
1878	1,752	40	1,712	1,242	303	166
1879	1,475	42	1,433	1,020	253	155
1880	1,470	61	1,409	918	340	151
1881	1,475	43	1,432	1,066	273	93
1882	1,183	50	1,133	955	138	4
1883	1,594	21	1,573	1,286	213	74
1884	1,731	40	1,691	1,427	217	47
1885	2,232	24	2,208	1,931	249	26
1886	2,050	37	2,013	1,715	254	34
1887	1,832	36	1,796	1,650	116	29
1888	1,905	31	1,874	1,713	149	10
1889	1,914	47	1,867	1,650	207	8
1890	1,367	25	1,342	1,255	81	
1891	1,303	24	1,279	1,188	86	
1892	947	16	931	819	110	2
1893	833	20	813	712	71	3
1894	1,073	32	1,041	973	58	10
1895	941	27	914	891	23	
1896	1,029	22	1,007	980	27	

Year	Persons proceeded against	Dismissed	Convicted	Fined	Imprisoned	Otherwise disposed of
1897	720	46	674	640	34	
1898	1,038	44	994	983	11	
1899	626	13	613	603	10	
1900	656	39	617	607	10	
1901	694	34	660	642	18	
1902	693	21	672	658	14	
1903	821	34	787	775	12	
1904	875	38	836	805	31	
1905	976	36	939	926	13	
1906	955	44	911	884	27	
1907	1,151	60	1,091	1,072	19	
1908	1,483	119	1,364	1,337	25	
1909	1,254	138	1,116	1,095	21	
1910	1,503	151	1,351	1,301	50	1
1911	1,241	216	1,023	978	45	2
1912	1,716	211	1,497	1,486	11	
1913	1,389	188	1,198	1,173	25	
1914	1,250	150	1,097	1,069	28	
1915	1,423	219	1,199	1,180	18	1
1916	1,072	142	927	901	26	4
1917	1,035	152	864	848	16	19
1918	776	200	567	567		
1919	582	170	410	402	8	
1920						
1921						
1922						
1923						
1924	490*					
1925						
1926						
1927	627					
1928	634 includes 5 men					
1929	600					
1930	457					
1931	327					
1932	273					
1933	247					
1934	307					
1935	196 includes 1 man					
1936	143					
1937	61 includes 1 man					
1938	57					
1939	68					
1940	63					

Year	Persons proceeded against	Dismissed	Convicted	Fined	Imprisoned	Otherwise disposed of
Convictions for Prostitution in Northern Ireland, 1922–40						
1922						
1923						
1924	229					
1925	256					
1926	198					
1927	175					
1928	123					
1929	101					
1930	60					
1931	63					
1932	65					
1933	40					
1934	42					
1935	31					
1936	61					
1937	96					
1938	99					
1939	27					
1940	2					

Sources: Criminal and Judicial Statistics, Ireland, 1863–1920; Saorstát Éireann: *Statistical Abstract, 1931–40*, Report of the Ministry of Home Affairs on the Administration of Local Government Services, 1924–46.
* Carrigan Committee, O'Duffy Evidence, D/JUS H247/41A, NAI

Appendix 2 Arrests for prostitution in Irish towns and cities, 1838–1919

Year	Dublin			Belfast	Cork	Limerick	Drogheda	Kilkenny	Galway	Kildare
	number taken into custody	Dismissed	Convicted							
1838	2,849	439	2,410							
1839	2,888	345	2,543							
1840	3,556	401	3,155							
1841	3,733	588	3,145							
1842	3,968	560	3,408							
1843	4,086	508	3,578							
1844	4,468	613	3,855							
1845	4,394	640	3,754							
1846	4,054	647	3,407							
1847	3,819	809	3,010							
1848	4,054	915	3,139							
1849	4.293	997	3,296							
1850	4,650	1,168	3,482							
1851	na									
1852	4,298	1,237	3,061							

Year	Dublin			Belfast	Cork	Limerick	Drogheda	Kilkenny	Galway	Kildare
	number taken into custody	Dismissed	Convicted							
1853	3,527	1,044	2,483							
1854	na									
1855	3,333	1,202	2,131							
1856	4,784	2,140	2,644							
1857	3,104	1,377	1,727							
1858	2,528	1,078	1,450							
1859	2,733	221	2,512							
1860	2,815	304	2,511							
1861	2,359	147	2,212							
1862	2,824	127	2,697							
1863	2,993	105	2,888	na	20	na	71	na	na	31
1864	3,241	41	3,200	na	36	na	25	32	3	36
1865	3,933	32	3,901	na	58	na	6	8	na	49
1866	3,848	125	3,723	8	28	na	22	na	na	82
1867	3,220	27	3,193	102	52	5	31	na	na	40
1868	3,836	133	3,703	71	na	na	44	16	na	23
1869	3,162	25	3,137	8	31	1	26	na	na	176
1870	3,255	35	3,220	38	67	na	23	na	na	39
1871	2,196	27	2,169	20	8	na	10	na	na	31
1872	1,929	4	1,925	22	na	na	17	na	na	10
1873	2,057	6	2,051	20	70	na	29	1	na	64
1874	1,522	9	1,513	46	11	1	18	2	3	35
1875	1,462	6	1,456	94	2	na	19	12	na	51
1876	2,015	11	2,004	113	na	na	na	31	na	52
1877	1,672	5	1,667	101	42	2	na	50	na	12

Year										
1878	1,393	15	1,378	101	43	3	na	na	na	16
1879	1,102	3	1,099	92	97	na	na	na	na	8
1880	1,009	9	1,000	225	81	na	7	12	2	1
1881	975	1	974	158	11	3	6	na	na	37
1882	785	2	783	129	9	4	2	na	10	32
1883	1,146	na	na	148	3	3	6	na	na	47
1884	1,202	5	1,197	151	21	14	8	na	na	69
1885	1,601	7	1,594	203	21	5	9	na	na	105
1886	1,563	6	1,557	118	9	11	10	na	na	66
1887	1,413	10	1,403	148	na	17	na	na	na	81
1888	1,407	11	1,396	165	30	11	4	na	na	91
1889	1,355	9	1,346	183	18	24	na	na	na	50
1890	1,077	1	1,076	131	9	na	na	na	na	3
1891	948	8	940	174	3	7	na	na	1	9
1892	684	3	681	94	12	12	1	na	na	50
1893	583	7	576	82	5	6	na	na	6	9
1894	753	4	749	129	12	8	na	8	34	99
1895	699	20	679	84	1	10	na	18	6	24
1896	681	15	666	95	8	6	na	22	5	108
1897	556	28	528	47	11	8	na	13	na	5
1898	806	14	792	98	na	22	na	na	na	na
1899	494	7	487	38	na	22	na	10	na	na
1900	431	13	418	86	na	35	na	na	na	5
1901	472	5	467	139	2	18	na	na	na	na
1902	517	6	511	76	9	16	na	na	na	na
1903	613	3	610	126	1	16	na	na	na	1
1904	586	6	580	185	na	28	na	na	na	na
1905	651	4	647	223	29	29	na	na	na	na
1906	601	9	592	227	29	27	na	na	na	na
1907	690	12	678	263	42	43	na	na	na	3
1908	724	16	708	474	129	47	na	na	na	na

Year	Dublin			Belfast	Cork	Limerick	Drogheda	Kilkenny	Galway	Kildare
	number taken into custody	Dismissed	Convicted							
1909	634	9	625	407	107	19	na	na	na	na
1910	785	18	767	453	128	31	na	na	na	7
1911	605	27	578	469	19	43	na	na	na	na
1912	1,067	34	1,031	456	63	24	na	na	na	3
1913	689	19	669	479	71	23	na	na	na	33
1914	645	13	631	446	55	10	na	5	na	20
1915	740	11	724	517	63	16	na	na	na	5
1916	552	4	548	391	45	2	na	na	—	na
1917	447	9	438	490	19	2	na	na	—	4
1918	260	5	246	431	16	2	na	na	—	6
1919	198	1	195	341	18	1	na	na	na	na

Appendix 3 Brothels in Dublin, 1838–94

	1	2	3	4	5	6	7	8
1838	81	157	861	164	758	402	1,630	
1839	na							
1840	na							
1841	27	215	260	113	963	355	1,187	
1842	26	237	981	89	182	352	1,163	
1843	35	253	1,103	95	184	383	1,287	
1844	39	269	1,145	97	192	405	1,337	
1845	37	262	1,250	120	244	419	1,494	
1846	38	240	1,166	114	193	392	1,359	
1847	42	235	1,116	121	198	398	1,314	
1848	39	247	1,127	99	216	385	1,343	
1849	31	203	1,108	96	236	330	1,344	
1850	25	200	1,122	47	93	272	1,215	
1851	32	216	1,042	51	128	299	1,170	
1852	20	158	1,001	98	288	276	1,289	
1853	15	134	754	58	132	207	886	
1854	17	171	941	89	187	277	1,128	
1855	15	134	651	47	94	196	745	77
1856	11	131	666	61	115	203	781	12
1857	10	85	479	50	106	145	585	50
1858	9	99	606	46	98	154	704	12
1859	7	114	796	28	63	143	865	15
1860	7	112	842	29	121	148	963	
1861	6	102	791	33	131	141	922	
1862	7	114	939	40	86	161	1,025	
1863	8	121	1,022	56	141	185	1,163	
1864	6	123	904	63	163	192	1,069	1
1865	6	135	943	53	132	191	1,075	2
1866	6	138	868	57	163	195	1,031	
1867	7	116	934	38	113	161	1,047	
1868	10	118	836	55	133	183	969	3
1869	8	116	738	49	104	173	842	2
1870	6	119	540	59	128	184	668	
1871	6	127	579	40	102	173	681	1
1872	3	102	495	49	94	154	590	
1873	3	90	422	45	83	138	506	4

	1	2	3	4	5	6	7	8
1874	4	102	469	37	59	143	531	
1875	4	86	448	34	89	124	537	
1876	6	76	381	49	103	131	493	
1877	7	81	400	83	128	171	539	
1878	7	75	407	57	106	139	513	
1879	5	60	200	62	108	127	308	17
1880	9	60	239	67	195	136	434	27
1881	9	65	261	64	159	138	420	8
1882	10	54	234	84	196	161	437	19
1883	5	57	248	168	277	230	525	12
1884	7	60	268	172	251	239	554	5
1885	3	74	315	182	302	259	617	17
1886	1	88	275	222	329	311	604	22
1887	3	75	275	125	219	203	494	2
1888	2	70	256	112	213	184	469	5
1889	2	76	274	105	198	183	472	4
1890	1	78	269	95	167	174	436	4
1891	2	79	274	100	165	181	439	6
1892		76	269	76	132	152	401	
1893	2	80	280	64	108	146	388	3
1894	1	74	249	71	118	146	367	5

Notes
1 brothels where prostitutes do not reside
2 brothels where prostitutes do reside
3 prostitutes residing in brothels
4 house, not brothels, where prostitutes reside
5 prostitutes lodging in houses not brothels
6 total number of houses occupied or frequented by prostitutes
7 total number of prostitutes
8 number of brothels repressed by the police
na = no figures available

Appendix 4 Some case histories of women who were residents of the Sancta Maria Hostel

M B was 26 years on the streets, living in a brothel in Elliott Place. She was hardly ever sober, and such an habituated methylated spirits drinker that she was known in the locality as the 'Queen of the Spunkers'. During these years she never approached the Sacraments. She was brought to the Hostel in March 1923, went through the exercise of the retreat, March 25th to 27th. On this date she went to confession and received Holy Communion. After a few months she was reconciled to her married sister from whom she had been estranged during all the time she had been living an immoral life. Having worked in different situations up to April 1930 she went to live with her sister who resides in 107 Gardiner Street. She is there at present and attends the Sacraments regularly.

H W living in Slickers lodging House came to the Hostel in July 1922. She was an absolutely notorious character and marked on the prison sheets 'not much chance of reform'. She remained in the Hostel as cook until 1929 when she left to return to her people who had not spoken to her for 15 years on account of the immoral life she had been leading. She is now quite reconciled to her relations and lives with them. During her stay in the hostel from 1922 to 1929 she made several retreats, the pilgrimage to Lough Derg on three different occasions and attended the sacraments regularly. She frequently calls to the hostel to give an account of herself.

S G came to the hostel in September 1922 from Lynches Lodging house, aged 26 years. She was the child of an Orangeman and a very notorious character with an almost hopeless prison record extending over three cities. She was expelled from Liverpool by the police. On three occasions she returned to her old life, each time being taken back into the hostel. For the past two years she is in a Magdalen Asylum, goes daily to Mass and Holy Communion, and is stated by the nuns to be a good example to the other penitents.

N C was admitted to the hostel in August 1928 aged 28 years. This girl was the child of a mixed marriage and brought up a Protestant. She expressed a wish to become a Catholic and was taken to the Little Sisters of the Assumption, Camden Street, for instruction. In 1929 she was received into the church, made her first Holy communion and Confirmation at Clonliffe college. Later she went into the Magdalen Asylum, High Park, where she has remained and is very happy and very contented.

B F came to the hostel in March 1923. She had been 15 years on the streets and a determined methylated spirits drinker. On March 25th 1923 she went through the exercises of the retreat, went to confession, and received Holy Communion. From this date she never looked back or took drink. On 26th May she married C F. They adopted a little boy of whom they are intensely fond.

I F came to the hostel in February 1924 aged 21 years. For about six years she had been connected with a man by whom she had two children, a boy aged 5 who was unbaptised and in Protestant hands since birth and a girl aged two years in the care of the Catholic Protection Society. She remained in the hostel until 1929 when she left to go to work. Since then she has been working in three different hotels and giving satisfaction. She is at present working in the Four Courts Hotel. During the time spent in the hostel she made several retreats and went regularly to the Sacraments. In March 1925 her little boy was rescued from the Protestants, brought to Dublin from Belfast and baptised in Westland Row Church. Later the children were placed in schools the boy in Carriglea Industrial School and the girl with the Sisters of Mercy in Booterstown.

K S came to the hostel from Slickers lodging house in July 1922 aged 39 years. She was greatly addicted to drink, of a very hard nature with no religion. On one occasion she was stabbed by a bayonet but when brought to hospital and at the point of death she refused to see a priest. She went through the exercises of the first retreat well. Later she left the hostel and returned to her old life. She was discovered in Slickers intoxicated and in great despair. She eagerly accepted the invitation to take part in the second retreat 11th to 14th September 1922. Again she became unsettled and left the hostel returning to Slickers. In 1925 she called to the home of one of the legionnaires who brought her back to the hostel. She made a third retreat and from this date has not looked back but took up work giving every satisfaction in the Sanatorium, Newcastle, Incurable Hospital, Donnybrook, and Peamount Sanatorium where she is working at present and has been for the past twelve months. She goes to the Sacraments regularly.

Appendix 5 Ballads and songs relating to prostitution in Ireland

'A MUCH ADMIRED SONG CALL'D TIE MY TOES TO THE BED' (DUBLIN? 1865?)

When I first came to Dublin I view'd barrack Street
I was a hearty young fellow and an art on my feet
I met with a girl call'd Bessey McCabe
She brought me to a lodging call'd sweet durty lane

I had two hundred & a good suit of c'oa'hs
And to tell you the truth I had a new pair of brogues
Id u lovely felt hat and my waistcoat was red
And young Bessey McCabe tied my toes to the bed

When I wakend next morning young Bessey was gone
And five drunken girls to work they began
The had black eyes broken noses their blood ran in stream
Faith sayes I to myself but they wil end my days

The mistress I ask'd her where was my cloaths
She told me my wife brought them of I suppose
Blugaronthers says I was I mared last night
And they told I was to a handsome young wife

Call her in my good people till I see her face
I just came to Dublin to renew my lease
She has my two hundred pounds and my darling fine purse
And if she be my wife she served me bad enough

When I thought fer to rise my 2 toes they are tied
And they told me it was tricks that was played by the bride
She coverd me snug in the bed with the cloaths
But she never came back for to loosen my toes

They brought me to en? And lock me up tight
Without sheet or blanket the length of the night
The dickens a bed was there to lie down
But walking about like a bull in a pound

So all you young fellows to Dublin does go
Take care of young Bessey lest she serve you so
She took my two hundred pound my big coat and my brogues
And she never came back for to loosen my toes

When she brought me to trial she swore to her shoes
Dev l a blaggard in Dublin but did me abuse
The justice he ta? tend to hang me dead
And he laught at my wife tying my toes to the bed

'A NEW SONG CALLED THE YOUNG MAN IN SEARCH OF HIS SISTER' (DUBLIN, *c.* 1869)

Good people now draw near and to me pay attention
And listen unto me the truth I am going to mention
For this maid I grieved ?? from the time I miss'd her
And the truth I'm going to tell it's all about my sister.

I soatlh' all I land [f]or my sister young and pretty
But not until once I found till I came to Dublin city
When walking up the strait my ? was nigh to blister
When a chap I chanc'd onest say ? did you see your sister

If you rove up and down you find her in the city
She as a comely smile and the damsels name is Kitty
She has two Ivory teeth and wears glosing whiskers
I stompt' upon the streets saying surely that's my sister

The sent me to Barrack Inne there fer to enquire
I there esp,ap the dame sitting by the fire
With a soldier by her side as I stept'd in he kis'd her
Then with a shout I cried young man let go my sister

The iuds they fel to and began to beat each other
The girl she run out ? to defend her brother
The police they came on us soon as they got the whiskey
Cried the youngsters at the door its all about my sister

They brought me before the more [mayor] being the ruler of the city
While twould relate hoing my case he'd pitty me
The more he smiled and said young man you're a fond jester
So he order'd me away to go and seck my sister

'ODE OF WELCOME'

The gallant Irish yeoman
Home from the war has come,
Each victory gained o'er foemen,
Why should our bards be dumb

How shall we sing their praises
Or glory in their deeds,
Renowned their worth amazes,
Empire their prowess needs.

So to Old Ireland's hearts and homes
We welcome now our own brave boys
In cot and hall; 'neath lordly domes
Love's heroes share once more our joys.

Love in the Lord of all just now,
Be he the husband, lover, son,
Each dauntless soul recalls the vow,
By which not fame, but love was won.

United now in fond embrace
Salute with joy each well-loved face.
Yeoman, in woman's hearts you hold the place.

This piece is attributed to Oliver St John Gogarty and appeared in the magazine *Irish Society* in 1900, when the Irish regiments returned from South Africa. The letters on the right side read 'The Whores will be busy'. See Ulick O'Connor, *Oliver St John Gogarty* (Dublin, 2000), pp. 22–3, where the verses are printed.

'SALONIKA' *c.*1918 POPULAR SONG

For they takes us out to Blarney
They lays us on the grass:
They puts us in the family way
And leaves us on our ass.

Now there's lino in the parlour
And in the kitchen too:
There's a glass-backed cheffoneur
That we got from Dicky Glue.

Now never marry a soldier
A sailor or a marine,
But keep your eye on the Sinn Fein boy
With his yellow white and green

And when the war is over
What will the slackers do?
They'll be all around the soldiers
For the loan of a bob or two.

And when the war is over
What will the soldiers do?
They'll be walking round with a leg and a half
And the slackers will have two.

Now they taxed their pound of butter
And they taxed their ha'penny bun,
But still with all their taxes
They can't bate the bloody Hun.

They taxed the Coliseum,
They taxed St Mary's Hall:
Why don't they tax the bobbies
Wi' their backs agin the wall?

And when the war is over,
What will the slackers do:
For every kid in America
In Cork there will be two.

Notes

INTRODUCTION

1 *First Report from his Majesty's Commissioners for Inquiring into the Condition of the Poorer Classes in Ireland, with appendix (A)*, HC 1835 (369) xxxii, p. 561.
2 *Ibid.*, pp. 66–8, 91, 92, 95.
3 *Alexis de Tocqueville's Journey in Ireland, July–August, 1835*, ed. Emmet Larkin (Dublin, 1990), p. 64. For other comments on the same lines, see *Observations on the Labouring Classes* (Dublin, 1836); Gustave de Beaumont, *Ireland, Social, Political and Religious* (London, 1839), vol. II, p. 35; F. B. Head, *A Fortnight in Ireland* (London, 1852).
4 Hugh Heinrick, *A Survey of the Irish in England (1872)*, ed. Alan O'Day (London, 1990), p. 27.
5 Harold Begbie, *The Lady Next Door* (London, 1914; reprint Dublin, 2006), p. 95.
6 *Irish Independent*, 22 January 1924. This was the opening phrase in a full-page advertisement taken by the Christian Brothers to promote their new publication, *Our Boys*.
7 See, for example, William Meagher, *Notices on the Life and Character of the Most Rev. Daniel Murray* (Dublin, 1853); W. S. Mason, *A Statistical Account or Parochial Survey of Ireland* (Dublin, 1819); Halliday Sutherland, *Irish Journey* (New York, 1958), mentions walking down Tyrone Street, part of the notorious red-light district of Dublin which existed until the mid-1920s.
8 C. S. Andrews, *A Man of No Property* (Cork and Dublin, 1982), p. 29.
9 *Irish Times*, 6 August 1928 cited in Mark Finnane, 'The Carrigan Committee of 1930–31 and the "moral condition" of the Saorstát', *Irish Historical Studies*, 32 (2001), p. 535.
10 *Irish Press*, 1 December 1926.
11 Hasia Diner, *Erin's Daughters in America: Irish Emigrant Women in the Nineteenth Century* (Baltimore, 1983), pp. 136–7.
12 K. H. Connell, *Irish Peasant Society: Four Historical Essays* (Oxford, 1968), pp. 51–86, 113–61. David Miller, in a review of Connell's book, pointed out that Connell's methodology in constructing illegitimacy figures was questionable. See *Journal of Modern History*, 42 (1970), pp. 387–8. For recent work on levels of illegitimacy in pre-famine Ireland, something which is notoriously difficult to gauge, see Sean Connolly, 'Illegitimacy and pre-nuptial pregnancy in Ireland before 1864: the evidence of some Catholic registers', *Irish Economic and Social History*, 6 (1979), pp. 5–23; Liam Kennedy and Paul Gray, 'Famine,

illegitimacy, and the workhouse in western Ireland: Kilrush, County Clare', in Alysa Levene, Thomas Nutt and Samantha Williams (eds.), *Illegitimacy in Britain, 1700–1920* (London, 2005), pp. 122–40. D. H. Akenson, *Small Differences: Irish Catholics and Irish Protestants, 1815–1922 – an International Perspective* (Kingston, 1988), questions many of Connell's findings.

13 William Acton, *Prostitution Considered in its Moral, Social, and Sanitary Aspects in London and other Large Cities* (London, 1857; 2nd edn 1869), p. 161.

14 *Report from the Select Committee on Dublin Hospitals; together with the Proceedings of the Committee, Minutes of Evidence, Appendix and Index*, HC 1854 (338), xii. Evidence of Mr Tufnell, Q. 397.

15 Frank Duff, evidence to the Inter-departmental Committee on Venereal Diseases, 1926, p. 38. File S4183, VD in the Irish Free State, 1924–7, NAI.

16 *Commissioners for Inquiring into the Condition of the Poorer Classes in Ireland* 1835, p. 84.

17 *Ibid.*, p. 74.

18 *Census of Ireland 1911, pt. 1: showing area, houses, and population; also the ages, civil or conjugal condition, occupations, birthplaces, religions and education of the people, vol. 1, province of Leinster* (Cd 6049), HC 1912–13 cxiv, 1.

19 See ch. 2.

20 For survey histories of women in nineteenth- and twentieth-century Ireland see Myrtle Hill, *Women in Ireland: a Century of Change* (Belfast, 2003); Rosemary Cullen Owens, *A Social History of Women in Ireland, 1870–1970* (Dublin, 2005). On women's role in the labour force see Mary E. Daly, *Women and Work in Ireland* (Dundalk, 1997).

21 See chs. 5 and 6.

22 *Annual report of the Local Government Board in Ireland*, 1900 (Cd 338) xxxv, p. 1.

23 Mary E. Daly, *A Social and Economic History of Ireland since 1800* (Dublin, 1981), p. 92.

24 Mary E. Daly, 'Women in the Irish Free State, 1922–39: the interaction between economics and ideology', *Journal of Women's History*, 6 (1995), pp. 102–3.

25 *Ibid.*, p. 105.

26 Jill Harsin, *Policing Prostitution in Nineteenth-Century Paris* (Princeton, 1985), p. xv.

27 *Ibid.*

28 See for example, Annet Mooij, *Out of Otherness: Characters and Narrators in the Dutch Venereal Disease Debates, 1850–1990* (Amsterdam and Atlanta, 1998); Peter Baldwin, *Contagion and the State in Europe, 1830–1930* (Cambridge, 1999), pp. 367–78.

29 For the regulation of prostitution and disease in the British colonies see Philippa Levine, *Prostitution, Race and Politics: Policing Venereal Disease in the British Empire* (London, 2003). This study excludes Ireland.

30 See S. J. Connolly, *Priests and People in Pre-Famine Ireland, 1780–1845* (Dublin, 1982); Emmet Larkin, 'The devotional revolution in Ireland', *American Historical Review*, 72 (1967), pp. 852–83; Emmet Larkin, *The Roman Catholic Church and the Creation of the Modern Irish State, 1878–1886* (Dublin, 1975); Mary Peckham Magray, *The Transforming Power of the Nuns: Women, Religion and Cultural Change in Ireland, 1750–1900* (Oxford, 1998).

31 Tom Inglis, *Moral Monopoly: the Rise and Fall of the Catholic Church in Modern Ireland* (Dublin, 1998), p. 140.

32 *Ibid.*, p. 145.

33 See Maria Luddy, 'Moral rescue and unmarried mothers in Ireland in the 1920s', *Women's Studies*, 30 (2001), pp. 797–817; Lindsey Earner-Byrne, 'The boat to England: an analysis of the official reactions to the emigration of single expectant Irishwomen to Britain, 1922–1972', *Irish Economic and Social History*, 30 (2003), pp. 52–70; Lindsey Earner-Byrne, ' "Moral repatriation": the response to Irish unmarried mothers in Britain, 1920s-1960s', in Patrick J. Duffy (ed.), *To and From Ireland: Planned Migration Schemes c. 1600–2000* (Dublin, 2004), pp. 155–73.

34 See for example, Cara Delay, 'Confidantes or competitors? Women, priests and conflict in post-famine Ireland', *Eire-Ireland*, 40 (2005), pp. 107–25.

35 See ch. 6.

36 Timothy J. Gilfoyle, 'Prostitutes in history: from parables of pornography to metaphors of modernity', *American Historical Review*, 104 (1999), p. 117.

37 For exceptions see Maria Luddy, 'An outcast community: the "wrens of the Curragh" ', *Women's History Review*, 1 (1992), pp. 341–55; 'Irish women and the Contagious Diseases Acts 1864–1886', *History Ireland*, 1 (1993); ' "Abandoned women and bad characters": prostitution in nineteenth-century Ireland', *Women's History Review*, 6 (1997), pp. 485–503; 'The army and prostitution in nineteenth-century Ireland: the case of the wrens of the Curragh', *Bullán: An Irish Studies Journal*, 6 (2001), pp. 67–83; Frances Finnegan, '*Do Penance or Perish*': a Study of Magdalen Asylums in Ireland (Piltown, Co. Kilkenny, 2001; New York, 2004); Elizabeth Malcolm, ' "Troops of largely diseased women": vd, the Contagious Diseases Acts and moral policing in late nineteenth-century Ireland', *Irish Economic and Social History Society Journal*, 26 (1999), pp. 1–14; Ciaran Ó Murchadha, 'Paphian nymphs and worshippers of the Idalian Goddess: prostitution in Ennis in the mid-nineteenth century', *The Other Clare*, 24 (2000), pp. 32–6.

38 Judith Walkowitz, *Prostitution and Victorian Society: Women, Class, and the State* (Cambridge, 1980).

39 *Ibid.*, pp. 3–6.

40 Ruth Rosen, *The Lost Sisterhood: Prostitution in America, 1900–1918* (Baltimore, 1982).

41 *Ibid.*, pp. 38–50.

42 *Ibid.*, p. xiv.

43 Luise White, *The Comforts of Home: Prostitution in Colonial Nairobi* (Chicago, 1990), pp. 7–10.

44 Gail Hershatter, *Dangerous Pleasures: Prostitution and Modernity in Twentieth-Century Shanghai* (Berkeley, 1997), pp. 3–4.

45 *Ibid.*, pp. 4–5.

46 *Sex in a Cold Climate*, Testimony Films Documentary for Channel Four, broadcast 16 March 1998.

47 *The Magdalene Sisters*, written and directed by Peter Mullan, Dublin, a PFP Films Production in association with Temple Film, 2002.

48 Jonathan Murray, 'Convents or cowboys? Millennial Scottish and Irish film industries and imaginaries in *The Magdalene Sisters*', in Kevin Rockett and

John Hill (eds.), *National Cinema and Beyond, Studies in Irish Film*, 1 (Dublin, 2004), p. 151.

49 Mary Raftery and Eoin O'Sullivan, *Suffer the Little Children: the Inside Story of Ireland's Industrial Schools* (Dublin, 1998), pp. 108–9.

50 See for instance, *Les Blanchisseuses de Magdalen* available as *Convents of Shame*, Marathon International Video, http://www.marathon.fr; *The Magdalens*, BBC 1993; *Sex in a Cold Climate*, Testimony Films Documentary for Channel Four, broadcast 16 March 1997; *Sinners*, Parallel Productions/BBC Northern Ireland, drama, broadcast 26 March 2002; *Washing Away the Stain*, BBC Scotland, broadcast 16 August 1993; Patricia Burke Brogan, *Eclipsed* (Galway, 1994) and *Stained Glass at Samhan*, (Co. Clare, 2003).

51 See for instance, Gary Crowdus, ' "The Sisters of no mercy": an interview with Peter Mullan', *Cinéaste*, 28 (2003), pp. 26–33; Nick James, 'Keeping it clean: an interview with Peter Mullan', *Sight and Sound* (March 2003), pp. 16–17.

52 Diarmaid Ferriter, *The Transformation of Ireland, 1900–2000* (London, 2004), p. 538. In 1953 the Magdalen asylum in High Park had almost two hundred inmates. See *The Order of Our Lady of Charity of Refuge 1853–1953: a Centenary Record of High Park Convent Drumcondra Dublin* (Dublin, n.d.), p. 65.

53 Finnegan, *'Do Penance or Perish'*.

54 See for instance, Jason Knirck's review in the *Catholic Historical Review*, 91 (2005), pp. 381–2; that by Mary Clancy in *Saothar*, 27 (2002), p. 94, and Caitriona Clear in *Women's Studies: An Interdisciplinary Journal* 30, 6 (2001), pp. 847–9.

55 Finnegan, *Do Penance or Perish*, p. 51.

56 For an insightful view of the film see Tom Dunne, 'Penitents', *The Dublin Review*, 9 (2003–4), pp. 74–82. There have also been novels, plays, poems and songs written and published on Irish Magdalen asylums. Two art installations, one by Irish artist Mannix Flynn, the other by American artist Diane Fenster, have been created around the subject of Magdalen asylums.

57 Lucy Bland, *Banishing the Beast: English Feminism and Sexual Morality, 1885–1914* (London, 1995), ch. 3.

58 Lucy Bland, ' "Guardians of the race": or "vampires upon the nation's health": female sexuality and its regulation in early twentieth-century Britain', in Elizabeth Whiteleg *et al.* (eds.), *The Changing Experience of Women* (Oxford, 1982), p. 382.

1 'FROWSY, SHAMELESS WOMEN': AN OVERVIEW OF PROSTITUTION IN IRELAND IN THE NINETEENTH AND TWENTIETH CENTURIES

1 Paphos, Mount Ida and Cyprus were places associated with the ancient cult of Aphrodite. See Ó Murchadha, 'Paphian nymphs and worshippers of the Idalian Goddess', p. 32.

2 See, for instance, Walkowitz, *Prostitution and Victorian Society*; Timothy J. Gilfoyle, *City of Eros: New York City, Prostitution, and the Commercialization of Sex, 1790–1920* (New York, 1992); Alain Corbin, *Women for Hire: Prostitution and Sexuality in France after 1850* (Cambridge MA, 1990); Rosen, *The Lost Sisterhood*.

3 From 1836 the Dublin Metropolitan Police (DMP) divided Dublin into five policing divisions (six from 1842) designated A, B, D, E, F, G divisions. By 1891 the DMP covered an area of 31.15 square miles; *DMP statistics*, 1891, p. xi.

4 *Criminal and Judicial Statistics for Ireland* 1896 (C8207) xciv 521.

5 See ch. 5.

6 *Census of Ireland for the year 1851, pt. I, vol. 4, province of Connacht*, HC 1852–3 (1542) xcii, 339–555.

7 *Galway Express*, 20 August 1881. Also in 1881 another constable referred to a building in the same street as a 'training house of ill fame', *ibid.*, 27 August 1881.

8 *Ibid.*, 19 March, 29 October 1881.

9 A hospital which treated venereal diseases; see ch. 4.

10 Summer Assizes, Crown and Peace Office, Co. Kildare 1885; Quarter Sessions, Naas (NAI).

11 *Munster News*, 25 October 1876. Cited in Caroline Conley, *Melancholy Accidents: the Meaning of Violence in Post-Famine Ireland* (Lanham, MD, 1999), p. 121.

12 *Report from the Select Committee on the Contagious Diseases Acts; with the Proceedings of the Committee, Minutes of Evidence, Appendix and Index, 1882*, HC 1882 (c340) ix, evidence of Mr James Curtis, Qs. 11,194, 11,203.

13 See ch. 3 for a discussion of Magdalen asylums in Ireland.

14 *DMP statistics*, 1838–94.

15 While it is not of central concern to this study it is also worth pointing out that many Irish women who emigrated also engaged in prostitution. William Sanger, in his famous study, *The History of Prostitution: its Extent, Causes, and Effects throughout the World* (New York, 1859), discovered from his inquiries that over 60 per cent of New York's prostitutes were foreign born and of these, Irish women were overrepresented. In a survey of the gaol register of Toronto between 1845 and 1890 Constance Backhouse found that of the 2,028 women imprisoned for prostitution 1,304 were Irish born. Of the 59 women imprisoned for keeping brothels between1865 and 1900, 27 were Irish born: Constance B. Backhouse, 'Nineteenth-century Canadian prostitution law: reflections of a discriminatory society', *Histoire Sociale/Social History*, 18 (1985), pp. 399–403. See also J. F. Maguire, *The Irish in America* (London, 1868), ch. 17. There is evidence to show that many Irish women worked as prostitutes in Liverpool and London. It was noted that of 1,123 prostitutes summarily punished for being disorderly on the streets of Liverpool in 1853, 497 were Irish. *Report of the Select Committee on Poor Removal, Proceedings, Minutes of Evidence, Appendix and Index*, HC 1854 (396) xvii, evidence of the Rev. A. Campbell, Q. 4,993. This is an aspect of Irish migration history that still awaits its historian.

16 *Criminal and Judicial Statistics for Ireland* 1886 (C4796) lxxii 233.

17 See his *Dear Dirty Dublin: a City in Distress 1899–1916* (Berkeley and Los Angeles, 1982), p. 193.

18 The list of convictions gives us some idea of where brothels existed in Limerick at that time: G. and Bridget Creagh, of Newgate Land; Mary

Duigh, of Mart Street; Mary Houlihan and Mary Fitzgerald of Post Office Lane; Bridget Deady of White Horse Lane; Catherine Hennessy and Mary Horrigan of Gibson's Lane, Red Lion Lane, and the Mother Abbess, Mary Gibson, of Gibson's Lane. *Limerick Chronicle*, 9 July 1836.

19 *Census of Ireland for the year 1861, pt iv, Report and tables relating to the religious professions, education and occupations of the people*, vol. I [3204-III], HC 1863 lix, I; vol. II [3204-III], HC 1863 lx, I.
20 For further information on this brothel see ch. 5.
21 CSORP 1835/2991, complaints re brothels in Dublin, NAI.
22 *Criminal and Judicial Statistics for Ireland* 1884 (C4181) lxxxvi 243.
23 *Ibid.*, 1914–16 (Cd 8077, 8006) lxxxii 451.
24 *Ibid.*, 1919 (Cmd 43, 438) lii.
25 Logan wrote a number of works on prostitution: William Logan, *An Exposure from Personal Observation of Female Prostitution in London, Leeds, Rochdale, and Especially Glasgow, With Remarks on the Causes, Extent, Results and Remedy of the Evil* (Glasgow, 1843); *The Moral Statistics of Glasgow* (Glasgow, 1849); and *The Great Social Evil: its Causes, Extent, Results and Remedies* (London, 1871).
26 Logan, *Great Social Evil*, p. 49.
27 *Ibid.*, pp. 48–52.
28 Rev. John Edgar, *Female Virtue: its Enemies and Friends* (London, 1841).
29 Michael J. F. McCarthy, *Priests and People in Ireland* (Dublin, 1903), p. 287. McCarthy's work is notably anti-Catholic.
30 *Cork Examiner*, 20 March 1876.
31 *Ibid.*, 16 September 1878.
32 Naas Union Poor Law minute book, 18 March 1868, Kildare County Library, Newbridge. In 1837 a prostitute in Westport, County Mayo, remarked that a fair day 'was good for her', *Mayo Constitution*, 28 March 1837.
33 *Report from the Select Committee on the Contagious Diseases Acts*, 1882, evidence of Mr James Curtis, Q. 11,211.
34 *Select Committee of Inquiry into Drunkenness among the Labouring Classes of the United Kingdom, Report, Minutes of Evidence, Appendix*, HC 1834 (559) viii, 315, letter of John C. Graves, p. 442. The police cited the recent suppression and abolition of the celebration of midsummer at St John's Well in Kilmainham 'where similar proceedings had been carried on for many years' as a precedent for repressing the Donnybrook Fair.
35 *Freeman's Journal*, 28 September 1837. See also 'Report of the Commissioners of the Metropolitan Police for the Information of His Excellency, the Lord Lieutenant, 1838'. CSORP, 1838/2642, NAI.
36 *Freeman's Journal*, 16 August 1841.
37 For an excellent account of the fair see Séamas Ó Maitiú, *The Humours of Donnybrook: Dublin's Famous Fair and its Suppression* (Dublin, 1995).
38 Fergus D'Arcy, 'The decline and fall of Donnybrook Fair: moral reform and social control in nineteenth century Dublin', *Saothar: Journal of the Irish Labour History Society*, 13 (1988), p. 17.
39 See ch. 5.
40 In 1860 an 'amazing influx of prostitutes' into Clonmel was attributed to the

town 'becoming headquarters to a regiment of the line'. *Tipperary Free Press*, 10 January 1860.

41 S. J. Connolly (ed.), *The Oxford Companion to Irish History* (Oxford, 1998), p. 29.

42 Padraic O'Farrell, *Irish Times*, 31 January 1987.

43 Quoted in W. S. Mason, *A Statistical Account or Parochial Survey of Ireland*, 3 vols. (Dublin, 1814–19), III, p. 79. In 1845 Athlone was again deemed to be 'infested with prostitutes'. See *Athlone Sentinel*, 21 March 1845.

44 Isaac Weld, *Statistical Survey of the County Roscommon* (Dublin, 1832), p. 407.

45 *Commissioners for Inquiring into the Condition of the Poorer Classes in Ireland*, 1835, p. 111.

46 Kilmainham Papers, MS 1054, p. 290, NLI.

47 MS book recording offences committed in Dundalk under the 17th and 18th Victoria, Chapter 103; D/2458/3, PRONI.

48 *Clare Journal*, 6 December 1858. Also cited in Ó Murchadha, 'Paphian nymphs', p. 35. For a valuable interpretation of the economic importance of prostitution to families and communities see White, *The Comforts of Home*.

49 *Clare Journal*, 1 May 1884.

50 Diary of Rev. Anthony McIntyre's visits to the poor Belfast, 1853–57. D1558/2/3 PRONI, pp. 6, 29, 34, 59.

51 *Ibid.*, p. 64.

52 Rev. W. M. O'Hanlon, *Walks Among the Poor of Belfast* (Memston, 1971, reprint of the original 1853 edition). For other information on the level of prostitution in Belfast in the period between 1800 and 1865 see Brian Griffin, *The Bulkies: Police and Crime in Belfast, 1800–1865* (Dublin, 1997), pp. 61–8.

53 *Ballymena Observer*, 8 September 1866.

54 *Belfast Newsletter*, 3 December 1860.

55 Reports and Printed Documents of the Corporation of Dublin, 1885, no. 149, quoted in Yvonne Whelan, *Reinventing Modern Dublin: Streetscape, Iconography and the Politics of Identity* (Dublin, 2003), p. 105.

56 Reports and Printed Documents of the Corporation of Dublin, 1888, vol. III, no. 110, quoted in Whelan, *Reinventing Modern Dublin*, p. 106.

57 Unsigned letter to Archbishop Walsh, 6 February 1889, Walsh Papers, 1889, File 404/1-3, DDA.

58 See ch. 5.

59 *Standing Orders and Regulations for the Government and Guidance of the Dublin Metropolitan Police* (Dublin, 1889), pp. 200–1.

60 *The Royal Irish Constabulary Manual or Guide to the Discharge of Police Duties* (Dublin, 1910), p. 48.

61 *Ibid.*

62 The Vagrancy Act, 1823, 5 Geo. 4, c.83.

63 Towns Improvement (Ireland) Act, 1854, 17 & 18 Vic., c.103, s.72. This Act conferred extensive powers of town management on those towns which adopted it. See Virginia Crossman, *Local Government in Nineteenth Century Ireland* (Belfast, 1994), pp. 67–9. The civic authorities in some towns also

introduced byelaws to curb prostitution. In Kilkenny in 1843 the local authorities ordered that 'females of ill fame, night walkers and other idlers be prevented from loitering or standing before any door or upon any footway from sunset to sunrise'. Kilkenny Borough Minute Book, X, 1843–55 (Kilkenny Borough Archives), p. 69, cited in Liam Bolger, 'The Military in Kilkenny 1800–1870' (unpublished doctoral thesis, National University of Ireland Maynooth, 2005), p. 67. Other Acts which assisted with controlling prostitution and provided police with powers against brothel-keepers included the Criminal Law Amendment Act, 1885, 48 & 49 Vic., c.69; the Refreshment Houses Act (Ireland), 1860; the Licensing Act of 1872, ss. 14 and 15; the Dublin Police Act, 1842, 5 & 6 Vic., c.24, s.7; and the Prevention of Crimes Act, 1871, 34 & 35 Vic., c.112.

64 See ch. 4.

65 'Return relating to the number of men in the [A, B, D, E, F] G Division, reports of being in brothels each year from 1 January 1838 to 1 January 1858, the number convicted and the punishment in each case', CSORP 1858/11753, NAI. For other corruption cases see CSORP 1883/13366, NAI.

66 See, for instance, *Irish News*, 6 July 1904.

67 *Freeman's Journal*, 30 July 1855. The DMP managed to close seventy-seven brothels that year. See appendix 3.

68 *Freeman's Journal*, 5 June 1857. According to the DMP figures they closed fifty brothels in the city that year. See appendix 3.

69 *Freeman's Journal*, 29 September 1878.

70 *Ibid.*

71 *Ibid.*, 9 September 1880.

72 *Report from the Select Committee on the Contagious Diseases Acts.* 1882, evidence of Mr Rawton McNamara, Q. 6,472. The DMP statistics only record the closure of twenty-two brothels in Dublin throughout the 1870s.

73 *Freeman's Journal*, 10 October 1877.

74 *Cork Examiner*, 11, 15 June 1864.

75 *Reports of the Royal Commission upon the Contagious Diseases Acts, 1866–69*, HC 1871, (c.408–1) xix, evidence of Rev. Maguire, Q 18,776. Many of the women had settled off Barrack Street, which was described as 'notorious and detested': *Cork Examiner*, 3 July 1876.

76 *Freeman's Journal*, 5 May 1880.

77 *Belfast Newsletter*, 27 August 1851. It was reported that 'when the outrage was at its height, some of the casual visitors of the place were seen scrambling like cats over the adjacent walls and roofs'.

78 *Ibid.*, 25 August, 2 September 1856. The association did not survive beyond a few months.

79 Town Clerk's Letter Book, LA/7/29AA/3 PRONI, 10 December 1872, p. 888.

80 *Reports of the Royal Commission upon the Contagious Diseases Acts, 1866–69*, evidence of Rev. Maguire, Q. 18,804.

81 *Limerick Reporter and Tipperary Vindicator*, 21 June 1850.

82 *Clare Journal*, 3 February 1851. Cited in Ó Murchadha, 'Paphian nymphs', p. 35.

83 *Clare Journal*, 18 April 1853.
84 Dunboyne Papers, MS 3,337, NLI. Emphasis in the original.
85 *Ibid.*
86 *Limerick Chronicle*, 12 September 1855.
87 Kieran Sheedy, ' "Soft, full day-trade blue", the diary of P. J. Dillon, Ennis Draper', *The Other Clare*, 18 (1994), p. 59; cited in Ó Murchadha, 'Paphian nymphs', p. 36.
88 James O'Shea, *Priests, Politics and People in Post-Famine Ireland* (Dublin, 1983), p. 222. See also Denis G. Marnane, *Land and Violence: a History of West Tipperary from 1660* (Tipperary, 1985), p. 112.
89 *Reports of the Royal Commission upon the Contagious Diseases Acts, 1866–69.* evidence of Rev. Maguire, Q. 18,864. One correspondent to the *Cork Examiner* observed in 1880 that Queenstown was now a moral seaport town, and that, although once it had been degraded by vice, there were now but 'groups of exiled daughters of Erin sitting here and there humming Irish ballads or Irish airs': *Cork Examiner*, 26 April 1880.
90 *Cork Examiner*, 3 July 1876.
91 It was later noted that the priests had closed down forty brothels in 1876. *Report from the Select Committee on the Contagious Diseases Acts, 1882*, evidence of John Kingston, Q. 2,656. Between 26 and 29 June 1876, Shinkwin sent fourteen women to the Good Shepherd asylum in the city. Of that number, six found themselves in hospital within months, five left of their own accord, one died in October, and two women appear to have remained within the asylum. Six other women, sent by clergymen, entered the asylum in July of the same year, none of these remained there. See MS Register of the Magdalen asylum 1876, Good Shepherd Convent, Cork, penitents 165–188.
92 McCarthy, *Priests and People in Ireland*, pp. 287–8.
93 *Ibid.*, p. 287. The 'pro-cathedral' was never designated a cathedral by the Pope.
94 *Report from the Select Committee on the Contagious Diseases Acts, 1882*, evidence of Rev. Thomas Morgan, Q. 11,347.
95 *Report of the Select Committee on the Contagious Diseases Acts, 1881*, HC 1881 (351) viii, evidence of Mr McNamara, Q. 6,476.
96 *Clare Journal*, 7 February 1848.
97 See 'Visitation notes of Bishop William Keane', Cloyne Diocesan Archives, Cobh, Co. Cork. My thanks to Sister Cabrini Delahunty for bring this material to my attention. It is not clear what the outcome of this case was.
98 E. Hayes to Bishop Keane, 16 December 1857. Bishop William Keane papers, Cloyne Diocesan Archives, 1796.07/49/1857. My thanks to Sister Cabrini Delahunty for bring this material to my attention.
99 See ch. 6. The North Wall in Dublin was noted as a place for prostitutes and foreign sailors. Residents had tried to end the nuisance over the years without success: *Freeman's Journal*, 11 November 1908.
100 *Kilkenny Moderator*, 27 October 1856.
101 For instance, a deputation from Fermoy met with the British military authorities in Cork to urge them to reconsider a decision to remove a battalion from the garrison in the town: *Freeman's Journal*, 21 September 1907.

The urban council promised to allow the army use of the technical school for the education of the soldiers when they needed; they also promised to provide suitable accommodation for the married soldiers in a housing scheme that was being developed in the town; the sanitary condition of Mess House Lane, which was close to the barracks, would be improved, and the deputation said they would get permission from the farmers of the area to allow the soldiers to train on their lands.

102 Letter to the District Inspector, RIC, 25 May 1886, in Petty Sessions Book, 14 October 1889, cited in Gerard Burke, 'The British Army and Fermoy' (unpublished MA thesis, National University of Ireland, Cork), p. 44.

103 Letter from Fermoy Urban District Council to CO Fermoy Garrison, 24 March 1890; Burke, 'The British Army and Fermoy', p. 45.

104 Letter from the Urban District Council to CO Fermoy Garrison, 10 June 1890 and letter from the Urban District Council to CO Fermoy Garrison, 10 June 1890; Burke, 'The British Army and Fermoy'. Similar problems existed in Tipperary Town where the town commissioners seldom had the support of the military authorities in dealing with prostitution. See Marnane, *Land and Violence*, pp. 72–3.

105 *Third Report of Her Majesty's Commissioners for Inquiring into the Housing of the Working Classes (Ireland)* (C4547) HC 1885 xxxi, evidence of the Rev. Robert Conlam, Q. 23,255.

106 *Ibid.*, Q. 23,256.

107 *Ibid.*, Q. 23,264.

108 'Name book, Dublin city: notes concerning the city of Dublin compiled during the progress of the ordnance survey in 1837', cited in Jacinta Prunty, *Dublin Slums, 1800–1925: a Study in Urban Geography* (Dublin, 1997), p. 297.

109 'Report of the paving and lighting committee', Reports and Printed Documents of the Corporation of Dublin, 1, 75 (1886), cited in Prunty, *Dublin Slums*, p. 315.

110 'Report of the Housing Committee . . .', Reports and Printed Documents of the Corporation of Dublin, 1, 13 (1918), cited in Prunty, *Dublin Slums*, p. 315. In 1901 a magistrate hearing a case of assault on a young girl commented on the fact that a school, managed by Catholic clergy, operated in Lower Tyrone Street which was 'such a shockingly immoral locality'. He was horrified that 'little girls were sent to school in such a vile place': *Evening Telegraph*, 18 November 1901, quoted in McCarthy, *Priests and People*, p. 295.

111 See O'Brien, *Dear Dirty Dublin*, pp. 193–4.

112 John Finegan, *The Story of Monto: an Account of Dublin's Red Light District* (Dublin, 1978), p. 7. In 1906 Montgomery Street was renamed Foley Street. Mabbot Street became Corporation Street in 1911. Tyrone Street Upper and Lower were renamed Railway Street and Waterford Street, respectively.

113 Bella Cohen was no longer running a brothel by 1904. Eliza Mack ran a second brothel at 90 Mecklenburgh Street: *Thom's Irish Almanac and Official Directory* (Dublin, 1904).

114 Sutherland, *Irish Journey*, pp. 17–18.

115 *Freeman's Journal*, 3 December 1914.

116 Suppression of prostitution, in Ad Hoc Committee on Prostitution, File 72/94/A, Department of Justice, NAI.

117 *DMP Statistics*, 1886, p. vii.

118 *Cork Constitution*, 1 September 1855.

119 Letter from Archbishop Walsh to Count Plunkett prostitution in Dublin dated 20 February 1886, MS 36,169, NLI.

120 *The Darkest England Gazette*, 12 May 1894, p. 8.

121 *Freeman's Journal*, 11, 25, 29 September, 3, 5 October 1866. As was usual when the police took an interest in prostitution they succeeded in moving the prostitutes from one area to another. In this instance it was observed that while 'the evil has abated in Sackville Street through the efforts of the police . . . [it] has increased in Grafton Street': *Freeman's Journal*, 3 October 1866. It was noted in *The Times*, 4 October 1866, that on the previous evening the Dublin papers reported that up to three hundred women were brought up at the head police office for 'walking the streets, and loitering'. It was reported that 'most of these persons were, on the confession of the police constables, innocent of any offence against the law and they were discharged. Upon a few of them additional imprisonment of 24 hours, or a fine of 2s and 6d was inflicted'. The newspaper correspondence had clearly forced the police into action.

122 *Cork Examiner*, 20 March 1876.

123 *Ibid.*, 20 October 1877.

124 *Ibid.*, 3 July 1876.

125 *Ibid.*, 21 March 1878. See Maura Cronin, 'Place, class and politics', in J. S. Crowley, R. J. N. Devoy, D. Linehan and P. O'Flanagan (eds.), *Atlas of Cork City* (Cork, 2005), pp. 204–5.

126 See ch. 4.

127 See ch. 6.

128 *Report on State Prisons and Other Gaols in Ireland*, 1809 vii (246), p. 66.

129 *Dublin Hospitals Commission, Report of the Committee of Inquiry 1887, together with Minutes of Evidence and Appendices* (C5042) HC 1887 xxxv, (c5042), p. 94.

130 'Reviews and bibliographical notices', *Dublin Quarterly Journal of Medical Science*, 28 (1859), pp. 207–25. Review of *The History of Prostitution*, by W. W. Sanger.

131 DMP office file, CSORP 1921–22/3395, NAI.

132 For a detailed study of this case see Peter Murray, 'A militant among the Magdalens: Mary Ellen Murphy's incarceration in High Park convent during the 1913 lock-out', *Saothar: Journal of the Irish Labour History Society*, 20 (1995), pp. 41–54.

133 *Freeman's Journal*, 15 August 1839.

134 *Cork Examiner*, 2 March 1859.

135 Maria Luddy, *Women and Philanthropy in Nineteenth-Century Ireland* (Cambridge, 1995), ch. 4.

136 See ch. 3.

137 See ch. 4.

138 The author pressed for closer guardianship of young children, especially illegitimate children, whom he believed should be watched over by charitable organisations. He argued that if young women were more closely monitored,

they would not so easily fall into prostitution. 'If they are not of an age to decide their fate irrevocably in marriage, neither are they of an age to make the no less serious decisions of devoting themselves to a vicious life'. 'Report of a local committee as to the best means of diminishing vice and crime in Dublin', *Journal of the Statistical and Social Inquiry Society of Ireland*, 5, 59 (1882), p. 309.

139 *Annual Report*, Dublin White Cross Vigilance Association, (Dublin 1898).
140 *The Vigilance Record*, 15 April 1887.
141 *Ibid.*, April 1888, p. 35.
142 *Ibid.*, April 1891.
143 Edward J. Bristow, *Vice and Vigilance: Purity Movements in Britain since 1700*, (Dublin, 1977), pp. 104, 163.
144 *The Vigilance Record*, 15 April 1892.

2 'LOOKING FOR MY LIVING': WOMEN, COMMUNITY AND PROSTITUTION IN IRELAND

1 See DMP Statistics and Criminal and Judicial Statistics.
2 *Ibid.*
3 *Report of the Royal Commission upon the Contagious Diseases Acts, 1866–69*, evidence of Rev. Maguire, Q 18,770.
4 *Belfast Newsletter*, 6 August 1851.
5 *Report from the Select Committee on the Contagious Diseases Acts, 1882*, evidence of Mr James Curtis, FRCSI, Qs. 11,256–7.
6 See below, pp. 61–70.
7 In 1911 wages for female mill workers in Belfast were between 9 and 12 shillings a week, while men earned between 20 and 40 shillings. See A. C. Hepburn, *A Past Apart: Studies in the History of Catholic Belfast, 1850–1950* (Belfast, 1996); Emily Boyle, 'Linenopolis: the rise of the textile industry', in J. C. Beckett (ed.), *Belfast: the Making of a City, 1800–1914* (Belfast, 1983), p. 54.
8 *Annual Report of the Inspectors of Factories for the half year ending 31 December 1863*, pp. 154–5, 538–9.
9 *Report of the Chief Inspector of Factories and Workshops for the year 1894* (C7745), HC 1895 xix, p. 18.
10 *Belfast Evening Telegraph*, 12 January 1907, cited in Michael Boyle, 'Women and crime in Belfast, 1900–1914' (unpublished doctoral thesis, Queen's University, Belfast, 1997), p. 219.
11 *Commissioners for Inquiring into the Condition of the Poorer Classes in Ireland*, 1835, appendix a, pp. 57, 67, 69.
12 *Irish News*, 24 July 1901.
13 The sentence was not implemented and the recorder said he would see what could be done for the woman: *Irish Independent*, 11 October 1911.
14 *Freeman's Journal*, 15 October 1841.
15 Belfast case, CSORP 1913/3348, NAI.
16 See O'Brien, *Dear Dirty Dublin*, p. 193. MS Census Dublin 39/86, 1901, NAI.
17 *Thom's Irish Almanac and Official Directory* (Dublin, 1904).
18 MS Census, Dublin 39/38, 1901, NAI.

19 MS Census, Dublin 40/49, 1911, NAI.

20 MS Census, Dublin 40/187, 1901, NAI.

21 Quoted in Ulick O'Connor, *Oliver St John Gogarty* (London, 1964; Dublin, 2000), p. 55.

22 MSS Census, Dublin 39/106, 1901, 40/128, 1911, NAI.

23 MS Census, Dublin 40/55, 40/49, 1911, NAI.

24 *Freeman's Journal*, 3 September 1834.

25 *Clonmel Herald*, 28 February 1838.

26 *Kilkenny Moderator*, 15 March 1871.

27 Case cited in Geraldine Curtin, *The Women of Galway Jail: Female Criminality in Nineteenth-Century Ireland* (Galway, 2001), p. 34.

28 *Clare Journal*, 19 September, 1842. Also cited in Ó Murchadha, 'Paphian nymphs', p. 33.

29 From 1787 Australia became a penal colony. Beginning in 1791, 40,000 Irish convicts were transported direct from Ireland; 9,104 of these were women. See Bob Reece (ed.), *Irish Convicts: the Origins of Convicts Transported to Australia* (Dublin, 1989), p. 2.

30 Criminal Record Files, 1840, Susanna Price, NAI (hereafter CRF).

31 CRF, 1841 Mc81, NAI.

32 *Kilkenny Moderator*, 7 January 1846.

33 CRF, 1851 M 57, NAI.

34 CRF, 1848 H 58, NAI. For other cases of criminal activity see *Clare Journal*, 30 January, 6 February, 3, 13, 24 July 1843: *Belfast Newsletter*, 25 April 1853, 17, 19 April 1854, 25 May 1855, 27, 31 October 1856, 28 June 1858, 14 May, 17, 22 September, 19 October, 12 December 1860, 2 May 1862.

35 CRF, 1841 Mc81, NAI. For another case see CRF, 1841 W3, NAI.

36 *Belfast Newsletter*, 16 June 1852. See also 21 March 1853, 18, 19, 25 January 1860.

37 See, for example, *Freeman's Journal*, 23 April 1878.

38 *Dublin Evening Post*, 5 August 1824.

39 *Irish News*, 11 November, 4, 23 December 1912.

40 *Irish News*, 4 December 1912. In 1871 Mary Considine was sentenced to five years for killing another prostitute in Limerick. Return of outrages, Limerick 1871, 37; 1883, 10, NAI. For other acts of violence within the community of prostitutes see *Belfast Newsletter*, 13 June 1855.

41 Conley, *Melancholy Accidents*, p. 120.

42 *Kilkenny Moderator*, 5 January 1856.

43 *Freeman's Journal*, 19 March 1835.

44 *Belfast Newsletter*, 8 October 1861.

45 *Kilkenny Moderator*, 5 April 1856.

46 *Galway Express*, 29 October 1881.

47 *Cork Examiner*, 20 March 1876.

48 *Clare Journal*, 8 November 1844. The case was later dismissed.

49 *Ibid.*, 3 November 1845. In Belfast in 1856 an old man was charged by a constable with using threatening and abusive language to a female of 'unfortunate condition'. The fact that the prisoner, alleged to be a brothel-owner, was about to attack the woman with a sword helped to convict him: *Belfast Newsletter*, 25 August, 1856.

50 *Clare Journal*, 2 March 1846; *Limerick and Clare Examiner*, 4 March 1846.
51 *Freeman's Journal*, 15, 19 October 1841.
52 Limerick Assize files 1890: *Limerick Reporter*, 8 July 1890; Kildare Assize files 1886; *Kildare Observer*, 12 March 1886; Tipperary Assize Files, 1892; *Clonmel Chronicle*, 2 March 1892. Also cited in Conley, *Melancholy Accidents*, pp. 102–3.
53 Extract from the visiting committee minute book, HMP Waterford made 1 December 1890; CSORP 1891/447, NAI.
54 See below, p. 67.
55 She was, instead, sent to jail for one month for an assault on a policeman; see Petition of a 'common prostitute', CSORP 1876/8460, NAI.
56 *Galway Pilot*, 30 March 1912.
57 *Freeman's Journal*, 7 September 1877.
58 *Ibid.*, 10 January 1839.
59 *Clare Journal*, 30 October 1843.
60 *Ibid.*, 14 October 1844.
61 *Kilkenny Moderator*, 8 July 1846.
62 *Clare Journal*, 4 August 1845.
63 *Freeman's Journal*, 3 March 1839.
64 The statistics for drunkenness were ones that the police were diligent in recording. Many of those summarily convicted for drunkenness had been convicted many times previously. Margaret Ann Rocks was perhaps unique in accumulating 200 such convictions. In despair over the possibility of a prison sentence she pleaded with the magistrate to 'hang me, do anything you like with me, but don't send me to jail, as I am jailed out': *Belfast Newsletter*, 24 May 1895.
65 Galway Assize Files, 1888, NAI. Cited in Conley, *Melancholy Accidents*, p. 121. Conley notes that five prostitutes in Galway had tried to commit suicide by the same means within a five-week period in 1888.
66 *Seventh Report of the General Prisons Board, 1884–85* (C4543) xxxviii, 783; *Eighth Report of the General Prisons Board, 1886* (C4817) xxxv, 281.
67 *Nineteenth Report of the General Prisons Board, 1896–7*(C8589) xl, 545.
68 Cited in Pauline Prior, 'Murder and madness: gender and the insanity defence in nineteenth-century Ireland', *New Hibernia Review*, 9 (2005), pp. 19–36.
69 For a general history of women in Ireland see Rosemary Cullen Owens, *A Social History of Women in Ireland, 1870–1970* (Dublin, 2005).
70 *Freeman's Journal*, 12 March 1881.
71 Jane McL. Côté, *Fanny and Anna Parnell, Ireland's Patriot Sisters* (Dublin, 1991), p. 207.
72 *The Nation*, 26 January 1882, cited in *ibid.*
73 John Kirby, Governor, Tullamore Gaol, 20 November 1890; Inspector Kirby, Athlone 10 December 1890: CSORP 1891/447, NAI.
74 Letter to the undersecretary, Dublin Castle, dated 30 December 1890: CSORP 1891/447, NAI.
75 *Cork Examiner*, 3 July 1876. The economic value of prostitution to the community is explored fully in White, *The Comforts of Home*. (Chicago, 1990).
76 Westport Union Minute Book, 18, 25 April 1861. MS 12,627, NLI.
77 Case noted in Curtin, *Women of Galway Jail*, pp. 92–4.

78 *Belfast Newsletter*, 27 November 1862.
79 Elizabeth Finnegan, Government Prisons Board, PEN 1885/99, NAI. For a similar case see *Clonmel Herald*, 26 July 1838.
80 See, for example, *Clare Journal*, 20 May 1844, 6 February 1846. See also CSORP 1876/6484 for a case in Clonmel.
81 Quoted in R. W. M. Strain, *Belfast and its Charitable Society: a Story of Urban Social Development* (Oxford, 1961), p. 283.
82 *Clare Journal*, 15 September 1847.
83 *Athlone Sentinel*, 7 March 1845. For another similar case see *ibid.*, 21 March 1845.
84 *Northern Standard*, 15 March 1876.
85 J. F. Burns, 'From whoredom to evangelism', *Lisburn Historical Journal*, 2 (1979), n.p.
86 The story of May Duignan, notorious as 'Chicago May', reveals the necessity prostitution was for some women. Nuala O'Faolain, *The Story of Chicago May* (London, 2005).
87 *Commissioners for Inquiring into the Condition of the Poorer Classes in Ireland*, 1835, appendix a, p. 562.
88 *Ibid.*, p. 93.
89 *Cork Constitution*, 5 September 1855.
90 [Thomas J. Haslam], *A few words on prostitution and the Contagious Diseases Acts* (Dublin, 1870).
91 *Cork Examiner*, 20 March 1876.
92 *Athlone Sentinel*, 24 May 1845.
93 Evidence of a girl paid 1 shilling and 6 pence by a farmer in *R. v Harte* Crown File at Belfast Recorder's Court, Belf 1/2/2/28, PRONI; and evidence of a ship's fireman paying 5 shillings in *R. v McIllhatton*, Crown File at Belfast Recorder's Court, Belf 1/2/2/24, PRONI.
94 *Kilkenny Moderator*, 13 February 1860.
95 See, for instance, the case of Elizabeth Wall who was transported for stealing from a man she had taken 'into the fields' near Mountmellick: CRF, 1841 w3, NAI.
96 *Freeman's Journal*, 21 September 1877.
97 *Belfast Newsletter*, 28 March 1853.
98 *Clare Journal*, 24 July 1843. Also cited in Ó Murchadha, 'Paphian nymphs', p. 34.
99 Quoted in Strain, *Belfast and its Charitable Society*, p. 281.
100 For problems with the children of prostitutes in the Cork foundling hospital see *Report from the Royal Commission on Conditions of the Poorer Classes in Ireland, Third Report, appendix C*, parts i and ii, HC 1836(43) xxx, p. 33.
101 See ch. 3.
102 Under the industrial schools legislation of 1868 children who frequented the company of prostitutes could be placed in such schools. See, for example, CSORP 1919/17970, NAI.
103 Though in 1849 the master of the Mountmellick workhouse refused to allow a number of women into the house because they were women of 'idle infamous lives debauching the youthful inmates': unnamed file, CSORP 1849/010175, NAI.

104 A committee was appointed to halt this process in the Cork union. It seems, however, to have failed in its purpose: *Cork Examiner*, 17, 22 September 1841. See also *Eighth Annual Report of the Commissioners for Administering the Laws for the Relief of the Poor in Ireland*, xxiv (1855), pp. 107–11, 587–8.

105 *Cork Constitution*, 2 February 1841; *Southern Reporter*, 2 February 1841.

106 Cork Union Minutes, 1 February 1841, CAI. Also reported in the *Dublin Medical Press*, 3 February, 1841.

107 *Cork Examiner*, 17 September 1841.

108 *Athlone Sentinel*, 12 December 1850.

109 Under the Poor Law Legislation of 1838 Ireland was divided into 130 unions, and by 1842, 130 workhouses were built or in the process of being erected in these unions; 33 new unions were created during the famine bringing the total to 163. There were two unions in Dublin City and the workhouses there are referred to as the North Dublin union and the South Dublin union. The workhouses were managed by an elected board of guardians. See Virginia Crossman, *The Poor Law in Ireland, 1838–1948* (Dundalk, 2006).

110 Deposition sworn by Catherine Harvey before John Campbell, JP of the County and City of Dublin, 1 May 1861: Cullen Papers, 43/8, DDA. See also the statements made by Lord Naas in the House of Commons in June 1850 about procuring in Irish workhouses: *Hansard*, 3, cxi, cols. 737–8. For other cases of procuring in workhouses see, 'Dangers of the Poor House to Young Females', 1859, Cullen Papers, File, Laity, July–December 1859, s.319/8, DDA; *Report from the Select Committee Appointed to Inquire into the Administration of the Relief of the Poor in Ireland*, HC 1861 (408) x, 1, evidence of Most Rev. Paul Cullen, Q. 3,973.

111 Cork Union Minutes, 30 January, 13 March 1843; *Southern Reporter*, 3 January 1844; *Cork Constitution*, 23 Jan 1844. See also Poor Law Commission Correspondence, 1844, 2/440/38, NAI.

112 Killarney Poor Law Union Minute Books, 1844–5, vol. v, p. 307. Kerry County Library, Tralee.

113 *Wexford People*, 12 January 1887. A committee was formed to see what could be done about the matter.

114 Women of bad character or bad reputation were often named as separation women in the Belfast workhouse. This is a label applied before the introduction of separation allowances in 1914 which were monies paid by the government to the dependants of soldiers fighting in the war. The women in receipt of these allowances were also known as 'separation women': See ch. 5.

115 *Nomad's Weekly and Belfast Critic*, 17 February 1900.

116 *Cork Examiner*, 20 March 1876. There were women who entered the workhouses suffering from venereal diseases who were not labelled prostitutes. From a small 1864 sample noted from the North Dublin Union workhouse these women were listed as having employment, most being servants. See Register of Admission and Discharge, North Dublin union, 1864, MFGS 52/7, NAI.

117 She may have entered more often, as a number of Catherine Clearys with different birth dates are to be found in the workhouse in these years. It is

likely that they are the same individual. Cork Indoor Register, 1869–72, CAI.

118 There is still considerable work to be done on those who entered workhouses in Ireland. We have no age, employment, or gender profile for the indoor recipients of relief for these institutions.

119 Belfast Board of Guardians Indoor Relief Book, October 1892–March 1893, BG7/G/20, PRONI.

120 *Eighth Annual Report of the Commissioners . . . for the Relief of the Poor in Ireland*, p. 111.

121 In 1859 the bishop of Sligo requested information from his priests about the classification system in operation in the workhouses in his diocese. While concerned with the religious issue he was also keen to hear about moral classification. For the responses see box marked section III C, Workhouses-Reforms, Elphin Diocesan Archives, Sligo.

122 Westport Union Minute Book, 6 September 1860, MS 12,626, NLI.

123 Westport 1890, Precedent Book LGBD2/1, PRONI.

124 *Fifteenth Annual Report of the Commissioners for Administering the laws for the Relief of the Poor in Ireland*, 1862 [2966] xxiv, 535, p. 622.

125 Classification in workhouses, CSORP 1883/7984, NAI.

126 D. Caulfield, 'Historical statistics of Ireland', *Journal of the Statistical and Social Inquiry Society of Ireland*, 3 (1862), p. 242. See also Anna Clark, 'Wild workhouse girls and the liberal imperial state in mid-nineteenth-century Ireland', *Journal of Social History* (2005), pp. 389–409.

127 *Report from the Select Committee Appointed to Inquire into the Administration of the Relief of the Poor in Ireland*, 1861, evidence of Mrs Woodlock, Qs. 4,631–47.

128 *Ibid.*, evidence of Rev. Paul Cullen, Q. 3,971.

129 See ch. 5. For information on the 1861 Select Committee see Helen Burke, *The People and the Poor Law in 19th Century Ireland* (Dublin, 1987), pp. 218–42.

130 Virginia Crossman's work on the Irish poor law has clarified the issue of rights and obligations operating within the poor law system. See her 'Viewing women, family and sexuality through the prism of the Irish poor laws', *Women's History Review* 15 (2006), pp. 541–50. For further information on Magdalen asylums see ch. 3.

131 Drogheda Union 1896, Precedent Book LGBD2/1, PRONI.

132 A case was apparently decided in the courts on this question: Precedent Book LGBD2/1, PRONI.

133 Edenderry Union 1889 Precedent Book LGBD2/1, PRONI.

134 *Galway Express*, 14 May 1881.

135 Letter from M. Seymour, Commandant, Curragh Brigade, 18 November 1879: Kilmainham Papers, MS 1071, p. 30, NLI.

136 Con Costello, *'A Most Delightful Station': the British Army on the Curragh of Kildare, Ireland 1855–1922* (Cork, 1996), p. 25.

137 James Greenwood, *The Wren of the Curragh* (London, 1867), p. 2.

138 Memorial to Colonel J. Colborne, Curragh camp, 1 September 1859, OPW 486/59, OPW files, NAI.

139 Letter from Major Bellaris to Headquarters, Curragh, 12 September 1859: *ibid.*

140 *All Year Round*, 26 November 1864.
141 *Leinster Express*, 27 October 1855.
142 *The Times*, 24 February 1857.
143 Jeffrey Richards, 'Introduction' to James Greenwood, *The Seven Curses of London* (London, 1869; reprinted Oxford, 1981), p. vi. For a fascinating insight into Greenwood's workhouse stay see Seth Koven, *Slumming: Sexual and Social Politics in Victorian London* (Princeton, 2004), ch. 2.
144 *Ibid.*, n. 25, pp. 304–5.
145 Greenwood, *The Wren*; Greenwood, *The Seven Curses of London*.
146 Greenwood, *The Wren*, pp. 11, 17.
147 *Ibid.*, pp. 14–15.
148 *Leinster Express*, 2 February 1865.
149 Kilmainham Papers, MS 1069, April 1878, p. 313, NLI.
150 *Report from the Select Committee on the Contagious Diseases Acts, 1882*, evidence of Mr James Curtis, Q. 11,277; Greenwood, *The Wren*, p. 25.
151 Greenwood, *The Wren*, p. 31.
152 *Ibid.*, p. 27.
153 *Leinster Expres*, 8, 15 April 1865.
154 *All The Year Round*, 26 November 1864.
155 *Ibid.*
156 *Leinster Leader*, 27 January 1890.
157 Ranger of the Curragh to Lord Lieutenant, 25 November 1859, OPW 486/59, NAI.
158 Kilmainham Papers, MS 1071, p. 105, NLI.
159 Costello, *Most Delightful Station*, p. 167.
160 Kilmainham Papers, MS 1069, p. 313.
161 *Ibid.*, MS 1071, p. 105.
162 Kilmainham Papers, MS 1071, p. 30, 19 November 1879.
163 *Ibid.*, p. 98, 10 February 1880.
164 *Ibid.*, p. 105.
165 *Ibid.*, MS 1069, p. 313.
166 *Ibid.*, MS 1072, pp. 106, 115.
167 *Ibid.*, MS 1071, p. 116, 27 February 1880.
168 Anonymous letter to Lord Spencer, 4 August 1876: Add. MS 77489, Althorp Papers, British Library, London.
169 Charles Brassington to Lord Spencer, 22 September 1876; *ibid.*
170 *Ibid.*
171 E. Maude to Brassington, 6 October 1876, *ibid.*
172 James R. Howard to the Lord Lieutenant, 7 December 1859, OPW 486/59, NAI. In 1860 the chaplain and the doctor at the Kildare infirmary wanted the women removed so that their health would not continue to suffer.
173 *Pall Mall Gazette*, 23 October 1867. Evidence given to the Curragh Commission in 1866 suggested it was relatively common for the soldiers to hunt both sheep and 'unfortunate girls'. Curragh of Kildare, Commission of Inquiry, transcript, 1866. Parts 1 and 2, 1, pp. 193, 195. Department of Defence, Property Management Branch, Dublin.
174 *Kildare Observer*, 8 January 1887.
175 Kilmainham Papers, MS 1051, 7 August 1860, p. 63.

176 *Leinster Express*, 2 July 1876.
177 *Ibid.*, 5 August 1876.
178 *Ibid.*, 5 August 1865.
179 *Kildare Observer*, 13 June 1885.
180 *Leinster Express*, 18 March 1865.
181 See, for instance, Shani D'Cruze, *Crimes of Outrage: Sex, Violence and Victorian Working Women* (London, 1998); Shani D'Cruze, (ed.), *Everyday Violence in Britain, 1850–1950* (London, 2000); Anna Clark, *Women's Silence, Men's Violence: Sexual Assault in England, 1770–1845* (London, 1987).
182 *Kildare Observer*, 25 October 1879.
183 *Ibid.*, 15 November 1879.
184 *Ibid.*, 2 August 1879. She was considered 'a great nuisance in the town of Naas'.
185 *Ibid.*, 27 December 1879.
186 Greenwood, *The Wren*, pp. 34–5. In evidence to a select committee on the Contagious Diseases Acts James Curtis, a surgeon at the Cork lock hospital, recalled that he had been in some brothels in Limerick City 'and the prostitutes were more like wild beasts. They were naked, and the cursing and swearing there was most abominable.' *Report from the Select Committee on the Contagious Diseases Acts, 1882*, Q. 11, 265.
187 Greenwood, *The Wren*, p. 26. Emphasis in the original.
188 *Ibid.*, pp. 34–5.
189 Greenwood, *The Seven Curses of London*, p. 294.
190 Greenwood, *The Wren*, p. 23.
191 *All the Year Round*, 26 November 1864.
192 Greenwood, *The Wren*, pp. 30–1.
193 *Ibid.*, pp. 31–2. Emphasis in the original.
194 Acton, *Prostitution Considered in its Moral, Social and Sanitary Aspects*; Henry Mayhew, *London Labour and the London Poor* (London, 1861/2).
195 Greenwood, *The Wren*, pp. 44–5.
196 *All the Year Round*, 26 November 1864.
197 Diary of a young soldier, MS 132,651, NLI. My thanks to Professor Kevin O'Neill for bringing this source to my attention.
198 Myna Trustram, *Women of the Regiment: Marriage and the Victorian Army* (Cambridge, 1984), p. 36.
199 *Ibid.*, p. 117.
200 Letter to military secretary, Curragh camp, 1 September 1859, OPW 486/59, NAI.
201 See *ibid.*, 27 October 1859; report on Curragh, 8 November 1869; letters from Curragh camp to the Ranger, 27 June, 24 July 1861
202 Kilmainham Papers, MS 1054, May 1878, pp. 327–8.
203 *Ibid.*, MS 1071, p. 31.
204 Greenwood, *The Seven Curses of London*, p. 300.
205 Naas Poor Law Union Minute Book, 7 March 1860. Kildare County Library, Newbridge. The memorial was sent to the Secretary of War in the week 30 May 1860.
206 *Ibid.*, 1, 8 August 1860.
207 *Ibid.*, 26 December 1860, 2, 16 January 1861. Between January and December

1865 there were on average thirty women in the auxiliary workhouse each week. The highest level of occupancy came in the winter months with between forty and fifty-four residents each week. In the summer months numbers went down as low as seventeen.

208 *Leinster Express*, 19 November 1862.

209 Poor Law Commissioners to Naas Board of Guardians, 16 November 1863, CSORP 1863/10089, NAI.

210 Letter from Robert Browne to E. L'Estrange 6 November 1863, OPW 486/59, NAI.

211 Naas Poor Law Union Minute Book, 27 January 1864.

212 *Ibid.*, 21 April 1880.

213 Greenwood, *The Wren*, pp. xi–xii.

214 Naas Union Poor Law Minute Book, 30 September 1863.

215 *Ibid.*, 11, 25 November 1863.

216 Poor Law Commissioners to Naas Board of Guardians 25 November 1863: CSORP 1863/10089, NAI. For a copy of the Poor Law Commissioners response to the case see Burke, *People and the Poor Law*, pp. 163–70.

217 *Irish Times*, 24 November 1863.

218 Poor Law Commissioners to Naas Board of Guardians, 25 November 1863: CSORP 1863/10089, NAI.

219 After the famine the numbers receiving relief declined to a very low level in the 1850s but numbers began to rise again in the 1860s and the duties of relieving officers became increasingly important.

220 For details of the case see, CSORP 1863/10089, NAI; Naas Union Poor Law Minute Book, November 1863, Kildare County Library; *Irish Times*, 24 November 1863; *Seventeenth Annual Report, Commissioners for Administering the Laws for the Relief of the Poor in Ireland*, 1864 [3338] xxv, 373.

221 Poor Law Commissioners to Naas Board of Guardians, 16 November 1863, CSORP 1863/10089, NAI.

222 *Leinster Express*, 18 November 1865.

223 Naas Union Poor Law Minute Book, 8, 22, 29 November, 1865. See also *Leinster Express*, 18, 25 November 1865.

224 *Ibid.*, 18 November 1865.

225 Greenwood, *The Wren*, p. 36.

226 *Saunders' Newsletter*, 24 September 1859; *Leinster Express*, 24 September, 8 October 1859.

227 *Saunders' Newsletter*, 24 September 1859.

228 *Leinster Express*, 24 September 1869.

229 *Ibid.*, 8 October 1859.

230 Curragh of Kildare, Commission of Inquiry, transcript notes, 1, p. 360.

231 Costello, *Most Delightful Station*, p. 171.

3 'BEHAVED VERY ILL': RESCUE WORK AND MAGDALEN ASYLUMS IN THE NINETEENTH AND TWENTIETH CENTURIES

1 See *Irish Times*, 4, 8, 13, 21, September 1993; *Sunday Tribune*, 5 September 1993, *Sunday Press*, 12 September 1993.

2 *Washing Away the Stain*, BBC Scotland, broadcast 16 August 1993.

3 *Les Blanchisseuses de Magdalen; Sex in a Cold Climate; Sinners; The Magdalene Sisters*. For other works see the bibliography.

4 For the work of Lady Denny in the Foundling Hospital see Robins, *The Lost Children: a Study of Charity Children in Ireland*, ch. 2 (Dublin, 1980). See also Beatrice Bayley Butler, 'Lady Arbella Denny, 1707–1792', *Dublin Historical Record*, 9 (1946–7), pp. 1–20.

5 *Rules and Regulations for the Asylum of Penitent Females:With an Account of the Receipts and Disbursements* (Dublin, 1785), p. 2.

6 MS Board of Guardian Minute Book, Magdalen asylum, Leeson Street, November 1841–January 1853, Representative Church Body Library, Dublin.

7 Quoted in J. D. H. Widdess, *The Magdalen Asylum, Dublin, 1766–1966* (Dublin, c. 1966), p. 5.

8 *The Dublin Guide, or, a Description of the City of Dublin and the Most Remarkable Places within Fifteen Miles* (Dublin, 1794), p. 51. The lock penitentiary in Dorset Street, Dublin, took in women from the Westmoreland lock hospital. Between 1794 and 1809 it had dealt with 380 women and it was claimed that there were ten applications for every vacancy. See *A Report upon Certain Charitable Establishments in the City of Dublin which Receive Aid from Parliament* (Dublin, 1809), p. 10.

9 *Connaught Journal*, 2 December 1824.

10 *Ibid.*, 28 December 1826, 4 June 1829, 3 June 1830, 16 May 1831, 4 June 1835, 26 May 1836.

11 *Ibid.*, 31 May 1827. The Sisters of Mercy took over the asylum in 1845.

12 *Report of the Committee of the Dublin Female Penitentiary to the General Meeting* (hereafter DFP), 1815, p. 19.

13 *Ibid.*, 1814, p. 12.

14 Rosa M. Barrett, *A Guide to Dublin Charities* (Dublin, 1884), part III, p. 4. The Rescue Mission Home established in the North Circular Road in 1875 stated that it was for the reformation of a 'better class, socially, of young women than those in other homes', p. 6.

15 *Report of the Ulster Magdalen Asylum, 1887*.

16 W. S. Leathem, *A History of the Church of Ireland* (Belfast, 1939), p. 46.

17 W. D. Killen, *Memoir of John Edgar, DD, LLD* (Belfast, 1867), p. 134.

18 An inquiry into the Ulster Female Penitentiary in the 1830s found that about eighty women had been taken in since its establishment in 1829. However, the inquiry also commented that the institution 'does not appear to afford any temptation to the unfortunate to seek it as a place of refuge. The food is of the plainest description, principally consisting of potatoes and oatmeal.' *Third Report of the Commissioners for Inquiring into the Condition of the Poorer Classes in Ireland*, p. 2.

19 Barrett, *Guide to Dublin Charities*, p. 3.

20 *Report of the Belfast Midnight Mission for 1874–75* (Belfast, 1875), p. 4.

21 *Ibid.* Of the 312 women who passed through the home in 1874–5, 29 were placed in situations, 4 emigrated, 4 married, 154 were sent to penitentiaries, 23 were restored to friends and family, 37 were sent to hospital, 37 returned to their 'evil ways' and 28 were unaccounted for.

22 For the work of the mission in this area see *Belfast Newsletter*, 8 January 1863, 7 January 1864; *Banner of Ulster*, 11 January 1862.

23 *An Address to the Ladies Forming the Committee of the Intended New Dublin Female Penitentiary in Consequence of their Appeal to the Public* (Dublin, 1813). The objections raised in the pamphlet were answered in *Four Letters in Answer to an Address to the Committee of the Dublin Female Penitentiary* (Dublin, 1813). The Rev. Mark Cassidy, in a private letter to the committee of the Ulster Female Penitentiary in 1816, objected to the composition of the committee. According to him the management of the asylum was entrusted to Protestant evangelicals and the interests of the home, being confined to one sect, could only be damaged because other religious bodies would be prevented from cooperating with the managers of the home. See Ulster Female Penitentiary, letter from Rev. Mark Cassidy, D 1088/22, PRONI.

24 DFP, 1814, p. 6.

25 Quoted in Butler, 'Arbella Denny', p. 10. The Magdalen asylum in Leeson Street was 'a shelter that will afford you time to reflect how gravely you have offended that gracious Author of all good': *Rules and Regulations of the Asylum for Penitent Females*, p. 10.

26 Murray Papers, File 31/1/4 undated, DDA.

27 Mr and Mrs S.C. Hall, *Ireland: its Character and Scenery*, 3 vols.(London, 1841–3), III, p. 62.

28 See the case histories in the annual reports of the DFP, 1814–16.

29 *New Edition of the Tract which gave Origin to the Institution of the Lock Penitentiary with an Account of its Progress and Present Circumstances earnestly Recommended to the Attention of the Humane and Affluent* (Dublin, 1805), p. 10.

30 In the registers of the seven Magdalen asylums I have seen children are never mentioned. Many of these women, however, did have children according to the census returns. For instance, the returns for the Good Shepherd asylum in Cork for 1911 reveal one woman who had been married for eight years, having five children. If the children were the product of the marriage then they would have been very young when their mother entered the asylum. In the same asylum there was another woman who had been married three years and had three children, and yet another, two years married with two children. See MS Census, Cork 85/1, 1911, NAI.

31 Minutes of the Penitent Relief Society, July 1858, M1133, NAI.

32 *Abstract Report and Statistical Sketch of the Magdalen Asylum, High Park, Drumcondra* (Dublin, 1881), p. 17.

33 *Annual Report*, Asylum for Penitent Females, 1831, p. 11.

34 *Ibid.*, 1816.

35 Murray Papers, File 31/7–9, 1840, DDA.

36 The newspapers of the period have numerous advertisements for sermons to aid Magdalen asylums. See, for example, *Freeman's Journal*, 26 December 1821, 15 March, 11 April 1822, 6 September 1823, 1, 30 January 1840, 12 December 1877, 26 January 1878; *Cork Examiner*, 8, 11 May 1915, 2, 5 February 1918. The archives of the Good Shepherd convent in Limerick contain a number of documents that list the proceeds from fund raising

efforts made for their asylum. These methods included bazaars, and circulars appealing for funds. In 1883, for instance, a local grocer offered the convent a case of champagne for the bazaar. Miscellaneous papers, GSC, Limerick.

37 *Freeman's Journal*, 6, 18 November 1878.

38 Killen, *Memoir of John Edgar*, p. 134.

39 Annual reports, DFP, 1812–25. The Dublin by Lamplight institution accounts show a similar pattern. In 1856 subscriptions and donations accounted for 98 per cent of income and laundry work 2 per cent. By 1867 subscriptions and donations had dropped to 39 per cent of income while laundry receipts had climbed to 56 per cent. See annual reports, Dublin by Lamplight Institution 1857, 1858, 1868. This institution also took over a 'concern known as Duffy's factory in Ballsbridge' in 1856, probably to use as a laundry and make the institution more self supporting. See *Irish Ecclesiastical Gazette*, (September 1856). Another source of income for an asylum was provided by the charity sermon which usually accounted for about 5 per cent of an institution's annual income.

40 Dublin by Lamplight, *Annual Report 1857* (Dublin, 1858), p. 7.

41 MS Magdalen asylum Register, 1809–28, RCB Library, Dublin.

42 Mrs 908 was recommended to the asylum from Steeven's hospital, where she may have been treated for venereal disease. She remained in the asylum for over seven years. Mrs 910 was also eight years old on entering the asylum.

43 *Ibid.* Mrs 669 was only thirteen when taken in. She stayed for eighteen months and was then taken home by her father. Mrs 759 was eleven when she was brought to the asylum by her mother.

44 *Ibid.*

45 MS Admission book, penitents, 105, 183, 753, 770. RCB Library, Dublin.

46 *Ibid.*

47 *Rules and Regulations for the Asylum for Penitent Females*, appendix, p. 3.

48 G. D. Williams (ed.), *Dublin Charities, Being a Handbook of Dublin Philanthropic Organisations and Charities* (Dublin, 1902), p. 60. The refuge admitted nineteen during the year 1899–1900. Of these four returned home, one married and eight were placed in situations.

49 *Ibid.*, p. 153. For the year 1899, 244 penitents were resident or admitted to the home. Of that number 178 left before the allotted probation period of eighteen months had expired, 31 were sent to situations and 2 were returned to friends. The remaining women were resident in the home when these figures were compiled.

50 See Francis Finnegan, *Poverty and Prostitution: a Study of Victorian Prostitutes in York* (Cambridge, 1979).

51 *An Appeal to the Public from the Committee of the Intended New Dublin Female Penitentiary* (Dublin, 1812), p. 20.

52 Annual reports, DFP, 1813–25, subscription lists.

53 See Dublin by Lamplight, *Annual Report 1868*.

54 The Salvation Army also engaged in rescue work. They dealt with prostitutes, unmarried mothers and other women in need. They ran a refuge in Belfast from 1905. For an excellent account of the work of the refuge see Leanne McCormick, 'Prostitutes, fallen women and friendless girls: policing

female sexual morality in Northern Ireland, 1900–1945' (unpublished doctoral thesis, University of Ulster, 2004), ch. 3.

55 Murray Papers, File 33/1/20, undated, DDA.

56 DFP, 1816.

57 *Report from the Select Committee on the Contagious Diseases Acts, 1881*, evidence of Rev. Henry Reed, Q. 6,231. The Good Shepherd nuns had approached Cardinal Cullen in 1870 with a proposal to establish a branch of their convent in Dublin, specifically to take over the care of the penitents in an asylum in Mecklenburgh Street. Nothing came of this proposal. See letter to Cullen from the superioress of the Good Shepherd convent, Limerick, 13 February 1872. Cullen Papers, File 335/1/6 (Nuns, 1872), DDA.

58 MS Annals of the Convent of Our Lady of Charity of Refuge. These annals are very detailed and provide a lot of information about the coming of the Order to Ireland and the difficulties the nuns had in wresting control of the asylum from the Rev. John Smith. *The Order of Our Lady of Charity of Refuge, 1853–1953* provides a synopsis of the information contained in the annals.

59 See for instance Rev. P. A. Sheehan, *Luke Delmege* (London and New York, 1901), pp. 367–8.

60 MS Annals, 1826–1909, GSC, Limerick. Likewise, when the Sisters of Charity took over an asylum in Cork, in 1846, it was observed 'that the state of the house as well as the habits of the inmates, then thirteen in number, was dirty and disorderly in the extreme.' Sisters of Charity Cork, Annals, pp. 46–7, RSCG, Milltown.

61 Between 1860 and 1900, 321 women entered this asylum, many being sent to it by priests. See Finnegan, '*Do Penance or Perish*', p. 152.

62 Letter from M. Chantal, Cork to Mother M. Aikenhead dated 14 June 1846, File 1/13/97 (RSCG, Milltown). The Magdalen asylum in Townsend Street was run by a Mrs Ryan, a niece of Archbishop Troy, from 1798. By the 1830s Mrs Ryan, through illness, was unable to control the penitents under her care. As a penance the penitents were not allowed to change the straw on their beds and to ensure that this rule would be kept Mrs Ryan had the ticken, which held the straw, nailed to the bedposts. When the Sisters of Charity entered the asylum they discovered that as a result of Mrs Ryan's action the beds were crawling with maggots. See typescript annals of the Sisters of Charity, Donnybrook, vol. I, 1833, pp. 277–9, RSC, Donnybrook.

63 The Sisters of Charity in Cork would not take over the asylum until they were guaranteed full control by the previous lay committee. See annals and letters of that convent kept at Milltown.

64 See Annals of St Mary Magdalen Asylum, RSCG, Milltown, for copies of the accounts sent to the bishop.

65 Sr M. Gertrude Howell to the Secretary, Charitable Donations and Bequests, 27 January 1875. Sr M. Gertrude Howell to Cardinal Cullen, 29 January 1875, Cullen Papers, File 322/1/4 (Nuns 1875), DDA.

66 There are six published accounts dealing with Our Lady of Charity Refuge in High Park in Drumcondra. The most detailed of these, *Abstract Report and Statistical Sketch of the Magdalen Asylum, Drumcondra* gives an insight into the running of the home. In rhetoric and style it is similar to the reports published

by the lay asylums and appears to have been published in an attempt to raise funds for the home. See also the *Report Showing the Foundation and Progress of the Monastery of the Order of Our Lady of Charity of Refuge* (Dublin, 1857); 'Second report of the Order of Our Lady of Charity of Refuge', *Irish Quarterly Review*, 9 (1860), appendix: 'The Magdalens of High Park', *The Irish Rosary*, I (April, 1897); *Souvenir of the Golden Jubilee of Our Lady of the Charity of Refuge, High Park, Drumcondra* (Dublin, 1903); *The Order of Our Lady of Charity of Refuge, 1853–1953*. All of these works were written anonymously.

67 The Gloucester Street asylum had 511 admissions between 17 February 1887 and 26 December 1897. At least half of these left the refuge voluntarily and at least 10 per cent entered the refuge more than once. See Prunty, *Dublin Slums*, pp. 269–70.

68 The registers usually give details about where the women were born. However, recommendations were generally made by the inhabitants of a particular town. In Cork, for example, most penitents were obviously operating in the city and were recommended by individuals from the city.

69 Penitent no. 427, MS Register of the Asylum, RSC, Donnybrook.

70 Penitent no. 346, *ibid.*

71 See *Practical Rules for the Use of the Religious of the Good Shepherd for the Direction of the Classes* (Angers, 1898). The guidance in this book appears not to have changed over the nineteenth or even the twentieth centuries.

72 *Conferences and Instructions of the Venerable Mother Mary of Saint Euphrasia Pelletier, Foundress of the Generalate of the Congregation of Our Lady of Charity of the Good Shepherd of Angers* (London, 1907), 2nd edn, pp. 372–78.

73 *Rules for the Direction of Classes*, p. 138.

74 Penitent no. 721, MS Register of the Asylum, RSC, Donnybrook.

75 MS Register of the Asylum, GSC, Limerick.

76 *Galway Express*, 29 October 1881.

77 Penitents 582, 601, 667, MS Register Good Shepherd Convent, Waterford.

78 MS Register, Good Shepherd asylum, Belfast, pp. 56, 64.

79 For a full and incisive account of convent laundry inspection see Desmond Greer and James W. Nicholson, *The Factory Acts in Ireland, 1802–1914* (Dublin, 2003), pp. 284–97. For an idealised portrait of a Magdalen laundry see Sheehan, *Luke Delmege*, this describes the laundry of an Irish Magdalen asylum as an up-to-date work space.

There was nothing repulsive or alarming here. Seven or eight long tables, running parallel to each other, filled the room; and at each table, eight or ten women, ranging from the young girl of fifteen to the woman of sixty, were silently occupied in laundry work. All modern appliances to save human labour were there. The workers were neatly dressed and happy, if one could judge by their smiles . . . it was a happy sisterhood, working in perfect silence and discipline . . . these poor girls took Luke around, and showed with intense pride the mighty secrets of the machinery; how steam was let on and shut off; how the slides worked on the rails in the drying-room, etc. And, moving hither and thither amongst them, in an attitude of absolute equality, were the white-robed Sisters . . . and they laboured and toiled like the rest, *Ibid.*, p. 522.

80 *Hansard*, xcix, 135 and 678, 13 August 1901, cited in Greer and Nicholson, *The Factory Acts*, pp. 290–1.

81 Quoted in *ibid.*, p. 293.

82 *Ibid.*

83 *Ibid.*, pp. 296–7. In 1905 the factory inspectors visited, 'with one or two exceptions, 24 penitentiaries in Ireland. They were refused admission to two Protestant and one Catholic asylum.' The total number of inmates at the time in all of the asylums was given as 1,238. See *Report of the Chief Inspector of Factories for theYear Ending 31 December 1905* [Cd 3036], HC 1906 xv, 405, p. 260.

84 MS Census, Limerick 45/111 1901, 62/13, 1911, NAI.

85 MS Census, Dublin 12/85; 1901, Galway 105/118, 1911, NAI. Unfortunately, the census returns for the Magdalen asylums do not enumerate the occupations of the women and tend to list them as laundresses or seamstresses, positions they would have held within the asylum.

86 DMP Statistics, 1911.

87 See ch. 2, pp. 44–6.

88 For the origins of prostitutes in England see Walkowitz, *Prostitution and Victorian Society*, ch. 1.

89 *Guide for the Religious Called Sisters of Mercy* (London, 1866), p. 58.

90 *Ibid.*, p. 60.

91 *Ibid.*, p. 61.

92 *Ibid.*, p. 59.

93 *Abstract Report and Statistical Sketch*, p. 181.

94 Murray Papers, File 31/9/30 (1840–42), DDA.

95 MS Annals of St Mary Magdalen, Cork, SC, Cork.

96 *Guide for the Religious Called Sisters of Mercy*, p. 56. Mother Francis Bridgeman, author of this guidebook, noted in 1859 that she 'made this subject [Magdalen asylums] the special object of enquiry in many travels. I was in favour of the principle that we followed while I had to do with the Asylum, that is, to encourage the penitents to remain in by every means, but not to make this a necessary condition, after a certain number of years, at least three, sometimes five or six, we provided those who did not wish to remain and were seemingly trustworthy with a situation.' Letter from Mother Mary Francis Bridgeman to unknown, December 1859, Convent of Mercy Archives, Baggot Street, Dublin.

97 *The Diaries of Mary Hayden*, 5 vols. (Killala, Co. Mayo, 2005), vol. I, 22 July 1882, p. 343.

98 Mary Costello, 'The sisterhood of sorrow, no. 1. – the Magdalens', *Lady of the House* 15 February 1897, p. 8.

99 See below, p. 121.

100 Mary Costello, 'The Sisterhood of Sorrow, no. 2' – the Magdalens', *Lady of the House* 15 March 1897, p. 7.

101 *Abstract Report and Statistical Sketch*, p. 25.

102 This system did not operate in those refuges run by the Sisters of Charity or the Sisters of Mercy.

103 *Abstract Report and Statistical Sketch*, pp. 26–7.

104 *Ibid.*, p. 25.

105 See n. 79 above.

106 The novel was published in London and New York and was issued in an

edition of 10,000 copies, translated into French in 1902 and German in 1904. See Catherine Candy, *Priestly Fictions: Popular Irish Novelists of the Early Twentieth Century* (Dublin, 1995), pp. 130–2.

107 Sheehan, *Luke Delmege*, p. 557.
108 Thomas Burke, *Ireland's Vindication: Refutation of Froude, and Other Lectures, Historical and Religious* (London, n.d.), p. 21.
109 'The Magdalens of High Park', p. 179.
110 Sheehan, *Luke Delmege*, pp. 221–2.
111 *Report of the Belfast Midnight Mission, 1874–75* (Belfast, 1875).
112 Minutes, 11 December 1907, Edgar Home, PHS.
113 Annual report, Edgar Home, 1909, PHS.
114 *Ibid.*, 1910.
115 At the annual general meeting each year the committee were informed of the numbers who passed through the home. These figures have been collated from those reports available in the minute book, Edgar Home, PHS.
116 Annual Report, Edgar Home, 1904, PHS.
117 *Ibid.*, 1924.
118 MS Cork 83/58, 84/12, Dublin 39/77, 57/1, Galway 42/22, 1901: Cork, 95/128, Dublin 56/5, 70/48, 40/53, 1911, NAI.
119 Belfast Midnight Mission, minutes 1944, Records of the Belfast Midnight Mission, 1934–1949, D/2072/1, PRONI.
120 *Ibid.*
121 *Ibid.*
122 *Northern Whig*, 15 March 1913, 10 October 1917.
123 *Englishwoman's Review*, 15 September 1881, pp. 414–16.
124 *Rotunda Girls' Aid Society, Annual Report 1887–8* (Dublin, 1888).
125 Church of Ireland Rescue League, Belfast, 13th Annual Report, 1924–5, D/1326/26/18, PRONI.
126 For more details on this society see lay organisations, Box 2, Byrne papers, DDA, which contains correspondence and the annual reports of this organisation.
127 Evidence of Miss Buchanan, Magdalen asylum, Lower Leeson Street to the Carrigan Committee, D/Jus 90/4, NAI.
128 Typescript report on unmarried mothers, unsigned, undated but *c.* 1924. Dr Bernard Hackett Papers, Waterford and Lismore Diocesan Archives, Bishop's House, Waterford.
129 Nora Tynan O'Mahony, 'In a Magdalen asylum', *The Irish Monthly*, 24 (1906), p. 374.
130 *Ibid.*, p. 375.
131 McCarthy, *Priests and People in Ireland*, p. 438.
132 See, for instance, *Souvenir of the Golden Jubilee of Our Lady of the Charity of Refuge, High Park, Drumcondra; The Order of Our Lady of Charity of Refuge, 1853–1953*. Halliday Sutherland, a Scottish medical doctor, visited and wrote about the Sisters of Mercy asylum in Galway in 1958: *Irish Journey*. Canon Sheehan paints a very sympathetic picture of the Magdalen asylum in Limerick in his novel *Luke Delmege* where Sister Mary of Magdala, a consecrated penitent, 'went around in her penitent's garb, and washed and scrubbed, and ironed, and did all kinds of menial offices for the aged and the

sick', p. 373; Similarly, Fanny Taylor, *Irish Homes and Irish Hearts* (London, 1867), praises the work done by the various religious communities with penitents.

133 Miscellaneous material regarding charity sermons and general funding; Good Shepherd convent, Limerick.

134 *Report of the Vice-Regal Commission on Poor Law Reform in Ireland, Minutes of Evidence* (Cd 3202) HC 1906 li, the Viscount Corry. Also the Presbyterian minister of the Monaghan workhouse described sending single, young and pregnant women to a reformatory as 'one of the greatest acts of mercy that could be performed'. The chairman of the Limerick Union also suggested that 'first offenders' should have the opportunity of going to a penitentiary but remarked that 'the Magdalen Asylum has a bad name and people don't like to go there': *ibid.*, Q. 25922.

135 We have no idea of the understanding of mental deficiency in Ireland in the late nineteenth or twentieth centuries. Certainly in Britian mental deficiency was believed to constitute a major social problem and some women were deemed mentally deficient as a consequence of their sexual behaviour.

136 These included (a) county homes (the former workhouses); (b) special institutions run by nuns; (c) maternity homes, privately run and considered expensive; (d) and the Regina Coeli hostel in Dublin. The Regina Coeli hostel was run by the Legion of Mary and opened its doors in October 1930. It took in women in 'grave difficulties for whom no alternative existed'. Typescript, 'The Regina Coeli Hostel, report 5 October 1930–11 May 1932', Byrne Papers, DDA. These were the principal resorts available to Catholic women. The Bethany Home in Rathgar dealt with Protestant women. The annual reports of the Department of Local Government and Public Health reveal that many of the women who entered these maternity homes left within two years, taking their children with them.

137 *Annual Department of Local Government and Public Health, Report 1931–32* (Dublin, 1932), p. 129.

138 Joseph A. Glynn, 'The Unmarried Mother', *The Irish Ecclesiastical Record*, 18 (1921), p. 463.

139 *Department of Local Government and Public Health, Annual Report*, 1932.

140 See, for instance, *ibid.*, 1935, pp. 146–8.

141 Unmarried mothers file, Criminal Law Amendment Act Committee, Minutes of Evidence, the Carrigan Committee, D/Jus 90/4, 1930, NAI.

142 Notice dated 22 February 1923, cited in James P. Murray, *Galway: A Medico-Social History* (Galway, 1997), appendix 7.

143 *Irish Times*, 7 September 1928.

144 See *Board of Superintendence of Dublin Hospitals, Reports* (Dublin, 1920–32).

145 CC box 6, July 1935–May 1937, Mrs B . . . to Archbishop Byrne, 21 July 1937, Byrne Papers, DDA. My thanks to Dr Lindsey Earner-Byrne for alerting me to this material.

146 Report of the Committee on the Criminal Law Amendment Acts (1880–5) and Juvenile Prostitution (1931), (The Carrigan Committee Report), p. 38: Department of the Taoiseach, S 5998, NAI.

147 Letter from Secretary, An Roinn Oideachais to Secretary, Department of Justice, 27 July 1933; Criminal Law Amendment Act, File Jus 8/20, NAI.

148 Margaret McNeill's report in Criminal Law Amendment Act, File Jus 8/20.
149 *Ibid.*
150 Frank Duff to Miss Shaw, 21 March 1935, Leon O'Broin Papers, MS 31,670, NLI.
151 *Ibid.*
152 Duff noted that of 176 cases in the Legion hostel, Sancta Maria, 58 were industrial school girls. See Minutes of the Ad hoc committee, Fourth meeting, held 17 January 1948, evidence of Frank Duff, Suppression of Prostitution, Ad Hoc Committee, Department of Justice, DJ 72/94/A, NAI.
153 For further information on the Legion of Mary see ch. 6. Duff remarked in an inquiry held into prostitution in 1947 that

> most institutions run by nuns tend towards the water-tight, little facilities are given for visitation and none for the sort of contact with the community which is so necessary . . . how often it is said that the management of nuns and a chaplain provide sufficiently for the moral uplifting of people! 'Officialism' can be 'officialism' even though it wears a religious habit. 'Officialism' seldom reforms.

Suppression of Prostitution, Ad Hoc Committee on Prostitution, evidence of Frank Duff, Department of Justice 72/94/A, NAI.
154 Information relating to the work of the Legion of Mary in File on St Vincent de Paul, Byrne Papers, DDA.
155 'Report on Rescue Work at Harcourt Street, Dublin 15 July 1922 to 15 October 1922 signed Rev. M. Creedon CC', p. 19. Report presented as a letter to Mr Cosgrave and dated 14 October 1922, Department of Justice file H266/40, Criminal Law Amendment Act, Bill, 1934, NAI.
156 Eleven were in Gloucester Street, two in Limerick, six in Cork, seven in High Park, seven in Donnybrook, seven in Dun Laoghaire. Of those who passed through the hostel, four were placed in Gloucester Street, four in High Park, five in Donnybrook, six in Cork, two in Limerick, two in Dun Laoghaire, and one in Waterford. Report of the Regina Coeli Hostel, 5 October 1930–11 May 1932, Byrne Papers, DDA.
157 Rev. R. S. Devane, SJ, 'The unmarried mother: some legal aspects of the problem, – the legal position of the unmarried mother in the Irish Free State', *Irish Ecclesiastical Record*, 23 (1924), p. 185.
158 These were crimes known to the police and exclude the figures for the abandonment of children under two years of age: *Statistical Abstracts of Ireland*, 1927–41. From 1923 the annual reports of the Registrar General enumerate the deaths of infants registered as 'homicide'. For 1923 this was nine; 1924 it was sixteen; 1925 it was nine; 1926 it was twenty. There is a discrepancy between the figures provided by the police from 1927 and those available in the Registrar General's reports. For instance in 1927, the criminal statistics reveal nineteen infant murders known to the police while the Registrar General's report numbered sixteen infant deaths due to homicide.
159 It is unclear how many cases were taken between 1923 and 1926.
160 Most of the girls assigned to the home were convicted of petty pilfering, but there were also some infanticide cases. Department of Justice file, Our Lady's House, Henrietta street, Dublin 16/62A, NAI.

161 These figures were compiled from infanticide and concealment of birth cases, Trials Record Book at the Central Criminal Court, 1925–1941, Department of Justice. The father of one woman, convicted of concealment of birth in 1927, requested that his daughter be sent to the Good Shepherd asylum in New Ross, a request that was granted. See letter from the Rev. John O'Connor, New Ross to the Central Criminal Court, 27 July 1927. Trial, Records Book, Central Criminal Court, June 1925 to June 1927, IC 88 61, NAI. The entry in the Trials Record Book, 27 July 1927, stated that the woman 'shall not leave the Convent of the Good Shepherd New Ross to which she is now being sent without the express permission of the Reverend Mother of the said Convent'.

162 *Cork Examiner*, 1 May 1936. For another similar sentence see *Irish Independent*, 29 May 1930; Central Criminal Court, 24 June 1935, Limerick, indict. no. 2; State File at Central Criminal Court, 18 April 1939, Longford, indict. no. 1. CCC 27 May 1940, Co. Cavan, indict. no. 1, NAI.

163 Department of Justice 8/128 Criminal Justice (Female Offenders Bill), 1942, File Jus 8/128, NAI.

164 The difficulties of placing women in Magdalen asylums was brought to light by a case in 1938. The 20-year old woman involved had a baby by her 48-year old uncle. She opted to carry out her sentence, of two years, in St Patrick's Refuge in Dun Laoghaire. She was visited in the refuge by her uncle and shortly after had a nervous breakdown. When she returned from Grangegorman to the refuge an incident occurred which saw the nuns transfer her to the Legion of Mary's Regina Coeli hostel in Harcourt Street. This move, however, broke the terms of her suspended sentence and a special court had to be convened to rectify the matter. The young woman decided at this stage that she preferred to complete her sentence in prison, a one-year sentence, while the convent sentence was for two years. However, before the hearing she was persuaded to go to High Park on the assumption that with good behaviour she would be released early. See ID 11 92, Trials record book at the Central Criminal Court, 26 April 1938, Department of Justice, NAI.

165 See file ID 11 96, Co. Galway, 1941, NAI.

166 By 1944 the Gloucester Street asylum had one probationer for 3 years, and four for 1 year; St Patrick's Refuge had one for 2 years, the Sisters of Mercy asylum in Dun Laoghaire had one probationer for 18 months, and eight on 12-month charges, the High Park Convent had one probationer for 3 years, two for 2 years and four for 1 year, the Good Shepherd convent, Cork, had two for an unspecified period, and the Sisters of Charity in Cork had one; the Good Shepherd convent, Limerick had one for 3 months. While Our Lady's in Henrietta Street was subsidised by the government none of these other institutions were. The cases assigned to the Good Shepherd convents, it was noted, were for the most part 'streetwalkers' and 'women of loose morals'. Letter signed F. C. Connolly, 2 November 1943, to Leas Runaidhe, Department of Justice file, Our Lady's House, 16/62A. Our Lady's House in Henrietta Street also sent some of its inmates to Magdalen asylums. In an annual report for 1933 it was noted that thirty-four were received into the home, seventeen from court and seventeen voluntary; four were provided with an outfit and went home to parents; one girl was very unsatisfactory and had to be transferred to

High Park; two were unable to be kept in and were sent to the South Dublin union. In 1932, forty-eight entered the home and three were sent to penitentiaries. In 1931, thirty-five were received and five sent to penitentiaries. In 1928, thirty received and none sent to penitentiaries, 1930, thirty-one received, five to penitentiaries, 1929, twenty-five received and one sent to penitentiary. In 1927, twenty-nine received and two sent to penitentiaries. Annual report for Our Lady's House in Department of Justice file, Our Lady's House, 16/62A, NAI.

167 Hand-written notes re convents, 'Suppression of prostitution', Department of Justice, Carrigan Committee Report, File 72/94A.

168 *The Reformatory and Industrial Schools Systems Report* (the Kennedy Report) (Dublin, 1970), pp. 37, 39, 77.

169 Though we have no idea how many women were in Magdalen asylums in the twentieth century the Magdalen asylum in High Park had almost two hundred inmates in 1953: *The Order of Our Lady of Charity of Refuge 1853–1953*, p. 65. In 1987 there were 69 women aged between thirty-five and eighty-eight resident in Our Lady of Charity Home in Gloucester Street: *A Centenary Celebration 1887–1987 Sisters of Our Lady of Charity, Sean McDermott Street* (Dublin, 1987), p. 7.

4 'THE BLACK PLAGUE': VENEREAL DISEASES IN NINETEENTH-CENTURY IRELAND

1 Robert McDonnell, 'Lectures on venereal diseases, lecture 1', *Medical Press and Circular*, 29 January 1868, p. 87.

2 Claude Quétel, *History of Syphilis* (Baltimore, 1992), pp. 82–3, 109–12.

3 It was not until 1909–10 that the first successful specific for syphilis, Paul Ehrlich's Salvarsan ('606'), an arsenical preparation which caused several unpleasant side effects, was introduced. Since the Second World War penicillin has been the most effective treatment against syphilis.

4 Kevin P. Siena, ' "The foul disease" and privacy: the effects of venereal disease and patient demand on the medical marketplace in early modern London', *Bulletin of the History of Medicine*, 75 (2001), pp. 199–224.

5 Martin Fallon (ed.), *The Sketches of Erinensis: Selections of Irish Medical Satire, 1824–1836* (London, 1979), p. 111. To 'catch cold' was a euphemism for contracting a venereal disease.

6 *Freeman's Journal*, 17 January 1820. Advertisements, some of them different from those appearing in the *Freeman's Journal*, also appeared in the *Athlone Sentinel* throughout the 1840s and 1850s.

7 *Freeman's Journal*, 18 December 1821. This same advertisement was repeated in the *Freeman's Journal* almost weekly between 1821 and 1823.

8 *Ibid.*, 22 November 1822. This advertisement was printed in the *Freeman's Journal* at least twenty-two times between December 1821 and December 1823.

9 *Kilkenny Moderator*, 11 February 1846.

10 *Freeman's Journal*, 20 August 1838. The book *The Silent Friend* advertised in the *Athlone Sentinel*, 23 May 1845, provided ten colour engravings 'representing the deleterious effects of mercury on the skin'. 'Perry's Purifying

Specific Pills' were available for sale through named premises in Athlone, Armagh, Ballina, Ballyshannon, Belfast, Cork, Clonmel, Dublin, Enniskillen, Kingstown, Killenal, Limerick, Waterford, Wexford, Roscommon and Derry: *Athlone Sentinel*, 22 August 1849.

11 *Freeman's Journal*, 25 May 1839.

12 *Ibid.*, 20 November 1822.

13 *Ibid.*, 28 June 1823, 20 November 1823. Other advertisements made it clear that remedies were available to men and women. A number of doctors from the London College of Surgeons distilled their knowledge in two publications, *The Aegis of Life for the Male Sex* and *Hygeiana*, exclusively addressed to females. It was noted that 'perusal . . . must prove beneficial to their moral happiness'. The books were available in a bookshop in Grafton Street, Dublin. They were also willing to send remedies to 'all parts of the world': *ibid.*, 4 June 1823 and other issues in 1823.

14 *Ibid.*, 14 March, 1837.

15 *Ibid.*, 20 August 1838. The advertisement for 'Perry's Purifying Specific Pills' appeared in the *Freeman's Journal* at least fifty-one times in 1840 and 1841. Although beyond the scope of this study folk remedies for venereal disease would be worth investigating.

16 There were, for instance, 120 women in the South Dublin union suffering from venereal diseases in 1853. See *Report from the Select Committee on Dublin Hospitals*, Qs. 2332–40.

17 John Brown, 'Medical report of the Dundalk "Destitute Sick Society" together with a sketch of the medical topography and statistics of the town and parish', *Dublin Journal of Medical Science*, 15 (1839), p. 415.

18 Cited in R. S. Allison, *The Seeds of Time being a Short History of the Belfast and Royal Hospital 1850/1903* (Belfast, 1972), p. 4. From the 1850s the hospital committee apparently on moral grounds, opposed the admission of patients with venereal disease and the lock ward was given over to other cases. By the 1870s, however, such patients were being treated on an inpatient and outpatient basis in the hospital. *Ibid.*, p. 67.

19 Thomas Woods, 'Report of cases which occurred in the Parsonstown workhouse infirmary', *Dublin Quarterly Journal of Medical Science*, 28 (1859), p. 17.

20 William John Geary, 'Report of St John's Fever and Lock Hospitals, Limerick', *Dublin Journal of Medical Science*, 11 (1837), p. 384. See also, William John Geary, *A Historical and Medical Report of the Limerick Fever and Lock Hospitals: Comprising a Period of Nearly Forty Years* (Limerick, 1820). The Limerick hospital was closed in 1849: see G. Pugin Meldon, 'Some notes on the admissions to the Westmoreland Lock Hospital, Dublin, since the year 1860', *Dublin Journal of Medical Science*, 137 (1914), p. 110.

21 Geary, 'Report of St John's Fever and Lock Hospitals', p. 384; see also Geary, *A Historical and Medical Report*.

22 John Fleetwood, *A History of Medicine in Ireland* (Dublin, 1951). The lock hospital in Cork was opened on Infirmary Road on 15 June 1869 and contained forty-six beds. See *Irish Medical Directory* (Dublin, 1879); *Report from the Select Committee on the Contagious Diseases Acts, 1882*, evidence of Mr James Curtis, FRCSI, Qs 11,205–7.

23 *The Irish Builder*, 1 May 1897, pp. 89–90. See also Westmoreland lock hospital, Department of Health, B135/22, NAI. For an interesting exploration of the changing geographical location of the hospital see Gary Boyd, *Dublin, 1754–1922: Hospitals, Spectacle and Vice* (Dublin, 2006), pp. 145–50.

24 *Report upon Certain Charitable Establishments in the City of Dublin*, p. 4. Repeating the findings of the 1809 report, W. J. Warburton, J. Whitelaw and R. Walshe, *History of the City of Dublin*, 2 vols. (London, 1818), record the

present unparalleled state of Europe: large standing armies have unhappily become necessary for our protection; in every large town, nay, in every small village, troops are now quartered permanently; and that to this circumstance, the more extensive propagation of the venereal disease in the capital, and throughout every part of the island is to be attributed, the sick reports of the army afford irrefutable proofs, ii, p. 696.

25 *Report upon Certain Charitable Establishments in the City of Dublin*. The authors of the report also observed that 'the number of claimants for admission is uniformly greater in the winter months than in summer, which is certainly not to be attributed to any cause than that these poor people are forced, by the inclemency of the season, to seek the shelter and comforts which the hospital affords': *ibid.*, p. xxviii.

26 Westmoreland lock hospital, report, 1829, OP/737/5, NAI. At the same time the outpatient clinic was closed. The reasons given for the closure of the clinic were 'that mercury given to outpatients may do harm, that outpatients will not attend the outpatients' department for a sufficient length of time; that the patients will spread the disease while under treatment'. *Royal Commission on Venereal Diseases, Reports and Minutes of Evidence, First report: Appendix: Minutes of Evidence* (1913–1914) HC 1914, evidence Dr Brian O'Brien, 27 February 1914, Q. 8047.

27 *Report of the Commissioners Appointed by the Lord Lieutenant of Ireland to Inspect Charitable Institutions, Dublin*, HC 1842 (337) xxxviii, pp. 53–4. Up to 1820, the surgeons who attended the hospital were unpaid and consequently their attendance was sporadic which did little for the value of the treatment received in the hospital.

28 *Report on the Select Committee on the Irish Miscellaneous Estimates*, HC 1829 (342) iv, 127, p. 172.

29 *Ibid.*

30 *Ibid.*, pp. 172–4.

31 *Report from the Select Committee on the Contagious Diseases Acts, 1882*, evidence of Dr McNamara, Q. 6,509–12. Dr McNamara stated that the Meath, St Vincents, the Mater and Jervis Street hospitals had strict rules against admitting patients with venereal disease. Usually such patients entered these hospitals without declaring the nature of their illness. The workhouse infirmary in Belfast treated up to fifteen cases of syphilis a year in the 1860s. See Belfast Board of Guardians Minute Book, 1861–2, BG/7/A/24, PRONI.

32 See the evidence of Dr T. Byrne who included this information in a letter from Dr Hamilton of the Richmond Hospital: *Select Committee on Dublin Hospitals*, 1854, Q. 59.

33 *Ibid.*, Q. 1,062. For other regulations governing the patients' behaviour see

Laurence M. Geary, *Medicine and Charity in Ireland, 1718–1851* (Dublin, 2004), pp. 103–4.

34 *Report of the Commissioners Appointed to Inspect Charitable Institutions, Dublin,* 1842, p. 52.

35 Westmoreland lock hospital, report, 1829, OP/737/5, NAI. The same claims for classification are made in *Report of the Commissioners Appointed to Inspect Charitable Institutions, Dublin,* 1842, pp. 54–5.

36 *Ibid.,* p. 41.

37 *Report from the Select Committee on Dublin Hospitals,* 1854, Q. 79, pp. 53–4.

38 *Dublin Hospitals Commission, 1885,* evidence of Mr Henry Fitzgibbon, Q. 2,313.

39 *Ibid.,* Q. 2,309.

40 *Ibid.,* Q. 2,309.

41 *Dublin Hospitals Commission, Report of the Committee of Inquiry, 1887, together with Minutes of Evidence and Appendices* (C5402) HC 1887, xxxv. Evidence of Mr Henry Fitzgibbon, Q. 2,337. Fitzgibbon refused to act on this rule seeing it as an 'absurdity'.

42 *Report of the Commissioners Appointed to Inspect Charitable Institutions, Dublin,* 1842, p. 52, *Dublin Hospitals Commission, 1887*: evidence of Mr Henry Fitzgibbon, Q. 174. It is not clear whether this policy applied to married women or not.

43 *Ibid.* Evidence of Mr Rawden McNamara, Q. 4,357. Mr Henry Fitzgibbon was to note that 'the variety of costume in which these ladies come in would give rise to a great deal of unpleasantness among themselves very often'. *Ibid.,* Q. 4,576.

44 *Ibid.,* Qs. 4,584–5. There was much discussion among the board of governors of the hospital regarding this matter. After requesting the opinions of both chaplains and doctors it was decided to continue the system as it was. The Catholic chaplain was in favour of retaining the system while the Protestant chaplain thought it 'an unnecessary humiliation of the patients'. See MSS Board minute books, Westmoreland lock hospital, vol. v, 6 March 1886; 13 March 1886; 3 April 1886, RCPI.

45 *Dublin Hospitals Commission, 1887*: evidence of Dr Henry Fitzgibbon, Q. 174.

46 See MS Visitors' Book, Westmoreland lock hospital, 1825–89, RCPI.

47 Westmoreland lock hospital, Report, 1829, p. 60. OP/737/5, NAI.

48 *Ibid.*

49 *Ibid.,* p. 50.

50 *Report of the Select Committee on Dublin Hospitals,* 1854, Qs. 121–4.

51 *Ibid.,* also *Dublin Hospitals Commission,* 1887, Q. 2,182.

52 There are a number of gaps when admittance figures were not produced.

53 *Dublin Hospitals Commission,* 1887, p. x; *Fifty-Second Annual Report of the Board of Superintendence of the Dublin Hospitals* (Cd 5335) HC 1910, xxii; *Dublin Hospital Reports* (Cd 8189) 1916, xvi, p. 23.

54 Elizabeth Malcolm, 'Troops of largely diseased women: vd, the Contagious Diseases Acts, and moral policing in late nineteenth-century Ireland', *Irish Economic and Social History,* 26 (1999), pp. 2–4.

55 Cormac Ó Gráda, *Black '47 and Beyond: the Great Irish Famine in History, Economy and Memory* (New Jersey, 1999), pp. 178–82.

56 *Report of the Select Committee on Dublin Hospitals*, 1854, Q. 114.

57 *Dublin Hospitals Commission*, 1887, Q. 2,220.

58 General Register of Patients, Westmoreland lock hospital, vol. IV, 1857–68, RCPI.

59 *Ibid.* One woman named Eliza Smith, aged nineteen, had been infected for three months before seeking treatment.

60 *Medical Press and Circular*, 17 February 1869, pp. 137–9. In one case he noted the woman 'was treated for three months in the hospital and left uncured, and resumed her mode of life for eight weeks, when another sore erupted and she was admitted again and subjected to a mildly mecurial treatment . . . this woman was, while suffering from this sore, living irregularly, and if the sore was contagious, must have caused frightful mischief among the community'.

61 *Report from the Select Committee on the Contagious Diseases Acts, 1881*, HC, evidence of Dr McNamara, Qs. 6,523, 6,546, 6,567, 6,569. McNamara stated that men were able to look after themselves, but the women needed protection.

62 *Report of the Select Committee on Dublin Hospitals*, 1854, Q. 39.

63 *Ibid.*, preface p. iv. M. H. C. Hime, *The Moral Utility of a Lock Hospital* (Dublin, 1872).

64 *Report of the Commissioners Appointed to Inspect Charitable Institutions*, Dublin, HC 38 1842, (337) xxxviii, p. 47.

65 Westmoreland lock hospital, report, 1829, p. 55. OP/737/5, NAI. Between July 23 and October 1829, forty-five women were admitted to the hospital laundry. Of these, six were returned to parents, six provided with situations, four restored to friends, two were returned to the hospital wards because of illness, eight left the laundry of their own accord, five were expelled for 'irregularity', two died and twelve were in the laundry in 1829.

66 *Dublin Hospitals Commission, 1887*, evidence of Mr Rawden McNamara, Q. 4359.

67 *Ibid.*, Q. 4,359. Of the 910 rescued patients, 417 were sent to other asylums or penitentiaries; 155 were returned to friends; 82 went to the workhouse; 250 were employed in the hospital as staff while 10 got situations outside the hospital. Of the 232 patients treated in 1877, 41 were sent to asylums or penitentiaries, 12 returned home, 19 went to the workhouse, 18 were given employment in the hospital, 2 were sent to other hospitals, the remaining 140 remained unaccounted. See *Twenty-First Report of the Board of Superintendence of the Dublin Hospitals for 1880* (C2565) xxiii, p. 22.

68 *Report of the Commissioners Appointed to Inquire into the Hospitals of Dublin*, 1856 xix, p. 10.

69 *Dublin Hospitals Commission, 1887*, Q. 2,312.

70 William Henry Porter, 'Essays on the natural history of syphilis', *Dublin Quarterly Medical Journal*, 24 (August 1857), p. 268.

71 See Mary Spongberg, *Feminizing Venereal Disease: the Body of the Prostitute in Nineteenth-Century Medical Discourse* (London, 1997).

72 See, for instance, John Morgan, 'On the occurrence of chronic genital sore of a peculiar nature', *The Medical Press and Circular*, 17 February 1869, p. 137.

73 John Morgan, 'An abstract of cases under treatment in the Westmoreland

Lock Hospital: with remarks as to the venereal affections in Dublin', *British Medical Journal* (15 May 1869), p. 440.

74 Robert McDonnell, 'Lectures on venereal diseases – lecture ii', *Medical Press and Circular*, 19 February, 1868, p. 154.

75 The *Lancet* was founded in 1823; the *British Medical Journal* had begun life as the *Provincial Medical and Surgical Journal* in 1840. The *Dublin Medical Press* appeared in January 1839, in 1866 it amalgamated with the *Medical Circular* which had been founded in London in 1852, and from 1868 it was transferred to London and became increasingly English. See Robert J. Rowlette, *The Medical Press and Circular 1839–1939: a Hundred Years in the Life of a Medical Journal* (London, 1939). The *Medical Press and Circular* contains many articles by Irish doctors and was a principal forum for the discussion of Irish medical politics and medical treatments throughout the century.

76 For the operation of and resistance to the CDAs in England see J. Walkowitz, *Prostitution and Victorian Society;* J. R. Walkowitz, 'The making of an outcast group: prostitution and working women in nineteenth-century Plymouth and Southampton', in Martha Vicinus (ed.), *A Widening Sphere: Changing Roles of Victorian Women* (London, 1977); J. R. Walkowitz, 'Male vice and female virtue; feminism and the politics of prostitution in nineteenth-century Britain', in A. Sninton *et al.* (eds.), *Desire: the Politics of Sexuality* (London, 1984); with D. J. Walkowitz, ' "We are not beasts of the field": prostitution and the poor in Plymouth and Southampton under the Contagious Diseases Acts', in M. S. Hartman and Lois Banner (eds.), *Clio's Consciousness Raised: New Perspectives on the History of Women* (New York, 1974).

77 In Cork the lock hospital was located at Infirmary Road. By 1881 it had relocated to Anglesea Place. According to the census reports there were twenty-five women resident in the hospital in 1871 and seventeen there in 1881: *Census of Ireland, 1881, vol. ii, Province of Munster* (C3148), HC 1882 xxvii, 1.

78 In the Curragh three such police were appointed.

79 War Office to Chief Secretary, 1 January 1869, CSORP 1884/27996/8, NAI.

80 CSORP 1884/27996/11, NAI.

81 CSORP 1884/27996/20, 5 October 1869, NAI.

82 Costello, *Most Delightful Station*, p. 134.

83 Letter from the Surgeon, Infirmary, Kildare, to War Office, 16 March 1860, OPW 486/59, NAI.

84 Previously he had noted that 'the health of the youth of the country, particularly that of the jockey boys, is materially injured by the rapid spread of venereal disease'. Letter from Robert Browne, dated 25 November 1859 to War Office OPW 486/59, NAI.

85 Hamilton LaBatt, *Observations on Venereal Diseases: Derived from Civil and Military Practice* (Dublin, 1858).

86 Kilmainham Papers, 22 October 1859, MS 10268, NLI.

87 Kilmainham Papers, MS 1060, letter dated 8 April 1867, p. 4. *Ibid.*, 19 December 1866, MS 1059, pp. 101, 207, 275, NLI.

88 *Leinster Express*, 18 February 1865.

89 *Ibid.*, 21 February 1865. Also quoted in Costello, *Most Delightful Station*, p. 157.

90 *Ibid.*
91 Many of these women, it was claimed, had been resident on the Curragh since the camp was established. 'Surgical society of Ireland', *Medical Press and Circular*, 14 December 1881, p. 516.
92 *Ibid.*
93 *Ibid.*, p. 517.
94 *Ibid.*
95 Sir Richard Airet, who had been Quartermaster General at the Curragh, noted in 1871 that 'we have been told that these women are almost in the habit of burrowing in the ground like rabbits, that they are in a constant state of filth, and covered in vermin', and that if the Acts were not in force the women would go back to their old ways. *Reports of the Royal Commission Contagious Diseases Acts, 1866–9*, 1871, Q. 15,815.
96 'Surgical society of Ireland', *Medical Press and Circular*, 14 December 1881, p. 517.
97 War Office to Medical Officer, lock hospital, 25 October 1884, CSORP, 1884/23660, NAI.
98 Hime, *The Moral Utility of a Lock Hospital*, p. 3.
99 *Ibid.*, p. 4. For a similar description of their habits in the hospital see 'Surgical society of Ireland', *Medical Press and Circular*, 14 December 1881, p. 517.
100 Hime, *The Moral Utility of a Lock Hospital*, p. 5.
101 Kilmainham Papers, MS 1066, p. 161. NLI.
102 *Report of the Royal Commission on the Contagious Diseases Acts, 1866–69*, evidence of Mr Henry Richardson, Q. 18,807.
103 Evidence of Rev. Maguire, Q. 18,807, *ibid. The Lancet* also argued that there had been a great improvement in the streets of Cork, declaring that where 400 women worked as prostitutes before the implementation of the Acts, by 1870 there were only 'about 77' in the city. *Ibid.*, 25 March 1871, pp. 418–19.
104 *The Medical Enquirer* (October, 1877), pp. 133–6.
105 *The Shield*, 15 April 1871. The same information is noted in *The Lancet*, 25 March 1871, pp. 418–19.
106 *Report from the Select Committee on the Contagious Diseases Acts, 1881*, appendix 15. Between June 1869 and February 1870, 215 patients had been admitted to the hospital. Of these 170 were discharged, with an average stay of fifty-three days in the hospital. It was argued that the hospital had effected a 50 per cent decrease in venereal disease infections among the troops in the garrison in the previous six months. See *The Lancet*, 19 February 1870, p. 279.
107 *Report from the Select Committee on the Contagious Diseases Acts, 1881*, appendix 15.
108 *Report from the Select Committee on the Contagious Diseases Acts, 1882*, appendix 27, p. 612.
109 *Reports of the Royal Commission on the Contagious Diseases Acts, 1866–9*, Q. 18,504.
110 *Report from the Select Committee on the Contagious Diseases Acts, 1882*, evidence of Mr Kingston, Q. 2,531.
111 *Report from the Select Committee on the Contagious Diseases Acts, 1871*, evidence of Mr Henry Richardson, Q. 18,484.

112 *Report from the Select Committee on the Contagious Diseases Acts*, 1882, evidence of Mr Kingston, Q. 2,531.

113 *Report from the Select Committee on the Contagious Diseases Acts, 1866–9*, evidence of Mr Henry Richardson, Q. 18,641.

114 *The Shield*, 21 April 1877.

115 'Association for the Extension of the Contagious Diseases Act, 1866, to the civil population of the United Kingdom', *Dublin Quarterly Journal of Medical Science*, 46 (1868), p. 169.

116 Charles A. Cameron, 'Report on public health: prevention of venereal disease', *Dublin Quarterly Journal of Medical Science*, 48 (1869), p. 623.

117 Charles A. Cameron, 'Half-yearly report on public health', *Dublin Quarterly Journal of Medical Science*, 52 (1871), pp. 476–9. Evidence to the CDAs inquiry of 1871 reported that syphilis was 'exceedingly rife' in Dublin and a surgeon at the Westmoreland lock hospital observed that 'he never recollected, in his experience, so much true syphilis at any time existing as there is now in Dublin'. *Report from the Committee on the Contagious Diseases Acts, 1866–9*, evidence of Mr William Henry Splogett, Q. 4,312.

118 *Dublin Medical Press and Circular*, 22 June 1881, p. 540.

119 'Report on public health', *Dublin Journal of Medical Science*, 48 (1869), p. 627.

120 Malcolm, 'Troops of largely diseased women', pp. 9–10.

121 Benjamin Scott, *A State Iniquity: its Rise, Extension and Overthrow* (London, 1890), pp. 297–328.

122 For meetings organised by the Irish branch of the NARCDA see *The Shield*, 7, 14 March, 16, 23 May 1870, 4 March, 27 May 1871, 31 January 1874, 1 February 1875, 1 August 1875, 26 February 1876, 11 March 1876, 3 February 1877, 11 December 1880; *Freeman's Journal*, 8 January 1878.

123 *The Shield*, 3 February 1877, p. 23.

124 *Report from the Committee on the Contagious Diseases Acts, 1871*, Q. 2,632.

125 *Select Committee on the Contagious Diseases Acts, 1882*, evidence of Canon Hegarty, Q. 11,035.

126 *The Shield*, 23 May 1870, pp. 92–3, 96.

127 *Ibid.*, p. 93.

128 Annual reports, Ladies National Association (hereafter LNA), 1871, 1889. In an interview she gave to the *Irish Citizen*, in 1914, Anna Haslam stated that the fight for the repeal of the CDAs 'threw the suffrage movement back for ten years, we were all so absorbed in it': *Irish Citizen*, 21 March, 1914.

129 *Annual Report of the National Association for the Repeal of the Contagious Diseases Acts*, 1880–1.

130 Annual reports, LNA, 1871–86.

131 Walkowitz, *Prostitution and Victorian Society*, pp. 137–9.

132 *Report from the Committee on the Contagious Diseases Acts, 1871*, evidence of Mr Maguire, Q. 18,798.

133 *The Shield*, 21 February, 1880.

134 *Ibid.*, December, 1878.

135 'Surgical Society of Ireland: session 1878–79', *The Medical Press and Circular*, 29 April 1879, p. 347. In another editorial the journal asked 'Might not the opponents of the Acts vary the monotony of their argument with a little proof.' *The Medical Press and Circular*, 15 January, 1879, p. 48.

136 'The Contagious Diseases Acts', *The Medical Press and Circular*, 30 April 1879, p. 354.

137 Thomas Wrigley Grimshaw, 'Address in state medicine to the state medicine sub-section of the Academy of Medicine in Ireland', *Dublin Quarterly Journal of Medical Science*, 77 (1884), pp. 216–18.

138 *The Shield*, 16 May 1870, p. 86, lists the names of a number of medical men who opposed the Acts in Ireland.

139 *Dublin Medical Press and Circular*, 1 March 1882, p. 193.

140 See annual reports of the LNA, 1871–88, for numerous references to these drawing-room meetings.

141 *Report from the Select Committee on the Contagious Diseases Acts*, 1882, appendix, p. 596.

142 *Annual Report*, LNA, 1877, p. 16.

143 Emily G. Patterson, Catherine Ross and Isabella M. S. Tod, *To the Members of the Belfast Committee for the Repeal of the Contagious Diseases Acts, And Others Interested in Public Morality* (Belfast, 1878), p.1.

144 *Ibid.*, p. 2.

145 *Annual Report*, LNA, 1874, p.13.

146 *Ibid.*, LNA, 1876, p. 15. *The Shield*, 26 February 1876, p. 67; 11 March 1876, p. 82; 1 April 1876, p. 106.

147 Bligh had organised a meeting in the town hall in Dundalk but this was cancelled by the clerk as an unsuitable subject for a public meeting: *The Shield*, 1 April 1876, p. 106.

148 'The Contagious Diseases Acts and their work', *The Medical Press and Circular*, 27 November 1878, p. 436.

149 For details of the meetings see *The Shield*, 16 November 1878, pp. 273–80; *Freeman's Journal*, 2 November 1878.

150 See annual reports, LNA 1871–86; NARCDA 1880–1.

151 *Ibid.*

152 [Haslam], *A Few Words on Prostitution*.

153 Quoted in Jane Jordan, *Josephine Butler* (London, 2001), p. 212.

154 Minutes of the General Assembly, 1871, PHS.

155 *Ibid.*, 1883, PHS.

156 *The Shield*, 6 July 1872, p. 999.

157 *Report from the Select Committee on the Contagious Diseases Acts, 1882*, evidence of Rev. Canon James Hegarty, Q. 10,983.

158 *Ibid.*, evidence of Rev. Thomas O'Reilly, Q.11,465.

159 *Englishwoman's Review*, 15 October, 1883, pp. 438–40.

160 Isabella M .S. Tod, 'The new crusade and women's suffrage', reprinted as a pamphlet from the *Pall Mall Gazette, c.* 1885.

161 Walkowitz, *Prostitution and Victorian Society*, p. 132.

162 *Annual Report*, LNA, 1885.

163 Luddy, *Women and Philanthropy in Nineteenth-Century Ireland* (Cambridge, 1995).

164 *The Shield*, 5 June 1886, p. 87. See also the 'Report of a meeting of the Ladies' National Association', *Women's Penny Paper*, 3 August, 1889, p. 8.

165 Walkowitz, *Prostitution and Victorian Society*, p. 246.

166 Rosa M. Barrett, *Ellice Hopkins: a Memoir* (London, 1908), *passim*.

167 Dublin White Cross Association, *Annual Report*, 1898.
168 See Lucy Bland, *Banishing the Beast: English Feminism and Sexual Morality* (London, 1995), pp. 58–9, 95–123.
169 *Report from the Select Committee of the House of Lords on the Law relating to the protection of young girls together with the proceedings of the committee, minutes of evidence, appendix*, 1881 [448] ix. Paper laid before the committee by Lord Ramsay from Superintendent Mallow to the Chief Commissioner of the DMP, G Division, 2 July 1881, p. 154. It was also noted that

> The agencies through which respectable girls of a superior class obtain employment are above suspicion, and are very careful, and the humbler class of girls of the Catholic religion generally rely on priests and sisters of charity to get suitable situations for them. Of course there are young persons of other religious denominations who look after and assist girls of their own faith. It often happens that when young girls are seduced in Dublin the brothel keepers send them to England out of the way of their parents, but such girls know well what they are about. They merely go from one brothel to another.

170 See appendices 1–3.
171 Rev. R. M. Gwynn, 'Some principles of social service', in Rev. William Bell and Rev. N. D. Emerson (eds.), *The Church of Ireland, AD 432–1932* (Dublin, 1932), p. 188.
172 Barrett, *Ellice Hopkins*, p. 166. The Church of Ireland Purity Society and the Dublin White Cross Association amalgamated soon after 1885.
173 *The Vigilance Record*, 15 April 1887, p. 19.
174 *Ibid.*
175 *Ibid.*
176 *Ibid.*, April 1891.
177 Edward J. Bristow, *Vice and Vigilance: Purity Movements in Britain Since 1700* (Dublin, 1977), p. 104.
178 *Ibid.*, p. 163. These claims are probably exaggerated. The Mecklenburgh Street area was a notorious red-light district in the city. The police rarely interfered in the business conducted in this area and it was only with the campaign organised by Frank Duff and the Legion of Mary from 1922 that prostitution declined in this district. For further accounts of the work of the WCVA in Ireland see *The Vigilance Record*, March 1888, p. 21; February 1888, p. 12; 15 April 1887, pp. 19, 51; August 1889, p. 77; April 1890, p. 29; April 1892, p. 23; May 1893, pp. 28–9. *The Sentinel*, June 1892, p. 75; June 1894, p. 79.
179 *The Vigilance Record*, April 1891, p. 36.
180 *Ibid.*, p. 37.
181 *Ibid.*, 15 April 1887, p. 19.
182 *The Dublin White Cross Association: Report for the Year Ending 31 December 1898* (Dublin, 1898).
183 See p. 32.
184 See ch. 5.
185 Mrs Charles Martin, 'Our young work girls', *The Irish Monthly* (1879), p. 469.
186 Anon., 'St. Martha's Home', *The Irish Monthly*, 10 (1882), pp. 157–60.
187 *Ibid.*, p. 158.
188 Pugin Meldon, 'Some notes on the admissions to the Westmoreland lock hospital', pp. 112–13.

5 'SOLDIER'S TOTTY': NATIONALISTS, SUFFRAGISTS AND THE SURVEILLANCE OF WOMEN, 1900–22

1 Ben Novick, *Conceiving Revolution: Irish Nationalist Propaganda during the First World War* (Dublin, 2001).
2 Margaret O'Callaghan, 'Language, nationality and cultural identity in the Irish Free State, 1922–7: the *Irish Statesman* and the *Catholic Bulletin* reappraised', *Irish Historical Studies*, 24 (1984), pp. 226–45.
3 *Freeman's Journal*, 28 October 1901.
4 *Ibid.*
5 *Ibid.*, 6 June 1904.
6 Quoted in O'Connor, *Oliver St John Gogarty*, p. 54. The allegation was not reprinted in the 11th edn of the *Encyclopaedia*.
7 *Sinn Féin*, 21 September 1907.
8 *Freeman's Journal*, 19 November 1908.
9 *Irish Times*, 10 October, 1910.
10 *Ibid.*, 20 October 1910.
11 *Ibid.*
12 *Ibid.* See also *Irish Times*, 18 October 1910.
13 *Ibid.*
14 *Ibid.*, 22 October 1910.
15 *Ibid.*, 21 October 1910.
16 *Ibid.*, 24 October 1910.
17 *Ibid.*, 29 October 1910.
18 *Ibid.*, 19 October 1910.
19 See p. 34.
20 *Irish Times*, 24 October 1910.
21 *Ibid.*, 25 October 1910.
22 *Ibid.*, 27 October 1910.
23 *Ibid.*, 29 October 1910.
24 *Ibid.*, 31 October 1910. This home opened 2 February 1910, and could accommodate twelve girls with their infants.
25 *Ibid.*
26 *Irish Worker*, 16 December 1911. The paper suggested it would like to report on 'The usual weekly meeting [which] was held last night of the Vigilance Society for exposing the inhumanity of sending starved children to school!'
27 *Ibid.*
28 Patrick Maume, *The Long Gestation: Irish Nationalist Life, 1891–1918* (Dublin, 1999), p. 130.
29 Evidence of Rev. R. S. Devane, 1926, Committee on Evil Literature, File Jus/7/2/14, NAI.
30 *Sligo Champion*, 11 November 1911, cited in Michael Wheatley, *Nationalism and the Irish Party: Provincial Ireland 1910–1916* (Oxford, 2005), pp. 92–3. Wheatley notes that one of the newspapers targeted was *Reynolds Weekly*. At the end of November, Sir Henry Daliziell, proprietor of the paper, claimed that his Irish sales had risen by 50 per cent since the campaign started. *Midland Reporter*, 23 November 1911, cited in Wheatley, *Nationalism and the Irish Party*, pp. 92–3. For the progress of other vigilance societies see *Irish*

Independent, 7 April 1909, 14 March 1916, 24 October 1917; *Freeman's Journal*, 31 January 1911, 7 March, 11 May, 20 August 1914, 8 September 1916, 2, 21, 28 June, 18 October 1919, 6 January, 11 October, 1920; 3 February, 9 November, 1 December 1921, 28 November, 4 December 1922, 5, 14 February, 11 May, 10, 15 December 1923; *Evening Telegraph*, 24 January 1920.

31 *Irish Times*, 9 December 1912.

32 The *Freeman's Journal* published a number of letters from Irish bishops calling for the suppression of evil publications, including 'socialistic publications read by the labouring classes': *Freeman's Journal*, 6 September 1915. A letter from the honorary secretaries of the Dublin Vigilance Committee to Mr Birrell, 24 September 1915, noted that it appears 'anomalous that while prosecutions have been successfully brought in England against some of these journals, no proceedings as far as we know have been taken in Ireland': CSORP 1915/16465, NAI.

33 For insights into the 'White Slave' issue see Rosen, *The Lost Sisterhood*; Gilfoyle, *City of Eros*; Bland, *Banishing the Beast*. M. E. Francis's novel, *The Story of Mary Dunne* (London, 1913), deals with the issue. While warning against Irish female emigration to England the novel highlights the occurrence of 'white slavery' and the danger to innocent, Catholic girls. As one character observes, 'A girl like her [Mary Dunne] coming, as I take it, from a remote village in Ireland, would be an easy victim. A good-natured man volunteers to show her the way to a registry office, or some kind, motherly woman takes a fancy to her on board the boat – offers to take her into her own service – it's all the same in the long run – the girl disappears!': *ibid.*, p. 93.

34 Alice Abadam (1856–1940) had been a member of the militant WSPU. In 1907, she was part of the group that broke away to form the Women's Freedom League. She was later associated with the Catholic Women's League: Obituary, *The Times*, 3 April 1940.

35 *Irish Citizen*, 12 October 1912.

36 *Ibid.*, 26 October 1912.

37 *Freeman's Journal*, 18 October 1912. The members of the Vigilance Association included Miss Rosa Barrett, Miss Buchanan PLG, Mrs Cherry, Mrs H. D. Connor, Lady Dockrell, Mrs Farquharson, Mrs Marcus Goodbody, Mrs Leit, Dr Kathleen Lynn, Dr Katherine Maguire, Mrs Fitzmaurice Manning, Miss Moses, Mrs Richardson and Dr Ella Webb: *Irish Times*, 18 October 1912.

38 *Irish Citizen*, 2 November 1912. The charges of proselytism were further refuted in letters to the *Irish Citizen*, 9 November 1912.

39 *Freeman's Journal*, 14 October 1912. Rosamond Jacob records in her diary attending an 'at home' suffrage meeting in Waterford where white slavery was discussed. Jacob Diaries 13 February 1914, MS 32, 582 (26), NLI.

40 *Irish Times*, 14 October 1912.

41 *Irish Citizen*, 2 November 1912. Susanne Day's one-act play *Toilers* deals with this issue of poverty and poor wages driving women to prostitution. The play was performed in Dublin in 1918 and published in *The Englishwoman* (1919), pp. 180–90.

42 *Irish Citizen,* 26 October 1912.

43 *Ibid.,* 26 October 1912.

44 *Ibid.,* 12 October 1913. Rosamond Jacob in her novel *Callaghan* reiterates the significance of women securing the franchise in order to tackle prostitution. F. Winthrop [Rosamond Jacob], *Callaghan* (Dublin, n.d., *c.* 1921), ch. 12.

45 *Northern Whig,* 13 March 1913.

46 *Ibid.,* 15 March 1913.

47 *Irish Citizen,* 12 July 1913.

48 *Irish Worker,* 25 May 1912.

49 *Irish Times,* 9 October 1912.

50 Miss Carden, Hon. Sec., *The Women's Patrol Committee* (London, n.d. *c.* March 1916), HO 45/10806/309485, National Archives, London. The *Irish Weekly Independent* argued for a close scrutiny of British labour exchanges that brought Irish girls over to work in English munitions factories during the war: *Irish Weekly Independent,* 24 March 1917.

51 *Irish Times,* 15 October 1912.

52 For fictional representations of this danger see, for example, Padraic O Conaire's short story 'Nora, Daughter of Marcus Beag', in *The Finest Stories of Padraic O Conaire* (Dublin, 1982), pp. 153–67; Alice Dease, *On the Broad Road* (Dublin, n.d.).

53 *Irish Citizen,* 12 July 1913.

54 Judith Walkowitz, *City of Dreadful Delight: Narratives of Sexual Danger in Late Victorian London* (London, 1992).

55 Alan Hunt, *Governing Morals: a Social History of Moral Regulation* (Cambridge, 1999), pp. 178–9. Criminal Law Amendment Act, 1912, 2&3 Geo. V. c.20. A synopsis of the provisions of the Act are provided in the Report of the Inter-Departmental Committee of Inquiry Regarding Venereal Disease, VD in the Irish Free State, 1924–7, File S 4183, Department of the Taoiseach, NAI.

56 *Irish Times,* 18 October 1912.

57 *Ibid.,* 11 October 1912. The committee of the Edgar Home in Belfast also supported the bill. See Edgar Home, Committee Minutes, 1913, PHS.

58 *Irish Times,* 15 October 1912.

59 *Ibid.,* 12 October 1912.

60 *Freeman's Journal,* 18 October 1912.

61 *Irish Times,* 25 October 1912.

62 *Ibid.,* 24 October 1912. The suffragist Anna Haslam sent a letter on behalf of the Irish Women's Suffrage and Local Government Association to the Home Secretary on the Criminal Law Amendment Bill: *ibid.,* 10 October 1910. The Irish Women's Suffrage Society held a meeting in the Ulster Hall in Belfast appealing for support for the Criminal Law Amendment Bill to be passed to help stop the white slave trade: *Northern Whig,* 11 March 1912.

63 See appendix 1.

64 *Irish Citizen,* 1 March 1913.

65 *Ibid.,* 10 May 1913.

66 *Ibid.* In Belfast three men were charged with an offence under the white slave traffic act: *The Irish News and Belfast Morning News,* 18 February 1913.

67 *Irish Times,* 18 February 1913.

68 The *Freeman's Journal* attempted, unsuccessfully, to reignite the white slavery

issue in its 'crusade' against vice in late 1922–3. See, *Freeman's Journal*, 4 August 1922, 17, 18, 24 August, 16 October 1923.

69 *Irish Times*, 18 February 1913.
70 *Ibid.*
71 Novick, *Conceiving Revolution*, p. 133.
72 S. J. Connolly (ed.), *The Oxford Companion to Irish History* (Oxford, 1998), p. 29.
73 Virginia Crossman, *Politics, Law and Order in Nineteenth-Century Ireland* (Dublin, 1996).
74 *Limerick Chronicle*, 9 February 1848. See also, Kilmainham Papers, MS 1306, pp. 114, 124, NLI.
75 Kilmainham Papers, 14 April, 1881, MS 1064, p. 217, NLI. For the anti-recruiting campaign during the Boer War see Donal P. McCracken, *Forgotten Protest: Ireland and the Anglo-Boer War* (2nd edn, Belfast, 2003), pp. 46, 50–2.
76 Miss Helena Molony, witness statement 391, Bureau of Military History, copy files, NAI; see also Mrs Sidney Czira, Witness Statement, 909.
77 Witness statement 273 of Mrs Margaret Keogh (née Quinn), treasurer Inginidhe na hÉireann, member of Cumann na mBan, Dublin. Bureau of Military History, copy files, NAI. A strong anti-recruitment campaign was carried out in the Inginidhe na hÉireann journal, *Bean na hÉireann*.
78 *The Hibernian*, 18 December 1915.
79 Novick, *Conceiving Revolution*, p. 151.
80 Quoted in *ibid.*, p. 152.
81 According to the 1911 census 52 per cent of the adult female population in Dublin were single. Many of the poorest of these shared rooms, with one or more women.
82 *Irish Times*, 16 November 1915.
83 *New Ireland*, 18 December 1915.
84 *Irish Times*, 16 October 1915.
85 *The Hibernian*, 13 November 1915; *Irish Citizen*, 20 October 1915.
86 *The Hibernian*, 13 November 1915; *Irish Times*, 16 October 1915.
87 *Irish Citizen*, 13 November 1915. There were about 130,000 inhabitants of tenement housing in Dublin in the first decade of the twentieth century and about 21,000 families occupied just one room. See O'Brien, *Dear Dirty Dublin*, p. 164.
88 Memoranda of interviews, Ireland, vol. III, October 1915–May 1916, p. 58: Sir Matthew Nathan Papers, Bodleian Library, Oxford.
89 *Freeman's Journal*, 4 January 1915.
90 These organisations included the Irish Women's Reform League, the Alexandra Guild, the National Reform Association, the National League for Opposing Women's Suffrage, the Franchise League, the Church League, the IWSLGA, the Philanthropic Reform Association, the United Irishwomen, the Irish Women's Temperance Association, the Irish Workhouse Association, the Irish Catholic Girls' Association, the Girls' Friendly Society, and the Irish Women's Christian Association.
91 In a 1919 report it was stated that one patrol should be Protestant and the other Catholic. *Report of the Irish Women Patrols, 1919* (Dublin, 1920), p. 5.
92 *Freeman's Journal*, 14 January 1915; *Irish Citizen*, 9 January 1915.

93 *Irish Times*, 12 January 1916.

94 For the work of these patrols in England see Philippa Levine, ' "Walking the streets in a way no decent woman should": women police in World War I', *Journal of Modern History*, 66–1 (March 1994), pp. 34–78; Angela Woollacott, ' "Kaki fever" and its control: gender, class, age and sexual morality on the British home front in the First World War', *Journal of Contemporary History*, 29 (1994), pp. 325–47.

95 *Irish Worker*, 9 January 1915. James Connolly also disapproved of the patrols remarking that the 'poor working-class girl will have a new terror added to her life'. Quoted in Novick, *Conceiving Revolution*, p. 152.

96 *Irish Citizen*, 13 February 1915.

97 *Ibid.*

98 *Ibid.*, 9 October 1915.

99 *Ibid.*, 23 October 1915.

100 *Irish Times*, 12 January 1916.

101 *Ibid.*

102 *Irish Citizen*, February 1916.

103 Carden, *The Women's Patrol Committee*. The women patrols were in operation in Dublin in 1920 where the area of greatest concern appeared to be St Stephen's Green. See *Freeman's Journal*, 1 November 1921. There is evidence that some work by the patrols was still being carried out in 1923. See *Freeman's Journal*, 21, 31 January 1923. Policewomen did make an appearance in Ireland in 1920 when a number of women from England, under the control of the RIC, were sent to act as searchers of women. These policewomen had been drawn from those who had served in the women's police service and who had worked during the war in the munitions factories, where they had to ensure that girls in the danger zone had no metal concealed in their clothes or hair. It was noted that these 'searchers learned to make skilful search with the least possible amount of unpleasantness': *Freeman's Journal*, 16 July, 24 August 1920, 18 February 1922, 2 February 1923. Irish women activists lobbied for years to have women police in Ireland, a request that was finally conceded with the appointment of the first Ban Gardai in 1958.

104 Minute Book of the General Committee, 22 November 1912–17 November 1921; Meeting of 17 November, 1916; Mother's Union, Dublin.

105 *Irish Citizen*, 18 April 1914. A similar scheme had been in operation in Cambridge from the 1 January 1913. See Evaline Hutchinson, 'Women in the police courts', *The Englishwoman*, 20 (1913), pp. 25–9.

106 *Irish Citizen*, 13 March 1915.

107 *Ibid.*

108 *Ibid.*, editorial, 14 August 1915.

109 *Irish Worker*, 18 July 1914.

110 *Irish Citizen*, April 1916. A Ladies' Vigilance Committee was formed in Dublin in January 1911 to 'aid the Dublin Vigilance Committee'. This appears to be a different organisation to any formed under the auspices of the suffrage campaign. See *Freeman's Journal*, 31 January 1911, 11 May 1914.

111 For various reports about the committee see *Irish Citizen*, December 1916, January, April, May, September, December, 1917, March, April, 1918, June/July 1919.

112 For a valuable discussion of these allowances see Susan Pedersen, *Family Dependence and the Origins of the Welfare State: Britain and France, 1914–1945* (Cambridge, 1993), pp. 107–16. Initially 1 shilling and 1 penny per day was paid to a serving soldier's wife, with an extra 2 pence a day for each dependent child. A wife also received 3 shillings and 6 pence a week out of her husband's pay while he was serving abroad. These allowances were increased in March 1915. Wives of privates and corporals were now paid 12 shillings and 6 pence a week, while allowances for children ranged from 5 shillings per week for the first child to 3 shillings and 6 pence a week for a second child, and 2 shillings for any other children. For details of separation allowance payments see CSORP 1914/14308, NAI.

113 Keith Jeffery, *Ireland and the Great War* (Cambridge, 2000), p. 7. In 1916 it was noted that between 1,000 and 1,200 cases relating to pensions were dealt with. See *Report to His Majesty the King of the War Pensions and Statutory Committee for the Year 1916* (Cd. 8750), 1917–18 xvii, p. 85.

114 File re Misuse of Separation Allowances to the wives of soldiers, 17 December 1914. CSORP 1914/22394, NAI. See also comments on the spending habits of the separation women in Athy in *Leinster Leader*, July 1916.

115 *Kerry Advocate*, 17 October 1914.

116 'Salonika' *c.* 1918, a popular song in Cork. For the entire song see appendix 5.

117 For cases of fraud re separation allowances see, for example, *Freeman's Journal*, 22 October 1914; *Cork Examiner*, 16 November 1915; *Irish Independent*, 11 February 1916; 25 July 1917; 28 March 1917, 14 February 1916; 25 February 1916; *Kerry Advocate*, 24 April 1915. Other fraud cases can be found in CSORP/1918/1478; CSORP 1918/749, this case also reported in the *Limerick Chronicle*, 12 January 1918. Ballymena fraud case, CSORP 1915/16018, case also reported in *Belfast Newsletter*, 25 September 1915; CSORP 1915/16187; CSORP 1915/16511; CSORP 1915/19150; CSORP 1915/19149; CSORP 1915/18907; CSORP 1915/19950; CSORP 1915/1911; CSORP 1915/17275; CSORP 1915/21829; CSORP 1915/17198; CSORP 1915/18756; CSORP 1915/17200; CSORP 1915/17199; CSORP 1915/19560.

118 Memoranda of interviews, Ireland, vol. III, October 1915–May 1916, p. 104: Sir Matthew Nathan Papers, Bodleian Library, Oxford. One of the groups who did this kind of investigative work was the Irish Association for the Prevention of Intemperance. This was supported by, among others, the Church League for Women's Suffrage, the Irishwomen's Reform League, the IWSLGA, the White Cross Vigilance Association and the women's patrols.

119 *Freeman's Journal*, 20 April 1915. We have, as yet, no history of women's use of the public house in Ireland.

120 Memoranda of interviews, Ireland, vol. III, p. 96, Nathan Papers. One deputation suggested that women should not be allowed to purchase drink for consumption off the premises, which would stop what was known as the 'jug and bottle trade'.

121 For cases of child neglect see *Irish Independent*, 16 August 1916, 25 August 1917, 31 January 1918. For other cases see *Meath Chronicle*, 12 February, 21 October 1916, 10 February 1917, *Cork Examiner*, 17 May 1915, 4 March 1918, *Derry Journal*, 14 March, 16 August, 3, 22 September 1915.

122 *Irish Independent*, 3 February 1915.

123 Captain J. C. Arnold, ' "Last post" of the separation woman', *War Pensions Gazette*, February 1920, p. 449.

124 Michael Laffan, *The Resurrection of Ireland: The Sinn Féin Party, 1916–1923* (Cambridge, 1999), pp. 126–7.

125 Máire Nic Shiúbhlaigh, *The Splendid Years* (Dublin, 1955), p. 167.

126 Quoted in Kenneth Griffith and Timothy E. O'Grady, *Curious Journey: an Oral History of Ireland's Unfinished Revolution* (2nd edn, Cork, 1998), p. 78.

127 William O'Brien, Bureau of Military History, witness statement, 1766, p. 12, copy files, NAI.

128 Rosamond Jacob Diaries, 9 July 1918, MS 32,582 (34), NLI.

129 *Honesty*, 15 January 1916, pp. 1–2.

130 *Ibid.*

131 *Cork Examiner*, 21 May 1915; *Irish Citizen*, 13 May, 10 July 1915.

132 Novick, *Conceiving Revolution*, pp. 158–9.

133 CO 904/204, National Archives, London. The real fear on the part of the government was that this would harm recruitment.

134 CO 904/207/238, National Archives, London.

135 *Meath Chronicle*, 2 May 1934.

136 *Northern Whig*, 23 January 1917. A response to this letter observed that the acquisition of the vote in other places had no impact on the morals of men or women. *Ibid.*, 27 January 1917.

137 Novick, *Conceiving Revolution*, ch. 4.

138 See ch. 6.

139 Margaret and James H. Cousins, *We Two Together* (Madras, 1950), p. 178. For other imprisoned women see *Irish Citizen*, 25 May, 22 June 1912.

140 Prisoner Record Sheets in File A, Box 1 and File C, Box 1 in Suffragette Files in Government Prisons Board, NAI.

141 See Cliona Murphy, *The Women's Suffrage Movement and Irish Society in the Early Twentieth Century* (Hemel Hempstead, 1999), pp. 100–6.

142 *Irish Citizen*, 6 December 1913.

143 Margaret O'Callaghan, 'Women and politics in Independent Ireland, 1921–68', in Angela Bourke *et al.* (eds.), *The Field Day Anthology of Irish Writing*, Vol. v: *Irish Women's Writing and Traditions* (Cork, New York, 2002), p. 126.

144 *Ibid.*

145 Jacob Diaries, 27 May 1918; MS 32,582 (33), 10 December 1917–1918, NLI.

146 Jacob Diaries, 22 April 1919, MS 32,582 (35), NLI.

147 Albinia Brodrick, 'The Black Plague', *The British Journal of Nursing*, 19 July 1913, pp. 45–7.

148 Quétel, *The History of Syphilis*, p. 142. In 1909 Ehrlich modified his formula and introduced '914' or neosalvarsan which was easier to use than salvarsan. It was not until the introduction of penicillin in 1943 that the treatment of venereal diseases was revolutionised.

149 *The British Journal of Nursing*, 8 June 1907.

150 This was the Women's National Health Association established to fight tuberculosis in 1907. Its originator was Lady Aberdeen, wife of the Viceroy. She was an unpopular figure for Irish nationalists.

151 Brodrick, 'The Black Plague', pp. 45–7, concluded in the same journal 26

July 1913, pp. 63–5. She had published an earlier paper on the subject and the significance of training nurses on this issue in Albinia Brodrick, 'Safeguarding the public health', *The Englishwoman*, 1 (1909), pp. 237–43. Brodrick (1863–1955) was the daughter of Lord Middleton and became an ardent nationalist. She gaelicised her name to Gobnait ni Bhruadair and was later a member of Cumann na mBan. Pádraig Ó Loingsigh, *Gobnait ni Bhruadair: Beathaisnéis* (Baile Átha Cliath, 1997).

152 *The British Journal of Nursing*, 14 June 1913, p. 419.

153 *Suffragette*, 8 August 1913, p. 737. In Pankhurst's book, *The Great Scourge and How to End it* (London, 1913) she argued that syphilis was 'the most potent single cause of physical degeneracy and of mortality'.

154 *Royal Commission on Venereal Diseases, Final Report* (Cd 8189) xvi, 1916. For a good general discussion of venereal disease see Lesley A. Hall, 'Venereal diseases and society in Britain, from the contagious diseases acts to the national health service', in Roger Davidson and Lesley A. Hall (eds.), *Sex, Sin and Suffering: Venereal Disease and European Society Since 1870* (London, 2001), pp. 120–36.

155 *Royal Commission on VD, First report: Appendix: Minutes of Evidence* (Cd 7475) HC 1914 xlix, p. iii.

156 Evidence of Dr Brian O'Brien, 27 February 1914, Q. 8,208, *ibid.*

157 *Ibid.*, Qs. 8,017–8.

158 *Ibid.*, Q. 8,022.

159 In Belfast, O'Brien noted that most of the patients with venereal disease treated in the infirmaries associated with the workhouses were men: 207 in 1911, 184 in 1912, and 119 in 1913: women: 83 in 1911, 102 in 1912 and 141 in 1913. For the South Dublin union the figures were men: 195 in 1911, 225 in 1912 and 173 in 1913. In the North Dublin union there were 84 in 1911, 96 in 1912 and 96 in 1913. Women, he noted, were not treated in the Dublin workhouse infirmaries and were sent instead to the Westmoreland lock hospital: *ibid.*, Qs. 8,117–20.

160 *Ibid.*, Qs. 8,198–8,206.

161 *Ibid.*, Qs. 7,992–8,295. His evidence was also reprinted in *The British Journal of Nursing*, 21 March 1914, p. 256.

162 *Royal Commission on Venereal Diseases, First Report*, evidence of Dr Brian O'Brien, 27 February 1914, Qs. 8,216–21, 1914.

163 *Ibid.*, Q. 7,828.

164 Evidence of Albinia Brodrick, also reported in *The British Journal of Nursing*, 28 March 1914, p. 280.

165 *Royal Commission on Venereal Diseases, First Report*, 1914, evidence of Sir William Thompson, 12 December 1913, Qs. 2,550–90.

166 *Ibid.*, evidence of Dr Brian O'Brien, 27 February 1914, Qs. 8,286–9. See also E. J. McWeeney, 'On the recent action of the state with regard to venereal disease', *Journal of the Statistical and Social Inquiry Society of Ireland*, 13 (1913–19), pp. 498–517.

167 *Royal Commission on Venereal Diseases, Final Report*.

168 See David Evans, ' "Tackling the hideous scourge": the creation of venereal disease treatment centres in early twentieth-century Britain', *Social History of Medicine*, 5 (1992), pp. 413–35.

169 *Irish Citizen*, 3 January 1914.

170 *Irish Independent*, 3 July 1917. Other references to venereal diseases occur in *ibid.*, 13 September, 24, 30 October 1917, 6 April, 14 August 1918, 19 June 1919, 18 October 1921, 4 June 1923, 21 May 1924.

171 *The British Medical Journal*, 23 December 1916, p. 885.

172 *The Lancet*, 27 January 1917, p. 156; *The British Medical Journal*, 27 January 1917, pp. 134–5.

173 *The Lancet*, 3 February 1917, p. 173.

174 *Ibid.*, 31 March 1917, p. 506. Men and women were given separate lectures. The report in *The Lancet* saw little value in such methods, believing that people often came away from such lectures with incorrect information.

175 *The British Medical Journal*, 28 April 1917, p. 563.

176 This had been done in England in July 1916. In Ireland this was effected by the passing of the Public Health (Prevention and Treatment of Disease) (Ireland) Act, 1917 7&8 Geo. V., c. 40. See *Venereal Diseases: Provision for Diagnosis, Treatment and Prevention*, Circulars Issued by the Local Government Board for Ireland (Dublin, 1918). See also *Irish Independent*, 24 October 1917; *The British Medical Journal*, 10 November 1917, p. 632.

177 *Irish Independent*, 30 October 1917.

178 *Ibid.*, 5 April 1918.

179 A Mr Garner was appointed by Belfast Corporation in January 1920 to act as an organising secretary for propaganda. He went to London to train with the NCCVD but had given up the position by September. See Leeanne McCormick, 'Prostitutes, fallen women and friendless girls: policing female sexual morality in Northern Ireland, 1900–1945' (unpublished doctoral thesis, University of Ulster, 2004), pp. 173–4.

180 *Irish Independent*, 16 March 1918.

181 St John Gogarty, *The Plays*.

182 *Ibid.*, p. 40.

183 Letter from Ulster Medical Society to the secretary, Antrim County Council, 15 November 1917, LA1/3AG/12, PRONI. Similar sentiments were expressed in the minutes of the County Londonderry VD Committee, 30 March 1918, LA5/9AK/1, PRONI.

184 *Irish Independent*, 11 June 1918, *Derry Journal*, 16 December 1918, 14 February 1919.

185 Letter from Waveney Hospital, Ballymena to secretary, Antrim County Council, 17 October 1919, LA1/3AG/13, PRONI.

186 Manager Midland Railway Company to secretary, Antrim County Council, 17 December 1919, LA1/3AG/13, PRONI.

187 *The British Medical Journal*, 25 May 1918, p. 602.

188 Local Government Board Ireland, *Annual Report for the Year Ended March 1920* (Cmd 1432), xiv, 1921, p. 1.

189 *Ibid.*

190 *Irish Independent*, 11 June, 14 August 1918; *Department of Local Government and Public Health, First Report 1922–25* (Dublin, 1927), p. 44. 'Venereal Diseases', Department of Health, B135/13, NAI. It was noted that the attempt to set up a scheme in County Louth was 'interrupted owing to the unsettled conditions in the country and never came fully into operation'. *Ibid.*

191 Susan R. Grayzel, *Women's Identities at War: Gender, Motherhood and Politics in Britain and France During the First World War* (Chapel Hill, 1999), pp. 146–51.

192 Minutes, 5 March 1918, Minute Book of the Women Delegates to the All Ireland Conference of 19 April 1917, MS 21,194 (47), NLI.

193 Minutes, 25 April 1918, A conference of the societies with reference to combating the spread of vd which was held in the Mansion House on 19 March 1918 under the auspices of Cumann na dTeachtaire (The Association of Women Delegates), Royal College of Physicians, Ireland.

194 *Ibid.*, minutes, 9 April 1918.

195 *Ibid.*

196 *Ibid.*, minutes, 5 September 1918, 7 November 1918. A lady who wished to remain anonymous had purchased 37 Charlemont St and let it to the committee at a reasonable rent until the committee could afford to buy it. See also, Margaret Ó hÓgartaigh, *Kathleen Lynn: Irishwomen, Patriot, Doctor* (Dublin, 2006), ch. 2.

197 Minutes, 28 May 1918, 'A conference of the societies with reference to combatting the spread of venereal disease', Royal College of Physicians Ireland. See also circular letter regarding the establishment of a hospital for infants in letters to Hanna Sheehy Skeffington, March–August, 1918, Sheehy Skeffington Papers, MS 22,682, NLI.

198 Richard Hayes and Kathleen Lynn, *Public Health Circular no. 1* (Sinn Féin public health leaflet, Dublin, February 1918).

199 See Jacob Diaries, 23 August 1918, MS 32,582 (33), NLI. The 'flu epidemic saw the clinic being used as a treatment centre for those afflicted with the illness. In May 1919 St Ultan's Hospital was established by Dr Kathleen Lynn and Madeleine ffrench-Mullen. It treated infants but did not specialise in syphilitic infants.

200 For those women imprisoned for their nationalist activities the fear of catching venereal disease was a constant worry. Constance Markievicz, while imprisoned in Aylesbury Prison in England commented 'one horror always hung over our heads, and that was the fear of catching loathsome diseases'. *San Francisco Examiner*, 7 December 1919 quoted in Sean McConville, *Irish Political Prisoners, 1848–1922* (London, 2003), p. 540.

201 *Northern Whig*, 24 April 1917.

202 Jacob Diaries, 16 August 1918, MS 32,582 (33), NLI. See also *Irish Citizen*, August 1918.

203 The Belfast Women's Political League, formerly the Belfast Suffrage Society, was formed on 25 February 1918. *The International Woman Suffrage News*, 1 April 1918, p. 110.

204 WO 32/11403, NAL. See also *Irish Independent*, 6 April 1918 and Minutes, 25 July 1918, 'A Conference of the Societies with reference to combatting the spread of venereal disease'. The Women's Political League, formerly the Belfast Suffrage Society, was also involved in the campaign. The Women's Political League had the support of labour organisations and the Irish Co-operative Guild in Belfast for the withdrawal of the regulation. *The International Suffrage News*, 1 September 1918, p. 188.

205 Sylvia Pankhurst, 'State regulation of vice', *Workers Dreadnought*, 6 April 1918, p. 980.

206 *Irish Citizen*, August 1918, February 1919.
207 *Hansard*, 24 July 1918, col. 1,957.
208 Government leaflet, 'Information on the dangers of venereal disease and on facilities for treatment', 1919. Antrim County Council, General Correspondence, LA1/3AG/13, PRONI.
209 Cases appended to the file noted that two soldiers had contracted venereal disease from going with women in the Park; neither had been paid any money. Phoenix Park, Undesirable Women Frequenting, CSORP 1921-22/3455/3 NAI.
210 Lieutenant Colonel H. C. Donald, 'The diagnosis and treatment of syphilis', *Dublin Journal of Medical Science*, 142 (1919), p. 77.
211 *Ibid.*

6 'HOPELESS CASES': PROSTITUTION AND SEXUAL DANGER IN THE IRISH FREE STATE, 1922–40

1 *The Report of the Committee on Evil Literature* (Dublin, 1927); *The Report of the Commission on the Relief of the Sick and Destitute Poor, Including the Insane Poor* (Dublin, 1928). The *Report of the Committee on the Criminal Law Amendment Acts (1880–1885) and Juvenile Prostitution* (1931), copy in Department of the Taoiseach, S 5998, NAI; 'Suppression of Prostitution Inquiry', Ad Hoc Committee on Prostitution Department of Justice File 72/94/A, NAI; the unpublished Report of the Inter-Departmental Committee of Inquiry Regarding Venereal Disease can be found in the file VD in the Irish Free State, Department of the Taoiseach File, S 4183, NAI. Officially the Irish Free State ceased to exist in December 1937 from which time the State was renamed Éire.
2 See, for instance, *Irish Times*, 23 April 1931; *Irish Independent*, 24 March 1931; *Evening Herald*, 3 March 1931.
3 There is nothing unique to Ireland about the pressure for women to return to the domestic sphere in this period. See, for instance, Aurora G. Morcillo, *True Catholic Womanhood: Gender Ideology in Franco's Spain* (Illinois, 2000).
4 Maryann Valiulis, 'Neither feminist nor flapper: the ecclesiastical construction of the ideal Irish woman', in Mary O'Dowd and Sabine Wichert (eds.), *Chattel, Servant or Citizen: Women's Status in Church, State and Society* (Belfast, 1995), p. 172.
5 *Ibid.*, p. 175. Valiulis makes the valuable point that the construction of the ideal Irish woman in this period had its counterpart in other European countries, such as Italy. Spain was also to the fore in reiterating the domestic as the natural sphere of women.
6 Sandra L. McAvoy, 'The regulation of sexuality in the Irish Free State, 1929–1935', in Elizabeth Malcolm and Greta Jones (eds.), *Medicine, Disease and the Irish State, 1650–1940* (Cork, 1998), p. 264.
7 J. H. Whyte, *Church and State in Modern Ireland, 1923–1879* (Dublin, 1971), ch. 2.
8 Evidence of R. S. Devane in 'VD in the Irish Free State', Department of the Taoiseach File, S 4183, NAI, p. 30.
9 *Irish Catholic Directory and Almanac*, 1920 (Dublin, 1920), p. 514. This

concern with clothing had surfaced in the first years of the twentieth century: issues of 'modest' dress, and 'traditional' dress had informed the nationalist movement. See, for example, Mary L. Butler, *Modern Fashions in Ladies' Dress* (Dublin, 1927; reprint of 1899 edition).

10 *Irish Independent*, 4 March 1930.

11 *Ibid.*, 12 May 1926. See also *Irish Catholic Directory and Almanac, 1927* (Dublin, 1927), p. 569.

12 *Irish Independent*, 13 October 1926.

13 Rev. M. Garahy SJ, *Idols of Modern Society* (Dublin, 1922).

14 *Ibid.*, p. 9.

15 *Irish Independent*, 12 February 1923.

16 *Ibid.*, 4 September 1925.

17 *Freeman's Journal*, 22 September 1923.

18 *Ibid.*, 4 August 1922, 18, 24 September, 16 October 1923.

19 *Ibid.*, 17 September 1923.

20 For unmarried motherhood in Ireland see, Maria Luddy, 'Moral rescue and unmarried mothers in Ireland in the 1920s', *Women's Studies*, 30 (2001), pp. 797–817; Paul Michael Garrett, ' "The abnormal flight": the migration and repatriation of Irish unmarried mothers', *Social History*, 25 (2000), pp. 330–43; 'The hidden history of the PFIs: the repatriation of unmarried mothers and their children from England to Ireland in the 1950s and 1960s', *Immigrants and Minorities*, 19 (2000), pp. 25–44; Lindsey Earner-Byrne, 'The boat to England: an analysis of the official reactions to the emigration of single expectant Irishwomen to Britain, 1922–1972', *Irish Economic and Social History*, 30 (2003), pp. 52–70; ' "Moral repatriation": the response to Irish unmarried mothers in Britain, 1920s to 1960s', in Patrick J. Duffy (ed.), *To and From Ireland: Planned Migration Schemes c. 1600–2000* (Dublin, 2004), pp. 155–73.

21 *Annual Report of the Registrar-General for Saorstát Eireann* (Dublin, 1924).

22 Whyte, *Church and State*, p. 31.

23 Memorandum from the Adoption Society of Ireland, 9 February 1950, in Department of the Taoiseach File, S 10815A. Adoption of Children: General File, NAI. For numbers of illegitimate and legitimate births from 1864 to 1945 see appendix 1 in E. W. McCabe, 'The Need for a Law of Adoption', Statistical and Social Inquiry Society of Ireland, p. 11, in the same file.

24 *Report of the Committee on the Criminal Law Amendment Acts*, 1931, p. 8.

25 Mrs J. McKean to An Runaidhe, Roinn Dli agus Cirt, 22 November 1926 in Department of Justice File, H 171/1, NAI.

26 *Ibid.*, pp. 12–14.

27 *Irish Independent*, 7 March 1931.

28 *Ibid.*

29 *Report of the Committee on the Criminal Law Amendment Acts*, 1931, p. 32.

30 *Freeman's Journal*, 3 March 1924.

31 *Irish Independent*, 7 October 1925.

32 *Ibid.*, 2 October 1925.

33 For further details on the iniquities of dancehalls see Rev. R. S. Devane SJ, 'The dance hall', *Irish Ecclesiastical Record*, 37 (1931), pp. 170–86.

34 *Irish Press*, 16 October 1931.
35 *Irish Independent*, 4 March 1935.
36 *Irish Press*, 9, 11 September 1935. For other cases see, *ibid.*, 23 September 1935.
37 *Irish Times*, 11 March 1931.
38 The Committee on the Criminal Law Amendment Acts suggested a series of legislation that might be enacted. Similar proposals for legislative action were made by the Committee for the Reform of the Laws Relating to the Protection of Women and Girls, the Dublin Christian Citizenship Council, and other organisations.
39 *Irish Press*, 6 September 1935.
40 *Ibid.*, 11 September 1935. At Carrick-on-Suir district court on 16 September, DJ McCabe, in granting dance licences, said that he thought the publication given of the alleged bad side of dancing had done much harm.

He was dealing there with the plain people, who come to the dances for the pleasure of a 'hop'. The people had self restraint and self control and a regard to virtue, and were simply enjoying themselves at dances. That was his experience of dancing. His position was to interpret the police code, and not to give an opinion on morals. He would not dictate to any person what kind of dances they should dance. Local enthusiasts could use their influence.

The Irish Law Times and Solicitors' Journal, 28 September 1935, p. 274. For a similar judicial view see *ibid.*, 7 November 1936, p. 294.
41 *Irish Independent*, 3 March 1930.
42 John Springhall, *Coming of Age: Adolescence in Britain 1860–1960* (Dublin, 1986), pp. 28, 34. For an enlightening discussion of the impact of views on adolescent women in Britain see Carolyn Oldfield, 'Growing up Good? Medical, Social Hygiene and Youth Work Perspectives on Young Women, 1918–1939' (unpublished doctoral thesis, University of Warwick, 2001).
43 R. S. Devane, SJ, 'The legal protection of girls', *Irish Ecclesiastical Record*, 37 (1931), p. 37.
44 *Ibid.*, p. 34.
45 See Oldfield, 'Growing Up Good', p. 69.
46 *Sagart* is the Irish word for priest.
47 An Sagart, 'How to deal with the unmarried mother', *Irish Ecclesiastical Record*, 20 (1922), p. 152.
48 For Catholic Church proposals regarding the care of unmarried mothers see Byrne Papers, Government and Politics, Department of Local Government, DDA.
49 Rev. M. H. McInerny, 'A postscript on the souper problem', *Irish Ecclesiastical Record*, 20 (1922), p. 141. In 1913 a Dublin cleric provided Archbishop Walsh with a list of proselytising institutions in Dublin. They included shelters for fallen women and unmarried mothers. See Box 377/4-7, Walsh Papers, 1913, DDA.
50 McInerny, 'Postscript on the souper problem', pp. 148–50.
51 *Annual Report of the Catholic Protection and Rescue Society of Ireland, 1923*, p. 3.
52 See ch. 3, and fn. 139, p. 284.

53 Typescript report entitled 'Unmarried Mothers', unsigned, undated but *c.* 1924. Dr Bernard Hackett Papers, Waterford Diocesan Archives, Bishop's House, Waterford.

54 Joseph A. Glynn, 'The unmarried mother', *Irish Ecclesiastical Record*, 18 (1921), p. 463.

55 *Relief of the Sick and Destitute Poor, Including the Insane Poor* (Dublin, 1928), p. 68.

56 R. S. Devane, SJ, 'The unmarried mother: some legal aspects of the problem – the legal position of the unmarried mother in the Irish Free State', *Irish Ecclesiastical Record*, 23 (1924), p. 183.

57 R. S. Devane, SJ, 'The unmarried mother: some legal aspects of the problem – the age of consent', *Irish Ecclesiastical Record*, 23 (1924), pp. 67–8.

58 Hugh Kennedy, *Dáil Debates*, vol. 33, 13 February 1930, col. 185.

59 *Relief of the Sick and Destitute Poor*, p. 69.

60 Devane, 'The unmarried mother: legal position', p. 179 (emphasis in the original).

61 *Department of Local Government and Public Health, Annual Report* (Dublin, 1932), p. 29. The Department of Local Government and Public Health organised a conference in consequence of 'several complaints from English rescue societies of the number of girls who having got into trouble leave the Free State and go to England'. The result of the conference was an agreement between the Irish rescue agencies to 'discourage girls going to England . . . and to bring them back when possible': *ibid.*, pp. 129–30.

62 *Relief of Sick and Destitute Poor*, p. 69.

63 Venereal disease, internal committee of inquiry, 1925 Department of Health, B135/13, NAI. The number of patients who presented at Steeven's clinic between January 1919 and December 1922 was 4,222, of whom 743 were women and children. By 16 March 1923, 4,473 individuals had been treated there. T. P. C. Kirkpatrick, 'The work of a venereal disease treatment centre', *Irish Journal of Medical Science*, 16 (1923), pp. 145–54.

64 See *First Report, Department of Local Government and Public Health 1922–25* (Dublin, 1927), p. 44.

65 Department of Health, Treatment of venereal disease in Waterford, 1926–29 B35/21, vol. 1, NAI.

66 Letter from the Department of Foreign Affairs to Department of Local Government and Public Health, 13 July 1935, Department of Health B135/11, vol. 1, NAI.

67 Venereal diseases, internal committee of inquiry, Department of Health, B135/13, NAI.

68 In 1937 it was noted that 'even up to this day vulgar opinion holds that all bad cases of venereal disease entering the [Westmoreland lock] hospital are destroyed by being smothered between mattresses'. File Westmoreland lock hospital, Department of Health B135/22, NAI.

69 Venereal disease returns prior to 1936, Department of Health, B135/14, vol. 1, NAI. One doctor noted that gonorrhoea was 'so rife in Dublin in 1939, that all babies born in the maternity hospitals had silver nitrate drops placed in their eyes to save them from gonococcal conjunctivitis which commonly

led to blindness'. John Walsh, 'Who was William Doolin?' *Irish Medical Journal*, 77 (1984), n.p.

70 For Northern Ireland available figures relate to the treatment of patients in Belfast.

71 The inquiry was referred to in the *First Report, Department of Local Government and Public Health*, p. 44.

72 *Inter-Departmental Committee of Inquiry Regarding Venereal Disease, Report* (Dublin, n.d., c.1926), p. 4. Though printed the report was never published. Department of the Taoiseach File, S 4183, NAI.

73 *Ibid.*, p. 3.

74 *Ibid.*

75 For a discussion of the issue in political terms see John M. Regan, *The Irish Counter-Revolution, 1921–1936* (Dublin, 1999), pp. 177, 196. For a discussion of the inquiry as a means of introducing a regulation system for prostitution in the Free State, and its role in a struggle for civil authority, see Philip Howell, 'Venereal disease and the politics of prostitution in the Irish Free State', *Irish Historical Studies*, 33 (2004), pp. 320–41.

76 *Inter-Departmental Committee of Inquiry Regarding Venereal Disease*, p. 19. The Army chaplain, in his annual report for 1926, observed that

> a considerable number of men who are suffering from the disease are married men. The results are appalling to contemplate, and they are going to have a very serious effect on the birth rate, and the health of the community. The urgent need of making clear to the soldier the dangerous consequences of debauch and fornication is evident. A prevalent saying in the Army is, that a soldier is not 'blooded' until he has contracted venereal disease; as a consequence, the Army is in danger of developing into a hot-bed of venereal disease.

Army Chaplain's Correspondence 1923–39, Byrne Papers, Box Government and Politics, DDA.

77 *Inter-Departmental Committee of Inquiry Regarding Venereal Disease*, p. 5.

78 *Ibid.*, p. 18–19.

79 *Ibid.*, p. 29. Emphasis in the original.

80 *Ibid.*

81 *Ibid.*, p. 33.

82 Devane, 'The unmarried mother – legal position', pp. 180–3.

83 'Report on the rescue work in Harcourt Street, Dublin, 15th July to 15th October, 1922 by Rev. M. Creedon', in Department of Justice, File H 266/40, NAI.

84 *Ibid.* Oral history sources tend to support Creedon's views of women who worked as prostitutes in Dublin at this time, and later. See Kevin C. Kearns, *Dublin Tenement Life: an Oral History* (Dublin, 1994), pp. 54–5, 69–70, and *passim*.

85 'Return giving particulars of women arrested for soliciting by the Dublin Metropolitan Police from 1 September 1924–20 October 1924'; Army Chaplain's Correspondence from 1923–39, Byrne Papers, Box Government and Politics, DDA.

86 Twenty-three were in their thirties, two were aged fifty, eight were in their forties, three were aged nineteen, forty-two were in their twenties: *ibid.*

87 The occupations included sixteen who were listed as servants, four as dealers, one as a draperess, one as a waitress, one as a shop assistant, one as a hotel worker, and the rest were unknown. *Ibid.*

88 Of the 78 arrested, 22 had no previous arrests, while 24 had one previous conviction, 11 had two, 11 had three, 2 had four, 2 had five, 1 had seven, 2 had nine, 1 had ten, 1 had twenty-five and 1 had thirty: *ibid.* Their 'habitual places of rendezvous' included the Phoenix Park, Bonham St and Quays, South Circular Road, Lamb Alley, Wexford Street, Islandbridge, Christchurch Place, Synge Lane, Grantham Street, Grafton Street, College Green, Stephen's Green and Dawson Street, Dame Street, Lower Leeson Street, Wellington Quay, Nassau Street, Westmoreland Street, Dawson Street, Kildare Street, Adelaide Road, Herbert Street and Canal, Summerhill, O'Connell Street, North Quays, Talbot Street, Lower O'Connell Street, Railway Street, the vicinity of Frenchman's Lane, North Wall, Drumcondra, Royal Canal, Dorset Street, Parkgate Street, Canal Bank, Wellington Road, Harcourt Terrace, Wilton Terrace, Earlsfort Terrace, Crown Alley and Corporation Street.

89 Frank Duff, 'The Story of the Legion', *Maria Legionis* (September 1940), p. 5.

90 Report submitted by Deputy Commissioner Murphy, 26 March 1925. Suppression of prostitution, Ad Hoc Committee on Prostitution, Department of Justice File, 72/94/A, NAI.

91 *Ibid.*

92 See ch. 5.

93 Report submitted by Deputy Commissioner Murphy, 26 March 1925; Suppression of prostitution, Ad Hoc Committee, Department of Justice File, 72/94A, NAI.

94 Inter-Departmental Committee of Inquiry Regarding Venereal Disease, 'VD in the Irish Free State', Department of the Taoiseach File, S 4183, p. 30, NAI.

95 Statement of Mr Frank Duff, *ibid.*

96 Evidence of Frank Duff to the Ad Hoc Committee, Department of Justice, DJ 72/94/A, NAI.

97 Devane, 'The unmarried mother: some legal aspects of the problem, part ii', p. 183.

98 *Ibid.*, p. 184.

99 *Report of the Inter-Departmental Committee of Inquiry Regarding Venereal Disease*, p. 34.

100 In their report the Committee stated that 'representatives of the organisations of social workers who appeared before us seemed to us to exaggerate the importance of prostitution as an influence in disseminating venereal disease': *ibid.*, p. 10.

101 *Ibid.*, p. 30.

102 Duff noted of the first meeting:

actually, my presence there constituted a difficulty inasmuch as we were declaring on the first night that we were not going to take men in for the present . . . The reason was that we were meeting in the St Vincent de Paul premises and if we started recruiting men, we were certainly entering into a competition with them. They were eagerly looking for men . . . but most definitely laid down was the fact that the Legion of Mary was not to be a women's organisation alone.

Charles T. Moss (ed.), *Frank Duff: a Living Autobiography* (Dublin, 1983), p. 19.

103 *Ibid.*, pp. 29–30. Frank Duff wrote a series of articles on the first years of the Legion and their work in Monto in the organisation's journal, *Maria Legionis*. See *Maria Legionis*, March 1937–Christmas 1942. The series ended abruptly in 1942 when Duff was advised by the archbishop of Dublin, Charles McQuaid, to desist from publishing any more material on the subject. The story of the early years of the Legion was retold by Duff in Moss, *Frank Duff.*

104 Creedon agreed to pay the owner-manager £4 a day *in lieu* of payment from the girls: Frank Duff, 'The history of the Legion of Mary', *Maria Legionis* (June 1937), p. 7.

105 To Leon O'Broin from Jack Nagle, 27 April 1981, Leon O'Broin Papers, MS 31,673, NLI. Creedon's nickname was 'Little dearie'.

106 *Ibid.*, pp. 31–2. In incurring the archbishop's disapproval Devane was fearful that he would be transferred out of Ireland. Moss, *Frank Duff*, p. 31.

107 *Ibid.*, p. 36; Frank Duff, *Miracles on Tap* (New York, 1961), p. 28.

108 Inter-Departmental Committee of Inquiry Regarding Venereal Disease, statement of Mr Frank Duff. Department of the Taoiseach File, S 4183, NAI.

109 Visitation of Dublin parishes, 1927 files, Byrne Papers, DDA. There appear to have been fewer than 200 women in the locality working as prostitutes.

110 Inter-Departmental Committee of Inquiry Regarding Venereal Disease, p. 33, statement of Mr Frank Duff. Department of the Taoiseach File, S 4183, NAI.

111 *Ibid.* There was almost no newspaper coverage of the raids conducted by the police.

112 Press reports of this raid were limited and very short. See *Irish Independent*, 13 March 1925.

113 Report submitted by Deputy Commissioner Murphy, 26 March 1925. Suppression of prostitution, Ad Hoc Committee, Department of Justice File, 72/94/A, NAI. Murphy also noted that the parochial clergy despaired of reforming the women 'and do not visit such areas. It is only by a vigorous police campaign, and the institution of homes for the reception of women found there that the evil can be eradicated'.

114 Inter-Departmental Committee of Inquiry Regarding Venereal Disease, pp. 31, 33. Department of the Taoiseach File, S 4183, NAI.

115 *Ibid.*, p. 33. Duff noted that 'the brothels were now occupied by fifty respectable families'.

116 See John Finegan, *The Story of Monto* (Cork, 1978).

117 See Hershalter, *Dangerous Pleasures*, pp. 313–20, which notes the organisational attempt at the reform of prostitutes in Shanghai similar in some ways to that carried through by the Legion of Mary.

118 Report on the work at 76 Harcourt Street in file on the St Vincent de Paul Society and miscellaneous papers in Byrne Papers, DDA. Between July and December 1922, six were married, three to a labourer, two to soldiers in the

British Army, one to a soldier in the Free State army. One proved a biga-
mous marriage and she later married again. Six were married in 1923, one
to a painter, three to labourers, one to a Free State soldier and one to a car
driver. Fourteen appear to have been married in 1924, two to a van driver,
one to an electrician, one to a bookmaker, one to a car driver, one to a
labourer, one to a carpenter, other occupations not given. Eight married in
1925, one to a labourer, one to a street musician (three of the men were
received into the Catholic Church before marriage). Ten married in 1926,
one to a newspaper seller, two to a labourer. Four married in 1927, no occupations given; two married in 1928 no occupations given; one married in
1929, no occupation given; two married in 1930, no occupations given; six
married in 1931, no occupations given.

119 In 1939 of the 364 women committed to Mountjoy Prison, 150 were
    known prostitutes. Of these, 53 were suffering from venereal disease. By 1945
    the number of women committed to the prison was 597of whom 210 were
    known prostitutes and 127 of these were afflicted with a venereal disease. See
    report of the governor of Mountjoy Prison, 12 October 1945, Suppression of
    prostitution, Ad Hoc Committee, Department of Justice, 72/94A, DDA.

120 For the considerable problems the Legion and Duff had with the church
    hierarchy see Legion of Mary file, Byrne Papers, DDA.

121 Report of the Regina Coeli hostel, 5 October 1930–11 May 1932, file on the
    St Vincent de Paul Society and miscellaneous papers in Byrne Papers, DDA.

122 Typescript c. 1924, 'The Work at 76 Harcourt Street' Lay Organisation, Box
    1, Byrne Papers, DDA.

123 Frank Duff to Miss Shaw, n.d. c. November 1926, Leon O' Broin Papers MS
    31,670, NLI.

124 File on St Vincent de Paul, Byrne Papers, Lay Organisations, Box 1, DDA.
    For another account of the regime within the hostel see evidence of Miss
    Shaw, February 1948, to the Suppression of prostitution, Ad Hoc commit-
    tee, Department of Justice, 72/94/A, NAI.

125 File on St Vincent de Paul, Byrne Papers, Lay Organisations, Box 1, DDA. It
    is likely that some of the children were adopted as a small number were
    placed with the Catholic Protection and Rescue agency in Dublin.

126 A study of Salvation Army work with unmarried mothers in England iden-
    tified significant differences between its published accounts and its unpub-
    lished records. See Anne R. Higginbotham, 'Respectable sinners: Salvation
    Army rescue work with unmarried mothers, 1884–1914', in Gail
    Malmgreen (ed.), *Religion in the Lives of English Women, 1760–1930*
    (Beckenham, 1986), pp. 216–33.

127 Frank Duff to Miss Shaw, 16 December 1926, Leon O' Broin Papers MS
    31,670, NLI.

128 *Ibid.*

129 Typed report from the Legion of Mary (undated) concerning Sancta Maria
    hostel, Byrne Papers, DDA.

130 *Ibid.*

131 Evidence of Miss Shaw, February 1948, to the Suppression of prostitution,
    Ad Hoc committee.

132 Department of Justice H247/41/A, NAI.

133 Liam O'Flaherty, *The Informer* (Dublin, 1999), pp. 158–9.
134 See Christopher Murray, *Sean O'Casey* (London, 2000), pp. 91–3. For an interesting analysis of the play see Lionel Pilkington, *Theatre and State in Twentieth-Century Ireland: Cultivating the People* (London, 2001), pp. 98–104.
135 The objections to the play were encapsulated in Sheehy Skeffington's letter to the *Irish Independent*, 23 February 1926:

> A play that deals with Easter Week and what led up to it, that finds in Pearse's words . . . a theme merely for the drunken jibe of 'dope', in which every character connected with the Citizen Army is a coward, a slacker or worse, that omits no detail of squalid slumdom, the looting, the squabbling, the disease, the degeneracy, yet that omits any revelation of the glory and the inspiration of Easter Week is a Hamlet shown without the Prince of Denmark.

136 Ria Mooney, 'Playing Rosie Redmond', *Journal of Irish Literature*, 6 (1977), p. 22.
137 *Ibid.*, p. 21.
138 Sean O'Casey, *Inishfallen, Fare Thee Well: Autobiography*. Book 4: *1917–1926* (London, 1972), pp. 176–7, quoted in Murray, *O'Casey*, p. 96.
139 Report of the Inter-Departmental Committee of Inquiry Regarding Venereal Disease, p. 4.
140 Resolution sent to Minister for Home Affairs from the Civic Committee of the Irish Women Workers' Union 2 November 1923. Department of Justice File, H 171/39, NAI.
141 Letter from the Irish Women Citizens' Association, from their Standing Committee on Children's Care, to Mr Kennedy, 11 January 1924, *ibid.*
142 Deputy Corish, *Dáil Debates*, vol. 11, 28 April 1925, col. 369.
143 Deputy Little, *Dáil Debates*, vol. 34, 27 March 1930, col. 257.
144 Richard Devane was to observe that the establishment of the Committee resulted in 'several years of persistent pressure'; see Devane, 'The legal protection of girls', p. 20.
145 Report of the Committee on the Criminal Law Amendment Acts (1880–85) and Juvenile Prostitution (Dublin, 1931), p. 4. Department of the Taoiseach, S 5998, NAI.
146 *Ibid.*
147 *Ibid.*, p. 7.
148 *Ibid.*, appendix for the list of witnesses. The committee recorded that the witnesses were 'specially qualified by their professions, duties or experience to testify authoritatively on the subject': Report of the Committee on the Criminal Law Amendment Acts, 1931, p. 6.
149 Carrigan Committee, Criminal Law Amendment Act, 1933–4, File H 247/41/B, evidence of Richard S. Devane (emphasis in the original).
150 *Ibid.*
151 *Ibid.*
152 This is the claim made by the accused that he believed the girl was of age.
153 Evidence of the Irish Women Citizen's and Local Government Association, *ibid.*
154 Evidence of Rev. Fitzpatrick, Limerick, *ibid.*

155 Evidence of Rev. John Flanagan, Fairview, Dublin, *ibid.*
156 Evidence of DJ Dermot Gleeson, *ibid.*
157 *Ibid.*
158 *Ibid.* He did so in a number of letters to the committee. See letters to the committee, 3 October 1930, 18 March 1931.
159 Carrigan met with the Minister for Justice to discuss widening the terms of reference of the committee in April 1931. A letter from Secretary to Little, 17 April 1931, reported that Carrigan had met with the Minister and

> it is considered that the terms of reference of the CLAC are sufficiently wide and elastic to have permitted the Committee to take evidence, examine documents, and to consider for the purpose of their report the several offences dealt with by the CLAA (1885) and its amendments which include the subject of gross indecency to which you have made special reference. It is an error to suppose that the Committee have been restricted to dealing with the problem of the age of consent.

160 Memo from the medical women to the CLAAC, 4 November 1930. *Ibid.*
161 Evidence of the Medical Women and Miss Kathleen M. Sullivan to the Committee. *Ibid.*
162 For an incisive examination of O'Duffy's evidence to the committee see Mark Finnane, 'The Carrigan Committee of 1930–31 and the "moral condition" of the Saorstát" ', *Irish Historical Studies*, 32 (2001), pp. 519–36.
163 O'Duffy's written evidence, Department of Justice file, H 247/41/A, NAI, p. 10.
164 *Ibid.,* p. 17.
165 *Ibid.,* p. 14.
166 Statistics presented by O'Duffy to the committee in *ibid.*
167 Finnane, 'The Carrigan Committee', p. 531.
168 O'Duffy's written evidence, Department of Justice file, H 247/41/A, NAI. 'There are in every district', he wrote, 'women known as "amateurs" who are willing to gratify the passions of any man while not requiring to be paid for their service', p. 10.
169 *Report of the Committee on the Criminal Law Amendment Acts,* p. 30. However, the age range of common prostitutes was much broader than this.
170 For a discussion of the Mental Deficiency Acts in England which argues for their humanitarian and philanthropic approaches, alongside concern with eugenics, see Mathew Thomson, *The Problem of Mental Deficiency: Eugenics, Democracy, and Social Policy in Britain c. 1870–1959* (Oxford, 1998).
171 There is no history of attitudes to 'mental deficiency' in Ireland and its impact on social and welfare policy.
172 *Report of the Committee on the Criminal Law Amendment Acts,* p. 33.
173 *Ibid.,* pp. 37–9.
174 *Ibid.,* p. 16.
175 *Ibid.*
176 Department of Justice memo on the Carrigan Report, 27 October 1932, Department of the Taoiseach, S 5998, NAI.
177 *Ibid.*
178 *Ibid.* There were objections raised to many of the proposals made by the committee.

179 Memo dated 23 February 1933, Department of Justice File, H 247/41/D, NAI.

180 Letter and memo from Keane to Geoghegan, 25 November 1932, Department of Justice File, H 247/41/B, NAI.

181 See Geoghegan to W. T. Cosgrave, 26 November 1932, Department of Justice file, *ibid.*

182 Geoghegan Committee Minutes, second to eighth meetings, Department of Justice file, H 247/41/D, NAI.

183 *Dáil Debates*, vol. 53, 21 June 1934, pp. 849–56, 1248–51, 1 August 1934, pp. 2,013–25, 9 August 1934, p. 2,401. *Seanad Debates*, vol. 19, 23 August 1934, pp. 95–6, 12 December 1934, pp. 793–7, 16 January 1935, pp. 941–2, 6 February 1935, pp. 1,217–60.

184 James Smith, 'The politics of sexual knowledge: the origins of Ireland's containment culture and the Carrigan report', *Journal of the History of Sexuality*, 13 (2004), p. 209.

185 See the evidence provided to the Suppression of prostitution, Ad Hoc Committee, Department of Justice File, 72/94/A, NAI.

186 Witness statements in Suppression of prostitution, Ad Hoc Committee, Department of Justice File, 72/94/A, NAI.

187 Enforcement of Criminal Law Amendment Acts 1885–1935, Garda Síochána seek instructions, File Jus 9/8, NAI. The first case brought under the Criminal Law Amendment Act (section 18) was heard in the Dublin District Court. A youth of 18 was summoned that

> on October 16, 1935, at Palmerston Park, being a place along which the public habitually pass as a right, did act in such a way as to offend modesty, contrary to the CLAA. The youth was fined 5/-. Inspector W. Maher, prosecuting, said that the defendant had his arms around a young woman. He was standing close to her, backwards to a wall, at Palmerston Park. This was a public place, but there was no one passing at the time, and the type of conduct was prevalent in the locality. The inspector said he was relying more on the words 'cause of scandal' than on the words 'offend modesty'. He alleged that the defendant was standing close to the woman and had her in his arms in a compromising attitude. The woman was young, had her arms on the defendant's shoulders. Defendant said he knew the girl about three or four months. She was 21 years of age, and he had admitted he had his arm around her. But not that he had any intention of committing offensive conduct. The district justice said that he did not think it was very serious for any young man to have his arm around a girl's waist paying attention to her. It was a section under which it would be difficult to dismiss the case, but the Inspector who was a man of great experience in the city, said that the position of the parties was such as to cause scandal.

The Irish Law Times and Solicitors' Journal, 7 December 1935, p. 341. In another case tried under section 18 relating to 'public decency', a Guard prosecuted a young man from County Roscommon alleging that he committed an offence when he embraced and kissed a girl outside a dance hall at 11.45 pm one night. The Justice declared that kissing in public was not public indecency. *The Irish Law Times and Solicitors' Journal*, 30 November 1935, p. 238. For the infamous Blackrock Kissing case see *ibid.*, 23 October 1937, p. 284.

188 See above, pp. 198–9.

189 In 1936, in an effort to refute claims made in a speech by Justice Hanna in which he stated, 'that in the Free State the normal standard has been far

exceeded in sexual offences, dishonesty in business, offences against public order and in juvenile crime', the Department of Justice compiled figures which instead revealed that 'unnatural offences and offences against young girls show a definite tendency to increase'. See Memorandum on Crime, 1936, Jus 8/451, NAI. The file also includes a copy of Hanna's speech. The figures (averaged over three years) for what were listed as sexual crimes were as follows:

	1927–9	1930–2	1933–5
Infanticide	223	194	163
Unnatural offences	99	154	256
Rape	69	44	41
Indecent assaults on females	245	243	243
Offences against young girls	86	92	132

See also Criminal Statistics, 1926–43, DJ 72/53, part 1, NAI. As Mark Finnane has noted this file contains a table that details the high number of sexual offences as compared to the same figures for the years before 1914. Mark Finnane, 'The Carrigan Committee', p. 533.
190 Suppression of prostitution, Ad Hoc Committee, and for venereal disease infections see Department of Health files B 135/11, B135/12.
191 See footnote 61 above.
192 Joint Committee of Women's Societies and Social Workers, Minute Book, 1935–9, 98/14/5/1, NAI. The Joint Committee was made up of the following organisations: the Women's National Health Association, Women Citizens Association, Irish Women Workers Union, National Council of Women, Mothers Union, Irish Schoolmistresses Association, Women Graduates Association, Irish Countrywomen's Association, Irish Save the Children Fund.
193 *Ibid.*
194 *Ibid.*, Minutes 24 September 1935.
195 Dr McDonnell's report on his interview with Archbishop and memo, 13 May 1927, in Department of the Taoiseach file, S 4183, NAI.
196 Unsigned memorandum, 27 October 1932, Department of Justice, H 247/41/C, NAI. See also Finnane, 'The Carrigan Committee', pp. 519–36.

CONCLUSION

1 *Irish Independent*, 2 February 1926.
2 *Irish Times*, 2 February 1926.
3 *Ibid.*, 4 February 1926.
4 *Irish Independent*, 4 February 1926.
5 See ch. 6, p. 210.
6 In the Irish case this is particularly evident in the work of Frances Finnegan, *Do Penance or Perish*.

Bibliography

MANUSCRIPT SOURCES

BODLEIAN LIBRARY, OXFORD

Sir Matthew Nathan Papers, Memoranda of interviews, Ireland, vols. I–III, October 1914–May 1916.

BRITISH LIBRARY, LONDON

Althorp Papers, Add. MS 77489.

CONVENT OF THE GOOD SHEPHERD, BELFAST

MS Register of the Entrants to the Magdalen asylum, 1851–1900.
Typescript history of the Good Shepherd in Ireland.

CONVENT OF THE GOOD SHEPHERD (GSC)

(The following records were seen originally in individual convents. These records have now been centralised in Limerick.)

MS Register of the Magdalen asylum, Good Shepherd Convent, Cork, 1872–1900.
MS Register of the Asylum of the Good Shepherd, Limerick, 1828–1900, 4 vols.
MS Book in which are written the Names of our Benefactors, 19th century.
MS Monthly Accounts, Magdalen asylum, Limerick, vol. I, 1866–76; vol. II, 1888–1901.
MS Statistics of the Province of Ireland, 1848–96.
MS Accounts of Laundry Receipts and How Placed, 1892–1913.
MS Annals of the Convent, 1826–1909.
Leaflet requesting funds for the Magdalen asylum, 1879.
Typescript history of the Convent taken from the Annals.
Scrapbook containing newspaper cuttings, miscellaneous documents, etc., relating to the Magdalen asylum, nineteenth century.
MS Register of St Mary's Magdalen asylum, Convent of the Good Shepherd, Waterford, 1842–1900.

MS Convent Annals, 1858–1900.
Typescript history of the Convent taken from the Annals.
Typescript history of St Mary's Home taken from the Annals.

CONVENT OF MERCY, BAGGOT STREET, DUBLIN

Mother Mary Frances Bridgeman letters.

CONVENT OF MERCY, TRALEE

MS Annals of the Convent, 1854–1927.

CONVENT OF OUR LADY OF CHARITY OF REFUGE, HIGH PARK,
DRUMCONDRA, DUBLIN

MS Annals of the Convent, vol. I, 1853–1939.
MS Register of the Magdalen asylum, 1839–1904.

CONVENT OF THE SISTERS OF CHARITY, DONNYBROOK, DUBLIN

MS Register of the Magdalen asylum, 1796–1899.

CONVENT OF THE SISTERS OF CHARITY, ST VINCENT'S, CORK

MS register of St Mary's Magdalen asylum, 1846–99.
MS Annals of St Mary Magdalen.

CORK ARCHIVES INSTITUTE

Cork Union Minutes, 19 July 1841–27 February 1843, BG 69/A1.
Cork Union Minutes, 6 March 1843–30 December 1844, BG 69/A3.
Cork Union Indoor Relief Register, 26 August 1867–9 May 1869, BG 69/G14.
Cork Union Indoor Relief Register, 7 December 1869–10 March 1873, BG
    69/G15.
Youghal Board of Guardians Minute Book, October 1887–April 1888, BG
    163/A75.

SISTERS OF CHARITY GENERALATE, MILLTOWN, DUBLIN

Typescript, Letters of Mary Aikenhead to Mother M. de Chantal Coleman from
    1837–52.
Typescript copy of the Annals, vol. I, 1816–36; vol. II, 1837–58.

DEPARTMENT OF DEFENCE, PROPERTY MANAGEMENT BRANCH,
DUBLIN

Curragh of Kildare, Commission of Inquiry; transcript, 2 vols. 1866.

DUBLIN DIOCESAN ARCHIVES

Byrne Papers.
Cullen Papers.
Murray Papers.
Walsh Papers.

ELPHIN DIOCESAN ARCHIVES, SLIGO

Uncatalogued papers, box III C. Workhouses – Reforms, includes queries regarding classification systems in the workhouse.

IRISH ARCHITECTURAL ARCHIVE, DUBLIN

Plans of St Joseph's Convent and Magdalen asylum.

KERRY COUNTY LIBRARY, TRALEE

Killarney Union Minute Books, 1844–5, vol. V.
Killarney Poor Law Union Minute Books, 15 April 1848–20 December 1851, 2 vols.
Tralee Poor Law Union Minute Book, 14 December 1861–6 December 1862.

KILDARE COUNTY LIBRARY, NEWBRIDGE

Naas Union Poor Law Minute Books, 6 July 1859–1868, 8 vols.

LIMERICK MUSEUM, LIMERICK

The Account of the Governors and Governesses of Saint John's Fever and Lock Hospital, Limerick, 1837–1844 (printed).

MILITARY ARCHIVES, DUBLIN

Plan of the lock hospital, County of Kildare, 1870.

MOTHERS' UNION, DUBLIN

Minute Book of the General Committee, 22 November 1912–17 November 1921.

NATIONAL ARCHIVES OF IRELAND, DUBLIN

Bureau of Military History, witness statements (copies)
Miss Helena Molony, witness statement 391.
Mrs Sidney Czira, witness statement 909.
Mrs Margaret Keogh (*née* Quinn), witness statement 273.

Census records
MSS Census of Ireland, 1901, 1911.

Chief Secretary's Office, Registered Papers
CSORP 1835/2991, Complaints re brothels in Dublin.
CSORP 1838/2642, Report of the Commissioners of the Metropolitan Police for the Information of His Excellency, the Lord Lieutenant, 1838.
CSORP 1849/010175, Unnamed file.
CSORP 1858/11753, Return relating to the number of men in the [A, B, D, E, F] G Division, reports of being in brothels each year from 1 January 1838 to 1 January 1858, the number convicted and the punishment in each case.
CSORP 1863/10089, Papers relating to the case of Rosanna Doyle.
CSORP 1869/16686, Case of family of William Burke Kirwan.
CSORP 1869/8121, no title.
CSORP 1872/2770, no title.
CSORP 1876/8175, Case of Mary Anne Curran.
CSORP 1876/8460, Petition of a 'common prostitute'.
CSORP 1883/7984, Classification in workhouses.
CSORP 1883/13366, Associating with a prostitute.
CSORP 1883/13466, Contagious Diseases (Women) Acts.
CSORP 1883/13487, Immorality in Belfast workhouse.
CSORP 1884/23660, Contagious Diseases Acts.
CSORP 1884/27996, Contagious Disease Acts, Ireland 1864–1884.
CSORP 1884/28103, Resolution passed by Ballymoney Board of Guardians.
CSORP 1891/447, Prostitutes, Harsh Treatment by Local Authorities, 1890.
CSORP 1896/15894, Lunatics in workhouses.
CSORP 1913/3348, Belfast case.
CSORP 1914/1691, Re 'derelict children'.
CSORP 1914/22394, Misuse of Separation Allowances to Wives of Soldiers.
CSORP 1914/22394, Police investigation into separation allowances.
CSORP 1915/1911, Fraudulent Separation Allowance Claim.
CSORP 1915/2654, Women's Patrols.
CSORP 1915/14269, General details regarding separation allowances.
CSORP 1915/16018, Fraudulent Separation Allowance Claim.
CSORP 1915/16142, Fraudulent Separation Allowance Claim.
CSORP 1915/16187, Fraudulent Separation Allowance Claim.
CSORP 1915/16465, Dublin Vigilance Committee, 1915.
CSORP 1915/16511, Fraudulent Separation Allowance Claim.
CSORP 1915/16866, Fraudulent Separation Allowance Claim.
CSORP 1915/17198, Fraudulent Separation Allowance Claim.
CSORP 1915/17199, Fraudulent Separation Allowance Claim.
CSORP 1915/17200, Fraudulent Separation Allowance Claim.
CSORP 1915/17275, Fraudulent Separation Allowance Claim.
CSORP 1915/18756, Fraudulent Separation Allowance Claim.
CSORP 1915/18907, Fraudulent Separation Allowance Claim.
CSORP 1915/19149, Fraudulent Separation Allowance Claim.
CSORP 1915/19150, Fraudulent Separation Allowance Claim.

CSORP 1915/19560, Fraudulent Separation Allowance Claim.
CSORP 1915/19950, Fraudulent Separation Allowance Claim.
CSORP 1915/21829, Fraudulent Separation Allowance Claim.
CSORP 1917/749, Separation case.
CSORP 1917/20995, Army Pensions.
CSORP 1917/24282, Fraudulent Separation Allowance Claim.
CSORP 1917/24736, Soldier assaulted by women.
CSORP 1918/1478, Separation case.
CSORP 1919/17970, Case of Mary and Hugh Straney.
CSORP 1920/, Case of Ellen Macken.
CSORP 1921–22/3455/3, Undesirable Women frequenting the Phoenix Park.
CSORP 1921–22/3395, DMP office file.

Department of Health
B13/134, vol. I , Venereal disease, Kildare.
B35/2, vol. I, Venereal disease, review of arrangements.
B35/21, vol. I, Treatment of venereal disease in Waterford 1926–29.
B135/3, vol. I, Venereal disease, Mater Hospital 1943–7.
B135/9, vol. I, Venereal disease, British information on, 1935–55.
B135/10, Venereal disease, correspondence with the press 1947–55.
B135/11, vol. I, Venereal disease, miscellaneous papers 1930–1953.
B135/12, Venereal disease returns for 1938 and 1943.
B135/13, Venereal disease, internal committee of inquiry, 1925.
B135/14, vol. I, Venereal disease prior to 1936.
B135/22, Westmoreland lock hospital.

Department of Justice
Trials Record Book, Central Criminal Court, IC 88 60, June 1925–June 1927.
Trials Record Book, Central Criminal Court, IC 88 61, June 1925–December 1926.
Trials Record Book, Central Criminal Court, ID 24 129, February 1928–November 1943.
Trials Record Book, Central Criminal Court, ID 33 68, November 1927–June 1933.
Trials Record Book, Central Criminal Court, ID 11 92, November 1933–April 1941.
Trials Record Book, Central Criminal Court, ID 11 96, 1941.
Trials Record Book, Central Criminal Court, ID 27 1, 1941–5.

Committee on Evil Literature, File Jus 7/2/9.
Committee on Evil Literature, File Jus 7/2/14.
Department of Justice, File Jus 8/20.
Criminal Law Amendment Act, correspondence, File Jus 8/20/1.
Criminal Justice (Female Offenders) Bill, 1942, File Jus 8/128.
Department of Justice, File Jus 8/451.
Criminal Law Amendment Acts 1885–1935, Enforcement of, Garda Síochána seek instructions, File Jus 9/8.
Our Lady's House, Henrietta Street, Dublin, grants 1920–60, File Jus 16/62A.

Dublin Catholic Male Discharged Prisoners' Aid Society (includes papers relating to St Joseph's Home for Girls, Belfast), File Jus 16/79.
Memorandum on Crime, 1936, Jus 8/451.
Crime Report 1936, File Jus 72/50.
Criminal Statistics, 1926–43, File Jus 72/53, part 1.
Suppression of Prostitution, Ad Hoc Committee on Prostitution, File Jus 72/94/A.
Minutes of Evidence, the Carrigan Committee, File Jus 90/4.
St Anne's Reformatory, 1944, File Jus 93/83.
Breach of v.d. regulations 1939–40, File Jus 116/45.
Department of Justice, File H 171/1.
Criminal Law Amendment Act, 1930, File H 171/31.
Criminal Law Amendment Act, 1926–30, File H 171/39.
Anonymous letter on immoral behaviour, c. 1930, File H 213/6.
Department of Justice, File H 247/41/A.
Department of Justice, File H 247/41/B.
Department of Justice, File H 247/41/C.
Department of Justice, File H 247/41/D.
Department of Justice, File H 247/41/E.
Department of Justice, File H 266/40.

Department of the Taoiseach
File S 2803, Summary Jurisdiction, Punishment of Solicitation Bill, 1932.
File S 2804, Criminal Law Amendment Acts, 1932–4.
File S 2864, Criminal Law Amendment Acts, 1932–4.
File S 4183, VD in the Irish Free State, 1924–7.
File S 4836, Propaganda for Combating Venereal Disease by Means of Cinema Films, 1925–6.
File S 5998, Criminal Law Amendment Bill, 1929–34.
File S 6134, Pastoral letters on immorality, 1930s.
File S 6489, Criminal Law Amendment Bill, 1934.
File S 6489A, Criminal Law (Amendment) Act, 1935.
File S 10815A, Adoption of Children: General File.
File S 13290A1, Children, Kennedy Report.
File S 16210, Women Police, 1938–58.

Government Prisons Board
Elizabeth Finnegan, Government Prisons Board, PEN 1885/99.

Joint Committee of Women's Societies and Social Workers
File 98/14/5/1, Minute Book 1935–9.
File 98/14/5/2, Minute Book 1939–48.
File 98/14/7/1, Miscellaneous papers.

Miscellaneous Files
Letter regarding the Magdalen asylum in Waterford, OP 298/4/4.
North Dublin Union Register of Admission and Discharge, 1864, MFGS 52/7.

South Dublin Union Minute Book 1860, BG79/A11–A14.
House for Fallen Women, Northcote Rescue Home, 1866–1920 Agreements of sale and appointment of trustees, 999/283/1–3.
Papers relating to the Asylum for Penitent Females, M1133.
Poor Law Commission Correspondence, 1844, 2/440/38.
Prisoner Record Sheets in File A, Box 1 and File C, Box 1 in Suffragette Files in Government Prisons Board.
Westmoreland lock hospital, report, 1829, OP/737/5.
Kildare Assize files 1886.
Limerick Assize files 1890.
Return of outrages, Limerick 1871, 37; 1883, 10.
Tipperary Assize Files, 1892.
Crown Files at Assizes 1883–4, 1c2632.
Crown Files at Assizes 1885–6, 1c2633.
Crown Files at Assizes 1890, Galway 1c19156.
Crown and Peace Office, Co. Kildare, appeals to quarter sessions 1868, 1877, 1881, 1885, 1c2630.
Crown Files at Assizes, Kildare 1890 1c2635.
Criminal Record Files, 1840–51.

Office of Public Works
Papers relating to the Curragh camp, 1853–70, OPW/486/59.

NATIONAL ARCHIVES, LONDON

Administration of regulation 40D of Defence of the Realm Act, HO 45/10893/359931.
Contagious Diseases Acts, 1866–9, HO 45/9512/17273C.
Colonial Office, CO 904/204.
File relating to Kathleen Lynn, CO 904/207/256.
History of Separation Allowances, WO 32/9316.
Protests against anti v.d. measures taken under Defence of the Realm Act, WO 32/11403.
Venereal disease in the army, 1914, HO 45/10724.
Women Police, HO 45/10806/309485.

NATIONAL LIBRARY OF IRELAND, DUBLIN

All Ireland Conference of 19 April 1917, Minute Book of the Women Delegates to, MS 21,194 (47).
Archbishop Walsh, Letter to Count Plunkett re prostitution in Dublin, 20 February 1886, MS 36,169.
Commission on the Relief of the Destitute Sick and Poor, Minutes of Evidence R27/2.
Dunboyne Papers, MS 3,337.
Mary Hayden, diaries, MS 16641.
Rosamond Jacob, diaries, MS 32,582.
Kilmainham Papers, MSS 1054, 1064, 1066, 1068, 1163, 1069, 1071, 1306.

Leon O'Broin Papers, MSS 31,670, 31,673, 31,676 (relating to his work on Frank Duff).
Sheehy Skeffington Papers, MSS 22,681; 33,621 (10).
Westport Union Minute Book, 5 April 1860–27 September 1860, MS 12,626; 18 April 1861–30 October 1861, MS 12,627.
Young soldier, diary MS 13,2651.

PRESBYTERIAN HISTORICAL SOCIETY, BELFAST

Annual Reports of the Edgar Home, 1900–26.
Minute Book of the Edgar Home 1900–48.
General Assembly minutes.

PUBLIC RECORD OFFICE OF NORTHERN IRELAND

Antrim County Council, 1919–45, LA/1.
Armagh Indoor Relief Register 1848–61, MIC: 15F/reel 6; MIC: 15F/reel 7.
Armagh Indoor Relief Register 1893, MIC: 15F/reel 8.
Belfast Board of Guardians, Minute Book, 1861–2, BG/7/A/24.
Belfast Board of Guardians, Indoor Relief Register February 1865, MIC: 15F/reel 28B.
Belfast Board of Guardians, Indoor Relief Book, October 1892–February 1893, BG7/G/20; February 1893–March 1893, BG7/G/21.
Book of Precedents, LGBD2/1 (summary of cases and queries re workhouse management).
Book recording offences committed in Dundalk under the 17th and 18th Victoria, Chapter 103, D/2458/3.
Crown File at Belfast Assize Court, Belf 1/1/2/39.
Crown File at Belfast Recorder's Court, Belf 1/2/2/28.
Crown File at Belfast Recorder's Court, Belf 1/2/2/24.
Circulars from the Local Government Board, Dublin 1917, LA1/3AG/12.
Diary of Rev. Anthony McIntyre's visits to the Poor of Belfast, 1853–7, D 1558/2/3.
Londonderry Board of Guardians, Minute Book, March 1859–November 1862, BG/21/A/11.
Minutes of the County Londonderry VD Committee, 1918, LA5/9AK/1.
Records of the Church of Ireland Rescue League, 1924–25, D/1362/26/18.
Records of Belfast Midnight Mission, 1934–49, D/2072/1.
Treatment of Venereal Disease in Northern Ireland 1919, LA1/3AG/13.
Town Clerk's Letter Book, LA/7/29AA/3.
Ulster Female Penitentiary, Letter from Rev. Mark Cassidy, D 1088/22.

REPRESENTATIVE CHURCH BODY LIBRARY, DUBLIN

MS Board of Guardian Minute Book, Magdalen Asylum, Leeson Street, 1841–53.
MS Magdalen Asylum, Leeson Street, Admissions Books, 1766–1986.

ROYAL COLLEGE OF PHYSICIANS OF IRELAND, DUBLIN

Records of the Westmoreland lock hospital, MSS General Registers of Patients, 4
vols., 1816–27; 1827–41; 1841–57; 1857–68.
MS Visitors' Book, 1825–89.
MS Chaplain's Visiting Book, 1861–4.
MS House Committee Books, 2 vols., 1862–71; 1871–5.
MS Registrar's Report Book, 1872–7.
MSS Board Minute Books, 2 vols., 1885–99.
Minute Book marked 'A conference of the Societies with reference to combating
the spread of venereal disease', 1918–19.

UNIVERSITY COLLEGE DUBLIN, ARCHIVES DEPARTMENT

Ernest Blythe Papers P24/119; P24/323.
Richard Mulcahy Papers P7/C/12; P7/C/15; P7/D/3.

WATERFORD AND LISMORE DIOCESAN ARCHIVES, WATERFORD

Dr Bernard Hackett Papers.
Typescript letter regarding unmarried mothers, 1924.
Typescript report on unmarried mothers, c. 1920.

WOMEN'S LIBRARY, LONDON

Annual Reports of the Ladies' National Association.
Annual Reports of the National Association for the Repeal of the Contagious
Diseases Acts.

OFFICIAL SOURCES

Dáil Éireann, Debates, 1922–60.
Seanad Éireann, Debates, 1922–60.

Criminal and Judicial Statistics for Ireland 1864 (3418) lvii 653.
Criminal and Judicial Statistics for Ireland 1865 (3563) lii 657.
Criminal and Judicial Statistics for Ireland 1866 (3705) lxviii 697.
Criminal and Judicial Statistics for Ireland 1867 (3930) lxvi 735.
Criminal and Judicial Statistics for Ireland 1867–8 (4071) lxvii 737.
Criminal and Judicial Statistics for Ireland 1867–8 (4071–1) lxvii 947.
Criminal and Judicial Statistics for Ireland 1868–9 (4203) lviii 737.
Criminal and Judicial Statistics for Ireland 1870 (753) lxiii C227.
Criminal and Judicial Statistics for Ireland 1871 (C443) lxiv 231.
Criminal and Judicial Statistics for Ireland 1872 (C674) lxv 235.
Criminal and Judicial Statistics for Ireland 1873 (C851) lxx 247.
Criminal and Judicial Statistics for Ireland 1874 (C291) liv 513.
Criminal and Judicial Statistics for Ireland 1875 (C1295) lxxxi 259.
Criminal and Judicial Statistics for Ireland 1876 (C1563) lxxix 273.

Criminal and Judicial Statistics for Ireland 1877 (C1822) lxxxvi 261.
Criminal and Judicial Statistics for Ireland 1878 (C2152) lxxix 265.
Criminal and Judicial Statistics for Ireland 1878–9 (C2389) lxxvi 279.
Criminal and Judicial Statistics for Ireland 1880 (C2698) lxxvii 251.
Criminal and Judicial Statistics for Ireland 1881 (C3028) xcv 243.
Criminal and Judicial Statistics for Ireland 1882 (C3355) lxxv 243.
Criminal and Judicial Statistics for Ireland 1883 (C3808) lxxvii 243.
Criminal and Judicial Statistics for Ireland 1884 (C4181) lxxxvi 243.
Criminal and Judicial Statistics for Ireland 1884–5 (C4554) lxxxvi 243.
Criminal and Judicial Statistics for Ireland 1886 (C4796) lxxii 233.
Criminal and Judicial Statistics for Ireland 1887 (C5177) xc 241.
Criminal and Judicial Statistics for Ireland 1888 (C5495) cviii 241.
Criminal and Judicial Statistics for Ireland 1889 (C5795) lxxxv 241.
Criminal and Judicial Statistics for Ireland 1890 (C6122) lxxx 253.
Criminal and Judicial Statistics for Ireland 1890–1 (C6511) xciii 251.
Criminal and Judicial Statistics for Ireland 1892 (C6782) lxxxix 253.
Criminal and Judicial Statistics for Ireland 1893–4 (C7189) ciii 279.
Criminal and Judicial Statistics for Ireland 1894 (C7534) xcv 105.
Criminal and Judicial Statistics for Ireland 1895 (C7799) cviii 323.
Criminal and Judicial Statistics for Ireland 1896 (C8207) xciv 521.
Criminal and Judicial Statistics for Ireland 1897 (C8616) c 517.
Criminal and Judicial Statistics for Ireland 1897 (8617) c 761.
Criminal and Judicial Statistics for Ireland 1899 (C99249) cviii, pt II, 351.
Criminal and Judicial Statistics for Ireland 1899 (C9492) cviii, pt II, 1.
Criminal and Judicial Statistics for Ireland 1899 (C9494) cviii, pt II, 445.
Criminal and Judicial Statistics for Ireland 1900 (Cd 225) civ 1.
Criminal and Judicial Statistics for Ireland 1900 (Cd 246) civ 353.
Criminal and Judicial Statistics for Ireland 1900 (Cd 313) civ 177.
Criminal and Judicial Statistics for Ireland 1901 (Cd 725, 682) lxxxix 463.
Criminal and Judicial Statistics for Ireland 1902 (Cd 185) lxxxiv 657.
Criminal and Judicial Statistics for Ireland 1902 (Cd 1208, 1187) cxvii 395.
Criminal and Judicial Statistics for Ireland 1903 (Cd 1746, 1676) lxxxiii 403.
Criminal and Judicial Statistics for Ireland 1904 (Cd 2218, 2149) cvii 431.
Criminal and Judicial Statistics for Ireland 1905 (Cd 150) lxv 929.
Criminal and Judicial Statistics for Ireland 1905 (Cd 2632, 2593) xcix 417.
Criminal and Judicial Statistics for Ireland 1906 (Cd 3112, 3050) cxxxv 405.
Criminal and Judicial Statistics for Ireland 1907 (Cd 3654, 3616) xcviii 447.
Criminal and Judicial Statistics for Ireland 1908 (Cd 4200, 3050) cxxiii 619.
Criminal and Judicial Statistics for Ireland 1909 (Cd 4793, 4747) civ 207.
Criminal and Judicial Statistics for Ireland 1910 (Cd 5320, 5264) cxi 359.
Criminal and Judicial Statistics for Ireland 1911 (Cd 5866, 5848) cii 367.
Criminal and Judicial Statistics for Ireland 1912–13 (Cd 6419, 6329) cx 703.
Criminal and Judicial Statistics for Ireland 1913 (Cd 6916) lxxvi 659.
Criminal and Judicial Statistics for Ireland 1914 (Cd 7064) c 349.
Criminal and Judicial Statistics for Ireland 1914 (Cd 7536, 7600) c 519.
Criminal and Judicial Statistics for Ireland 1914–6 (Cd 8077, 8006) lxxxii 451.
Criminal and Judicial Statistics for Ireland 1917–18 (Cd 8636) xxxvii 283.
Criminal and Judicial Statistics for Ireland 1918 (Cd 9065) xxv 29.

Criminal and Judicial Statistics for Ireland 1919 (Cmd 43, 438) lii.
Criminal and Judicial Statistics for Ireland 1921 (Cmd 1431) xli 591.

Report on State Prisons and Other Gaols in Ireland, 1809 vii (246).
Report on the Select Committee on the Irish Miscellaneous Estimates, HC 1829 (342) iv.
Report of the Commissioners Appointed to Inspect Charitable Institutions, Dublin, HC 38, 1842.
Select Committee of Inquiry into Drunkenness among the Labouring Classes of the United Kingdom, Report, Minutes of Evidence, Appendix, HC 1834 (559) viii, 315.
First Report from his Majesty's Commissioners for Inquiring into the Condition of the Poorer Classes in Ireland, with appendix (A), HC 1835 (369) xxxii.
Report from the Royal Commission on Conditions of the Poorer Classes in Ireland, Third Report, appendix C, parts i and ii, HC 1836 (43) xxx, 1.
Report of the Commissioners Appointed by the Lord Lieutenant of Ireland to Inspect Charitable Institutions in Dublin, HC 1842 (337) xxxviii.
Census of Ireland for the year 1851, pt. I, vol. 4, province of Connacht, HC 1852–3 (1542) xcii, 339–555.
Report from the Select Committee on Dublin Hospitals; together with the Proceedings of the Committee, Minutes of Evidence, Appendix and Index, HC 1854 (338) xii.
Report of the Select Committee on Poor Removal, Proceedings, Minutes of Evidence, Appendix and Index, HC 1854 (396) xvii.
Report of the Commissioners Appointed to Inquire into the Hospitals of Dublin, HC 1856 xix.
Report from the Select Committee Appointed to Inquire into the Administration of the Relief of the Poor in Ireland, HC 1861 (408) x, 1.
Census of Ireland for the year 1861, pt iv, Report and Tables Relating to the Religious Professions, Education and Occupations of the People, vol. I (3204-III), HC 1863 lix, I; vol. II (3204-III), HC 1863 lx, I.
Report of the Committee Appointed to Enquire into the Pathology and Treatment of the Venereal Disease with the View to Diminish the Injurious Effects on the Men of the Army and Navy, with Appendices, and the Evidence Taken before the Committee, HC 1868 xxxvii.
Report from the Select Committee on the Contagious Diseases Acts (1866): together with the Proceedings of the Committee, Minutes of Evidence and Appendix, HC 1869 vii.
Reports of the Royal Commission upon the Administration and Operation of the Contagious Diseases Acts, 1866–9, HC 1871 (C408–1) xix.
Twenty First Report of the Board of Superintendence of the Dublin Hospitals for 1880 (C2565) xxiii.
Report from the Select Committee on the Contagious Diseases Acts, 1881, HC 1881 (351) viii.
Copies of the Minutes of Evidence taken at the Recent Inquiry held at Belfast Workhouse by Inspectors Bourke and Brodie, together with their Report thereon, and Final Decision by the Local Government Board, HC 1881 (123) lxxix, 69.
Report from the Select Committee of the House of Lords on the Law relating to the Protection of Young Girls Together with the Proceedings of the Committee, Minutes of Evidence, Appendix. HC 1881 (448) ix.
Report from the Select Committee on the Contagious Diseases Acts; with the Proceedings

of the Committee, Minutes of Evidence, Appendix and Index, 1882, HC 1882 (C340) ix.

Census of Ireland, 1881, vol. ii, Province of Munster (C3148) HC 1882 lxxvii, 1.

Seventh Report of the General Prisons Board, 1884–85 (C4543) xxxviii, 783.

Third Report of Her Majesty's Commissioners for Inquiring into the Housing of the Working Classes (Ireland) (C4547) HC 1885 xxxi.

Eighth-Report of the General Prisons Board (C4817) HC 1886 xxxv, 281.

Dublin Hospitals Commission, Report of the Committee of Inquiry, 1887, together with Minutes of Evidence and Appendices (C5042) HC 1887 xxxv.

Report of the Chief Inspector of Factories and Workshops for the year 1894 (C7745) HC 1895 xix.

Nineteenth Report of the General Prisons Board, 1896–7 (C8589) xl, 545.

Report of the Chief Inspector of Factories for the Year Ending 31 December 1905 (Cd 3036) HC 1906 xv, 405.

Report of the Vice-Regal Commission on Poor Law Reform in Ireland (Cd 3202) HC 1906 li, 1.

Census of Ireland 1911, pt. 1: showing area, houses, and population; also the ages, civil or conjugal condition, occupations, birthplaces, religions and education of the people, vol. 1, province of Leinster (Cd 6049) HC 1912–13 cxiv, 1.

Army Reports, Increased Rates of Separation Allowances for the Wives and Children of Soldiers, 1914 (Cd 7623).

Royal Commission on Venereal Diseases, Reports and Minutes of Evidence, HC (Cd 7475) xlix, 1914; 1916 (Cd 8189) xvi; 1916 (Cd 8190) xvi.

Report to His Majesty the King of the War Pensions and Statutory Committee for the Year 1916 (Cd 8750) 1917–18 xvii.

REPORTS FROM GOVERNMENT DEPARTMENTS

Annual Reports of the Commissioners for Administering the Laws for the Relief of the Poor in Ireland, 1849–72.

Annual Report of the Inspectors of Factories for the half year ending 31 December 1863.

Annual Reports of the Local Government Board in Ireland, 1873–1920.

Annual Report of the Registrar-General for Saorstát Éireann (Dublin, 1924).

Department of Local Government and Public Health Reports (Dublin, 1922–41).

Dublin Metropolitan Police Statistics, 1855–1919 (Dublin, 1856–1921).

Local Government Board, Report on Venereal Diseases (London, 1913).

Report of the Commission on the Relief of the Sick and Destitute Poor, Including the Insane Poor (Dublin, 1928).

Report of the Committee on Evil Literature (Dublin, 1927).

Statistical Abstracts of Ireland, 1927–41 (Dublin, 1927–42).

GOVERNMENT OF NORTHERN IRELAND

Report of the Ministry of Home Affairs on the Administration of Local Government Services for the period 1st December 1921 to 31st March 1923 (Cmd 30 (n.d)).

Report on the Administration of Home Office Services, 1928 (Cmd 107) (1929).

Report on the Administration of Home Office Services, 1929 (Cmd 120) (1930).

Report on the Administration of Home Office Services, 1930 (Cmd 134) (1931).

Report on the Administration of Local Government Services, 1930–31 (Cmd 137) (1932).
Report on the Administration of Home Office Services, 1933 (Cmd 163) (1934).

CIRCULARS, DIRECTORIES, GUIDES, MANUALS

Belfast and Province of Ulster Directory for 1858–9 (Belfast, 1858).
The Dublin Guide, or, a Description of the City of Dublin and the Most Remarkable Places within Fifteen Miles (Dublin, 1794).
Guide for the Religious Called Sisters of Mercy (London, 1866).
Instructions for the Guidance of Resident Magistrates (Dublin, 1877).
Irish Catholic Directory and Almanac, 1869–1940 (Dublin, 1870–1941).
Irish Medical Directory (Dublin, 1879).
Pettigrew and Oulton, Dublin Almanac and General Register of Ireland (Dublin, 1834–49).
Reed, Sir Andrew, The Irish Constable's Guide (Dublin, 1901).
Religious Orders and Congregations in Ireland (Dublin, 1933).
The Royal Irish Constabulary Manual or Guide to the Discharge of Police Duties (Dublin, 1910).
Standing Orders and Regulations for the Government and Guidance of the Dublin Metropolitan Police (Dublin, 1889).
Thom's Irish Almanac and Official Directory, 1844–1941 (Dublin, 1844–1941).
Venereal Diseases, Provision for Diagnosis, Treatment and Prevention, Circulars, etc., issued by the Local Government Board of Ireland (Dublin, 1918).

NEWSPAPERS AND JOURNALS

Athlone Sentinel
Bean na hÉireann
Belfast Newsletter
Belfast Telegraph
British Journal of Nursing
British Medical Journal
Clare Journal
Connaught Journal
Cork Constitution
Cork Examiner
Derry Journal
Dublin Journal of Medical Science
Dublin Quarterly Journal of Medical Science
Dublin Medical Press and Circular
Freeman's Journal
Hibernian
Irish Builder
Irish Citizen
Irish Independent
Irish Law Times and Solicitors' Journal
Irish Monthly

Irish News
Irish People
Irish Press
Irish Statesman
Irish Theological Quarterly
Irish Times
Irish Worker
Kerry Advocate
Kildare Observer
Kilkenny Moderator
Lady of the House
Lancet
Leinster Express
Leinster Leader
Limerick Chronicle
Londonderry Sentinel
Maria Legionis
Medical Press and Circular
New Ireland Review
Northern Whig
Northern Standard
Pall Mall Gazette
Southern Reporter
The Lady of the House
The Shield
The Times
The Vigilance Record
Ulster Medical Journal
Wexford People

REPORTS RELATING TO CHARITABLE ORGANISATIONS

ASYLUM FOR PENITENT FEMALES

Report of the Asylum for Penitent Females, 1830 (Dublin, 1831).
Report of the Asylum for Penitent Females, 1831 (Dublin, 1832).
Report of the Asylum for Penitent Females, 1842 (Dublin, 1843).

BELFAST MIDNIGHT MISSION

Report of the Belfast Midnight Mission for 1874–75 (Belfast, 1875).

DUBLIN FEMALE PENITENTIARY

Report of the Committee of the Dublin Female Penitentiary to the General Meeting, 1814 (Dublin, 1814).
Report of the Committee of the Dublin Female Penitentiary to the General Meeting, 1815 (Dublin, 1815).

Report of the Committee of the Dublin Female Penitentiary to the General Meeting, 1816 (Dublin, 1816).
Fourth Report of the Committee to the General Meeting, 1817 (Dublin, 1817).
Report of the Committee of the Dublin Female Penitentiary to the General Meeting, 1819 (Dublin, 1820).
Report of the Committee of the Dublin Female Penitentiary to the General Meeting, 1820 (Dublin, 1820).
Report of the Committee of the Dublin Female Penitentiary to the General Meeting, 1823–24 (Dublin, 1825).

DUBLIN BY LAMPLIGHT

Report of Dublin by Lamplight, 1856 (Dublin, 1857).
Report of Dublin by Lamplight, 1857 (Dublin, 1858).
Report of Dublin by Lamplight, 1858 (Dublin, 1859).
Tenth Annual Report Dublin by Lamplight (Dublin, 1868).
Report of Dublin by Lamplight, 1879 (Dublin, 1880).

DUBLIN WHITE CROSS VIGILANCE ASSOCIATION

Dublin White Cross Vigilance Association, Report for the Year Ending 31 December 1898 (Dublin, 1898).

ULSTER FEMALE PENITENTIARY

Sixth Annual Report of the Ulster Female Penitentiary (Belfast, 1828).
Ulster Female Penitentiary, First General Report of the Committee Since Its Commencement in the Latter Part of the Year 1831 (Belfast, 1835).

ULSTER MAGDALEN ASYLUM

Ulster Magdalen Asylum, Report 1887 (n.p., 1888).
Ulster Magdalen Asylum, Annual Report (Belfast, 1906).

MISCELLANEOUS

Abstract Report and Statistical Sketch of the Magdalen Asylum, High Park, Drumcondra (Dublin, 1881).
Catholic Protection and Rescue Society of Ireland, Annual Report 1923 (Dublin, 1924).
Dublin Midnight Mission and Home, Report for the Year Ending 1876 (Dublin, 1877).
Geary, MD, William John, *A Historical and Medical Report of the Limerick Lock Hospital: Comprising a Period of Nearly Forty Years* (Limerick, 1820).
'Report of St John's Fever and Lock Hospitals, Limerick', *Dublin Journal of Medical Science*, 11 (1837), pp. 378–90.
'Report of St John's Fever and Lock Hospitals, Limerick', *Dublin Journal of Medical Science*, 12, 34 (1838), pp. 94–104.
Irish Women Patrols, Report 1919 (Dublin, 1920).

Magdalen Ayslum, in Leeson Street, Dublin, Receipts and Expenditure in the Years 1796–179 (Dublin, 1800).
Report upon Certain Charitable Establishments in the City of Dublin which Receive Aid from Parliament (Dublin, 1809).
Report Showing the Foundation and Progress of the Monastery and Order of Our Lady of Charity of Refuge (Dublin, 1857).
'Report on public health', *Dublin Journal of Medical Science*, 48 (November 1869), pp. 622–7.
Rotunda Girls' Aid Society, Annual Report, 1887–8 (Dublin, 1888).
'Second report of the Order of Our Lady of Charity of Refuge', *The Irish Quarterly Review*, 9 (1860), pp. i–viii.

CONTEMPORARY PUBLISHED SOURCES

Acton, William, *Prostitution Considered in its Moral, Social, and Sanitary Aspects in London and other Large Cities and Garrison Towns with Proposals for the Control and Prevention of its Attendant Evils* (London, 1857; 2nd edn 1869).
The Contagious Diseases Acts: Shall the Contagious Diseases Act be Applied to the Civil Population? (London, 1870).
An Address to the Ladies Forming the Committee of the Intended New Dublin Female Penitentiary in Consequence of their Appeal to the Public (Dublin, 1813).
Alexis de Tocqueville's Journey in Ireland, July–August, 1835, ed. Emmet Larkin (Dublin, 1990).
An Historical Guide to the City of Dublin (2nd edn, London, 1825; reprinted Dublin, 1980).
An Appeal to the Public from the Committee of the Intended New Dublin Female Penitentiary (Dublin, 1812).
An Appeal to the Public on Behalf of the Ulster Female Penitentiary (n.p., 1834).
An Sagart, 'How to deal with the unmarried mother', *Irish Ecclesiastical Record*, 20 (1922), pp. 145–53.
Arnold, Captain J. C., ' "Last post" of the separation woman', *War Pensions Gazette*, February 1920, p. 449.
'Association for the Extension of the Contagious Diseases Act, 1866, to the civil population of the United Kingdom', *Dublin Quarterly Journal of Medical Science*, 46 (1868), pp. 165–9.
Barrett, Rosa M., *A Guide to Dublin Charities* (Dublin, 1884).
Ellice Hopkins, A Memoir (London, 1908).
Begbie, Harold, *The Lady Next Door* (London, 1914; reprint Dublin, 2006).
Brodrick, Albinia, 'The Black Plague', *The British Journal of Nursing*, 19 July 1913, pp. 45–7.
'The Black Plague', *The British Journal of Nursing*, 26 July 1913, pp. 63–5.
Brown, John, 'Medical report of the Dundalk "Destitute Sick Society", together with a sketch of the medical topography and statistics of the town and parish', *Dublin Journal of Medical Science*, 15 (1839).
Burke, Rev. Thomas, *Ireland's Vindication: Refutation of Froude, and Other Lectures, Historical and Religious* (London, n.d.).
Butler, Beartice Bayley, 'Lady Arbella Denny, 1707–1792', *Dublin Historical Record*, 9 (1946–7).

Butler, Josephine E., *Personal Reminiscences of a Great Crusade* (London, 1896).
Butler, Mary L., 'Modern fashions in ladies' dress' (Dublin, 1927; reprint of 1899 edition).
Cameron, Charles A., 'Report on public health: prevention of venereal disease', *Dublin Quarterly Journal of Medical Science*, 48 (1869).
'Half-yearly report on public health', *Dublin Quarterly Journal of Medical Science*, 52, 104 (November, 1871), pp. 476–79.
'Report on public health', *Dublin Quarterly Journal of Medical Science*, 62 (1876), pp. 133–46.
Carter Battersby, J., 'On the variety and differential diagnosis of primary venereal sores', *Dublin Journal of Medical Science*, 89 (June 1890), pp. 499–506.
Caulfield, D., 'Historical statistics of Ireland', *Journal of the Statistical and Social Inquiry Society of Ireland*, 3 (1862).
Cavendish, L. C. F., 'Laundries in religious houses', *Nineteenth Century*, 41 (1897), pp. 89–97.
Cherry, J. C., 'The control of v.d. in Ireland', *Irish Journal of Medical Science*, 6 (1943), pp. 161–70.
Clarke, A. M., *Life of Reverend Mother Mary St. Euphrasia Pelletier* (London, 1895).
Conferences and Instructions of the Venerable Mother Mary of Saint Euphrasia Pelletier, Foundress of the Generalate of the Congregation of Our Lady of Charity of the Good Shepherd of Angers (London, 1907, 2nd edn).
Constitution of the Irish Vigilance Association (Dublin, n.d., c.1920).
'The Contagious Diseases Acts and their work', *The Medical Press and Circular*, 27 November, 1878.
Corrigan, Dominic, 'Medical report of the North Dublin Union', *Dublin Journal of Medical Science*, 21, 63 (1843), pp. 508–16.
Costello, Mary, 'The sisterhood of sorrow, no. 1, The Magdalens', *Lady of the House* (15 February 1897), pp. 6–8.
'The sisterhood of sorrow, no. 2, The Magdalens', *Lady of the House* (15 March 1897), pp. 7–8.
'The sisterhood of sorrow, no. 3, The Magdalens', *Lady of the House* (15 April 1897), pp. 7–8.
'The sisterhood of sorrow, no. 4, Conclusion of the Magdalens', *Lady of the House* (15 May 1897), p. 15.
Cousins, Margaret and James H., *We Two Together* (Madras, 1950).
de Beaumont, Gustave, *Ireland, Social, Political and Religious* (London, 1839), 2 vols.
Devane, SJ, Rev. R. S., 'The unmarried mother: some legal aspects of the problem – the age of consent', *Irish Ecclesiastical Record*, 23 (1924), pp. 55–68.
'The unmarried mother: some legal aspects of the problem – the legal position of the unmarried mother in the Irish Free State', *Irish Ecclesiastical Record*, 23 (1924), pp. 172–88.
'Indecent literature: some legal remedies. Introductory: the bishops' views', *Irish Ecclesiastical Record*, 25 (1925), pp. 182–204.
'The unmarried mother and the poor law commission', *Irish Ecclesiastical Record*, 31 (1928), pp. 561–82.
'The dance hall', *Irish Ecclesiastical Record*, 37 (1931), pp. 170–86.

'The legal protection of girls', *Irish Ecclesiastical Record*, 37 (1931), pp. 20–39.

Donald, H. C., 'The diagnosis and treatment of syphilis', *Dublin Journal of Medical Science*, 142 (1919), pp. 70–8.

Duff, Frank, *Miracles on Tap* (New York, 1961).

Edgar, Rev. John, *Female Virtue: its Enemies and Friends* (London, 1841).

Fallon, Martin (ed.), *The Sketches of Erinensis: Selections of Irish Medical Satire, 1824–1836* (London, 1979).

Fleetwood, John, *A History of Medicine in Ireland* (Dublin, 1951).

Four Letters in Answer to an Address to the Committee of the Dublin Female Penitentiary (Dublin, 1813).

Garahy, Rev. M., *Idols of Modern Society* (Dublin, 1922).

Glynn, Joseph A., 'The unmarried mother', *Irish Ecclesiastical Record*, 18 (1921), pp. 461–7.

Giollamhuire, 'Do Irish girls know?', *The Catholic Bulletin*, 12 (1922), pp. 38–9.

Greenwood, James, *The Wren of the Curragh* (London, 1867).

The Seven Curses of London (London, 1869).

Grimshaw, Thomas Wrigley, 'Address in state medicine to the state medicine subsection of the Academy of Medicine in Ireland', *Dublin Quarterly Journal of Medical Science*, 77 (1884).

Hall, Mr and Mrs S. C., *Ireland: its Scenery and Character*, 3 vols. (London, 1841–3).

(Haslam, Thomas J.), *A Few Words on Prostitution and the Contagious Diseases Acts* (Dublin, 1870).

Hayes, Richard and Kathleen Lynn, *Public Health Circular no. 1* (Sinn Féin public health leaflet, Dublin, February 1918).

Head, F. B., *A Fortnight in Ireland* (London, 1852).

Heinrick, Hugh, *A Survey of the Irish in England (1872)* ed. Alan O'Day (London, 1990).

Hime, H. C., *The Moral Utility of a Lock Hospital* (Dublin, 1872).

Hopkins, Ellice, *The Purity Movement* (London, 1885).

Present Moral Crisis: an Appeal to Women (London, 1883).

Immoral Legislation: A Few Facts for the Consideration of the Irish Clergy (Dublin, 1880).

Hutchinson, Evaline, 'Women in the police courts', *The Englishwoman*, 20 (1913).

Killen, W. D., *Memoir of John Edgar, DD, LLD* (Belfast, 1867).

Kirkpatrick, Frederick, 'On the epidemic ophthalmia in the Irish workhouse', *Dublin Quarterly Journal of Medical Science*, 21, 42 (1855), pp. 335–48.

Kirkpatrick, T. P. C., 'Syphilis and the state', *Dublin Journal of Medical Science*, 145 (1918), pp. 339–57.

'The work of a venereal disease treatment centre', *The Irish Journal of Medical Science*, 16 (1923), pp. 145–54.

LaBatt, Hamilton, *Observations on Venereal Diseases: Derived from Civil and Military Practice* (Dublin, 1858).

Leathem, W. S., *A History of the Church of Ireland* (Belfast, 1939).

Letter to the Public on an Important Subject (Dublin, 1767).

Logan, W., *The Great Social Evil: its Causes, Extent, Results and Remedies* (London, 1871).

Lowndes, Frederick, *Prostitution and Venereal Diseases in Liverpool* (London, 1886).

Lurgan Union, *Report of the Committee Appointed by Order of the Board 14th September 1848, Presented to the Board 14th December 1848* (Dublin, 1849).

MacInerny, Rev. M. H., 'The souper problem in Ireland', *Irish Ecclesiastical Record*, 18 (1921), pp. 140–56.

'A postscript on the souper problem', *Irish Ecclesiastical Record*, 19 (1922), pp. 140–56.

Maddison, Arthur J., *Hints on Rescue Work: a Handbook for Missionaries* (London, 1898).

The Law Relating to Child-Saving and Reformatory Efforts (London, 1909).

Maguire, J. F., *The Irish in America* (London, 1868).

Martin, Mrs Charles, 'Our young work girls', *Irish Monthly* (1879).

Mason, W. S., *A Statistical Account or Parochial Survey of Ireland*, 3 vols. (Dublin, 1814–19).

Mayhew, Henry, *London Labour and the London Poor* (London, 1861/2).

McCarthy, Michael, *Priests and People in Ireland* (Dublin, 1903).

McClure, H. I., 'Diagnosis and treatment of gonorrhoea in the female', *Ulster Medical Journal*, 5 (1936), pp. 36–40.

McDonnell, Robert, 'Lectures on venereal diseases – lecture ii', *Medical Press and Circular*, 19 February 1868.

McWeeney, E. J., 'On the recent action of the state with regard to venereal disease', *Statistical and Social Inquiry Society of Ireland*, 13 (1913–19), pp. 498–517.

Meagher, William, *Notices on the Life and Character of the Most Rev. Daniel Murray* (Dublin, 1853).

Meldon, G. Pugin, 'Some notes on the admissions to the Westmoreland Lock Hospital, Dublin, since the year 1860', *Dublin Journal of Medical Science*, 137 (1914), pp. 109–18.

Minchin, H., 'Observations on the mortality of infants born in workhouses', *Dublin Quarterly Journal of Medical Science*, 29, 57 (1860), pp. 70–80.

Morgan, J., 'A new view of the origin and propagation of the venereal disease – successful treatment by inoculation, derived from a hitherto unknown source, with illustrative cases', *Dublin Journal of Medical Science*, 1 (1870), pp. 49–93.

'Clinical review of cases under treatment at the Westmoreland Lock Hospital, during the past six months', *Dublin Journal of Medical Science*, 48 (1869), pp. 506–29.

Practical Lessons in the Nature and Treatment of the Affections Produced by the Contagious Diseases (London, 1872).

Practical Rules for the Use of the Religious of the Good Shepherd for the Direction of the Classes (Angers, 1898).

New Edition of the Tract which gave Origin to the Institution of the Lock Penitentiary with an Account of its Progress and Present Circumstances Earnestly Recommended to the Attention of the Humane and Affluent (Dublin, 1805).

Nic Shiúbhláigh, Máire, *The Splendid Years* (Dublin, 1955).

Observations on the Labouring Classes (Dublin, 1836).

O'Hanlon, Rev. W. M., *Walks Among the Poor of Belfast* (1853; reprint Memston, 1971).

'On the sanitary condition of Dublin', *Dublin Quarterly Journal of Medical Science*, 3, 6 (May 1847), pp. 470–84.

'On sanitary progress', *Dublin Quarterly Journal of Medical Science*, 15, 29 (1853), pp. 203–207.

Pankhurst, Christabel, *The Great Scourge and How to End it* (London, 1913).

Pankhurst, Sylvia, 'State regulation of vice', *Workers Dreadnought*, 6 April 1918, p. 980.

Patterson, Emily G., Catherine Ross and Isabella M. S. Tod, *To the Members of the Belfast Committee for the Repeal of the Contagious Diseases Acts, And Others Interested in Public Morality* (Belfast, 1878).

Peter, A., *The Magdalen Chapel* (Dublin, 1907).

Porter, William Henry, 'Essays on the natural history of syphilis', *Dublin Quarterly Journal of Medical Science*, 23 (1857), pp. 88–99, 257–70.

Practical Rules for the Use of the Religious of the Good Shepherd for the Direction of the Classes (Angers, 1898).

Rankin, J. C., 'Syphilis', *Transactions of the Ulster Medical Society* (1921–2), pp. 33–6.

Religious of the Congregation of the Good Shepherd of Angers, *Blessed Mary of Saint Euphrasia Pelletier* (London, 1933).

'Report of a local committee as to the best means of diminishing vice and crime in Dublin', *Journal of the Statistical and Social Inquiry Society of Ireland*, 5, 59 (1882), pp. 309–16.

Report of the Committee on Evil Literature (Dublin, 1927).

'Reviews and Bibliographical Notices', *Dublin Quarterly Journal of Medical Science*, 28 (August and November 1859), pp. 207–25, review of *The History of Prostitution* by W. W. Sanger.

Rowlette, Robert J., *The Medical Press and Circular 1839–1939: a Hundred Years in the Life of a Medical Journal* (London, 1939).

Rules and Regulations for the Asylum of Penitent Females: With an Account of the Receipts and Disbursements (Dublin, 1785).

Sanger, William, *The History of Prostitution: its Extent, Causes, and Effects throughout the World* (New York, 1859).

Scott, Benjamin, *A State Iniquity: its Rise, Extension and Overthrow* (London, 1890).

Sheehy, Rev., *The Influence of Women in Catholic Ireland* (Dublin, 1922).

Shirley Deakin, C. W., *The Contagious Diseases Acts* (London, 1872).

Souvenir of the Golden Jubilee of Our Lady of the Charity of Refuge, High Park, Drumcondra (Dublin, 1903).

Stephens, Rev. Walter, *An Address to the Guardians and Governesses of the Magdalen Asylum, Leeson Street* (Dublin, 1805).

'Stoning the desolate', *All the Year Round*, 12 (1865), pp. 369–72.

Sutherland, Halliday, *Irish Journey* (New York, 1958).

Taylor, Fanny, *Irish Homes and Irish Hearts* (London, 1867),

The Magdalen: a Tale of Real Life (Dublin, 1832).

'The Magdalens of High Park', *The Irish Rosary*, 1897, pp. 176–84.

The Order of Our Lady of Charity of Refuge, 1853–1953: A Centenary Record of High Park Convent Drumcondra Dublin (Dublin, n.d.).

To the Members of the Belfast Committee for the Repeal of the Contagious Diseases Acts (Belfast, 1878).

Tynan O'Mahony, Nora, 'In a Magdalen asylum', *The Irish Monthly*, 24 (1906), pp. 374–5.

Warburton, W. J., Whitelaw, J. and Walshe, R., *History of the City of Dublin*, 2 vols. (London, 1818).

Weld, Isaac, *Statistical Survey of the County Roscommon* (Dublin, 1882).

Williams, G. D., *Dublin Charities: Being a Handbook of Dublin Philanthropic Organisations and Charities* (Dublin, 1902).

Woods, Thomas, 'Report on cases which occurred in the Parsonstown workhouse infirmary', *Dublin Quarterly Journal of Medical Science*, 28 (1859), pp. 17–26.

Woodward, Henry, *A Charity Sermon, Preached at the Magdalen Asylum, on Sunday, the 20th of February, 1825* (Dublin, 1825).

SELECTED BOOKS AND ARTICLES PUBLISHED SINCE 1960

Allison, R. S., *The Seeds of Time Being a Short History of the Belfast and Royal Hospital, 1850/1903* (Belfast, 1972).

Arnold, Mavis and Heather Laskey, *Children of the Poor Clares: the Story of an Irish Orphanage* (Belfast, 1985).

Backhouse, Constance B., 'Nineteenth-century Canadian prostitution law: reflection of a discriminatory society', *Histoire Sociale/Social History*, 18 (1985), pp. 387–423.

Bourke, Angela, Siobhán Kilfeather, Maria Luddy, Margaret MacCurtain, Gerardine Meaney, Máirín Ní Dhonnchadha, Mary O'Dowd, and Clair Wills (eds.), *The Field Day Anthology of Irish Writing*, vols. IV and V, *Irish Women's Writing and Traditions* (Cork, 2002).

Boyd, Gary, 'Legitimising the illicit: Dublin's Temple Bar and the Monto', *Tracings*, 2 (2002), pp. 113–25.

Dublin 1745–1922: Hospitals, Spectacle and Vice (Dublin, 2006).

Bradshaw, Robert, *Frank Duff: Founder of the Legion of Mary* (New York, 1985).

Burke Brogan, Patricia, 'The Magdalen experience', in Patricia Kennedy (ed.), *Motherhood in Ireland: Creation and Context* (Cork, 2004), pp. 160–9.

Clark, Anna, 'Wild workhouse girls and the liberal imperial state in mid-nineteenth century Ireland', *Journal of Social History*, 39 (2005), pp. 389–409.

Connell, K. H., *Irish Peasant Society: Four Historical Essays* (Oxford, 1968).

Cohen, Sherrill, *The Evolution of Women's Asylums since 1500* (New York, 1992).

Conley, Caroline, *Melancholy Accidents: the Meaning of Violence in Post-Famine Ireland* (Lanham, MD, 1999).

Costello, Con, *'A Most Delightful Station': The British Army on the Curragh of Kildare, Ireland, 1855–1922* (Cork, 1996).

Crowdus, Gary, ' "The sisters of no mercy": an interview with Peter Mullan', *Cinéaste*, 28 (2003), pp. 26–33.

Crossman, Virginia, *Local Government in Nineteenth Century Ireland* (Belfast, 1994).

'Viewing women, family and sexuality through the prism of the Irish poor laws', *Women's History Review*, 15 (2006), pp. 541–50.

Curtin, Geraldine, *The Women of Galway Jail: Female Criminality in Nineteenth-Century Ireland* (Galway, 2001).

Daly, Mary E., 'Women in the Irish Free State, 1922–39: the interaction between economics and ideology', *Journal of Women's History*, 6 (1995), pp. 99–116.

Damousi, Joy, *Depraved and Disorderly: Female Convicts, Sexuality and Gender in Colonial Australia* (Cambridge, 1997).

Davidson, Roger, *Dangerous Liaisons: a Social History of Venereal Disease in Twentieth-Century Scotland* (Amsterdam, 2000).

Davidson, Roger and Lesley Hall (eds.), *Sex, Sin and Suffering: Venereal Disease and European Society Since 1870* (London, 2001).

Dunne, Tom 'Penitents', *The Dublin Review*, 9 (2002–3), pp. 74–82.

Earner-Byrne, Lindsey, 'The boat to England: an analysis of the official reactions to the emigration of single expectant Irishwomen to Britain, 1922–1972', *Irish Economic and Social History*, 30 (2003), pp. 52–70.

'"Moral repatriation": the response to Irish unmarried mothers in Britain, 1920s–1960s', in Patrick J. Duffy (ed.), *To and From Ireland: Planned Migration Schemes c. 1600–2000* (Dublin, 2004), pp. 155–73.

Fagan, Terry, and the North Inner City Folklore Project, *Monto: Madams, Murder and Black Coddle* (Dublin, 2002).

Ferris, Kathleen, *James Joyce and the Burden of Disease* (Lexington, 1995).

Finnane, Mark, 'The Carrigan Committee of 1930–31 and the "moral condition" of the Saorstát', *Irish Historical Studies*, 32 (2001), pp. 519–36.

Finnegan, Frances, *Poverty and Prostitution: a Study of Victorian Prostitutes in York* (Cambridge, 1979).

'Do Penance or Perish': a Study of Magdalen Asylums in Ireland* (Piltown, Co. Kilkenny, 2001; New York, 2004).

Fleming, David, 'Public attitudes to prostitution in eighteenth-century Ireland', *Irish Economic and Social History*, 31 (2005), pp. 1–18.

Garrett, Paul Michael, 'The abnormal flight: the migration and repatriation of unmarried mothers', *Social History*, 25 (2000), pp. 330–43.

Gilfoyle, Timothy, *City of Eros: New York City, Prostitution, and the Commercialisation of Sex, 1790–1920* (New York, 1992).

'Prostitutes in history: from parables of pornography to metaphors of modernity', *American Historical Review*, 104 (February 1999), pp. 117–41.

Grayzel, Susan R., *Women's Identities at War: Gender, Motherhood and Politics in Britain and France During the First World War* (Chapel Hill, 1999).

Greer, Desmond and James W. Nicolson, *The Factory Acts in Ireland, 1802–1914* (Dublin, 2003).

Griffin, Brian, *The Bulkies: Police and Crime in Belfast, 1800–1865* (Dublin, 1997).

Griffith, Kenneth and Timothy E. O'Grady, *Curious Journey: an Oral History of Ireland's Unfinished Revolution* (Cork, 1998, 2nd edn).

Hearn, Mona, *Thomas Edmondson and the Dublin Laundry: a Quaker Businessman, 1837–1908* (Dublin, 2004).

Hershatter, Gail, *Dangerous Pleasures: Prostitution and Modernity in Twentieth-Century Shanghai* (Berkeley, 1997).

Inglis, Tom, *Moral Monopoly: the Rise and Fall of the Catholic Church in Ireland* (Dublin, 1998).

'The struggle for control of the Irish body: state, church and society in nineteenth-century Ireland', *Eire/Ireland*, 40 (2005), pp. 9–37.

James, Nick, 'Keeping it clean: an interview with Peter Mullan', *Sight and Sound* (March 2003), pp. 16–17.

Jeffery, Keith, *Ireland and the Great War* (Cambridge, 2000).

Jordan, Jane, *Josephine Butler* (London, 2001).

Kennedy, Finola, *From Cottage to Crèche: Family Change in Ireland* (Dublin, 2000).

'Frank Duff's search for the neglected and rejected', *Studies*, 91 (2002), pp. 381–9.

'The suppression of the Carrigan reports: a historical perspective on child abuse', *Studies*, 89 (2000), pp. 354–62.

Kennedy, Liam, 'Bastardy and the Great Famine: Ireland, 1845–1850', *Continuity and Change*, 14, 3 (1999), pp. 429–52.

Kennedy, Liam and Paul Gray, 'Famine, illegitimacy, and the workhouse in Western Ireland: Kilrush, County Clare', in Alysa Levene, Thomas Nutt and Samantha Williams (eds.), *Illegitimacy in Britain, 1700–1920* (London, 2005), pp. 122–41.

Koven Seth, *Slumming: Sexual and Social Politics in Victorian London* (Princeton and Oxford, 2004).

Levine, Philippa, ' "Walking the streets in a way no decent woman should": women police in World War 1', *Journal of Modern History*, 66 (1994), pp. 34–78.

'Venereal disease, prostitution, and the politics of Empire: the case of British India', *Journal of the History of Sexuality*, 4 (1994), pp. 579–602.

'Rereading the 1890s: venereal disease as "constitutional crisis" in Britain and British India', *Journal of Asian Studies*, 55 (1996), pp. 585–612.

Prostitution, Race and Politics: Policing Venereal Disease in the British Empire (London, 2003).

Luddy, Maria, 'An outcast community: the "wrens of the Curragh" ', *Women's History Review*, 1 (1992), pp. 341–55.

'Irish women and the Contagious Diseases Acts 1864–1886', *History Ireland*, 1 (1993), pp. 32–4.

' "Abandoned women and bad characters": prostitution in nineteenth-century Ireland', *Women's History Review*, 6 (1997), pp. 485–503.

'Moral rescue and unmarried mothers in Ireland in the 1920s', *Women's Studies*, 30 (2001), pp. 797–817.

'The army and prostitution in nineteenth-century Ireland: the case of the wrens of the Curragh', *Bullán: An Irish Studies Journal*, 6 (2001), pp. 67–83.

MacAvoy, Sandra L., 'The regulation of sexuality in the Irish Free State, 1929–1935', in Greta Jones and Elizabeth Malcolm (eds.), *Medicine, Disease and the State in Ireland, 1650–1940* (Cork, 1999), pp. 253–66.

Mahood, Linda, *The Magdalenes: Prostitution in the Nineteenth Century* (London, 1990).

Maume, Patrick, *The Long Gestation: Irish Nationalist Life, 1891–1918* (Dublin, 1999).

McHugh, Paul, *Prostitution and Victorian Social Reform* (London, 1980).

McConville, Sean, *Irish Political Prisoners, 1848–1922* (London, 2003).

McLoughlin, Dympna, 'Women and sexuality in nineteenth-century Ireland', *Irish Journal of Psychology*, 15 (1994), pp. 266–75.

Malcolm, Elizabeth, ' "Troops of largely diseased women": vd, the Contagious Diseases Acts and moral policing in late nineteenth-century Ireland', *Irish Economic and Social History*, 26 (1999), pp. 1–14.

Mooij, Annet, *Out of Otherness: Characters and Narrators in the Dutch Venereal Disease Debates 1850–1990* (Amsterdam and Atlanta, 1998).

Mooney, Ria, 'Playing Rosie Redmond', *Journal of Irish Literature*, 6 (1977), pp. 21–7.

Mullin, Katherine, *James Joyce, Sexuality and Social Purity* (Cambridge, 2003).

Mumm, Susan, ' "Not worse than other girls": the convent-based rehabilitation of fallen women in Victorian Britain', *Journal of Social History*, 29 (1996), pp. 527–47.

Murphy, Paula, ' "A prison of the mind": the Magdalen laundries in popular culture', *Doctrine and Life*, 54 (October 2004), pp. 7–15.

Murray, Jonathan, 'Convents or cowboys? Millennial Scottish and Irish film industries and imaginaries in *the Magdalene Sisters*', in Kevin Rockett and John Hill (eds.), *National Cinema and Beyond, Studies in Irish Film, 1* (Dublin, 2004), pp. 149–60.

Murray, Peter, 'A militant among the Magdalens: Mary Ellen Murphy's incarceration in High Park convent during the 1913 lockout', *Saothar*, 20 (1995), pp. 41–54.

Novick, Ben, *Conceiving Revolution: Irish Nationalist Propaganda During the First World War* (Dublin, 2001).

O'Brien, Brendan, *Athlone Workhouse and the Famine* (Athlone, 1995).

O'Brien, John V., *Dear Dirty Dublin: a City in Distress, 1899–1916* (Berkeley, 1982).

O'Connor, Ulick, *Oliver St John Gogarty* (London, 1964; Dublin, 2000).

Ó Gráda, Cormac, *Black '47 and Beyond: The Great Irish Famine in History, Economy and Memory* (Princeton, 1999).

O hÓgartaigh, Margaret, *Kathleen Lynn: Irishwomen, Patriot, Doctor* (Dublin, 2006).

Ó Maitiú, Séamas, *The Humours of Donnybrook: Dublin's Famous Fair and its Suppression* (Dublin, 1995).

Ó Murchadha, Ciarán, 'Paphian nymphs and worshippers of the Idalian Goddess: prostitution in Ennis in the mid-nineteenth century', *The Other Clare*, 24 (2000), pp. 32–6.

O'Shea, James, *Priests, Politics and Society in Post-Famine Ireland: a Study of County Tipperary, 1850–1891* (Dublin, 1983).

Pedersen, Susan, *Family Dependence and the Origins of the Welfare State: Britain and France, 1914–1945* (Cambridge, 1993).

Prior, Pauline, 'Murder and madness: gender and the insanity defence in nineteenth-century Ireland', *New Hibernia Review*, 9 (2005), pp. 19–36.

Prunty, Jacinta, *Dublin Slums, 1800–1925: a Study in Urban Geography* (Dublin, 1997).

Quétel, Claude, *The History of Syphilis*, trans. Judith Braddock and Brian Pike (Baltimore, 1992).

Regan, John, *The Irish Counter Revolution, 1921–1936* (Dublin, 1999).

Rosen, Ruth, *The Lost Sisterhood: Prostitution in America, 1900–1918* (Baltimore, 1982).

Ryan, Louise, *Gender, Identity and the Irish Press, 1922–1937* (Lampeter, 2001).

Smith, James M., 'The politics of sexual knowledge: the origins of Ireland's containment culture and the "Carrigan Report" (1931)', *The Journal of the History of Sexuality*, 13 (2004), pp. 208–33.

Spongberg, Mary, *Feminizing Venereal Disease: the Body of the Prostitute in Nineteenth-Century Medical Discourse* (London, 1997).

Strain, R. W. M., *Belfast and its Charitable Society: a Story of Urban Social Development* (Oxford, 1961).

Trustram, Myna, *Women of the Regiment: Marriage and the Victorian Army* (Cambridge, 1984).

Valiulis, Maryann Gialenella, 'Power, gender and identity in the Irish Free State', *Journal of Women's History*, 1.4, 2.1 (Winter/Spring, 1994/95), pp. 117–36.

'Neither feminist nor flapper: the ecclesiastical construction of the ideal Irish woman', in Mary O'Dowd and Sabine Wichert (eds.), *Chattel, Servant or Citizen: Women's Status in Church, State, and Society* (Belfast, 1995), pp. 168–78.

Walkowitz, Judith, *Prostitution and Victorian Society: Women, Class and the State* (Cambridge, 1980).

City of Dreadful Delight: Narratives of Sexual Danger in Late-Victorian London (London, 1992).

Whelan, Yvonne, *Reinventing Modern Dublin: Streetscape, Iconography and the Politics of Identity* (Dublin, 2003).

White, Luise, *The Comforts of Home: Prostitution in Colonial Nairobi* (Chicago, 1990).

Whyte, J. H., *Church and State in Modern Ireland, 1923–1879* (Dublin, 1971).

BALLADS

'A New Song Call'd the Young Man in Search of his Sister' (Dublin, *c.* 1869).

'A New Song Call'd Brother Bill and Jamina Brown' (Dublin, *c.* 1865).

'A Much Admired Song Call'd Tie My Toes to the Bed' (Dublin?, 1865?).

UNPUBLISHED THESES

Bolger, Liam, 'The military in Kilkenny 1800–1870' (unpublished doctoral thesis, National University of Ireland, Maynooth, 2005).

Boyle, Michael, 'Women and crime in Belfast, 1900–1914' (unpublished doctoral thesis, Queen's University, Belfast, 1997).

Burke, Gerard, 'The British Army and Fermoy' (unpublished MA thesis, National University of Ireland, Cork, 1999).

Hughes, Peter E., ' "Cleanliness and godliness": A sociological study of the Good Shepherd refuges for the social reformation and Christian conversion of prostitutes and convicted women in nineteenth-century Britain' (unpublished doctoral thesis, Brunel University, 1985).

Oldfield, Carolyn, 'Growing up good? Medical, social hygiene and youth work perspectives on young women, 1918–1931' (unpublished doctoral thesis, University of Warwick, 2001).

Townsend, Joanne, 'Private diseases in public discourse: venereal disease in Victorian society, culture and imagination' (unpublished doctoral thesis, University of Melbourne, 1999).

Van Iersel, Linda, ' "Beware of the Flash Girls": discourse on prostitution and mechanisms of control in post-famine Ireland (1850–*c.* 1890)' (unpublished MA thesis, Catholic University, Nijmegen, 1995).

TELEVISION DOCUMENTARIES AND DRAMA

Les Blanchisseuses de Magdalen available as *Convents of Shame*, Marathon International Video, http://www.marathon.fr.
The Magdalens, BBC 1993.
Sex in a Cold Climate, Testimony Films Documentary for Channel Four, broadcast 16 March 1998.
Sinners, Parallel Productions/BBC Northern Ireland, drama, broadcast 26 March 2002.
Washing Away the Stain, BBC Scotland, broadcast 16 August 1993.

FILM

The Magdalene Sisters, written and directed by Peter Mullan, Dublin, a PFP Films Production in association with Temple Film, 2002.

NOVELS AND PLAYS

Broderick, John, *The Irish Magdalen: A Novel* (London, 1991).
Bruen, Ken, *The Magdalen Martyrs* (Dingle, 2003).
Burke Brogan, Patricia, *Eclipsed* (Galway, 1994).
    Stained Glass at Samhan (Co. Clare, 2003).
Conlon-McKenna, Marita, *The Magdalen* (London, 1999).
Day, Susanne R., *The Amazing Philanthropists* (London, 1916).
    'Toilers', *The Englishwoman* (1919), pp. 180–90.
Egerton, George, *Keynotes and Discords* (London, 1893).
Francis, M. E., *The Story of Mary Dunne* (London, 1913).
Grand, Sarah, *The Beth Book* (London, 1898).
Joyce, James, *Ulysses* (London, 1992).
Laffan, May, *Flitters, Tatters and the Counsellor* (Dublin, 1879).
Laverty, Maura, *Never No More: the Story of a Lost Village* (London, 1942).
Ni Ghráda, Mairéad, *On Trial: a Play* (Dublin, 1966).
O'Flaherty, Liam, *The Informer* (London, 1925).
Sheehan, Rev. P. A., *Luke Delmege* (London and New York, 1901).
Smith, Paul, *The Countrywoman* (London, 1962).
St John Gogarty, Oliver, *Blight: the Tragedy of Dublin*, in James F. Carens, *The Plays of Oliver St John Gogarty* (Newark, n.d.).
Winthrop, F. [Rosamond Jacob], *Callaghan* (Dublin, n.d., c. 1921).

MEMOIRS

O'Beirne, Kathy, *Katy's Story: a Childhood Hell Inside the Magdalen Laundries* (Edinburgh and London, 2005).

Index